Credit Management Kit
FOR
DUMMIES®

by Steve Bucci

Foreword by Durant S. Abernethy, Esq.
Former president, National Foundation for Credit Counseling
Former General Counsel, CUNA

WILEY

John Wiley & Sons, Inc.

Credit Management Kit For Dummies®

Published by
John Wiley & Sons, Inc.
111 River St.
Hoboken, NJ 07030-5774
www.wiley.com

Copyright © 2011 by John Wiley & Sons, Inc., Hoboken, New Jersey

Published simultaneously in Canada

For general information on our other products and services, please contact our Customer Care Department within the U.S. at 877-762-2974, outside the U.S. at 317-572-3993, or fax 317-572-4002.

For technical support, please visit www.wiley.com/techsupport.

Wiley also publishes its books in a variety of electronic formats and by print-on-demand. Not all content that is available in standard print versions of this book may appear or be packaged in all book formats. If you have purchased a version of this book that did not include media that is referenced by or accompanies a standard print version, you may request this media by visiting http://booksupport.wiley.com. For more information about Wiley products, visit us at www.wiley.com.

Library of Congress Control Number: 2011934641

ISBN: 978-1-118-01385-4 (pbk); 978-1-118-14559-3 (ebk); 978-1-118-14560-9 (ebk); 978-1-118-14561-6 (ebk)

Manufactured in the United States of America

10 9 8 7 6 5 4 3 2 1

WILEY

About the Author

Steve Bucci has been helping people decode and master personal financial credit and debt issues for the last 20 years.

For nearly a decade he has authored a popular, biweekly personal finance column as the Debt Advisor for the financial mega-site Bankrate.com. His column is featured frequently on America Online, Yahoo! Personal Finance, and other websites. The Scripps-Howard News Service syndicates his column to newspapers nationally. He's also a regular contributing columnist for the Providence Journal newspaper.

Steve was formerly president of several nationally and internationally respected nonprofit organizations dedicated to helping the consumer wisely use credit. They include the Consumer Credit Counseling Service (CCCS) of Rhode Island, the CCCS of Southern New England, and the Money Management International Financial Education Foundation. He began his career in counseling at the Yale Psychiatric Institute before switching to business careers in management consulting and then finance, developing and bringing to market both publicly and privately traded investment products. Steve returned to his first love, helping individuals, in 1991, this time using his financial and management experience to launch Rhode Island's first private, nonprofit, financial counseling agency.

Steve has served as director of the CDNE Education Foundation, the URI Center for Personal Financial Education, the National Foundation for Credit Counseling, the Better Business Bureau of Rhode Island, and National Network Non-Profit Services, and he's currently the treasurer at Saint Peter's By-The-Sea Episcopal Church. He was named Visiting Executive in Residence at the University of Rhode Island in 2005. Steve graduated from the University of Rhode Island at Kingston, where he received his BA and MA degrees. He and his wife, Barbara, live with their two cats, Pea-head and Stinky, at Sand Hill Cove in the seaside community of Narragansett, Rhode Island.

Dedication

This book is dedicated to all those concerned about personal financial issues in today's turbulent economy: personal financial professionals and credit counselors who choose to work with one family at a time rather than seek fame and/or fortune, and consumers looking for a way to understand and intelligently use credit as a tool for a better life in the 21st century.

Author's Acknowledgments

I want to thank John Wiley & Sons for asking me to write this book, not only because so much has changed in credit management recently but also because being asked to write and share my viewpoint represents a vindication of sorts of the holistic approach to managing credit that I've been espousing for the last two decades. Credit can only be managed from the bottom up, not the top down. That is to say, you can only build and maintain excellent credit by beginning with a strong foundation and then adding on more layers in stages. This process delivers both enviable credit and a better life for you and your family. The two are inseparable!

No successful person I know works alone. Certainly, that is so in my case; I received the support, help, encouragement, and at times great tolerance from many people in my life. My thanks to them all, and my particular thanks to Susan Spurgeon, whose cheery disposition, rare insight, and gifted memory have kept me on course and on schedule with this book and my activities at Bankrate.com. I also want to thank my credit reporting and scoring gurus Craig Watts at Fair Isaac, Sara Davies at VantageScore, and Rod Griffin at Experian; Jessica Faust, my agent; and my editors at John Wiley & Sons, especially Alissa Schwipps and Tracy Boggier. Finally, I would be remiss if I didn't acknowledge and thank my dear wife Barbara for her irrational and unshakable belief in my ability to do anything and for putting up with my mercurial behavior during the research and writing of this book.

Publisher's Acknowledgments

We're proud of this book; please send us your comments at http://dummies.custhelp.com. For other comments, please contact our Customer Care Department within the U.S. at 877-762-2974, outside the U.S. at 317-572-3993, or fax 317-572-4002.

Some of the people who helped bring this book to market include the following:

Acquisitions, Editorial, and Media Development

Senior Project Editor: Alissa Schwipps

   (Previous Edition: Chad R. Sievers)

Acquisitions Editor: Tracy Boggier

Copy Editor: Todd Lothery

   (Previous Edition: Christy Pingleton)

Assistant Editor: David Lutton

Editorial Program Coordinator: Joe Niesen

Technical Editor: Barbara O'Neill, PhD, CFP

Vertical Websites Assistant Project Manager: Jenny Swisher

Vertical Websites Associate Producer: Josh Frank

Vertical Websites Quality Assurance: Doug Kuhn

Editorial Manager: Christine Meloy Beck

Editorial Assistant: Rachelle S. Amick

Cover Photo: © iStockphoto.com / Feng Yu

Cartoons: Rich Tennant (www.the5thwave.com)

Composition Services

Senior Project Coordinator: Kristie Rees

Layout and Graphics: Carl Byers, Corrie Socolovitch

Proofreaders: Melissa Cossell, Lisa Young Stiers

Indexer: Valerie Haynes Perry

Special Help
Jennifer Tebbe

Publishing and Editorial for Consumer Dummies

   Kathleen Nebenhaus, Vice President and Executive Publisher

   Kristin Ferguson-Wagstaffe, Product Development Director

   Ensley Eikenburg, Associate Publisher, Travel

   Kelly Regan, Editorial Director, Travel

Publishing for Technology Dummies

   Andy Cummings, Vice President and Publisher

Composition Services

   Debbie Stailey, Director of Composition Services

Contents at a Glance

Table of Contents

Foreword

· ·

I've been a leader with consumer credit lenders and credit management foundations at the national level for more than 30 years. I'm often quoted as saying, "How to manage money and credit are fundamental life skills, and if you don't learn those skills, it will greatly diminish or ruin your life." *Credit Management Kit For Dummies* is just what you need to help you understand and prosper from using credit. Having the right information can make or break your financial life, and Steve Bucci's book has a real leg up on making it.

As CEO of the National Foundation of Credit Counseling (the oldest, largest, and most respected nonprofit credit counseling association in the country), I've worked with more than 200 state and regional CEOs of member consumer credit counseling services (CCCS). Steve was front and center in every significant area, helping people avoid or get out of serious credit problems. We worked with others to require all CCCS members to become accredited by the National Counsel on Accreditation, a significant quality-assurance exercise that required considerable effort over several years. Steve ran an outstanding CCCS in Rhode Island that was one of the leaders in developing new and effective credit-education affiliations with universities and services, including online Q&As, budgeting worksheets, and in-school programs. Steve has always been compassionate for those in need, creative in how to help them, and continually focused on what can be done to make a real difference in consumers' knowledge of money and credit so that credit topics are no longer neglected in homes and in schools. His commitment to the quality and depth of the *For Dummies* books he has written speaks volumes about this man I admire.

In the early 1990s, about 25 percent of Americans had a credit card. Today, more than 90 percent carry plastic money. More than 60 percent of these credit-card carriers have an average unpaid monthly balance of approximately $10,000 and are trapped in serious credit card debt. Add in upside down mortgages and other credit problems and it's clear that a huge number of families and individuals can benefit from *Credit Management Kit For Dummies* and avoid or limit losses by following the advice in this book. For them and all the rest who aren't in trouble and want to stay that way, this book is an absolute must-read.

Credit Management Kit For Dummies offers you the essentials of the many different types of credit you use during your lifetime, with realistic examples set in real-life situations. More important, this book gives you plain and concise explanations and tips for all the dramatic changes in the laws and rules for consumer credit scoring, lending, borrowing, fees, interest rate changes, and collection practices since Steve's book *Credit Repair Kit For Dummies* came out three years ago.

Steve Bucci creatively uses contemporary, consumer-friendly examples to help readers understand credit by introducing the concepts of your credit wall, green credit, and how negative credit pollutes your credit environment. However, this technique is far from cosmetic. *Credit Management Kit For Dummies* is more comprehensive than any book of any size I've seen that attempts to cover the complicated subjects within consumer credit management. Further, it is in-depth and current on the essential information and new developments regarding consumer credit.

If you read this book, both you and your lenders will benefit!

Durant S. Abernethy, Practicing Attorney
Former President and CEO of the National Foundation for Credit Counseling (NFCC) for 8 years
Senior Vice President and General Counsel of the Credit Union National Association (CUNA) for 15 years

Introduction

*I*t's not news to any of you that the credit environment has been in turmoil over the last couple of years. We're in the middle of what I call a *credit winter*. You've heard about the meteor that killed off the dinosaurs by causing a prolonged global winter environment? Well, you're living through a financial explosion that has caused a credit winter that has frozen lending, caused massive unemployment, and wiped out hundreds of thousands of mortgages and pension accounts.

This book is meant to be your guide to successfully managing your credit in this new environment. It looks at credit as an integral part of your life, not something that has a life of its own. Seeing your credit as an outcome of the decisions you make every day in your normal life makes attaining great credit a part of your pursuit of life and happiness. I call it your *credit-life connection*.

Tighter credit availability means you need better credit and higher credit scores to access today's credit products, which are essential in leading a rewarding life in today's society. Not only have the criteria for the best access to credit become much more selective, but the penalties for ignorance and failure have also soared.

You hear every day about the high number of foreclosures that are occurring. You don't hear about the penalties these families will face for years to come. A credit score drop of 100 to 150 points that can take up to seven years to rebuild means years of more-expensive credit, reduced employment opportunities, and more. Plus, for the uninformed, the loss of a home can prove to be a taxable event, putting them deep in debt to the IRS. Tens of thousands walk away from mortgages without realizing that they'll be shut out of the conventional mortgage market for the next seven years under Fannie Mae rules.

And if all this isn't enough, credit reporting is growing more powerful by the day. Updates in this book tell you about new consumer databases that collect information about your medical history, prescription drug use, rental history, and more. Employers, insurance companies, and lenders use this information to decide whether to hire or promote you, what insurance rates to give you, and whether to offer you new convenient banking products. You need to know what's in these files, and in this book, that's one of many things I tell you how to do.

Credit Management Kit For Dummies comes at a critical time for everyone. Credit continues to play an ever-changing and increasingly important role in your life, whether you use a credit card or not. Insurance, employment, entertainment, home buying or renting, and getting an education with student loans are more dependent than ever on you having good credit. Plus, while the rewards for good credit have never been higher, the penalties for failure — foreclosure, eviction, fighting, divorce, job problems, debts, collections — have never been greater. For these reasons and more, millions are looking for up-to-date, useful, and proven answers from a trusted and knowledgeable resource. This book contains the best of my experiences and research. I firmly believe that if you know the rules of the credit game, you stand a much better chance of getting a winning score. That's why I'm here, and that's why I wrote this book.

About This Book

I'm pleased to be able to share my experience to help you build and manage your credit, determine what works and what doesn't, and figure out what you can do to help yourself when things don't go as planned. Over the last two decades, I've helped and advised thousands of people just like you to understand how credit works and what the simple steps are that everyone can take to have great credit. I've helped some people through the advice in my popular Internet column that appears in newspapers all over the country, and I've helped many others through one-on-one coaching and counseling. In *Credit Management Kit For Dummies,* I give you the best of what I've learned so you can avoid the pitfalls and problems of a complex and powerful credit industry.

The *For Dummies* approach is different because it's low cost, simple, and drives right to the heart of the matter. With this book you can manage your credit simply by applying just a few key concepts. Unlike the celebrity mass-media approach of making one philosophy fit all after a 15-second question-and-answer period, I find that by taking the time to give you the concepts and tools you need, you can apply them to your specific detailed situation and come up with the answer that's perfectly custom-tailored just for you.

So, why this book?

 ✔ Because though credit can at first seem incredibly complex and unfair, the basis for successful credit is grounded in a few simple actions that anyone can master. I give you all the tools and insight you need to build, rebuild (if necessary), and manage great credit.

 ✔ Because you may need the advice of an experienced advisor to guide you through a mortgage problem, and this book tells you how to find a good credit-, HUD-, or bankruptcy-counseling agency.

✔ Because if you want to get a job or promotion; buy a reliable car to get to your job; start a business; insure your home, apartment, or car; or get a good higher education, you need a good credit record.

✔ Because you may be one of the millions of people who this year will be victims of personal data theft, and this book provides valuable information to protect your identity.

✔ Because you may be on the brink of credit trouble, and this book gives you budgeting and spending advice that can pull you back from the edge.

✔ Because the time is right for you to take control of your credit and your financial peace of mind, and this book helps you do just that.

Conventions Used in This Book

To make this book as simple to follow and as convenient as possible, I use the following conventions throughout:

✔ All web addresses and e-mail addresses appear in `monofont`.

✔ I use **bold** for all keywords in bulleted lists and for steps in numbered lists.

✔ New terms appear in _italics_ and are closely followed by easy-to-understand definitions.

What You're Not to Read

Although I hope you read every word I've written, I understand that your life is busy and that you want to read only the need-to-know info. So in this book, you can safely skip the sidebars, those shaded gray boxes that contain text. Sidebars provide supporting or entertaining information that isn't critical to your understanding of the topic. You can also skip anything marked by a Technical Stuff icon. This icon accompanies text that goes into additional detail about a subject, and though I hope you find these details fascinating, you can skip this text and still grasp the subject at hand.

Foolish Assumptions

I assume that you're reading this book because you know that credit is important in today's life but you may not know all the ins and outs of making credit work for you. Whether your credit is great and you want to keep it that way, not so great and you want to know how to improve it, or just plain non-existent and you want to establish it on your own terms, you'll benefit from this book. An understanding of your credit and how the credit system works may be especially important during some of life's transition points. I assume that this book is of value to you if you're

- Wanting to understand how to maintain your good credit
- Concerned about your credit report, what's in it, and who may be looking at it
- Concerned about the credit status of a loved one
- Unsure of the credit impact of remaining in your home or walking away
- Establishing credit for the first time
- Already in or will soon be in a marriage or partnership
- Taking on or paying back a student loan
- Hunting for a job or hoping for a promotion
- Concerned that your personal info may be compromised or stolen
- Wondering how to deal with medical issues and bills
- Reestablishing credit after the loss of a spouse or life partner
- Recently divorced or soon will be
- Considering what to do about overwhelming debt

I assume that you don't have a formal education in credit or personal finance. If you do, however, I believe you can still find practical insights in this book based on my experience and that of others whom I've helped.

How This Book Is Organized

This book is divided into five major parts with numerous chapters. At your fingertips is everything you need to establish, manage, correct, and improve your credit, with simple, easy-to-understand tips and action steps.

Part 1: Credit Management: An Essential 21st-Century Skill for Financial Success

In this part I show you the simple ways to build a lasting foundation for your credit and financial life in today's tightened credit environment using the concept of green credit as a renewable resource. You also find out about new protections in a post–financial meltdown world.

Part II: Writing on Your Personal Credit Wall: Credit Reporting and Scoring in the Facebook Age

In this part I help you understand your credit reports and scores, show you how to get access to and monitor them for free, and give you the information you need to correct the all-too-common errors that often appear on credit reports and may be lowering your score. I also tell you what you need to know about little-known consumer reports that have information about your medical history, drug use, and more.

Part III: Creating Solid Credit Strategies for Every Stage in Life

Your life changes as you mature, and so do your credit needs. In this part, I cover credit at every stage of your life, from when you're a credit newbie to when you're hunting for a job, buying a home, and getting married. I also discuss the credit implications in the unfortunate situations of divorce and the death of a spouse. I help you control access to your personal data and give you tips to keep your identity secure and avoid scams.

Part IV: Navigating Negative Credit

This part is for all of you with less-than-perfect credit. I show you how to handle minor delinquencies and major collectors while minimizing damage to your credit. I also deal with more serious credit issues, like bankruptcy, foreclosure, and identity theft. I give you all the information you need to clean up a messy credit report and find free help if you want it.

Part V: The Part of Tens

If you like pithy information when it comes to credit, this part is for you. I summarize the significant consumer protections available to you that can help you manage your credit. I also include my best ten tips for stellar credit and some advice on handling financial emergencies.

But that's not all! In the appendix, I fill you in on the CD-ROM that comes with this book, letting you know what you can find there and how to access the info.

Icons Used in This Book

Icons are those little pictures you see sprinkled in the margins throughout this book. Here's what they mean:

The CD that comes with this book is jam-packed with all kinds of useful information that I reference throughout the chapters ahead. Whenever I mention a useful tool available on the CD, I use this icon.

Whether you're new to this country or just new to credit, this symbol alerts you to important concepts and actions that are vital to properly establishing credit.

This icon denotes critical information. Considering the state of my own over-crowded memory, I wouldn't ask you to remember anything unless it was really important.

This image of a credit professional — okay, fine, of a Dummies Man — shows up whenever I go into more detail on a concept or rule. If you don't care about the details of how something works or where it came from, feel free to skip these gems.

This bull's-eye lets you know that you're reading on-target advice — often little-known insights or recommendations that I've picked up over the years.

This icon serves as a warning, telling you to avoid something that's potentially harmful. Take heed!

Where to Go from Here

You get to choose what happens next. This book is packed with information to help you at whatever state or stage your credit is in. You can use the index and table of contents to go directly to the topics of most interest to you or you can start at the beginning and take it from there. With the information in *Credit Management Kit For Dummies,* I'm confident you can get great credit and successfully manage it for the long haul. I wish you all the best in achieving your life dreams, which increasingly require a good credit history to realize. You and your loved ones deserve it.

Part I
Credit Management: An Essential 21st-Century Skill for Financial Success

The 5th Wave   By Rich Tennant

"I take it this is your first car loan."

In this part . . .

1 begin by showing you how to make a firm foundation on which to build your good credit in today's unforgiving and very tight credit environment. I give you a new and easy way to understand how credit fits into your daily life using the concept of green credit as a renewable resource.

Also in this part, I explain how your own personal goals and a spending plan are the essential ingredients to successfully managing your credit. And I cover in detail some consumer protections you're entitled to as a result of some recent credit-oriented legislation.

Chapter 1

Introducing Credit Management Essentials in a Tightened Credit Market

. . . .

In This Chapter

▶ Discovering how to manage your credit

▶ Knowing ways to protect your credit

▶ Keeping your credit solid in each stage of life

▶ Handling credit problems

▶ Rebuilding your credit after a crisis

. . . .

Managing your credit in today's tight credit environment is more important than ever. Why? Because of the huge excesses and losses of the last several years, credit is tight and unforgiving. If that's not enough, credit reports play a larger role than they used to in your noncredit life, affecting more decisions than ever before. This combination of scarcity and value make managing your credit one of the most important things you can do to be successful in achieving your life goals and personal happiness.

In this launchpad chapter, I start with the basics of credit management, which include how credit works, how you can apply that knowledge to get what you want, how to deal with life's inevitable setbacks, and how to recover from those setbacks as quickly as possible. Subsequent chapters build on this information and go into much more detail, helping to make your credit the best it can be and keep it that way. Why? Because life's too short to put up with bad credit, to be taken advantage of by unscrupulous financial companies, and to waste years recovering from credit problems that you can avoid or minimize with the proper actions on your part.

Managing Credit in Today's Unforgiving Economy

The concept of *credit* is easy to understand. It goes like this: You receive something *now* in return for your believable promise to pay for it *later*. That's it. Mortgages, credit cards, auto loans, and other types of credit all fit this definition.

Some people think that credit is a way to increase their income. It's not, although credit can help you manage your income. Others see credit as a way to enhance status — I have a platinum card and you don't! These distinctions are just ways to wrap additional products, features, and profits into the same credit instrument. Credit allows you to conveniently spend money that you've already earned or saved or to spend the money today that you'll earn tomorrow.

But spending tomorrow's money today gets more people in more trouble than they ever dreamed of — trouble that, at a minimum, can cost them some huge interest payments and fees and shut them out of future opportunities. For those with a combination of poor credit management and bad luck, the trouble can take the form of collectors, lawyers, and the loss of peace of mind that comes with financial stability. But not for you! Managing your credit and finances is easy if you know the rules of the game, do some basic painless planning, and know where you stand.

Planning for success

Behind every successful person or venture is a plan. Whether detailed or general, a plan for your money and credit is one of the basic criteria for success. Why? Because others have a plan for your money, and if you don't have one, their plan will win.

Your financial plan begins with envisioning your future as you'd like it to be. Do you desire a home, an education, vacations, a family? The basis of your plan consists of your personal dreams and vision expressed as goals. Long- and short-term goals form a firm base on which to build a plan, and they give you the incentive to fund your plan with savings and targeted spending. Counting up all your income and making decisions on how much you spend and how much you put toward your goals comes next. Called a *budget* or *spending plan,* this becomes your road map to financial success. In Chapter 4 I provide you with step-by-step instructions on how to set up your goals and plans.

After deciding on your goals and setting up your spending plan, you want to consider how credit can help. Using credit cards for convenience and auto and home loans for big-ticket items helps accomplish your goals. Each has differing criteria to qualify you for the best, lowest priced products. That criteria is found in your credit report and credit score.

Reviewing your credit report

Your credit is increasingly used to predict your future value as a customer, employee, and insurance risk. Why? Because there's a strong and proven link showing that if you have bad credit, you're more likely to have insurance claims and a diminished job performance. Research shows that employees with credit problems are less productive and have more absences than those with good credit. The result is that employers use credit reports during the hiring process to complete their assessment of candidates. In a competitive job market, a bad credit report can make the difference between an offer and the employer moving on to the next candidate.

Your *credit report* is a financial snapshot of your life so far. In most cases, every time you use credit, it gets reported to a data storehouse known as a *credit bureau.* This information ends up on a credit report for at least the next seven years. The good, the bad, and the ugly are all there for anyone you do business with to see and for FICO and VantageScore to summarize in a three-digit number (known as your *credit score,* which I discuss in the next section).

Lending decisions used to be based on who you were. For example, a local banker would typically know you personally and could approve or deny your application based on your reputation and his prior experience with you. Today, few borrowers have a personal relationship with their lenders. Even if they did, most loans go before a committee that requires more than a personal reference to approve your loan. Using the information in a credit report enables a group of strangers to objectively assess your payback record. Lenders still like to see evidence of character, capacity, and collateral, known as the three Cs of lending. Credit reports show your character (whether you keep your promises) and help to measure your capacity (how much credit you've handled before).

The information in your credit report is essential to good credit management, but what if your file contains mistakes? Credit-reporting errors are more common than you may think. Research has shown that 25 percent of all credit reports have errors in them that are significant enough to affect your credit score!

Your credit report contains personal information, account information, and public legal records about you. After you know what information is in your report, you can take simple steps to delete out-of-date or erroneous negative information and add positive data that polishes your credit image to get you what you want and need.

Under the Fair and Accurate Credit Transactions Act (the FACT Act or FACTA), you're entitled to a free copy of each of your reports every 12 months. Your state law may entitle you to many more free credit reports. In Chapter 7 I tell you how to get your free reports from each of the three major credit-reporting bureaus, how to get additional free reports, and how to get reports from specialty reporting bureaus, such as those that collect information on your medical history. I also tell you how to clean up your reports so you get the highest score you deserve.

Knowing your credit score

Your *credit score* is a numerical analysis of the years of credit data contained in your credit report. The organizations that calculate your credit score use a proven algorithm (formula) that can predict the likelihood of you defaulting on your next loan over the next two years. Your score doesn't take into account characteristics like gender, race, nationality, or marital status. The result is a discrimination- and prejudice-free assessment of you as a credit risk. Further, by boiling down the decision-making process to a three-digit score, you get the speed and convenience of a quick approval or denial of your application.

Two main scoring models are in use today: FICO and VantageScore. Your FICO score ranges from 300 to 850. Your VantageScore ranges from 501 to 990. Several weighted factors make up your score. By understanding these factors, you can avoid any surprises when you apply for that car or other loan.

I give you detailed definitions of each of these factors in Chapter 6 and tell you how you can get the maximum boost to your score with some simple credit-management techniques, like keeping your card balances under 50 percent of your maximum limit and using your savings account to help secure a low-interest-rate loan. The differences in interest payments over a number of years can run from hundreds of dollars on a credit card to tens of thousands more for a home mortgage.

All the information used to determine your credit score is contained in only one place: your credit report. You have at least three credit reports (from TransUnion, Equifax, and Experian), and the result is that you probably have at least three different credit scores! How can you be sure the information in each of your credit reports is accurate and as positive as possible? Great credit begins by knowing what's in your report and what's not. Check out the "Protecting Your Credit" section later in this chapter as well as Chapters 6, 7, and 8 for more information about monitoring your credit reports and scores.

Considering credit a renewable resource

Some people have a block when it comes to math, and that block can carry over into credit, which is based on seemingly confusing and endless numbers. I've helped some of my clients understand credit by relating it to something everyone understands: the environment. Everyone knows that pollution is bad for the environment. Everyone knows that resources in the environment can either be overused and diminished or managed well and renewed. And finally, everyone knows that a balance among all the environment's parts is necessary for the environment to be healthy and sustainable. The same principles apply to credit; I call this credit environment your *credit ecosystem*.

Credit ecosystem

You may find understanding your credit easier if you view it as its own ecosystem. Each of the credit-scoring components affects the others, and pollution in the form of negative reported behavior hurts your ecosystem. Like the real-world ecosystem, pollution takes time to clean up. If the damage is bad enough, it causes severe systemic damage for years before the environment can recover.

Balancing components

You manage your credit environment by limiting overuse of credit and monitoring your credit's health by being aware of your credit score and the information flowing into your reports. Doing so keeps everything in harmony, and the resulting balance strengthens your credit ecosystem. Overspending and overusing credit depletes your resources faster than you can replace them, much like overfishing or overlogging. An ever-increasing accumulation of debt from using more credit than you have income to support strains your credit ecosystem, perhaps to the point of collapse.

Credit pollution

Defaulting on payments introduces pollution into your credit report and score. Like an oil spill, this pollution can't be covered up and hidden; you have to clean it up properly and put safeguards in place so it doesn't happen again. Credit pollution, like its environmental counterpart, has effects beyond your credit report. A polluted report can hurt your job prospects, require larger payments (and a larger stain on your finances) for insurance and loan products, and more.

Green credit

I call using credit wisely, in accordance with your plan to build a positive credit history and score, *green credit*. In Chapter 3 I give you more insight into this way of understanding your credit and managing it like a renewable resource. Green credit is part of a balanced spending and income system that's reflected in your spending plan. By using credit judiciously, like you would organic fertilizer, you increase the buying power of your present income in a responsible way and replenish the resources you're using before they run out.

Protecting Your Credit

Credit is increasingly used for more than just getting a good rate on your credit card. It affects your ability to compete for a job or a promotion; get affordable insurance; qualify for some licenses, military service, and security clearances; and even find a decent place to live. At the same time, data breaches have exposed the credit and personal information of millions of people to identity thieves. These thieves can use stolen identities to establish credit in your name without your knowledge and then overuse and default on that credit.

Getting familiar with credit laws

Over the last several years, Congress has passed new laws to give you, the consumer, more protections. Knowing about and taking advantage of these safeguards can help you keep your credit safe. If your identity is ever stolen, knowing your rights is essential to a quick resolution. Among the laws I discuss in Chapter 5 are the

- ✔ **Dodd-Frank Wall Street Reform and Consumer Protection Act,** which created a single consumer watchdog agency and allows consumers free access to their credit scores under certain conditions.

- ✔ **CARD Act,** which restricts lenders from raising your rates on existing balances and more.

- ✔ **FACT Act,** which gives you access to free credit reports and ID theft protection and remedies.

- ✔ **Fair Debt Collection Practices Act (FDCPA),** which spells out your rights and the rules that collectors must follow in debt collection.

Knowing your rights: Collection protection

Collectors have a reputation for being demanding and sometimes abusive. If your plan hits a snag and a collector comes calling, knowing the rules and your rights makes all the difference between successfully resolving the problem and being terrified of the unknown.

One little-known solution to a debt-collection problem is the statute of limitations. Each state has a time period after which a debt can't legally be collected in court. Knowing your state's rules can take the teeth out of a collection attempt.

In Chapter 18 I go into detail about other ways to handle collectors, and I offer solutions that work. From how to handle calls and threatening letters to how to craft repayment proposals, I walk you through how to keep a small collection annoyance from becoming a major and upsetting life event.

Receiving free reports and filing disputes

I mention earlier in this chapter that you can get free copies of your credit reports annually to check for errors. I strongly recommend that you get these reports every chance you can. Besides the one annual free report from each of the three credit-reporting bureaus allowed by the FACT Act, your state may require the bureaus to give you more — sometimes many more! In addition, you're entitled to free extra reports, and sometimes even free credit scores, if you've been turned down for credit, didn't get the top rate offered, or had any adverse action (like a limit cut) to your credit card. All these situations are opportunities to check, dispute, and clean your credit reports for free and help make credit management a breeze.

Signing up for credit monitoring

Every time I turn around, someone is offering to monitor my credit for me. Do you need this service, and are you willing to pay for it? In Chapter 8 I get into the details of credit monitoring, and with a few exceptions, I find that it's an unnecessary expense. With all the opportunities you have for free reports (see the preceding section), paying for more may be overkill. As for score monitoring, expect it to change frequently as new data comes into and leaves your credit report. Unless you're planning a big purchase like a house in the near future that requires new credit, knowing your score every day is like knowing the value of your home when you don't intend to sell it — relatively interesting but useless information.

In addition, if you have a credit card, you may already have good fraud-monitoring in place without your knowing it. Most cards monitor spending patterns to sniff out fraud and identity theft before they cost a fortune. The result is one less reason to pay to monitor your credit.

Setting alarms, alerts, and freezes

If you're still worried about too much access to your credit data, you have the right to limit access to only those you approve. Chapter 8 covers how to limit access, along with the pluses and minuses of doing so. Among your options:

✔ You can set up alerts with your creditors to spot new activity on your account.

✔ You can place an alert on your credit file so that lenders use more caution before approving any changes.

✔ If you're a member of the military, you can place an active-duty alert on your files.

✔ You can freeze access to your account so that no new creditors can access your information without your express permission (except if you owe the government money).

Identifying identity theft

Still the number one reported crime at the Federal Trade Commission, identity theft isn't going away. The number of cases reported is small in relation to the huge amount of identity information that hackers get every time you hear of a database compromise. This leads me to believe that your identity may be in jeopardy for years to come as thieves warehouse your data for a future time. Some simple vigilance can help you stop a theft in its early stages before serious damage is done. Follow these tips from Chapter 12:

✔ Protect your information at home. Most identity theft is low-tech and committed by people that you invite into your home.

✔ Shred financial documents with account and Social Security numbers.

✔ Use electronic bill paying to avoid bill theft from your mailbox.

✔ Check your credit report at least once a year to look for unfamiliar credit lines. If you see accounts you don't recognize, take the actions I suggest in Chapter 12.

If the unthinkable happens and you become an ID theft victim, you need to take fast, effective steps as soon as you find out you've been victimized. Chapter 20 walks you through what you need to do and who you need to contact. It also helps you reestablish your credit afterward.

Maintaining Good Credit throughout Life

I say earlier in this chapter that your credit report presents a financial snapshot of your life . . . so far. So as your life changes, your credit report changes, too. If your life is filled with positive news like a steady job, a good income, a promotion, controlled expenses, and maybe even a partner, then your credit report should reflect that stability. If, however, you have a reversal of fortune with a job loss, income interruption, illness, or divorce, expect your perfect credit to show the stress of your life.

Establishing credit for the first time

Getting credit doesn't need to be scary. You have easy ways to establish credit for the first time or, in some cases, the second time around as a single person. Knowing what to do and what to avoid makes this process simple and foolproof. In Chapter 9 I cover the essentials of getting your new credit up and running. Using simple techniques like borrowing your own money and using retail store cards and authorized user accounts, you can establish good credit in no time. Your credit score can be figured on the history of just a month or two, and then you're on your way.

Here are a few ways to build credit for the first time:

✔ Open a savings account at a bank that reports to all three bureaus. Then take out a loan using the account as security and make monthly payments on time.

✔ Have a relative add you as an authorized user on her credit card. Her history will flow into your credit report.

✔ Apply for a secured credit card with a bank that reports monthly to all three bureaus.

Credit changes at life's stages

As you move through life, you find new needs for credit and new challenges in keeping your credit strong when life gets bumpy. Chapters 10 and 11 give you detailed help in negotiating life's often turbulent credit waters without capsizing your boat. Credit plays a strong role in every aspect of your life, including getting a job, buying a home or renting an apartment, purchasing a car, getting insurance on your home and car, getting married, getting divorced, paying medical bills, planning for retirement and end-of-life expenses, and more!

Many people know that because a prospective employer may check your credit in the hiring process, having good credit during your job hunt is important. But how can you keep your credit in good shape when you've been laid off and don't have enough income to handle all your bills while job hunting? Chapter 11 tells you how. It also gives you practical tips for safeguarding your credit before, during, and after a divorce.

Avoiding pitfalls

Whether you're new to credit or you're a credit veteran, you need to be careful of counterproductive actions and scams. Some examples of things I advise you to avoid, if at all possible, are payday lenders, refund-anticipation loans, check cashers, and credit-repair companies.

You won't go blind from using a payday lender once for an emergency, but the very concept of this type of high-interest loan is flawed. If you have no savings and you're living paycheck to paycheck and an emergency expense comes up, does getting a payday loan make sense? You have to pay back a short-term (two weeks or so) loan on your next payday. But all that money is already committed, so how can you pay it back? Chances are you'll need more than one loan and owe lots of money in interest charges.

Refund-anticipation loans are another borrowing mistake. These loans accelerate an e-filed tax refund by a very short period of time for a very large fee when calculated as an annual percentage rate (APR). Plus, if your refund is held up or reduced, you owe more money on the loan than you expected.

Check cashers perform a valid but expensive function for people with no bank accounts who need to cash checks. But I suggest that you get a bank account so you have a place to begin saving and stop paying for unnecessary check cashing.

Credit-repair companies have a horrid reputation. Legislation called the Credit Repair Organizations Act has tried to limit the damage caused by fraudulent actions that some companies advise to rig the credit-reporting system. If you're thinking of credit-repair companies, think again.

Repairing Bad Credit

After you've had a rough patch and fallen behind on your credit payments, you may think that you'll never recover. Between the interest expense, the negative credit reporting, and maybe even collection actions, the situation can be overwhelming. But I assure you that you can reverse the cycle. You can not only reestablish good credit but also keep good credit forever. Forever is a long time, but if you follow my advice in this book, you'll banish the credit blues from your history permanently! It's not magic, and it won't cost you another dime. By realistically assessing your situation, using free help if you need it, setting goals, planning your spending and savings, and using credit as part of your overall plan, you'll quickly rebuild your credit.

Settling debts

You hear the ads everywhere today: "Settle your debt for pennies on the dollar!"; "You have a right to pay less than you owe!"; and more. Debt settlement is an often misunderstood option that may work for you, but only if you handle it properly. Many companies that offer debt settlement help themselves a lot more than they help you. You can avoid the huge fees and potential credit damage you incur by dealing with many debt-settlement companies if you reach a settlement agreement with your lender on your own or if you use your own attorney.

Most people don't know that they're personally responsible for the actions of the debt-settlement company they hire and that their credit will be ruined in a protracted and adversarial settlement process.

In Chapter 18 I give you the information you need about debt settlements to decide whether debt settlement is for you and, if so, what your best options are.

Resetting your goals

Just as you did when you first started establishing credit, I want you to revisit your goals from time to time as your life changes. When your life changes, your goals should reflect that new reality. Some goals that seemed so easy may now move from short-term goals to long-term ones. Others may change as you mature. That red Corvette may not be as important as it was in your 20s. Take the time to reset your sights, as I explain in Chapter 13.

Begin by envisioning your life as you'd like it to be over the short, medium, and long term. Next, update your budget/spending plan so you know your current financial resources. Then begin to see how long it will take to fund your goals and when using credit may be appropriate.

To be sure your credit is up to the job of supporting your goals for the future, check your credit report and dispute any inaccuracies or out-of-date information. To rebuild a solid credit report, you need to start on solid credit history, not errors that may hold you back. After you check your reports, look for opportunities to review them for free every time you can (see Chapter 7 for extra free opportunities).

As you build your plan to clear up any past-due loan payments, take a minute to find out which creditors report your credit history to the bureaus and which don't. You need to pay all your creditors, but you sure don't want to miss paying a bill that reports late payments to the bureaus while paying one that doesn't report. Chapter 6 has a list of who reports and who doesn't.

Rebuilding credit by using it

The best way to rebuild your credit is to exercise it! Using your goals and spending plan as a guide, start making those payments as agreed, on time and for the correct amount. Every month you do so, you build better credit while your older, bad credit either counts for less or drops off your credit report altogether.

Consider opening a *secured credit card* (backed by a bank account deposit) or a *passbook loan* to add a revolving and installment account to fatten your credit history and score.

Using cosigning and authorized users

I normally don't recommend cosigning for a loan, but in your case, the opposite is true — you aren't cosigning, someone else is! Cosigning is one way to get access to credit so it can be reported to the bureaus. But you need to keep in mind a few important rules. First, you have to make all the payments on time. Second, if you can't make a payment when it's due, you have to tell the cosigner in advance so he can make the payment and protect his credit. You can pay him back later. Third, you can't ever get mad at the cosigner while you still owe him money. He's doing you a huge favor at great personal credit risk!

Another way to help rebuild your credit is to become an authorized user on someone else's credit card. After you're added to the person's account, her good credit history will flow on to your credit record as a positive account and payment stream, beefing up your record and score. The person needs to have good credit, though, or her bad credit will negatively affect yours. I suggest that you decline getting a card for the person's account so that only her charges appear on the account. That way, if she has a bad memory — like I do — you're spared monthly calls asking whether this charge or that charge is yours. Although you won't have access to any new credit, your score will get a boost.

Finding sources of free help

Though you can do a lot of things on your own, sometimes having a pro on your side to give you tips helps. You can find that help in three main places, and it can range from inexpensive to free. Nonprofit credit counseling, pro bono lawyers, and HUD-approved counseling agencies offer priceless insight, help, and advice. The trick is to ask for it.

Nonprofit credit counselors help by working with you to set goals, develop a spending plan, and assess your ability to repay your debts. They can set up a repayment plan in concert with your lenders to lower payments and interest rates and get positive credit back on your reports faster than you can do on your own. They're funded by creditors but work for you, and I recommend the good ones highly. You can discover where to find the good ones in Chapter 15.

Lawyers sometime offer free or pro bono help if you can't afford to pay. I have a list of resources to help you find one in your area in Chapter 15.

Mortgages are a different and dangerous type of loan. The rules for handling delinquent mortgages are different from those for regular consumer debts, and the penalty for a mistake is much more severe. So I strongly recommend that if you have a mortgage problem you get professional, HUD-certified help. You can find an agency at the HUD website: www.hud.gov.

Lastly, watch out for bad help. In a nutshell, if someone approaches you and offers to help for a fee, don't do it. The free resources work well. The costly ones too often are just ways to separate you from your money while you're under stress.

Dealing with collectors

Sometimes, you have to take the call. You know it's a collector, but you don't know what to say, do, or offer. In Chapter 16 I spell out how to take control of the collection process. Collectors have rules that they must follow, and if you know the rules, you'll feel more confident in dealing with a stressful situation. The Fair Debt Collection Practices Act (FDCPA) regulates what can and can't be done in a collection action. In general, this law protects you from abuse and threats. For example, a collector can't threaten an action that it can't or doesn't intend to take, it can't make harassing calls, and it can't use abusive language or swear at you. When you know your rights and insist that you be treated fairly, you can negotiate a payment schedule that fits your budget. If you need help, you can always ask a credit counselor (see the preceding section) for assistance.

Debts are subject to your state's statute of limitations. After a debt is past the date, you can't be sued for it. Collectors won't waste their time on a debt that can't be enforced.

Weathering a Severe Mortgage Crisis

Some credit problems are worse than others. In my experience a mortgage crisis is among the most upsetting, expensive, and damaging to your credit and relationships. Your home is your castle. When you may lose it you likely feel as though your very existence is under attack. It may be difficult to think matters through and come up with the best solution for you and your family. Here I preview the major options to help guide you along the best path. Check out Chapter 17 for more mortgage information.

I've said that mortgages are different from other types of debts and credit. They're different because of a number of factors, including the size of the debt, the importance lenders attach to a debt secured by your home, the fact that the debt is probably packaged in a security that's been resold many times and is subject to inflexible collection rules, and more. Mortgage delinquency can have a very large negative effect on your credit score for a very long time. For example, just being 30 days late on your mortgage payment can cost you 100+ points on your FICO score and take three years to recover from. The upshot is that if you're in danger of falling behind on your payments or you're already behind, you're better off with some professional help.

Opting for help

In a bad mortgage situation, the sooner you get help the better. The reason is simple: The stakes are high and the help is free. Most people who have a mortgage payment due on the first of the month know they have until the 15th to pay it. Do you? If you miss that payment on the 15th, you're 45 days late. Mortgages are paid in arrears, so the bill is 30 days old when you get it. Miss the pay date and the 15-day grace period goes away until you catch up. By the 15th of the next month, you're 15 days away from a foreclosure action. Fast, isn't it! So I suggest you don't delay in contacting a HUD-approved counseling agency. These agencies are often housed in credit-counseling agencies so they can address all your debt issues at once.

Doing it on your own

I realize some of you won't take help and insist on working your mortgage problems out on your own. The process is tricky and long but it can be done. In Chapter 17 I go into details on the steps and time frames for action. Besides acting quickly, you need to keep excellent notes about who you speak with, when, and what was said. You're dealing with a bureaucracy, and bureaucracies love to forget they ever heard from you and send you all over the place to avoid responsibility for helping. So notes are essential. In Chapter 17, I list terms and things to ask for so you can sound like you know what you're talking about.

Just because a bank doesn't want to take your home doesn't mean it won't.

As in any debt-resolution process, you need to do your homework before you make a call to your mortgage servicer. Know what you really need in terms of help to take care of your missed payments and what you can offer. You may be able to make additional payments over a six-month period to catch up. Or you may not be able to make your current payment at all but need to ask for a reduced payment for a certain amount of time. Whatever you need, you have to be specific. Chapter 17 helps you understand the major options, but they change frequently, so you may have to rely on your servicer (the bureaucrat) to advise you on options.

If it looks like you can't work out a compromise, you have some ways to leave your home that result in less credit damage. Among them are a

- ✔ **Deed-in-lieu of foreclosure:** You give the house back, saving the bank foreclosure expenses.
- ✔ **Short sale:** You get the bank to agree to let you try to sell the house for less than the mortgage value.
- ✔ **Friendly foreclosure:** You cooperate with the bank and leave the house in good shape on a timely basis.

Strategic mortgage default

Strategic mortgage default isn't an option anyone likes. However, the realities of the current mortgage market have more people considering walking away from their homes as an alternative to foreclosure. What happens is that, based on what you owe, you may be very, very unlikely to ever get back the money you're putting into payments every month. According to the Federal Reserve, strategic default is particularly popular as a remedy for people who lose 50 percent or more of their property values and owe large mortgages. Say that you owe $200,000 on your mortgage but the property is only worth $100,000. Why waste $100,000 in overpayments? Following that reasoning, many people are mailing the keys back to the bank and walking away from their former homes.

Credit damage from a strategic default is significant and lasts a long time. You can expect really bad credit for seven years and a FICO score drop of 140 to 160 points. Plus, Fannie Mae won't guarantee a future loan for you for the next seven years, which means that you'll pay more for a new mortgage and you'll need expensive mortgage insurance to buy another home in the next seven years.

Filing Bankruptcy

There are times in life when you just can't cope. This is also true in credit matters. If you're unable to come to terms with the aftermath of being over-extended on credit, bankruptcy may enable you to hit the reset button and start over again. But there is no free lunch, and while you pay a price in terms of future credit, bankruptcy for the right reasons and in the right cir-cumstances may be your best bet. In this section I give you a quick look at an often misunderstood and misused tool so you can decide if the cure for your debts is worth the damage to your credit. Chapter 19 has more information on the updated bankruptcy process, what it means to you, and what your alternatives are.

You need to pass a means test to see which type of bankruptcy you can file for. Chapter 7 bankruptcy gets rid of some of your debts but not others. Chapter 13 bankruptcy requires you to pay what you can afford to your creditors over a five-year period if you don't qualify for a Chapter 7. In a nutshell, if you earn too much money, you have to pay your bills in a Chapter 13.

Even worse, from my point of view, is that filing for bankruptcy may not solve your problem. If you're in debt trouble because you spend more than you make, or to put it another way, because your expenses exceed your income, then filing won't change that situation. Before long, you may be back in debt but without the option of refiling.

You face a waiting period between filing for bankruptcy and being able to file again. This period can range from two to eight years, depending on the type of bankruptcy you file and the type you want to file next.

In today's tight credit market, expect a long recovery time from a bankruptcy. Recent FICO research indicates that a Chapter 7 filing can lower a good credit score by up to 240 points and that it takes seven to ten years for the score to recover to its original level. Ouch! That's a long stay in the bad credit hotel. Be sure it's worth it!

Chapter 2

Gaining Control of Your Credit

. . . .

. . . .

*W*hen Henry Ford decided you could have any color you wanted for your new Model T Ford, as long as it was black, it wasn't because car buyers liked black. It wasn't even because Henry liked black. It was because drying the paint on cars coming off the assembly line took the longest time of all the operations, and black dried the fastest of all the colors. By sticking with black, Ford could ship more cars each day and make more money, faster.

Credit issuers operate pretty similarly; they care more about making themselves money than meeting your needs. They shovel out credit offers by the truckload based on very cursory reviews of your relative creditworthiness. Sure, some of the things they tell you may be true (for instance, you may indeed have earned the right to exclusive privileges and benefits), but the only thing you can be sure of is that the offer is good for them. Whether you need the credit product in question or whether it's even remotely advantageous to you is just not a question that the marketers of the credit world consider. Like the black paint on the Model Ts, you get what makes the most money for the lender. Unless, of course, you put yourself in control of your financial and credit future.

This chapter is all about helping you take control of your credit away from the issuers. In it, I unmask the plans others have for your financial future and introduce you to the tools you need to chart your *own* course to success. I also help you figure out how to balance your spending, savings, and credit use; perk up your credit score; and gauge your credit style.

The Importance of Planning When It Comes to Your Credit

Imagine a football quarterback saying that he plays the big game based on how he feels that day. If he sets no goals, practices no plays, has no trainer, and doesn't monitor his finish times or scores after each practice, would you want to bet on him winning a top spot in his division? In the sport known as credit management you need to follow a plan if you want to succeed.

But you don't have any competition, you say? Wrong! Lenders, credit grantors, insurers, landlords, and employers are constantly measuring your credit performance, and the cost of a substandard performance can be higher interest rates and fewer opportunities. All these players and others use your credit profile as a gauge of your potential for success or failure, so having a plan and goals for your credit makes real sense.

In the following sections, I reveal the plans others have for your money and introduce you to the steps you can take to seize control of your funds so that you don't fall prey to plans that only benefit credit issuers.

Zeroing in on the plans others have for your money

People constantly plan to get you to spend money that you don't really need to spend. Just think of the credit offers I'm sure you receive. These offers may ebb and flow with the economy and lenders' appetites for new customers, but inevitably they continue to show up from your bank, investment companies, and even strangers. Rest assured that issuers design these offers to be great for them without regard for your particular situation. If you answer many (or all!) of the offers you receive, your credit score would take a hit each time your report was reviewed for an offer, and you'd get a further score reduction every time you were approved for new credit. Trust me, the issuers don't care that their plans are winning at the expense of your credit.

If the credit issuers' hidden goals seem a bit nebulous to you, consider what happens when you set foot in your local grocery store. The fact that the milk is located on the *opposite* side of the store from the door is no accident. This forces you to walk through the entire store and past an array of tempting products to get the one thing you need. The potential for an impulse buy is greatly enhanced, to the delight of the store owner and at your expense.

The bottom line is that if you have no plan for your finances and others do, you're more likely to fail and they're more likely to win.

Developing your own plans for your future

To avoid being a pawn in some credit issuer's chess game, you need to start crafting a plan for your finances and credit. Specifically, you need to identify what you want to spend money on (goals), develop a spending and savings plan reflecting your goals, and then determine how credit fits into those plans. Chapter 4 presents the process of developing a spending and savings plan in detail, but the key tasks are as follows:

- ✔ Set and prioritize your financial goals.
- ✔ Take simple steps to create a workable plan.
- ✔ Adjust your plan as you go along.

The same overall process applies with your credit but with a few differences. Yes, you still need to set credit goals, but they can be simpler. For example, perhaps you want to buy a home in three years. You need to save for a down payment, and you need to have good credit to get a good interest rate and terms. This won't happen overnight, so you need to do your planning to make it happen. First, find out where you stand by obtaining free copies of your credit report and ordering your credit score; I explain how to do both in Chapter 7. Review your report for inaccuracies and then dispute them, as well as any out-of-date items you find, using the pointers in Chapter 7.

After you take care of the incorrect information, you can use the correct information in your report as a starting point for planning to build the credit you want. Make some adjustments to your credit usage based on the four statements your credit-score report shows about how you can improve your credit. These four statements are called *reason statements*. They may indicate that you have too many active cards or you have too much credit available. Both situations can hurt your credit.

Next, use the spending plan you create to determine which of your goals (say, buying a home or taking a cruise) needs to be funded using credit. Then find out what the credit criteria are for a low-interest mortgage rate and what kind of credit card you want to use on your cruise. Perhaps consider a card that gives you points toward a cruise as an incentive. (See Chapter 22 for my top ten ways to build great credit.) Now you're making the decisions about which type of credit offers to accept or turn down instead of just accepting those preapproved offers that show up, whether they fit your needs or not.

When you match your spending goals to a credit or lending need, you'll take charge of your finances in no time.

Balancing Spending, Savings, and Credit Use

An orchestra is beautiful to hear. A great meal is a delight to eat. What makes each a pleasure is balance. Whether it's the balance of instruments or the balance of ingredients and spices, if each component isn't in harmony with the others, if the balance is wrong, the outcome can be a disaster.

The same idea of balance applies to your finances and credit management. Your spending, savings, and credit use must all work together for the most pleasing result. The next sections show you how to take baby steps toward achieving that all-important balance. (For full details about crafting your future vision into achievable goals, turn to Chapter 4.)

Spending on your terms

If your spending is under control and you have money for periodic expenses in your plan, chances are you've built a strong foundation for your financial house, and your credit will be safe and strong when you need it. Say that your car has a mechanical problem; where does the money come from to fix it? If your spending is planned, then you should have a spending category for periodic auto maintenance and repairs. So the money comes from there and not your available credit on a credit card.

When you use credit, you use tomorrow's money, money that you haven't yet earned and may not earn. Look at it as using tomorrow's money today. But when tomorrow comes around, how will you pay for tomorrow if you've already spent tomorrow's money yesterday? The more you shelter your credit from surprises or overuse by planning where and how to spend your money, the stronger your credit history, credit score, and future will be.

Ending financial emergencies

If a spending plan gives you a firm foundation on which to build, then emergency savings provides the roof for shelter. Saving for emergencies and your goals is essential for financial success. Let me say that again. If you don't save, you'll fail. In other words, you'll constantly be spending tomorrow's money and becoming more and more vulnerable to money shortages and the stress they bring.

I'm sure you don't want to live paycheck to paycheck, but perhaps money is tight and you're wondering how on earth you can possibly save enough. Here are four essential ways to manage saving your hard-earned moola:

- ✔ **Make savings painless.** Use direct deposit to put money in a savings account every paycheck. Start small with what little you can afford — $5 a week or more. The amount doesn't matter.

- ✔ **Make savings a habit.** Automatic deposits slowly build. Your confidence in seeing savings where there were none before will build faster. Soon you'll have enough to handle a small emergency or even just a part of one.

- ✔ **Add to savings with money you don't have yet.** Put half of new raises, IRS tax refunds, and other windfalls like birthday money and the like into the account. This is money that you never had, never counted on, and won't miss.

- ✔ **Consider joining a savings club or organization.** Groups like America Saves (www.americasaves.org) and the Women's Institute for Financial Education (www.wife.org) can offer valuable ideas and support to keep you on track.

Using credit to enhance your life

With spending under control and money in the bank for emergencies and expected big-ticket items, you can use your excellent credit to get the best offers and give you an edge in life. You get the best deal terms on loans and credit cards thanks to a solid credit history and score. Even better, you free up thousands of dollars for trips, school, and other expenses when you get the lowest interest rates on mortgages, car loans, and more. Great credit also gives you lower insurance rates, access to better apartments, and even an edge at work. This last point is because a normal part of hiring and promotional decisions often involves a credit report review. Your good credit can give you a competitive edge over other applicants or co-workers who have blemished credit.

Improving Your Credit Score

To get the best deals on credit, you need to have a good credit score as well as a good credit report. Your credit score is developed from the data in your credit report and is a strong determinant of the interest rate and deal terms for which you qualify.

Having a perfect credit score is extremely rare. The FICO 850 and the VantageScore 990 scores are the top scores, and I've never seen a validated case of a perfect score. So it's just as well that a perfect score has very little influence on your loan approval as long as you have a good enough score for the credit for which you're applying.

Each type of credit — such as revolving (credit cards) or installment (car loans and mortgages) — has different score cutoffs or buckets into which credit grantors divide their customers and the rates and terms they offer them. For example, the rate for a 30-year mortgage may be the same for a person with a score between 760 and 850, all other underwriting criteria being the same (such as income and job stability). Any score in the range may be priced the same. A car loan provider may group anyone with a 720 to 850 score in the same category.

Your goal is to get into the best bucket you can by the time you need to get the type of credit in question. You do this by building a plan that gets you to your goal of good enough credit. Take some quiet time and include anyone with whom you're sharing your life. List each of your credit-oriented goals and then check a resource like www.bankrate.com to find out what credit score gets you in the next-highest tier of borrowers. Unless you're in the top tier, come up with actions you need to take based on what you find in your credit report. You can find details on how a score is built in Chapter 6.

Another way to pump up your credit score is to remove any errors you find on your credit report. Because credit scores normally look back over a two- to three-year period to develop an accurate picture of your risk profile, it takes time to offset any negative data in your credit report that may be hurting your score. Removing errors has an immediate effect on your score.

Watch out for companies that promise to remove accurate negative information from your credit report and thereby improve your score. They can't do what they claim and may get you in even more trouble if, for example, you're approved for a loan based on a fraudulently altered credit report. Avoid them like the plague!

Determining Your Credit Style

Lenders, particularly banks, divide their credit card customers into two main categories: transactors and revolvers. The people in these categories have different needs from their credit, so identifying your type of use is important in the process of picking a credit instrument that best fits your lifestyle needs.

Transactors, also referred to as *convenience users,* are pretty straightforward in their credit use. You fall into this category if you primarily use your credit cards for convenience in place of cash. This reduces your need to carry a wad of bills with you that would spoil the line of your trousers or invite a bump on the head. You pay balances in full every month and avoid fees and interest charges.

If you think you may be a transactor, focus on the incentives a card offers you for use, like airline tickets or hotel nights instead of a low interest rate. No balance means no interest, so who cares if it's 19.8 percent over prime; if you don't carry a balance, the interest rate is irrelevant to you. Be sure that you use the card enough to actually get a benefit from it. For example, if you choose an airline mileage card that requires you to charge $25,000 annually to get you the equivalent of a free ticket and you only spend $10,000 a year on the card, it may not be a good choice. You may want to consider a cash-back card instead. Some of these cards have an annual fee. Again, be sure that you get more out of the card than you pay into it.

Revolvers frequently carry a balance from month to month. If you're one of these most desirable customers (from the lenders' point of view), you consider your credit card as a line of credit to use to pay for purchases over time. You make payments on time, often for the minimum or more, but rarely in full. You pay interest every month and may not look too carefully at what the interest costs you over the long haul. Your bank loves you and could only love you more if you missed a payment or two!

A revolver's best choice is a card that offers a low interest rate. A low rate does a lot to help you keep balances down because your interest charges are included in the minimum payment you make each month. The result is that you carry debt for much longer if your rate is high and you make minimum payments. Shopping for a zero-APR card makes sense, but expect to change cards more often, as these rates are usually for limited periods of time. Be careful also about incurring a 3 to 5 percent fee for transferring balances from an old card with expiring rates to a new one. Changing cards often may also have a negative effect on your credit score (see the list of score components in Chapter 6).

In addition to the usual card user categorizations, I have a few of my own that you may find helpful in identifying yourself — read on.

The quicksand charger

You qualify as a *quicksand charger* in my book if you spend on impulse and don't notice that you're slowly sinking into a debt hole that may overwhelm you. Using credit without knowing how or when you'll be able to pay the bill is a bad habit that usually has an unhappy ending.

Use short-term installment loans for expenses that you plan to carry for six months or more. The fixed payment helps you get the debt paid off more predictably, and the additional type of credit use helps your score. Plus, every time you apply for a new installment loan you get a free reality check from your lender.

The clueless charger

If you find that you continue to have unpleasant surprises on your credit card statement (like unexpected balance transfer fees and penalties) and don't know why this is happening to you, you may be a *clueless charger*. Students and other credit newbies tend to find themselves being taken advantage of because they lack a plan for using credit.

Read and understand the terms that come with your credit card. Believe that you have to make payments on time as your card agreement says and not what other clueless chargers may tell you. For example, you can and will be sued in court if you don't make the payment required by the card issuer even though you're making a lesser payment and it's all you can afford. Get some financial education from a responsible provider. Lenders and credit counseling agencies can help.

The great pretender

With apologizes to the Platters, who released the hit song "The Great Pretender" in 1955, this category includes millions who extend their income or lack thereof by using credit as if it gives them additional income. This approach may help make ends meet in the short term but is often a disaster in the end.

The tighter your finances are, the tighter you need to control your use of credit. Start with a budget, trim expenses, increase income, and only use your credit when you know you can pay it off in a reasonable length of time (90 days or less is best). If you can't say when a charge will be paid off, don't charge it. It's better to cut back now rather than later, when your credit is trashed.

Chapter 3

Taking a Sustainable Approach to Your Financial Environment

In This Chapter

▶ Understanding the connections in your credit ecosystem

▶ Keeping your credit ecosystem in balance

▶ Avoiding credit pollution

▶ Recovering from credit damage

*N*ot everyone is comfortable with numbers. I know this from personal experience. My wife is one of those nonmath types. Now don't get me wrong, she can count her change and has money in the bank, but she sees the world differently from the way I do. So for the large number of people who don't see the world through a financial lens, I want to offer another way to understand credit management. I recently gave a keynote address on this topic to 200 teachers, and they agreed that their students need a better way to relate to credit that isn't just dollars and cents. Everyone in America understands the environment, so why not draw a parallel? Well, I did. And I call it the ecology of credit, or green credit.

Not long ago, Americans didn't understand the connection between their actions and their environment. They didn't get that something as seemingly minor as spraying for mosquitoes could upset the ecological balance of nature, or that throwing trash into the ocean could harm sea creatures and endanger whole species. Today, you all see the connections, and although you can disagree about whether humankind is experiencing global warming or climate change, everyone understands that actions have consequences, sometimes for years to come. Most people don't see this type of connection in their use of credit, but the reality is that credit decisions can create both negative and positive feedback loops, just like you see in the environment. For example, paying only the minimum payment on a credit card means you pay more interest, which means you have less money to deal with emergencies, which may make it more likely that you accumulate more debt as you go along.

In this chapter, I help you better understand credit by drawing parallels between your natural environment and your credit environment. Green credit advocates a sustainable approach to managing your financial resources and the stewardship of your credit ecosystem/environment through self-interested individual behavior. I help you recognize that credit is an integral part of modern-day life, not just an accessory. So come along with me as I take you on a field trip to the wilds of credit and beyond by exploring your financial environment.

Going Green: Treating Credit as a Renewable Resource

Looking at credit as a renewable resource changes your perspective. Treating a resource so that it lasts your entire lifetime makes you want to better understand how it works so you don't unknowingly harm it. Doing so also makes you responsible for not overusing or abusing this important resource to the point of endangerment or even extinction. To be a good steward of your credit, you need to understand how credit coexists with all the other parts of your financial ecosystem and how it fits into the rest of your life. In this section I show you how to recognize the parts of your credit environment, their relationships to one another, and ways to keep them all in sync so they complement one another.

Recognizing your credit environment

You've all heard about ecology or ecosystems at one time or another. What is an *ecosystem,* really? It's a unit that consists of a number of factors that function together in your environment. Each participant in the ecosystem depends on the others to survive. Together, they sustain one another in a routine pattern of give and take. Their balance can be delicate at times and easily upset. Major disruptions to the ecosystem can be disastrous to all the participants and can take years to undo. For example, in the ecosystem of the natural world, if too many fish are born, they use more than their share of water and plants, affecting the delicate balance.

Similarly, your credit ecosystem has a number of parts — lines of credit, emergency savings (to fund unexpected expenses without relying solely on credit), mortgages, credit cards, car loans, a payment history, and so on — that function and interact together. If one part is out of control, it impacts the others. A late payment on a bill can cause your credit to deteriorate and start a ripple effect through your credit ecosystem, as sure as a forest fire causes damage to more than the trees it burns. Each factor in your credit ecosystem has an effect on the rest of your life, such as your job, insurance, borrowing capabilities, housing options, and so on. Central to the credit ecosystem concept is the idea that your credit, savings, and spending are continually engaged in a highly interrelated set of relationships with other financial elements that need to be kept in balance to be healthy.

When you take a walk through any environment, you like to know what to look for. If you're at the beach, you look for footprints in the sand that tell you whether seagulls or terns have been there recently. The presence of horseshoe crabs, clam shells, or broken lobster pots tells you other things about the tide, currents, or passing storms. The same applies in the world of credit. Does your financial beach have excess income? Is your credit score rising or is it falling, like a barometer indicating a brewing storm? Does your credit report show healthy activity or signs of stress? The signs are there for you to read if you know where to look and what they mean. In the sections that follow, I help you predict tomorrow's financial weather and your long-range forecast in no time!

Taking a closer look at the parts that make up your credit ecosystem

The major components of your credit ecosystem include your net income, your debts, the types of credit you have available, your payment history, and any major financial missteps (toxic spills) you've made over the last seven to ten years. You may think that some of these items aren't strictly credit-related, like your income. And you'd be right in a narrow sense, but as in any ecosystem, all the parts have an influence on one another and their environment, both positive and negative.

On the left, Figure 3-1 shows the interdependencies of a typical financial ecosystem. Beginning with income, this figure visually depicts the relationship among the financial factors that make up your ecosystem. On the right, Figure 3-1 details the credit portion of your ecosystem. Beginning with offers and building to credit scores, if any part of the system is out of whack, the others are compromised.

Figure 3-1:
Your
financial
environment
is made up
of inter-
dependent
parts.

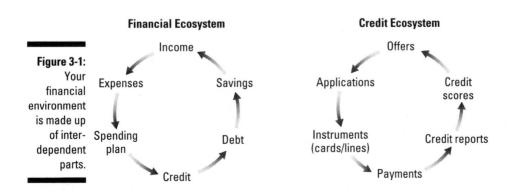

Financial Ecosystem

Income · Savings · Debt · Credit · Spending plan · Expenses

Credit Ecosystem

Offers · Credit scores · Credit reports · Payments · Instruments (cards/lines) · Applications

Counting your income

Income is always my favorite topic, so I want you to start there. Every biosystem needs nourishment in order to support its inhabitants. Krill are a type of small shrimp that form the basis on a food chain. The krill found at the South Pole are nourishment for migrating fish, birds, and mammals. No krill? No chain of life as we know it.

Your credit ecosystem's nourishment is income. Because you have income, you can support spending, debt, and credit. Knowing how much income you have tells you what you have to work with and what you can support. If you don't know what your spendable income is, you can only guess and hope you don't harm your environment by guessing wrong and overspending or overtaxing your resources. Surprisingly, many people don't have a clear picture of how much income they have available or whether they're losing some income through leaks in their paycheck. You can find examples of leaks and things you can do to maximize your income in Chapter 4.

Balancing your expenses

If income is your fertile resource, then your expenses represent what you take out of your environment. If you're a farmer, you need to balance the types of crops you grow or the types of animals you graze on your fertile land. Too much of either and you won't be successful. If you're a fisherman, knowing how many fish you can catch and what kinds you need to leave for balance is important for a sustainable ecosystem.

Knowing what you're spending and how fast you're depleting your income enables you to manage your income resources so they're healthy and productive for a lifetime. For tips on focusing your expenses, see Chapter 4.

Managing your resources

How can you be sure you're managing your resources for maximum yield? It's easy. You use a plan that accounts for all your income and all your expenses. I call it a *spending plan*. Making and sticking to a spending plan — sometimes called a *budget* — assures that you don't overextend your income resources. Doing so also allows you to be in charge of what resources you use and how fast you use them so that you stay in control of your environment. Just like knowing how many fish a pond can support, you want to know how many expenses you can afford before you commit to them. Failure to plan properly may result in an ecosystem collapse!

You can find help and tips on creating a spending plan that works for you in Chapter 4.

Introducing credit

Using credit in your environment can be a powerful way to increase yields in the present. The use of credit can be a great thing as long as you don't over-stress your environment to the point of doing long-term damage. A farmer may add fertilizer to the soil and growth hormones to cattle feed. This can enhance growth and yield, but too much of either can damage resources and cause a failure down the road. Knowing the right time to use credit and the right amount to borrow to improve your credit environment rather than harm it is your goal.

Sustaining Your Credit Ecosystem for Life

In this section I show you how financial goals and planning help keep your eco-system in balance. I talk more about goals in Chapter 4, but in brief, you want to set goals for life's major credit-related financial milestones and then create a plan to reach those goals. Among your goals may be funding college, buying a home, or buying a car. Here I take an ecological look at each of these.

Funding college

Unless you're fortunate enough to have a trust fund, you may have to take out a student loan to pay for your higher education. How does this type of loan fit into your overall financial environment and credit ecosystem? Be sure it fits well, because like an invasive species, you can't eradicate this type of loan by ordinary means. Student loans are exempt from most bankruptcy proceed-ings, so be sure you understand what your payments will be and what income stream you can expect from your chosen career field. If this loan is going to eat up too much of your future income — if, say, you're going to be a mod-estly paid social worker — you may want to supplement the loan by working part time. Or you could pass on that expensive Ivy League school in favor of a lower-priced community/state college to lessen the future stress on and damage to your income. Balancing your current spending with your future ability to make payments keeps this loan sustainable. This advice works in the case of parents as well as students. How much would you pay for a mystery item hidden in a box? Not much, I bet. How much would you borrow to fund an education leading to an unknown job with unknown income?

Home sweet home

In the past, millions of Americans bought a home as soon as they were able. Today, with home value appreciation no longer a certainty in the minds of many, the goal of homeownership warrants a second look to see how it fits into your credit and overall financial landscape. Beyond making sure that you can afford the payments on a mortgage and that your job is secure enough to allow you to make a long-term commitment to these payments, consider this: Homeownership isn't a good fit for everyone's financial environment. Changes to employment and income and opportunities to move or travel can all make a long-term commitment more uncertain today. Owing more than your home is worth (referred to as being *upside down* on a loan) can keep you from relocating for an opportunity. Having your own place is great, but it may not be all roses for your career, finances, or credit. Homeownership complements and fits best into a stable environment.

Credit on wheels

Most of you will use credit to make a purchase as large as a car. Making a down payment that's large enough to keep you from owing more than your car is worth when you drive it off the lot keeps your options open. Too small a down payment keeps you from selling your car without a big hit to your savings to make up the difference between the sale price and what you owe. Like homeownership, if you owe more than the car (or any asset) is worth, you're upside down on your loan. You don't want to turn a big part of your credit ecosystem upside down — it's as uncomfortable as it sounds!

Steering Clear of Credit Pollution

Your credit report offers you a graphical representation of your credit ecosystem. Each account listed on your report is like a tree that grows in a forest. The older it is, the better for you and your credit score because its age indicates strength and stability. As negative items appear on your report, they can spread from one account to another as defaults increase your cost of credit. Late payments can cause damage that weakens your credit and its ability to play its role in supporting your goals. This damage is the equivalent of pollution seeping into your natural ecosystem. Just as too much pollution can create a toxic environment, too many negative items on your credit report can cause major credit problems before you realize what has happened. So how do you recognize this situation and what can you do to restore your credit to a healthy balance? Read on!

Endangering your payment history

In most cases, every time you make a payment on your credit card or loan, the payment is reported to one or more of the credit bureaus. A payment that's on time and for the amount due helps your credit report and score grow stronger. Missing a payment or paying too little dumps toxic data onto your credit file. The effects can go far downstream in your financial environment. Bad credit can cost you a new job or promotion opportunity, licenses in some fields, higher insurance costs, and the opportunity to buy or rent decent housing. After damage is done to your credit forest, regrowth may take from two to seven years, or even ten years, as I explain in the next section.

Paying off a delinquent account or bringing it to a current status doesn't undo the damage already done, but doing so does stop future damage and allows you to begin to rebuild your credit over time.

Your payment history can harm your credit environment in many ways:

- ✔ Overspending using credit means higher payments. Higher payments limit the amount of money you can devote to savings and place a strain on your credit from overuse and lack of replenishment.

- ✔ Drying up your savings can cause a damaging cash-flow drought that weakens your ability to respond to new or unexpected expenses.

- ✔ Although creditors can no longer raise your interest rates on existing balances if you miss a payment on another loan, you damage your payment history as soon as you're 30 days late, and creditors can raise the rate on new purchases (see Chapter 5 for more information).

- ✔ If you miss two payments on a credit card (in other words, you're more than 60 days late), your existing-balance interest rate will explode like a wind-driven wildfire and consume more of your income than you can imagine when you can least afford it.

Clear-cutting your credit in bankruptcy

Among the most damaging things that can happen to a forest environment is overlogging — clear-cutting all the trees and leaving a wasteland behind. When you're forced to declare bankruptcy, you're clear-cutting your credit. All those credit accounts and lines that had previously been the strong and growing trees on your credit report are all chopped down. The resulting wasteland takes years to regrow, just as in nature.

Despite the devastation of a credit clear-cut, you may still owe a lot of money. Bankruptcy may not wipe out *all* your debt, and what remains can be the most tenacious and longest-surviving debt of all. Like plastic bags and inorganic products that can live on in the environment for years and years, some debts just don't disappear, including

- ✔ Federal, state, and local taxes
- ✔ Child support
- ✔ Alimony
- ✔ Student loans from the government or a lender
- ✔ Money owed as a result of drunk driving

Some bankruptcy-resistant debts continue to grow and consume precious resources from your financial environment. For instance, unpaid student loans can result in seizure of tax refunds or even part of your Social Security until they're satisfied.

Some lenders, however, specialize in giving new loans to people with a damaged credit ecosystem. Why? Because they can charge super high rates, and because, under the law, you can't clear-cut your debt in a second Chapter 7 bankruptcy filing for eight long years. My experience with these types of bottom-feeding lenders is that they verge on the predatory, and you're better off not doing business with them in the first place. They make risky loans all the time, so they're ready, willing, and very able to hammer you for any delayed, missed, or short payment.

Living in a post-bankruptcy wasteland has other challenges. You're unlikely to be able to buy a home, and renting an apartment is more difficult. Job opportunities for new employment or promotions may become an endangered species, as some employers check your credit before making any offers. Insurance costs rise with your perceived credit environment instability. Actuarial studies show a strong link between an unstable credit ecosystem and higher insurance claims. Finally, most people are buoyed by success and weighted down by failure. A bankruptcy often represents a major life failure, one that can deplete you of an important resource: self-confidence.

If you need to wipe out all your debts because you're overwhelmed, be sure that this extreme measure solves your problems. For example, if your defaults were caused by overuse of credit to supplement your income for basic living expenses, a bankruptcy won't solve your problem.

People tell me that it's unfair that they're penalized for the damage they've done by filing for bankruptcy. After all, they had no choice, and the situation genuinely may not have been their fault. Still, the trees are all gone, and it takes time to regrow your credit and regain the confidence of lenders and others that you'll take better care of your environment next time.

Outlasting a long, cold credit winter

As if the damage that you can do to your personal credit ecosystem isn't enough, I want you to consider one more aspect of your financial environment. You're in an environment that has seen a major shift in climate. No, I'm not talking about climate change, but about credit change! Like the oversized dinosaurs, millions of people have had a meteor-like financial meltdown hit their financial lives. Beginning in late 2007, the economy tanked, housing prices dropped, and unemployment gushed like an angry volcano spewing darkness over the sky. The result? A credit winter. Credit is frozen in many places and will be slow to thaw. It may take years before credit flows as it did before the last bubble.

You can avoid a dinosaur-like fate for your credit and financial dreams by adding new credit only when you need it, by making payments on time and for the full amount due, and by keeping balances low to remain nimble.

Surviving and Reviving after a Credit Catastrophe

Whether your credit has taken a toxic hit from delinquencies or has been wiped out in a clear-cutting from a bankruptcy, you can do some things to minimize ongoing damage and foster a recovery. To recover from a credit crisis and avoid a relapse, I have three suggestions that help speed your credit ecosystem's revival. But while your credit is recovering, you still need to manage your way through your financial environment, so I also give you tips to get you through the rough spots until your credit is healed.

Understanding what happened to your credit

To begin to recover your credit resource, the first thing you need to do is to understand what happened and why. For most people, the problems can all seem like a blur. Like a storm seen from the middle, figuring out where the chaos came from and when it will end is difficult. But credit problems can usually be traced to two main causes: gradual accumulation of debt by an extended period of overspending, or an event such as an illness or accident.

Planning for your next challenge

You can remedy the slow and easy overspending trap that happens to so many people by developing a spending plan that accounts for all your income and expenses. A spending plan helps you make conscious decisions about where you spend your money and keeps you from slowly sinking deeper and deeper into debt. I go into the nuts and bolts of how to set up a spending plan that works for you in Chapter 4.

A number of different tsunami-like events can wash out your finances. Medical illness, even if you're insured, can cause you to incur huge amounts of debt. Unexpected and uninsured or underinsured calamities like a home fire or a car accident can make a serious dent in your finances. The way to avoid a repeat of this type of unexpected expense is to insure for what you can and save for the rest. Be sure that your auto, home, and disability insurance policies are adequate to protect you in the event of a loss. Establish a plan to save between six months to a year of living expenses in an emergency account to last you through income interruptions from a job loss or to fund deductibles and expenses not covered by insurance.

Minimizing your damage as you move forward

With your credit crisis behind you, you still need to live through the months that follow despite the complications that damaged credit can cause. It's important to recognize and to be proactive about situations where your damaged credit may hurt you when someone checks your credit report. Realize that your credit ecosystem is part of your larger financial environment and that each affects the other.

When your credit is damaged, it can affect you far beyond not being able to get a credit card. Some events trigger a review of your damaged credit report while you're in the process of restoring your financial environment. These events include getting a new job, being considered for a promotion, moving to a new apartment, buying a car, and getting new credit. Here are some details about some of these events:

- **Employment/promotions:** Employers commonly pull a credit report as part of the hiring or promotional process. If you're up for a job or promotion, be sure to have an explanation of what happened in your credit history and what you've done since to ensure that it won't happen again. Mistakes are common; showing that you learned from them is not.

- **Moving:** Landlords want to know if you'll pay your rent, not just if you're able. Bad credit causes them concern unless you can explain what happened. You may want to offer a larger security deposit for a period of time to set your landlord's mind at ease.

✔ **Car financing:** A reliable car is an essential part of making a living for many of you. Getting to work predictably and on time is essential. If you're buying a car with damaged credit, be prepared to put down more money than usual so that the financing company is protected against a default. Be careful of dealers who charge high interest rates and penalties for prepaying your loan. Establishing a relationship with a credit union can be a good way to get a loan at a reasonable rate, even with blemished credit.

Rebuilding your credit ecosystem

Is rebuilding a damaged credit ecosystem a chicken-or-the-egg puzzle? Or is it a Catch-22 situation, where the catch is that you can't do what you want from where you are? It's neither, although it can sure seem that way.

Following an oil spill or other disaster, naturalist experts show up and analyze the damage. They come up with a plan for what needs to be done to restore the lost balance, and they tell you how long it will take for the damage to heal. Your credit score is your indication of the health of your credit ecosystem. A low score means that your credit environment has had some damage that will take time to repair. In times like these, getting new credit to show you can handle it can be challenging. But if you heed the following simple steps, you'll be growing healthy credit lines and growing a garden full of different blooms in no time.

When oil spilled into the Gulf of Mexico, experts predicted that it might take years for the fragile coastal ecosystems to recover. They began work to clean up the damage and built berms as protection against future damaging events. A toxic credit report and score takes time to restore as well. Slowly rebuilding your report with fresh accounts that you pay on-time and as agreed leads to a thriving credit ecosystem again. Also, showing that you can handle different types of credit can favorably impact your score.

Try planting the following for diversity and a speedy recovery:

✔ **Secured credit card:** Tough underwriting standards may make it impossible to open new accounts right away to regrow your credit. Use of a secured credit card may help rebuild your credit when other products aren't available. No one will know you have a bank account securing this card. Secured by a cash deposit, many of these cards report every time you make an on-time payment to the credit bureaus, just like an unsecured card does. Check to be sure the secured account is reported to the credit bureaus before you open the account. This will boost your score and credit over time.

✔ **Passbook loan:** Open a savings account and borrow the amount you have on deposit. Just make all your payments on time and this personal loan is inexpensive and grows your credit.

✔ **Retail store cards:** Usually easier to get than an unsecured bank card, this revolving credit line can even get you sale prices. But only use it when you're shopping for a need, not when you feel the need to shop. For more tips, see Chapter 22.

Monitoring your credit report and score periodically can offer you a simple measure of progress. You can get a free copy of your credit report annually at www.annualcreditreport.com. For measuring growth in your credit saplings, I suggest that you check one report every four months. That way you can have three free looks each year. Finally, you want to periodically monitor your progress and make adjustments to ensure a quick regrowth of your credit ecosystem.

Chapter 4

Creating a Spending (And Savings) Plan for Your Future

- -

In This Chapter

▶ Recognizing the importance of a spending plan

▶ Setting and prioritizing your financial goals

▶ Taking simple steps to create a workable plan

▶ Tapping into some financial resources

▶ Making adjustments to your plan as you age

- -

*I*magine that you're competing in the Olympics. The other athletes entered in your event have a trainer and a training plan to keep them focused and on track. You'd be severely handicapped if you just made up your training as you went along, practicing some days when you felt like it and not others. Well, consider this book your trainer and this chapter a training regimen to help you develop an easy spending and savings plan for financial success.

So what does a spending plan have to do with credit management? Everything! Your credit is a financial reflection of your life. If your life is out of control, chances are your finances are, too, and your credit isn't far behind. But if you successfully manage your spending and savings, your credit will never get overextended, you'll be able to pay the full balance of all your bills on time, and your credit score will be great as a result. Without a plan for your finances, you're destined to fail, but if you make a spending and savings plan part of your life and follow it, you'll succeed big time.

In this chapter, I show you how some simple planning helps focus your spending and credit use to achieve the goals you set for yourself and your family, to protect and build your credit, and to sleep soundly at night. The plan I'm talking about isn't about sacrifices that keep you from doing the things you want to do and can afford. It's a plan that will make your dreams into reality. Plus, it will keep others from diverting your financial future into their pockets. I take you through the process of figuring out how much you're spending and where your money is going now, and how you'd like to spend your income in the future. You accomplish this task by allocating your income to spending areas that you choose and by selecting the most advantageous type of credit for your needs. I help you get your plan in shape so you can win the gold in your financial Olympics!

Appreciating the Benefits of a Solid Spending Plan

A *spending plan* (formerly known as a *budget*) is a powerful tool that lets you decide how to spend your money to your greatest advantage and build your credit at the same time. It's your personal road map for spending your income, building up your savings, and using credit to save you money and to enhance your credit profile. A spending plan can be as detailed or as general as you want. To create a plan, you need to know your income and expenses and have a general idea of your financial goals over various periods of time. Your plan helps you organize your financial life and gives you rewards in the near and long term by attaining your goals.

Many people incorrectly think that a spending plan is restrictive and may cramp their style or ability to be spontaneous. Actually, a well-thought-out plan has the opposite effect — you get to enjoy *exactly* what *you* want. How is this possible? You discover how to eliminate wasteful spending while focusing your hard-earned money on those things you really want to spend money on.

As I explain in Chapter 3, credit is a tool. It doesn't give you more money to spend; it simply allows you to spend the money you haven't earned yet. If you borrow to cover emergencies or big-ticket items, you're spending money today that you won't earn until tomorrow.

So what happens when you get to tomorrow and find that you spent all the money that was supposed to be there? Nothing pleasant, I can assure you. You can't use credit to extend your income indefinitely. Sooner or later, over using credit catches up with you. Why do people keep spending money that they don't have or can't afford? For many reasons, one of which is because they listen to other people's ideas regarding what will make them happy instead of relying on their own plan and goals. But not you. You and I are going to develop a winning plan that helps you attain all *your* goals!

Here's a short list of things that a good plan can help you do:

✔ **Reach your financial and personal goals:** Your plan is a GPS that keeps you on track, helping you put aside money to reach your goals without getting sidetracked. Whether your goals include an exotic vacation, an addition to your home, or a new car, a plan assures that you get there.

✔ **Master your finances:** Deciding in advance where to spend your money helps assure that you spend it on those things that are most important to you. In addition, your plan builds your credit record and score with timely credit payments for those items you plan to purchase with credit. For everything you need to know about credit reports and credit scores, including how to improve your score, flip to Chapters 6 and 7.

✔ **Save more than you thought possible:** You may notice when you begin the planning process that your expenses are the same as — or, in some cases, more than — your income. Spending less than you make is a great way to ensure you don't become overextended, because the money you don't spend allows you to save for inevitable unplanned expenses and emergencies.

One of the best ways to live within your means is to have a plan for what you do with extra money such as tax refunds, raises, promotions, and so on. When a chunk of cash shows up, save half and spend half. Before you know it, your bank account will be buff!

✔ **Uncover extra cash:** The best bonus of having a spending plan is that you end up with more money to spend. Eliminating waste puts more money in your pocket every month. Instead of spending money on things you don't remember buying or don't really want or need, you can use that cash anyway you want from new toys to building savings.

✔ **Share common goals:** An effective spending plan pertains to your entire family. For example, your children are much more likely to go along with renting a movie rather than going to the movie theater for several months if they understand that doing so will allow them to go on a cruise! The same is true of your sweetie: If the two of you decide that an update to your home is your top financial priority, you'll both be on the same page when it comes to making necessary financial adjustments.

✔ **Be as prepared as an eagle scout:** As part of your plan, you grow your emergency savings account. This account covers unexpected expenses such as major car repairs, large appliance replacements, or big medical bills.

✔ **Keep debt in its place:** Because planning helps you bring your expenses in line with your income and builds savings, you don't need to use credit unless it's in your best interest to do so.

✔ **Manage your credit:** Keeping your debt down improves your credit and builds your credit score. Your score improves with lower amounts owed, fewer accounts with balances, and a lower proportion of your credit limit being used. For more details on your credit score and how to manage it successfully, check out Chapter 7.

✔ **Give yourself peace of mind:** Being in control of your money helps you avoid the financial stress that causes others sleepless nights, reduced productivity at work, and even physical symptoms (like headaches or ulcers). You'll have a smile on your face instead of worry lines.

Deciding on Goals: Imagining Your Future as You Want It to Be

Imagining your future is the fun part of building a spending plan. Many people wander through life without goals, letting events take them where they will. Well, there's a better way, and setting goals is a key first step. The first part of managing your finances and credit is to decide what you want to do and when. Don't worry — this isn't a test, and you can't fail. In fact, you can change your goals as often as you want.

Setting the stage for planning

Set aside an hour or so — more if you can — to envision your future as you'd like to live it. If you're sharing your life with another, be sure to involve that person in the discussion. Heck, make it a date! Over a glass of wine or a cup of tea, get comfortable and dare to dream. Or go to a favorite quiet place — a nearby park, the steps of a monument, a scenic overlook — and let your surroundings inspire you.

At this point, the sky's the limit! Dream as big as you want. Have you always wanted to take a year off and sail around the world? Jot it down. Do you yearn to go back to school or launch a new career? Add it to the list. Buying a home, owning a sports car — this goal-setting stage is your opportunity to indulge yourself in *all* your financial fantasies. Getting them down on paper and discussing, assessing, and prioritizing them is an important part of the process of tailoring your spending plan to meet your own personal goals.

Be sure to include some details. For example, you may have written down, "Go to Disney World." But to flesh it out a bit more and bring it alive, be more specific. Will you stay at the Grand Floridian or the Days Inn? Will you go for a week — or two? Try to be as specific as possible. This level of detail not only gives you a clearer target but also keeps communication about your goals clear.

 Wherever you do your planning, record your goals and put a date next to them. If you're in the mood, you can have some fun with this: Get out the scissors (or your computer mouse) and cut and paste pictures from magazines, calendars, and other sources to illustrate your goals. These images can be powerful motivators. Put them up on your refrigerator (or turn them into a screensaver) so that you can refer to them as you go along.

Categorizing your goals

I like to say that you eat an elephant one bite at a time. I suggest that you separate your goals into categories to keep from being overwhelmed. Otherwise, you may focus only on short- or long-term goals. For the best results I recommend that you use four general categories:

- **Short-term goals** are no longer than one year. They may include taking that vacation to Disney World, starting a retirement plan or an emergency fund, or even reducing your debt.

- **Intermediate-term goals** require one to five years to accomplish. These may include saving enough money to buy a new car, to begin a family, to purchase new furniture, or to pay off your debts.

- **Long-term goals** are at least five years down the road. These may include saving for your kids' education, starting your own business, or buying a home or boat.

- **Life goals** don't have a time frame, because you'll probably never *fully* achieve them. These goals aren't necessarily money-driven but capture the imagination. For example, you may want to be more content in your life. Imagine what it would take and write it down. Have at least one goal you can pursue that may be unattainable through money. Who knows? You won't succeed if you don't try.

Pay attention to how many goals you have in each category. Are all your goals focused on the short term? If so, spend some time thinking a little farther into the future. Also, remember that not all goals require money to realize. Adding some nonmonetary goals to your list can help take some of the financial pressure off the ones that do. For example, spending more time doing a shared activity, such as volunteering to assist the elderly or helping out at the local library, may offer a nonfinancial respite — and can be a great exercise in togetherness. Look for other opportunities to work "free" into your future.

Putting your goals in order

After you list all your goals and sort them into categories, the next step is to prioritize them. I suggest that you assign a high priority to short-term goals that you think you can reach easily or that are particularly motivating. That way you can experience the thrill of victory early on and provide a source of energy for the next goal.

If you have goals that you know will be difficult to achieve or will take a lot of saving to accomplish, I suggest you segment them. By breaking large goals into smaller chunks, you're better able to see progress. Plus, you'll have more reasons to celebrate.

This process shouldn't be a slog to the finish. You need to have fun along the way. Don't forget to celebrate every milestone. Also, don't be afraid to make adjustments as you go along. An unexpected bonus can move up a timeline; a layoff or illness can set it back. Adjust your plan accordingly.

Building Your Vision of Your Future in Seven Steps

Now that you've set and prioritized your goals, you've established a powerful incentive for turning easily swayed immediate gratification into a plan that puts you, not others, in control of your finances and your life. Now what you need is a tool, or a series of tools, to help you achieve your goals. That's where the spending plan that I discuss in detail in the following sections comes in.

You're not creating a plan to *restrict* your spending but rather to put you in charge of directing your money to where you want it to go.

Identifying resources and eliminating waste are great places to begin. You want to start with your current income and expenses. After all, you can't decide how much money to spend and where to spend it until you know how much you have to go around.

Step 1: Counting up your income

Figuring out how much you earn in a year can be easy or tricky, depending on how you're paid. If you earn a regular salary or work a set number of hours per week, the task is easy — just multiply your regular pay by the number of pay periods in a year. On the other hand, if you earn commissions or tips, or if you're, say, a fisherman or landscaper, you need some basis on which to project your income. Perhaps your work is seasonal (you sell ice cream or prepare tax returns, for example) and you bring in more income at certain times of the year, or maybe you work extra hours at inventory time, and that affects your income. I suggest that you look at last year's income as a starting point. Your old tax return should have most of the information you need.

Whatever your situation, try to estimate a year's worth of income. If you find it helpful to come up with a monthly average, start with a high-earning month rather than a low-earning one. That way you can save some of that month's extra income to tide you over in a low-income month.

You can use Table 4-1 (or the "Monthly Income Worksheet" on the CD) to list all the sources of income you expect each month. Be sure to use your take-home, or *net,* pay rather than your *gross* pay (your salary before taxes and other deductions). For example, if you earn $60,000 per year, your gross income is $5,000 per month — but you probably only take home about $3,600 or so after Social Security, federal and state taxes, and other deductions are made. You may also want to list the expenses that are deducted from your paycheck. Be sure to consider any ways that you can reduce or eliminate some deductions.

Many people over-withhold for taxes. If you got a $2,400 tax refund last year, that money is an interest-free loan to the IRS that you can put to better use. I suggest that you reduce your withholding by half of the amount of your refund. For a $2,400 refund, you're overpaying $200 a month in taxes. Reduce your withholding by $100 a month. That still leaves you a cushion with the tax man but adds some extra cash to your budget.

You may have income from other sources besides your regular paycheck. Don't forget to include child support, alimony, overtime pay, bonuses, investment income, royalties, or rental-property income. If you have income from part-time activities such as playing in a band, selling on eBay, and so on, add it to the pile!

Table 4-1   Income Worksheet for _____

Source of Income	Planned	Actual	Difference
Salary 1			
Salary 2			
Bonus			
Interest			
Dividends			
Other periodic income			
Child support/alimony			
Rental income			
Gifts			
Deduction changes/other			
Total Income	$	$	$

After you list all your income sources, come up with an average monthly income. Why monthly? Because you pay most of your major expenses on a monthly basis — your utilities, mortgage or rent, phone, and even many charitable contributions are often portioned out in monthly increments.

Step 2: Tallying what you spend

After you know what's coming in, you need to calculate what's going out — and where it's going. Determining your monthly spending isn't difficult, but for some of you it may require a little digging. Many of your major expenses — mortgage, credit-card bills, utilities, car loans, and so on — hit monthly. If you have an expense that occurs other than monthly, prorate it to a monthly amount. For example, a $2,000 homeowner's insurance bill due once a year is $166.66 a month. For frequent yet varying expenses, such as electricity and entertainment, gather several months to a year of history and then determine a monthly average.

Table 4-2 helps you get started (fill it out here or use a copy of "Monthly Expense Worksheet" on the CD). Using your checking- and savings-account statements, credit-card statements, cash receipts for significant purchases, other financial records, and/or a financial planning program (such as Quicken), enter and categorize all your expenses to figure out what you spend each month. If you don't have complete financial records, don't worry — just use your best estimates to fill in the blanks.

Table 4-2   Expenses Worksheet for _____

Expense	Planned	Actual	Difference
Rent/mortgage			
Property tax			
Renters/homeowners insurance			
Home maintenance			
Water			
Sewer			
Garbage			
Gas/oil for heating			
Electric			
Telephone			
Car payment			
Car insurance			
Gasoline			
Car repairs/maintenance			
Clothing			
Groceries/household supplies			
Doctor/dentist			

Expense	Planned	Actual	Difference
Prescriptions			
Health insurance			
Life/disability insurance			
Childcare			
Tuition/school expenses			
Child support/alimony			
Personal allowance			
Entertainment			
Eating out/vending			
Cigarettes/alcohol			
Newspapers/magazines			
Hobbies/clubs/sports			
Gifts			
Donations			
Work expenses			
Cable/satellite			
Internet connections			
Cellphone			
Student loan			
Pet/veterinary			
Other:			
Other:			
Total Expenses	$	$	$

If you're like most people, you'll be able to account for around 80 to 90 percent of where your money is spent. But you're likely to find that some fraction of your income just seems to vanish into parts unknown. I call these items "money gobblers" — small cash expenditures that never seem to register in your memory, let alone make it to the check register or any account ledger. I've assembled a list of some of the more common of these expenses (you may be able to add to this list, and not every item will apply to your life). These are all areas where your money may be leaking out without your knowledge or conscious intent, and each item is something you may be able to save on if you decide you'd rather reallocate the money:

✔ **Allowances:** Your kids will hate me for this, but you don't have to give them set allowances.

✔ **Family photos:** Try taking these yourself. You'd be surprised at what great pictures you can snap with your own digital camera. Dress the kids up as if they were seeing a pro. Drape a pastel bedsheet behind them and snap away. The shots you get will be even more special because of the time you spent together.

✔ **Babysitting:** See if you can work out a deal with friends or neighbors to watch their kids one day in exchange for them watching yours the next. Or take shameless advantage of the grandparents — most are only too happy to volunteer their services.

✔ **Salon:** Instead of going to a high-priced salon, look in the Yellow Pages for a beauty school in your area. You may be able to get your hair done for free (or for a very small charge), and the attention to detail you get is phenomenal — the students are supervised by teachers, and they're working to impress.

✔ **Beer, wine, and soda:** For some people, the thought of giving up brewskis, a favorite cabernet, or soft drinks may seem like a real hardship. But when you add up how much money you're spending, it may be enough of a motivation to abstain or cut back if you can attain a goal with the proceeds.

✔ **Fast food and vending machines:** The stuff is bad for not only your body but also your wallet. Shop at the grocery store instead; use coupons for amazing savings.

✔ **Books, magazines, newspapers, CDs, and movies:** One of the greatest resources at your disposal is your public library. You can get all the books, magazines, and newspapers you want — free of charge. Most libraries also lend out audio books, music CDs, and movies for free.

✔ **Car washes:** Now, I'm not suggesting that you never wash your car. I'm just suggesting that, when you need to do it, you do it yourself or toss a sponge, some soap, and the hose at your kids and set them loose. They have fun, your car gets a little cleaner, and you save significant dough.

✔ **Cards, gambling, and lottery tickets:** A dollar in the bank is much more valuable than a dollar spent gambling. End of story.

✔ **School fundraisers:** When your neighbor kids come a-knockin', just say no. If you want to be of help to your local school, you can volunteer at the library, coach a sports team, or lead a scouting troop.

✔ **Entertainment (concerts, movies, sporting events, and so on):** Look for ways to entertain yourself and your family free of charge. Instead of going to a professional baseball game, go out in the yard or to the park and toss a ball around with your kids or your friends. Instead of going to a movie, check out a DVD from the library.

✔ **Health foods:** Eating healthfully is important, but health foods can be pricey. Shop the produce department of your grocery store, stick to whole grains and lean meats, and you and your spending plan will be fine.

✔ **Hobbies:** Most hobbies cost money, and although they're fun, so is saving money. Make *that* your new hobby.

✔ **Eating out:** Even if you're eating at fast-food restaurants, eating out costs a lot. You can save big money by preparing your food at home.

✔ **Pets:** If you're in financial trouble, getting a new pet isn't a good idea. (Let me tell you about my free cat!) Even healthy pets cost money, and if your pet gets sick, you're in for more expenses. If you already have pets, stick to the necessities (food, vaccinations, hugs) and avoid the store-bought toys. You can make a rope bone out of old T-shirts or throw a tennis ball around in the yard — all your pet cares about is you (and food).

✔ **Tobacco:** You already know you shouldn't be smoking. Add up the financial costs, and you can see the damage it's doing *beyond* the damage to your health.

✔ **Yard sales:** If your idea of a fun Saturday morning is going from one yard sale to the next looking for bargains, wash the car instead. Most people think they're getting bargains, but they usually end up buying things they don't really need.

You don't have to cut all the preceding items out of your life. Just be aware that you're spending discretionary money and consider how important the items that aren't top priority really are. For example, you may not be willing to scrimp when it comes to Fido's organic, super-premium dog food — if that's the case, just make sure to budget for it every month.

To get to the point where you're able to identify that last 10 to 20 percent of expenses, track your daily expenditures. Record all those cash expenses that are such a part of your routine that you hardly notice them — items such as the morning coffee, newspaper, snacks, kids' allowances, and so on. Again, I'm not saying you shouldn't *have* them — the goal is just to be aware of where your money is going so you can decide whether that's the best use of your funds.

Was eating breakfast at the coffee shop every morning on your short-term goals list? I bet not. Did you know that if you take the $9 a day that breakfast costs and multiply that times 260 business days in a year, you get $2,340 — which could translate to a five-night Caribbean cruise for two? You get to make the choices here.

The really good news about this tracking is that you only need to do it for two months to catch most everything. After that you'll have a good handle on what's gobbling up your free cash, and you can either plug the hole or include it as an expense in your budget.

And now, a word from the Bureau of Labor Statistics: Are you an average spender?

You may be looking for some guidelines to tell you whether your spending is in line with that of others. Look no further. The nice people at the Bureau of Labor Statistics have been hard at work adding up grocery-store tapes and watching how often you fill up at the gas station. Their report is available at www.bls.gov/news.release/cesan.nr0.htm. I'm only kidding about them watching you at the gas station, but they do have their ways of getting the stats on what Americans are spending and for what. The latest data is a year or so old but probably still fine for your purposes.

To help simplify your spending plan discussions, I summarize some of the main items as percentages of income (see the aforementioned website for the full details). I arrived at the percentages by taking an average expense as a percentage of an average income. I use percentages based on after-tax or take-home income, because most people live on what's left over after Uncle Sam gets his share. I'm not suggesting that you plan according to these percentages, but you may find them useful as guidelines to see whether you're way out in left field on your estimates. For example, your

family may spend more on housing and less on entertainment, and I may do the opposite. The key to remember is that you get to decide.

- ✔ **Housing:** 26.9 percent of income after taxes

- ✔ **Transportation:** 15.6 percent (includes vehicles, gasoline and motor oil, and other transportation)

- ✔ **Food:** 13.0 percent (at home: 7.6 percent; away from home: 5.4 percent)

- ✔ **Personal insurance and pensions:** 11.1 percent (includes premiums for whole life and term insurance; endowments; income and other life insurance; mortgage guarantee insurance; mortgage life insurance; and premiums for personal liability, accident and disability, and other nonhealth insurance other than for homes and vehicles, pensions, and Social Security)

- ✔ **Healthcare:** 6.4 percent

- ✔ **Entertainment:** 5.5 percent

- ✔ **Apparel and services:** 3.5 percent

- ✔ **All other:** 10.5 percent

Step 3: Making savings part of your spending plan

How can *savings* be part of a *spending* plan? Easy — consider savings as an allocation of your available money. Then it becomes an expense, even though you aren't actually spending it.

Most people don't budget for savings, and that's a huge mistake. To be successful, you need to save money for emergencies beyond your identified goals. Add up what you need to save in a year to reach your prioritized financial goals and divide by 12. That's the monthly amount you need to save and include in your plan. If you don't have that much to allot for savings, you have a decision to make — spend less in another area(s), increase your income, or rearrange your goals.

The old saying "Pay yourself first" is a wise one, indeed. If you only save what drifts to the bottom line, you're significantly shortchanging yourself and losing out on an essential way to protect your credit — an emergency savings cushion.

Taking the direct (deposit) approach

The best way I've found to save is to have money directly deposited from your paycheck into a savings or checking account. After you get into the habit, it will become self-reinforcing. Seeing that balance rise will inspire you to do more when you can. You won't think to spend money if you can't see it. I do this myself and have found it to be painless.

Have your paycheck set up so that the amount of money you need to run your household (your monthly budget minus savings) goes directly into your checking account every pay period. I suggest that half of any pay raise, bonus, or leftover money above that amount be left to automatically go directly into your savings. You never see it and never spend it — unless, of course, you want to. You get half and the savings account gets half. What could be fairer!

Your savings plan is really two-pronged: You're saving to achieve the goals you've set for yourself, and you're saving so that you have money in case of an emergency. I cover both in the following sections.

Saving the easy way: The grown-up's version of the piggy bank

Remember when saving consisted of getting change and putting it into a piggy bank? Remember the happiness you experienced as those quarters and dimes clinked into your personal treasure chest? Well, you will have that feeling back plus more once you start a savings plan that works for you. Security, confidence, and the sheer potential of a pile of money waiting for you to transform it into your fondest wish make your childhood excitement pale. All you need is a little encouragement and a tip or two and you'll have savings for emergencies and the good things in life in short order.

A technique that helps me make the most of my spare pennies is to roll change. No, I don't mean pretending that you're someone else. At the end of the day, I place my loose pocket change into a neat little bank that my wife bought me that separates the coins by denomination so I can put them in those cute little tubes you can get (for free) at the bank. Stay away from the machines that change coins into dollars for a fee. For guys, this is easy, as the coins usually fall out onto the floor when you hang up your trousers. For the ladies, not only will you be saving money, but you'll also save the expense of physical therapy on your shoulder from damage caused by a purse weighted down with coins. Expect that this exercise will yield about $200 a year per person.

Another way to save is to use your credit cards less. Using cash more often helps reinforce the link between paying, earning, and the cost you're paying. Paying for a $100 item is easy with a swipe of your favorite, mileage-accruing credit card. If you have to peel off ten $10 bills, the experience is different. It's real money — and a lot of it! Plus, when your roll of cash is nearly gone, you may find yourself really thinking about a purchase twice.

You can also save money by bagging your lunch. Going out to lunch every day costs you thousands! Check out the math: 260 business days in a year, a $10 lunch special becomes $15 per lunch (including tax, tip, and gas/taxi), which equals $3,900 a year. If you pay 25 percent federal income tax, 7 percent state income tax, and 7 percent Social Security, bringing your lunch to work and saving $3,900 after taxes is the equivalent of nearly a $6,400 pre-tax raise [$6,400 − $1,600 (25 percent of $6,400) − $448 (7 percent of $6,400) minus another $448 (7 percent of $6,400) = $3,904 take-home]. Think of the goal you can realize with that money instead!

Finally, buy a Sunday paper and cut coupons. I know, newspapers are dying. So you'll be saving jobs and doing a public service in the process. Or visit one of the online sites (www.coupons.com) where you can browse and print coupons that you need. If you can put in a half-hour and come up with $20 in savings every week, you've made a great trade. How much? How about the equivalent of a $1,445 raise!

Managing to actually save for a goal

Now that you've agreed on your goals, know your income, and tracked your spending, the next task is to break down a goal into bite-size pieces to make it more easily attainable. If you can do this with *all* your goals, you'll be closer to a plan that works for you.

Take an intermediate-term goal as an example. Say you want to take a trip, and the cost of the trip is $2,000. If your goal is to go in 18 months, you divide the $2,000 by the 18 months. The result — $111.11 — is what you must put aside each month to pay for the trip by the time you're driving to the airport and waving goodbye to the cats.

But $111.11 a month isn't chopped liver. So where will the money come from? You need to either increase income or reduce expenses by the amount needed. Again, taking the vacation example, if you can get overtime at, say, $20 an hour, you'll need 100 hours in the next 18 months, or 5.55 hours a month, to swing it. On the expense side, you're looking to redirect $5.13 per workday ($2,000 ÷ 390 days) or $3.65 per day ($2,000 ÷ 548 days). Maybe your trip really is as easy as passing up that coffee and doughnut on your way to work!

With some of your longer-term plans, it's fair to apply income that you're pretty sure will show up but hasn't yet. Say you expect a 4 percent raise in six months. You may want to count that raise in your figuring.

Building an emergency fund

As one of your major long-term goals, you should have between 6 and 12 months of living expenses in an unallocated emergency account for unforeseen financial emergencies. A number that big can seem impossible to achieve. But remember: You only need to cover *expenses,* not income. You don't have to replace your entire annual salary, just the expenses you'd have during, say, a lengthy period when you may not be working. You now know what your expenses are — thanks to your spending plan — so the number is at least a real one and not just some unknown amount.

Some people used to say that a line of credit is as good as an emergency savings fund. They've learned otherwise. Using credit to cover an emergency can leave you much worse off if the emergency (such as a layoff) lasts longer than your credit does. Use up your savings and you're back to square one. Use up all your credit and have no savings, and you're at the bottom of a deep hole.

To start, shoot for something — even *one* month or one *week.* All you need to do is start building today. Having one week of expenses saved can be a world of difference from having none. Two weeks is divine. And a month — you're ahead of most people. So relax, get started, start small, and keep at it.

Put aside money for emergencies while you're saving for other things. But if you're saving for three things at once, won't it take three times as long? No! Because you'll be more likely to stick with a savings plan if you're saving for three things at once and at least two of them are things that have a personal payoff to you — like that vacation. When you have that emergency cash socked away, turn those savings dollars toward achieving one of your other planned goals.

I mention this strategy earlier but it bears repeating: Automate your savings plan. Arrange to automatically deposit part of your pay into different savings, checking, or investment accounts. If you never see the money in your check, you won't miss it. As you get those raises or bonuses, put at least half into your savings account. Tax refunds get the same treatment. Make it easy and automatic, and your savings will grow faster than you can imagine.

Step 4: Managing your credit to improve your spending plan

Credit and the loans that credit make possible have a place in your plan. Credit is a tool to be used — as long as the tool fits the job. In fact, credit can make things easier. It can allow you to defer a payment to a more convenient time or to make a payment in such a way that it benefits you more than paying cash. However, you should only use credit cards for spending money you already have or know you'll have soon.

What I'm talking about here is consumer credit. A number of different incarnations of consumer credit exist, and you can use each type to your advantage:

✔ **Noninstallment credit:** This is the type of credit I grew up with. My dad had a charge account at the local gas station. I gassed up the family car, and he stopped by the station and paid the bill in full at the end of the month. With noninstallment credit, you pay the entire balance each month. This type of credit is used in some retail stores, membership clubs, and the like. It is credit in its simplest form, available as a convenience to you — and a benefit to the merchant. You're not deterred from spending simply because you don't have the cash in your pocket. You get what you want, the merchant makes a sale, and everybody's happy — which is the essence of using credit properly.

You can use this type of credit in your plan to handle expenses for local services like trash removal, gardening, or lawn care. An extra benefit here is that you get the service first, so if it's faulty, you're more likely to get it fixed.

✔ **Installment, closed-end credit:** Frequently used by department or furniture stores, in this type of credit, an amount equal to the amount of a specific purchase is lent to you for repayment in installments.

Here's an example of how you can use this type of credit: You buy a new bedroom set at a local furniture store, and the store offers you installment credit allowing you 12 months to pay for the furniture in full. Normally, interest is associated with this type of loan, but the McKay boys were having a special sale — no payments for six months, and no interest for the next six. A sweet deal from your perspective, and a sweet sale from theirs.

If you use this type of credit, make sure you pay off the entire amount before the end date or you may be charged a high rate of interest starting from the date of purchase.

✔ **Revolving, open-end credit:** This is how most credit cards work. You're granted an amount of credit — with a limit, say, of $5,000 — to be used any way you want. You can choose how much of the limit you use at any point in time. As you use the card, you must make payments on time and for the amount agreed. As you make payments, the amount that goes to principal recharges the line. You can pay off the entire amount, which restores the credit line to its original and full amount, or you can just pay what your spending plan will allow — or even make only a minimum payment. You get to decide.

An example of using this type of credit in your spending plan is to help spread the cost of airline tickets. You'd need to have a set time frame for paying off the purchase (90 days or fewer, preferably) and make sure the needed monthly amount is available in your spending plan before making the purchase. Don't forget to include the interest that's charged for carrying the balance when you come up with your monthly payment amount.

You're supposed to benefit from the use of credit — you aren't supposed to get taken advantage of. Choose credit cards as a tool when they fit the short term need at hand and you can pay them off quickly and with certainty. Remember that bedroom set? You could have used your credit card to finance the bedroom set, but you would have paid 18 percent interest and you'd have had to make payments right away. Clearly, the installment, closed-end type fits the job better.

Step 5: Looking at your insurance options

Insurance is dull — until you need it! It is, however, an essential part of planning successfully for your future. Catastrophic illness, an accident, or loss of property can crush the best-conceived plans. I don't advocate insurance for every little thing that comes up — what amount of insurance you buy is a personal decision. To a degree, it depends on your resources and willingness to absorb the cost of some lower-level exposures in your life, such as car-insurance deductibles.

But you should be concerned about the major life events and expenses that can dramatically affect your finances at all stages of your life — from the death of a spouse, to a major medical disability that prevents a wage-earner from working, to being responsible for a serious car accident.

Here are a few critical coverage areas you want to consider as you pull together your plan for the future:

- ✔ **Life insurance:** If you have someone who will miss your income if you die, you need life-insurance coverage. *Term life insurance* covers you for a specified term or time frame, but you can usually renew it at an increasing expense as you age. It has no cash or investment value — your beneficiary gets paid when you die, not before. Make sure you have enough coverage to bridge the gap your death will cause to the household budget. A little bit of thought should identify the shortfall. And, of course, you want to have appropriate coverage on your partner as well. *Note:* A good credit rating can reduce your life insurance costs.

- ✔ **Disability insurance:** If you're unable to work for a period of time, disability insurance helps cover your expenses. It's available to cover both long- and short-term problems. Be good to yourself and your loved ones, and be sure that you get this.

- ✔ **Homeowner's insurance:** One of your biggest assets and one of your biggest liabilities is your home. As an asset, you'd have a tough time replacing it if an uninsured accident took away part or all of your home. Keep up with building-code changes that affect your replacement costs, and add insurance that covers the unlikely stuff. If it happens, you'll be glad you did. Some examples of the types of insurance you should have include flood insurance, earthquake insurance, and umbrella coverage on top of your limits (to insure you for personal and medical liability if someone falls down your front stairs and you get to become the long-term disability insurer by default). Be sure to deduct the value of your lot from your insured value.

I favor high limits and as high a deductible as you can be comfortable with. The best use of insurance is not to reimburse you for everything that may go wrong — just the big things that you can't handle on your own. So if can you handle a $1,500 or even a $3,000 surprise, using your emergency fund you'll have saved enough in lower premiums to cover the deductible. After that, you get to keep it all.

✔ **Car insurance:** Insuring yourself against being sued for running someone over, medical payments, and uninsured motorists is actually more important than having coverage to replace or repair your damaged car. Many states require certain levels of insurance to drive. Your insurance rep can help you choose a policy that meets your needs. *Note:* In a number of states, bad credit can increase your auto premiums.

For much more information on insurance policies, check out *Insurance For Dummies* by Jack Hungelmann (John Wiley & Sons, Inc.).

Step 6: Planning for the IRS

Okay, I understand that this may be like planning for the dentist, but as in the case of the dentist, pretax flossing and brushing make this unpleasant subject a lot easier to swallow. No spitting now! Without getting into Novocain-like numbing details, you're better off if you look at this issue as an important component of budget planning. Why? Because if you owe tax money, if you're counting on your tax refund to fill out your budget, or if you're considering bankruptcy, then drilling down into this subject can save you from a real financial toothache.

Typically, you pick a number of deductions and your employer withholds money from your paycheck and sends it to the IRS. The deductions reflect an *estimate* of what you'll owe, but most people end up either owing too much to the government on April 15 or getting too large a tax refund.

Not all income is subject to withholding. Among the exceptions are dividends, interest, income from side businesses, tips, stock gains, gambling winnings, money paid to you as an independent contractor, small-business income, forgiven debts, hobby income, rents, and gifts above a certain dollar level. But that doesn't mean you don't have to pay taxes on them! Be sure that you know what you owe and prepare yourself for that inevitability.

As you do your planning, you can choose one of three approaches to what I very generally call Goldilocks tax planning:

✔ Overpay

✔ Underpay

✔ Strive to pay just the right amount

You can probably already guess which strategy is the right one, but just in case, I cover them all in the following sections.

Overpaying your withholdings

Many people tell me, "I don't want to owe any money" or "I use my refund to pay down my cards after holiday shopping," so they deliberately overpay their taxes as a budget-balancing strategy.

Overpaying is too hard on your budget. At a minimum, you're giving the IRS an interest-free loan of your money, money that you could be using to soften up your debt, build up savings, or achieve any of a zillion good purposes. If you've overpaid all year and an emergency comes along in November, you can't ask the government for an advance of your refund to cover it. But you could use that money if you had it in a savings account, or even in your mattress.

If you're consistently getting a refund check, go over your situation with a qualified tax preparer. You can likely find a better way to not owe something on April 15 without overpaying every pay period.

Underpaying your withholdings

A too soft approach to taxes will end up with a nasty surprise. If you under withhold and owe a big tax bill in April, you may find your credit cards absorbing more unplanned items than just taxes, including tax penalties, interest, and a fat convenience fee. Ouch! Plus, your card may well be full already.

Most local, state, and federal taxes usually can't be discharged in a bankruptcy, nor can credit-card debt incurred from paying your taxes.

Paying just the right amount of withholdings

Oh, this feels just right! Adjusting your withholdings so you either give a little or get a little is not as difficult as it may first seem. You may be surprised to discover that you can have more deductions than you have people in your household. It's true. I don't recommend adding the cat as a dependent, but a deductible mortgage payment can count as one or two additional deductions. I suggest that you at least consult with a tax preparer to get a good forecast of your tax commitments for the year. You may get an early budget bonus if you find you're over-withholding and can decrease your deductions, which may allow you to fund some of those short-term goals you've been saving for.

On the other hand, if some nasty bears are in your future, you're much better off knowing about them in advance so you can be prepared and not be caught asleep when they come in the front door.

The right amount isn't a precise number. Until all the figures are in, there's no way to know exactly what you'll owe. I suggest that you pad your estimates with a cushion of $600 to $1,000 in excess of what you think you'll owe in April. An amount of $50 to $80 a month won't make a big difference to your monthly budget, and as long as your income is relatively stable and your deductions from last year haven't changed a lot, tax time may be a stroll in the woods.

Step 7: Planning for retirement

Unless you're one of those people who can't imagine not working, planning for retirement is important stuff. In fact, even if you can't imagine it, pay attention, because the choice of staying or leaving may not be up to you. Health issues, economic contractions, and more often influence when you leave your job. If you're like me, you can't wait!

I suggest that you find either a Certified Financial Planner (CFP), a Chartered Financial Consultant (ChFC), or, if you're in the heavy-duty-investment end of things, a Chartered Financial Analyst (CFA) to help you develop a plan that will meet your retirement goals. Using the budget and goals you developed earlier, you'll look like a star when you walk into a planner's office. If you tend to be more of a do-it-yourself person, you can find good resources on this topic at both Charles Schwab (www.schwab.com) and Fidelity (www.fidelity.com).

Compounding interest: Investing for the future

One of the key components of successfully budgeting for your future is having your limited savings earn as much as possible for your future needs. You've all seen the charts that loudly proclaim that if you had only saved xx dollars a year from the time you were 10 years old until you retired, you'd have a zillion dollars.

Well, behind all the smoke and mirrors is a grain of truth. Prudent investing is an important tool. However, you have the right to feel comfortable with the process. So, if you haven't started, it's never too late. Check out some of the resources in this chapter and start at your own speed and with your own goals in mind.

Whether you do it yourself or use a paid professional doesn't matter. The compounding of interest and tax advantages available today from some types of investments makes investing too great an opportunity to miss.

Face to face or over the Internet, you're better off if you have an idea of what you need to save to fund your retirement plans. Here are some simple tips for you as you look into the near or distant future:

- ✔ **Estimate your life expectancy.** Chances are it's longer than that of your parents. Just don't guess too short. The Centers for Disease Control (CDC) estimates between 78 and 80. You can also find some fun web calculators that can help you with an estimate. I tried www.livingto100.com/ as an example. Those of you, like me, who weren't born yesterday and are still in reasonably good health are looking at more than that. You can check out the good news at www.cdc.gov/nchs/fastats/lifexpec.htm.

- ✔ **Pick the right retirement date.** The difference between the age at which you want to retire and your last birthday is the time period you need to budget for.

- ✔ **Consider inflation.** After you have a number that you think you'll be comfortable living on in retirement, be sure to increase that number for future inflation — the further out your retirement, the happier you'll be if you increase it. A number of good websites or financial planning programs adjust for inflation and investment experience (how much your investments will earn).

- ✔ **Don't underestimate medical expenses.** The good news is that you've got years to go. The not-so-good news is that medical expenses can be a big part of your future. No one knows for sure how the government's actions to reduce medical costs will work out, so it pays to do some preparing on your own by getting your medical expenses and insurance coverage budgeted in your retirement planning.

- ✔ **Remember that time will still cost money.** If you end up with too little money and too much retirement, I recommend three courses of action: Save more for the same amount of time, save the same for longer, or spend less in your retirement budget. You can increase your current savings by earning more or spending less today. You can just keep pushing out the retirement date until the surplus you've accumulated or an increased retirement benefit makes your numbers work. Or you can do with less later. The choice is up to you.

Using Cool Tools to Help You Build and Stick to a Spending Plan

With the advent of the computer and the smart phone, tools to help you develop a spending plan — and stick to it — fill the shelves of most office-supply outlets.

But not all budgeting tools have to be electronic to be cool or even useful. If you want a less technologically based approach to budgeting, here are some suggested tools to add to your budgeting kit:

- ✔ **Pencil:** Lead, not ink, is the tool to use when developing a plan that you'll be changing throughout the process.

- ✔ **Sticky notes:** An easy way to supplement your planning ideas. They can be moved around to different places on a planning board or document as you make changes.

- ✔ **Envelopes:** They're handy for keeping dollars to be spent or receipts for what was spent, by category. You may consider one envelope for tax-deductible receipts, for example. Filing by expense categories or pay periods can be helpful.

- ✔ **Accordion files:** They work similarly to envelopes, but they're more portable — and you're less likely to misplace them.

This section takes a closer look at different tools you can use when keeping good records.

Web-based financial calculators

Web-based financial calculators are a cool way to help you figure out where you stand and what it will take to get you where you want to be. They're a great tool to help manage your money because they give you the information you need to make informed choices about what a course of action or purchase will actually cost you and for how long.

You can find calculators to help you figure out your mortgage payments at different interest rates, calculators to tell you the true cost of a loan and its impact on your budget, and even calculators that tell how much you need to budget for how long to get those credit cards paid off.

If you need a Web-based calculator, check out the following:

- ✔ **www.choosetosave.org:** A nonprofit clearinghouse, this site has a large number of calculators from many different sources such as the investment regulators at the Financial Industry Regulatory Authority (FINRA), the American Institute of CPAs (AICPA), and others.

- ✔ **www.myfico.com:** Fair Isaac or FICO developed the original (FICO) credit score. This website has excellent tools for determining what effect differing credit scores have on loan interest rates and the total costs to you.

- ✔ **www.bankrate.com:** Bankrate.com is a trusted financial resource and megasite that has general calculators for many financial functions. Plus, it's the home of the Debt Adviser, yours truly, at www.bankrate.com/brm/archive_debtadviser.asp.

Budgeting websites

You can find some easy-to-use, basic budgeting and spending advice and tools online. The following are a few of my favorites:

- ✔ **www.moneymanagement.org/financialtools:** Money Management International's website is a good start.

- ✔ **www.consumerlaw.org:** The National Consumer Law Center site has a large amount of consumer-oriented material that you may find helpful in sifting through the competing claims of those who want to help you deal with financial issues.

- ✔ **www.militaryonesource.com:** This is a good site for military personnel. Military OneSource is provided at no cost by the Department of Defense to all active-duty, National Guard, and Reserve members and their families. The 24/7 service provides information and referrals, plus private, local, face-to-face counseling. Call 800-342-9647. The site has good tips and online budgeting tools tailored to service personnel, plus a lot more — just look under the "Budgeting and Basic Money Management" tab.

Smart phone apps

Every smart phone has a zillion different apps that you can download (some for a price) that will jazz up your spending planning. Apps are so numerous and coming on the scene so quickly that I suggest you do a search for your phone's financial apps when you're ready to go to have the widest choice possible. User reviews are readily available.

Spending plan assistance

There's no shortage of places you can go to get free help building a spending plan that will work for you. But beware of scammers that promise help and just help themselves. Here are two great nonprofit associations whose members can help for free:

- ✔ **www.debtadvice.org:** The National Foundation for Credit Counseling has good advice and referrals along with a good, high-level budgeting calculator that plots your spending, based on income, against national averages to let you know whether you're in the ballpark of your peers. Their member-agency network offers budgeting assistance as well as debt-management solutions.

✔ **www.aiccca.org:** The Association of Independent Consumer Credit Counseling Agencies has a listing of member agencies, many of which can help you with budgeting issues, but all of which have debt-management products.

Adjusting Your Priorities and Your Plan

Depending on your stage of life, your primary budget needs vary. The basic tools remain the same, but the emphasis shifts. Your priorities are different in each stage:

✔ **In your first job:** Chances are you have big ideas and little money. At this stage, just establishing habits, such as developing a spending plan and beginning a small savings program, are most important. Be sure to keep current on student loan payments, or get deferrals if needed.

✔ **As a couple:** Your focus may be paying off old debts, finding out how to communicate about money, agreeing on financial goals and a spending plan, establishing joint and separate credit and savings accounts, setting up a household account, and preparing for a family.

✔ **With a growing family:** Adjusting to a stay-at-home spouse or childcare expenses, paying for your kids' sports programs and braces, expanding living expenses, and saving for education and weddings are just some of the issues a family faces.

✔ **Going solo:** Whether you never marry or you go through a split-up, you're likely to confront situations such as living and saving on one income, taking care of children solo, and perhaps paying off divorce expenses and dealing with alimony and child support.

✔ **In an empty nest:** As the kids fly the coop, it's time to confirm your vision for the future and recast your budget for a new lifestyle. This may include enjoying retirement, exploring estate planning, considering Social Security and Medicare issues, and having some fun with your savings.

Credit and financial challenges await you at different times and under differing circumstances. You'll be so much better prepared to weather any turmoil the future may bring and to take advantage of opportunities if you have a plan that allows you to know where your money is going and how to maximize your savings. As you move to new priorities or stages in your life, a dust-off of your goals, income, and expenses offers you all you need to make the most successful adjustments possible. A good rule of thumb to follow is when one of life's events shows up, it's time for you to revisit your plan.

Chapter 5

Protecting Your Credit in the Post–Financial Meltdown World

. . . .

In This Chapter

▶ Understanding your consumer protections

▶ Demystifying the CARD Act

▶ Realizing the implications of the Dodd-Frank legislation

▶ Knowing your rights under the FACT Act

▶ Using the Fair Debt Collection Practices Act with collectors

. . . .

You've heard it more than once: "I'm never going to use credit again." Whether this statement comes from a perception that credit grantors, bankers, or Wall Street tycoons have fixed the game in their favor or because you've been burned with loans that should never have been made, the truth is that you'll continue to have to deal with credit in one shape or another for the rest of your life.

Because credit is used for so much more than lending and because fine print matters, you need to understand what protections you have to help level the playing field. You need to be prepared when dealing with multibillion-dollar organizations that have proven themselves difficult to deal with after a transaction is closed or even less than fully reliable as a long-term partner. Maybe the financial services industry has changed. But until you know how it may have changed, speak softly and carry a big stick. Where do you find that big stick? Right here in this chapter. I explain your protections and what you have a right to expect from lenders, credit reporters, and collectors just in case they forget.

Why You Have the Right to Credit Protections

Americans value fair play. Many of you were brought up being told that good guys never start a fight, that the hero only shoots in self-defense and only after the bad guy shoots first, and that lenders don't lend money to just anyone or lend you more than you can possibly afford to repay. Whether you agree that the first two are still part of our culture, most people who've lived through the last few years agree that no one ever fully trusts a lender to be conservative, to offer only loans that people can afford, or to fully disclose all the terms of a deal.

What caused this big change in lending? I could tell you that it was just greed, pure and simple, but the situation was more complex than that. In a few words, these lending changes resulted from the decoupling of the ability to make money from being held responsible for results. Lenders were able to originate (make) a loan, get paid for it, and then turn around and package and resell the loan (and the risks of default) to people thousands of miles away. So if your bank can give you a mortgage, package it with others in a security, sell it on Wall Street to a hedge fund, and that fund sells your mortgage to investors in Spain, I think you'll agree that you need more protections than you might if your local credit union owned the mortgage on your home! Millions of you have been frustrated by credit decisions made in the 2001 to 2007 boom that preceded the recession that began at the very end of 2007. Your frustration has filtered down to Washington and resulted in new regulations and an extension of consumer protections.

The Credit Card Accountability, Responsibility, and Disclosure (CARD) Act of 2009 was designed to curb lending practices that many perceived as unfair and unfriendly to consumers. If that wasn't enough, and it wasn't, the CARD Act was followed by the Dodd-Frank Wall Street Reform and Consumer Protection Act, which established the Consumer Financial Protection Bureau (CFPB). This new bureau has the power to regulate a wide range of financial products and services, including credit counseling, payday loans, mortgages, credit cards, and other bank products. These new pieces of legislation join older consumer-protection laws such as the Fair Credit Reporting Act (FCRA).

Table 5-1 gives you an at-a-glance look at the best and most important consumer-protection laws and what they cover. I provide details on most of these in the rest of the chapter.

Table 5-1	Consumer-Protection Laws
Law	*Main Areas Covered*
CARD Act	Credit cards
Dodd-Frank	Wall Street regulation, consumer protection
FACT Act	Identity theft
Fair Credit Reporting Act	Credit reporting
Fair Debt Collection Practices Act	Debt collection

The CARD Act: Shielding You from Credit Card Abuse

The Credit Card Accountability, Responsibility, and Disclosure (CARD) Act of 2009 focuses specifically on your protections from credit card industry practices that have been deemed to be either unfair or just plain tricky. Among the key protections you can expect to see evidence of in your daily financial life are easier-to-understand terms, fewer retroactive interest rate increases on existing card balances, more time to pay your monthly bills, more notice of changes in your credit card terms, and the right to opt out of many changes in terms on your accounts.

Here's a list of the top protections that you as a consumer are due:

- ✔ **No more bait and switch:** Card issuers can't hike interest rates on existing balances except under certain conditions (such as when a promotional rate ends, or when an index used to set your variable rate goes up, or for a late payment of 60 days). Consequently, interest rates on new card charges can't change in the first year, major terms of the agreement can't change overnight, and you get 45 days' advance notice of any big changes.

- ✔ **No more universal default gotcha:** You may have heard of people having their rates raised on one card when they have a problem with another one. This practice has ended. Card issuers may only use universal default on future credit card balances that exist at the time of the default, and they must give you at least 45 days' advance notice of the change. You can then change cards, get other financing, or pay off the balance.

✔ **Limits on interest rate increases:** Card issuers may only raise your interest rate on existing balances if

- The rate was part of a promotional period that ended

- The index used to set your variable interest rate rises

- You're at the end of a workout agreement

- You have late payments of 60 days or more

✔ **Credit-granting restrictions for young adults:** Creditors can't give credit cards to kids with no income. People under 21 must show that they have enough income to repay the card debt or have a cosigner who does. What a concept! Additionally, credit card companies must stay at least 1,000 feet away from colleges if they offer free pizza or other gifts to entice students to apply for credit cards.

Avoid cosigning like the plague. In addition to high rates of default, your credit gets hurt, as does your relationship, when a payment is missed for any reason. Rather than cosigning, make the kid(s) an authorized user on your account or get the student a debit card.

✔ **Graceful grace periods:** Card issuers must give you "a reasonable amount of time" (at least 21 days after the bill is mailed) to make payments on monthly bills. More time to get your payment in should result in fewer late fees.

✔ **No tricky due dates or times:** Card issuers can no longer set early morning deadlines (before their mail is delivered) for payments. Cutoff times must be 5 p.m. or later on the date due, and due dates can't be on a weekend, a holiday, or a day when the card issuer is closed for business.

✔ **Payments must be fairly applied:** If you owe money at different rates on the same card (many cards have different rates for regular purchases versus cash advances and balance transfers), payments over the minimum due must go to the balance with the highest interest rate first. Consequently, your payment will reduce more of your balances faster than under the old practice.

✔ **Easy on the over-limit fees:** Card issuers can't charge you over-limit fees without your permission. If you opt out, or say no, transactions exceeding your credit limit are rejected. This is good news for controlling over-limit fees. Plus, if you opt in, no fees can be larger than the amount of over-spending. For example, going $10 over your limit can't incur a fee of $39.

✔ **No double-dealing double-cycle billing:** Interest on outstanding balances must end when you pay off the balance. *Double-cycle billing* used to cost you more if you paid off your balance because you'd have charges from the previous cycle even though you paid the last bill in full.

✔ **Disclosing minimum payment impact:** Card issuers must indicate how long paying off the entire balance will take if you only make the minimum monthly payment. They must also indicate how much you need to pay each month to pay off a balance in 36 months, including interest. Seeing the high cost of credit card minimum payments allows you to make better-informed decisions about how you pay for the use of credit.

✔ **Restricted late fees:** Late fees are limited to $25 or less unless you're late more than once in a six-month period. Your late payment is still reported to the credit bureau, but this restriction will result in fewer and lower fees charged to your account.

✔ **Right to opt out of changes:** Card issuers must give you advance notice of changes to the terms of use for your credit card. Therefore, you now have the right to reject many significant changes in terms to your credit card accounts.

If you opt out of some changes to your account, you may be required to close your account and pay off any balance under the old conditions.

Although the CARD Act provides a lot of consumer protections, it's not all-encompassing. It doesn't cover business and corporate accounts or interest rates on future card purchases. Cards with variable or floating interest rates (most cards) are subject to interest increases as the prime rate goes up. And card issuers can still close your account or lower your limits without advance warning.

If you believe your card issuer has violated any of the provisions of the CARD Act, contact customer service and ask for an explanation or a rebate. If you disagree with the answer you can contact the Federal Trade Commission (www.ftc.gov) or your state's attorney general or consumer protection department. After July 21, 2011, you can also complain to the Consumer Financial Protection Bureau's Consumer Response Center (www.consumerfinance.gov).

The Consumer Financial Protection Bureau, a Consumer's New Best Friend

The Consumer Financial Protection Bureau (CFPB) is a direct result of the Dodd-Frank Wall Street Reform and Consumer Protection Act. It's a new and powerful executive agency that has a substantial budget and broad consumer protection powers. The CFPB has the power to regulate a wide range of financial products and services, from smaller players like credit counseling agencies and payday lenders to the big guys like mortgage originators, underwriters and servicers, credit card issuers, and various bank products. The CFPB is vested with exclusive rulemaking authority over all federal consumer financial law. This authority extends to new rules to prohibit unfair, deceptive, or abusive acts, practices, and disclosures for financial products and services.

So who's protected by the CFPB? You, that's who! The CFPB is dedicated to making sure that you as a consumer are treated fairly and protected when dealing with the U.S. financial system. Through the use of strict regulations, the CFPB seeks to protect you from any person or organization that offers or provides a consumer financial product or service for personal, family, or household purposes. It also has specific authority to crack down on a person or company identified as being unlawful, unfair, deceptive, or abusive to any consumer financial product or service transaction.

Think of the CFPB as a tough but consumer-friendly cop on the financial product and services beat that aims to level the playing field so you know what you're buying. Following are several of the covered products and services that may affect you in today's financial marketplace:

- Issuers of everything from credit cards to mortgages need to improve disclosure and present fee data more clearly, from the point of sale to payoff.

- All that paperwork you sign when closing on a real estate investment needs to be understandable, by you!

- When you buy or sell a real estate or personal property asset, you should be assured of fair and consistent valuations.

- If you're one of the millions who use prepaid or reloadable cards or money orders, you'll get clearer disclosures and fee information.

- Providers of check cashing, check collection, and check guaranty services are subject to limits and disclosure requirements.

- Credit card transaction fees must be reasonable.

- The responsibilities of your financial advisor/broker will be clearer to you regarding individual financial matters or proprietary financial products or services.

- Credit counselors will have more oversight to be sure you're protected from mistakes or abuse.

- Debt settlement services will have CFPB oversight beyond recent Federal Trade Commission (FTC) rulings on upfront fees.

- Servicers of mortgages can't make up rules as they go along.

- Debt collection activity will be more tightly regulated.

Safeguarding Your Credit Data through the FACT Act

The Fair Credit Reporting Act (FCRA) and its update, the Fair and Accurate Credit Transactions Act (the FACT Act or FACTA), were put in place to make sure that any time your record of credit use is reported to the credit bureaus, the record is accurate, timely, fair, and private. The FACT Act applies to a large number of specialty consumer-reporting agencies, not just the three big bureaus (Experian, Equifax, and TransUnion). Some agencies accumulate and sell information about your check-writing history, medical records, and rental history. For more information on the different reporting bureaus, see Chapter 7.

So what are your rights and protections? Here's a summary of the biggies (for the full story, check out the FACT Act on the CD or visit www.ftc.gov/credit):

- ✔ **You must be notified if anyone takes a negative action based on your credit report.** Anyone using a credit report or specialty-bureau consumer report to deny your application for credit, insurance, or employment — or to take any adverse action against you — must tell you and give you access to the information by telling you how you can get a free copy of the credit report used to make the decision.

- ✔ **You have the right to know what's in your file.** You can get a copy of all the information about you in the files of a consumer-reporting agency.

- ✔ **You can get a free copy of your reports annually or if there's been an adverse action against you because of information in your credit report.** A free copy of your credit report every 12 months from each of the nationwide consumer-reporting companies is just what the doctor ordered for good credit health.

You can get your free copy at www.annualcreditreport.com. You can also get a free report if you're the victim of identity theft, if your file contains inaccurate information as a result of fraud, if you're on public assistance, or if you're unemployed but expect to apply for employment within 60 days. See Chapter 7 for details on specialty reporting agencies.

Beware of imposter websites! When you order your free annual credit reports online, be sure to correctly type in www.annualcreditreport.com to avoid being misdirected to other websites that offer supposedly free reports but only with the purchase of other products and services such as credit monitoring. Also, be aware that while you're on the authorized free site, you'll be offered additional products or services for a price. You're not required to make a purchase to receive your free annual credit reports.

✔ **You have the right to know your credit score.** Believe it or not, this didn't used to be the case. Your score was secret from you, but not from your creditors! Well, that's changed, and now you have the right to get your score from consumer-reporting agencies, but you'll have to pay for it. (See Chapter 7 for more info.)

✔ **You have the right to dispute incomplete, out-of-date, or inaccurate credit information and have it removed from your reports.** After you report an issue to the consumer-reporting agency, the agency has to investigate (they call it reinvestigate). Unless your dispute is frivolous, the agency must correct or delete the erroneous information, usually within 30 days.

✔ **You have the right to limit access to your file to only those who have a legitimate business purpose for requesting it.** A consumer-reporting agency may sell information in your file only to people with a valid use, called a *permissible purpose* — usually to consider an application with a creditor, insurer, employer, landlord, or other business purpose. You must give your approval for anyone to access your information, and you can limit access to your information for unsolicited prescreened offers for credit and insurance.

You can opt out of such preapproved credit offers with the nationwide credit bureaus at 1-888-5-OPTOUT (1-888-567-8688).

✔ **You have the right to collect damages for violations of your rights under the FACT Act.** If a credit-reporting agency or user or furnisher of information violates the FACT Act, you can sue the party in state or federal court.

✔ **You have additional rights if you're an identity theft victim or an active-duty military service person.** For example, you can appoint a personal representative to handle your affairs while you're deployed outside the U.S. Additionally, you may place an active-duty alert on your file, which requires that creditors exercise greater caution and verify your identity before making any credit decisions. For more information, see Chapter 12.

Although the FACT Act is a federal law and is enforced by the FTC and the CFPB, states may also enforce the law, and some states have their own consumer-reporting laws. You may have additional rights under your state's laws. To find out what applies in your state, contact your state or local consumer-protection agency or your state attorney general. Explain your concerns and ask what your rights are and how you can get help. Be sure to record names, dates, and actions in case you need to follow up.

The FDCPA, Providing Protection against Debt Collectors

What do you do when a debt collector sends you a letter or calls saying how much he misses seeing your payment? Whether you're feeling helpless or angry, knowing the rules that apply is important — specifically, what collectors can really do and what's not allowed. The Fair Debt Collection Practices Act (FDCPA) is the key piece of legislation that regulates debt collectors and your rights. It prohibits debt collectors — meaning collection agencies, lawyers who collect debts, and companies that buy delinquent debts and try to collect them — from using abusive, unfair, or deceptive practices to attempt to collect from you. The following sections get you better acquainted with the FDCPA.

The FDCPA covers most personal, family, and household debts, such as a personal credit card account, a car loan, a medical bill, or a mortgage. Notably, the FDCPA doesn't cover debts incurred in running a business.

Controlling the contacts

A collector may contact you at a reasonable time, such as after 8 a.m. or before 9 at night. If these times don't work, you get to define what a reasonable time to contact you is. But you must allow collectors to do their job, so you can't be too restrictive. A collector also may not contact you at work if you tell the collector (orally or in writing) that you're not allowed to get calls there.

Be sure to follow up any oral conversations or agreements in writing as soon as possible. Doing so documents what you and the collector have agreed to and helps eliminate miscommunications in a stressful environment.

Got an attorney? Let the collector know. After you do, the collector must contact the attorney and only the attorney, rather than you or anyone else. If you don't have an attorney, a collector has the right to contact others to get your address, home phone number, and place of employment. However, collectors can't tell anyone else why they're calling or that they're debt collectors.

Finding out about the debt

You have the right to receive a validation notice from the collector within five days of contact that tells you how much money you owe. The notice must include the name of the creditor to whom the collector claims you owe the money and procedures to follow if you don't think you owe the money.

If you don't owe the money or an error has been made, send the debt collector a letter (certified mail with a return receipt) within 30 days of receiving the validation notice and state that you're disputing the debt. If you're not 100 percent sure whether you owe the money, ask for verification of the debt. The good news is that, until the debt is verified, the law prohibits further collector contacts.

Collectors can begin contacting you again after they send you written verification of the debt, like a copy of a bill for the amount you owe.

Stopping a collector from contacting you

When a collector first contacts you about a debt, it usually comes as a surprise. If you decide after being contacted by the collector that you don't want to hear from the collector again, you have the right to tell the collector (in writing) to stop contacting you. Here's how.

Keep copies of everything you send or receive. Send an original copy of your demand by certified mail, and pay for a return receipt so you can document what the collector received. After the collector receives your letter, the collector may not contact you again. Well, there are two exceptions: The collector may contact you to tell you there will be no further contact. I know, it sounds silly, but that's the law. Second, the collector may let you know that the collector or the creditor intend to take a specific action as a result of your ending the conversation, like filing a lawsuit.

Sending a letter to a debt collector stopping all contact doesn't get rid of the debt, but it should stop the collector from contacting you. The creditor or the debt collector still can, and often will, sue you to collect the debt.

Spotting prohibited behavior

Debt collectors aren't allowed to get away with certain behaviors. Here are some highlights, or lowlights, of what a collector may not do:

- ✔ **Harass or threaten you:** Debt collectors may not harass, oppress, or abuse you or any third parties they contact. They may not threaten violence or harm, publish your name as someone who refuses to pay his debts (but they can report you to a credit bureau), use obscene or profane language, or repeatedly call to annoy you.

✔ **Lie to you:** Like Pinocchio, debt collectors who lie get in trouble. Their noses may not grow, but they can be sued if they pretend to be attorneys, government representatives, or employees of a credit bureau. They also get in trouble if they claim that you've committed a crime or lie about the amount you owe. They also can't pretend that the papers they send you are legal forms if they aren't or indicate that papers they send you aren't legal forms if they are.

✔ **Be unfair:** Collectors may not engage in unfair practices when collecting a debt. So what's not fair play? Trying to collect more than what's due unless the contract that created your debt — or your state law — allows an additional charge; depositing a post-dated check early; or contacting you by postcard to unfairly embarrass you with the mail carrier or your family. That's really not fair!

If a collector violates any of the provisions of the FDCPA, contact your local consumer protection agency, attorney general's office, or your own lawyer. The first two public resources should be able to stop the abusive or unfair behavior with a phone call or a letter. Your attorney may also file suit for damages against the collector/collection agency.

Suing the collector

You (hopefully your attorney and not actually you) have the right to sue a collector in a state or federal court within one year if the collector violates the law. If you win, you can win big. You can be awarded any damages you can prove resulting from the illegal collection practices, like lost wages and medical bills. You also can be reimbursed for your attorney's fees and court costs.

If a debt collector violates the FDCPA in trying to collect a debt and you win a lawsuit against that collector, the debt doesn't go away if you owe it. Also, if you lose your suit, you may owe more in fees and costs.

Exploring Other Protections

People turn to payday lending and debt settlement when they find traditional financing difficult or even impossible to obtain. These industries weren't tightly regulated before the 2007 recession, but nowadays, new protections are available if you know where to look. In the next sections, I take you on a quick tour of these businesses and the protections you can take advantage of if you decide to use them. I also introduce you to an age-old protection, called the statute of limitations, that's worth knowing about.

The ins and outs of payday loans

Astronomical interest rates, predatory lenders, and unsuspecting people forever in debt. That's generally what comes to mind when people think of payday loans. Well, the reality isn't as simple as that picture. Payday loans are short-term cash loans secured by your personal check. Say you need a short-term loan to cover some unexpected expense. You may not have access to credit lines or cards. Your bank won't give you a short-term loan. So you go to your local payday lender. You write a personal check for the amount you want to borrow, plus a fee, and you receive cash. Your check is held for future deposit or electronic access to your bank account, usually on the date of your next payday. Hence the term *payday loan* and the short period of the loan (usually one or two weeks). Payday loans charge extremely high fees: Using a not untypical $17.50 for every $100 borrowed up to a maximum of $300, the interest rates run 911 percent for a one-week loan, 456 percent for a two-week loan, and 212 percent for a one-month loan.

These loans are small in dollars and high in transaction costs. Many banks find them unprofitable and won't make them. The result is the payday loan industry. As expensive as these loans are, they can be less expensive than overdraft charges on your bank account, which are now limited by law but used to be so steep and unfairly applied that payday loans were cheap by comparison.

Payday lenders claim that their loans aren't high-cost if they're used properly. Here's an example of their thinking: You take a taxi for short distances and a plane for long ones. You wouldn't take a taxi coast to coast, nor would you take a plane to the local grocery store. Just because the taxi's rate per mile is higher than the plane's cost per mile doesn't necessarily mean that the taxi is overcharging for its service. Unless, of course, the taxi takes you from Times Square to Lincoln Center via Los Angeles.

Looking at the rules of payday loans

Lenders are required to quote the cost of payday loans as both the dollar finance charge and the annual percentage rate (APR). In addition, many states have rules and limits for payday lenders.

The website `www.credit.com/credit_information/credit_law/ PaydayLoanLaws.jsp` includes a list of the current state regulations for your protection, but I list the rules for the five largest states here:

- ✔ **California** allows loans of 31 days of up to $300. Fees allowed are up to 15 percent of the amount loaned.

- ✔ **Florida** allows loans of 7 to 31 days of up to $500 exclusive of fees. Fees allowed are up to 10 percent of the loan plus a $5 fee. The APR for a 14-day, $100 loan is 390 percent.

✔ **Illinois** allows loans of 13 to 45 days of up to the lesser of $1,000 or 25 percent of the borrower's gross monthly income. Fees allowed are $15.50 per $100 loaned. The APR for a 14-day, $100 loan is 403 percent.

✔ **New York** has no specific payday-lending legislation and permits payday lenders to charge any interest rate or fees that the borrower agrees to pay.

✔ **Texas** allows loans of 7 to 31 days without limitation. Fees allowed are 10 percent of the loan amount plus 48 percent annual interest and a $12 monthly fee. The effective APR for a 14-day, $100 loan is 309 percent.

On the federal level, the Department of Defense provides protections for men and women in the armed forces and their families. Specifically, lenders may not charge more than 36 percent annual interest, including fees. Additionally, if you're in the Navy or Marine Corps, the Navy and Marine Corps Relief Society will pay off your payday loan if you're having a problem repaying it, and then you can pay the organization back on better terms.

Getting help if a lender violates the rules

If you think a payday loan lender has taken advantage of you, you have a couple places to turn:

✔ **Your state's lender regulation agency:** Regulators may be able to help you work out a payment arrangement with lenders. And if you live in a state that doesn't allow payday lending, the state regulator can take action against lenders. Check out the following link to find the right agency: www.paydayloaninfo.org/state-information.

✔ **The Community Financial Services Association of America (CFSA):** More than half of payday lenders are members of the Community Financial Services Association of America, or CFSA, an organization that requires its members to subscribe to a code of conduct that goes beyond state laws. You may complain to the CFSA (www.cfsa.net) if you feel you've been treated unfairly or abused. Under its code of conduct, you can request and receive an extended payment plan that allows you to extend your loan for four payday cycles without any additional fees or charges.

Many nonmember payday lenders don't offer a payment plan. Their idea of a payment plan is a loan rollover until you collapse under the weight of fees and cumulative interest charges.

The details of debt settlement

Wouldn't it be nice if you didn't have to pay back all that money you owe? That's the premise behind the debt settlement industry. Don't get me wrong: Debt settlers expect you to pay them all you owe them, but they don't expect you to pay others to whom you owe money! In a nutshell, debt settlers try to get lenders to settle or accept a lower payment than is due to satisfy a debt. Why would lenders accept less? Because less is better than nothing!

Debt settlers generally collect a monthly amount from you, but instead of paying your creditors, they hold onto the payments for at least three to six months, depending on your circumstances and your creditors. Next, they try and negotiate with your creditors on your behalf to settle the account for less than the full balance. During this lengthy process, nothing is being paid to your creditors, and they use all the remedies they have to collect the debt from you, including judgments and garnishments. The settlement process seriously damages your credit whether it's successful or not.

The CFPB and the FTC regulate debt settlement. Debt settlers can't charge fees before actually settling a debt. The FTC's debt settlement rules apply to for-profit debt settlement and credit counseling, debt negotiation companies, and companies that falsely claim to have nonprofit status.

The new rules don't apply to in-person or Internet-only debt settlers, nor do they set a limit on how much you can be charged for a debt-settlement service.

Debt settlers must

- ✔ Represent their services accurately.

- ✔ Tell you how long paying off your debt will take, inform you of the conditions under which the settlers will negotiate a settlement with creditors, and tell you how much money you must pay before a settlement offer is made.

- ✔ Disclose that debt settlements will trash your credit rating and potentially expose you to lawsuits from creditors.

- ✔ Successfully settle or negotiate at least one of your debts, with at least one payment going to a creditor before you're charged any fees.

- ✔ Provide you with a written contract, debt settlement plan, or oral agreement outlining the pay-back strategy, as well as details of the potential pitfalls of debt-relief services.

If you think you've been taken advantage of, you have a couple places to turn. Your state agency that regulates debt settlers may be able to help. Look for the agency in the consumer protection department or the attorney general's office. Also, the CFPB expects to have a Consumer Response Center set up in late 2011 (it may already be in operation by the time this book is published) to help with your complaints and to answer any questions about consumer financial products and services, including debt settlement. Visit the CFPB website (www.consumerfinance.gov), answer a few simple questions, and at least find out which of the seven federal agencies to contact for enforcement issues.

You can also contact the Better Business Bureau, but doing so may not be an effective alternative because it relies on cooperation from the debt settler to help you.

The scoop on the statute of limitations

The *statute of limitations* (SOL) provides that you aren't held accountable for past mistakes forever. When I was in third grade, Sister Mary Assunta told me that this exemption didn't apply in her class. But elsewhere, each state has a law that restricts the time that legal proceedings may be brought against you to collect a debt. Each state sets a maximum period for a creditor to file a lawsuit, depending on the type of loan or claim. The periods vary by state. Federal statutes set the limitations for suits filed in federal courts. If you're not sued before the statutory deadline, the lenders lose their right to sue you.

If you're looking for a website that lists SOL laws for different states, check out www.nolo.com/legal-encyclopedia/statute-of-limitations-state-laws-chart-29941.html.

Statutes of limitations go way back to early Roman law and were designed to prevent fraudulent and stale (really old as opposed to dull or smelly) claims from arising after all evidence was lost or after the facts became obscured through the passage of time, defective memory, death, or the disappearance of witnesses.

To use this protection, you must show up before the court and answer the lender's complaint. If you don't, you waive the use of this defense and aren't permitted to use it in any subsequent proceedings.

Here's what you need to keep in mind about the SOL:

✔ If your debt is older than allowed under your state's SOL, you can't be sued in court to collect it.

✔ The SOL has nothing to do with the time a debt stays on your credit report. A debt can be on your credit report for seven years but be uncollectible in a much shorter period of time.

✔ The SOL begins to run from the day the debt — or payment on an open-ended account — was due and not paid.

✔ The SOL doesn't eliminate your debt after it expires. It keeps you from being sued in court. A collector can still ask that you repay the debt.

✔ Depending on your state's law, making a partial payment may restart the SOL clock and extend the time you may be sued.

✔ States that specify that a partial payment doesn't restart the clock on the SOL, unless there's a new written promise to pay, include Arizona, California, Florida, Iowa, Kansas, Maine, Massachusetts, Michigan, Minnesota, Mississippi, Missouri, Nevada, New York, Texas, Virginia, West Virginia, and Wisconsin.

Part II

Writing on Your Personal Credit Wall: Credit Reporting and Scoring in the Facebook Age

The 5th Wave   By Rich Tennant

"I'm entering all the bank's requirements for a mortgage, and I have to either buy a computer with more memory or start looking for a smaller house."

In this part . . .

I focus on bringing your credit reports and credit scores to life so you can easily understand what they say about you. I show you how to get access to your credit report for free, tell you when it's best to do so, and explain what your credit report and credit scores really mean to you and your future. I give you the details on what your credit report contains, how the information gets there, how you can make it look the best it can, and who can see your information besides you.

I discuss the various components that you need to know to build a good FICO score and VantageScore. I help you determine whether your credit scores measure up and how you can improve them. I tell you about the other bureau reports that credit reporters use in the sectors of insurance, medicine, gambling, employment, banking, checking, and even renting. Finally, I cover monitoring your credit — when it makes sense to do so and when it doesn't, as well as who to turn to for assistance.

Chapter 6

Discovering How Credit Reporting Works

Some people who use credit sparingly (or not at all) think that knowing their credit history is unimportant. But your credit history doesn't just come into play when you want to borrow money. Landlords, insurers, and even employers review credit reports and make decisions about you based on the information contained in your credit history. Heck, even a particularly finance-conscious romantic prospect may want to review your credit history before saying yes to moving in or tying the knot! A poor credit history can therefore cost you thousands of dollars and deny you opportunities you never even knew you missed.

Anytime lenders and others take a look at you to determine your credit risk — but especially during a tight credit cycle — knowing what they'll see is important. What's in your credit report and credit score, the two pieces of information that reveal your credit history, can make a difference in whether you even qualify for a loan, as well as how much you pay for interest or other terms of the loan and for your auto and homeowners/renters insurance. Don't worry though. In this chapter, I help you understand why you need to be on intimate terms with your credit report and credit score, what these pieces of info actually are, and how they're compiled.

After you're up to speed on credit reports and scores, challenge your friends to a credit score quiz found at www.creditscorequiz.org. Hint: This quiz was co-authored by VantageScore and the Consumer Federation of America!

Grasping the Importance of Your Credit Report

Perhaps you're wondering where all the data about your credit history comes from. Would you think I've seen too many spy movies if I told you that your personal information is being accumulated every day? Or would you think that the government is overstepping its boundaries again? Well, the truth is that your credit history is being compiled courtesy of credit issuers, banks, insurers, pharmacies, and landlords with whom you do business. Chances are they're reporting your financial transactions to the three major credit bureaus (Equifax, Experian, and TransUnion) and many other specialty bureaus that store information.

Each month when you pay your car payment, mortgage payment, and credit card bill, the creditors report your payment history to the credit bureaus. If you miss a monthly payment, your creditor reports that as well. Creditors review the information in your credit report or other specialty reports to determine the terms they may offer you for a credit card, loan, apartment, or insurance.

Clearly, what you don't know *can* hurt you. Consider two hypothetical life situations to illustrate my point:

- ✔ Say you sign up for one of those Internet dating services to meet that special someone. Now, what if all the information available to your prospective dates is given to them by people you've dated in the past? What if the quality of the dates you get in the future is directly tied to what all the people you've dumped (or have been dumped by) say about you? Starting to get concerned?

- ✔ Say you're applying for a job. Your salary, job title, and office size are tied directly to what's on your résumé. But what if you didn't write your résumé but your past employers did instead, and what if they mixed up your personnel file with the file of a person who was fired for punching the boss in the nose? Can you imagine walking into that job interview without having any idea what your former boss may have reported or whether it was correct?

I'm not saying that you're guaranteed to *like* the outcome of your date or the job interview, but at least you know it's based on information that's accurate and timely. Likewise with your credit report. You can't report your own credit history to the bureaus, but you *can* be knowledgeable about what your credit report says and anticipate how it influences you and others as you try to negotiate your way through the financial universe. You *can* head off situations that could cost you thousands of dollars or deny you opportunities. And you *can* catch inaccuracies on your report (a common situation) and correct them.

You have no excuse for not knowing what's in your credit report because you can get free copies of your report annually from all three credit bureaus. Getting the information is fast and easy. Simply visit www.annualcredit report.com or call 877-322-8228 to order your reports.

What Is a Credit Report, Exactly?

In its most basic sense, your credit report is your financial life history. Credit-reporting bureaus or agencies manage, maintain, and share this information. As many as 20 credit-reporting bureaus are out there; most are specialty reporting agencies (I introduce you to some of these in Chapter 7). The following three are considered the biggies:

- ✔ **Equifax** (www.equifax.com; 800-685-1111)
- ✔ **Experian** (www.experian.com; 866-200-6020)
- ✔ **TransUnion** (www.transunion.com; 800-888-4213)

You can rest assured that your rights are protected in the reporting process because of the Fair and Accurate Credit Transactions Act (the FACT Act or FACTA). You can find more details on the FACT Act in Chapter 5 and even a copy of the law on the CD.

The following sections explain what the details in your credit report reveal.

Revealing the facts about your financial transactions

You may think that your credit report contains the intimate personal details of your life, ferreted out from interviews with your neighbors, your ex, and your business associates. Not true! You can rest assured that your credit report doesn't reveal whether you tend to drink too much at office parties, whether you sport a tattoo, or any other personal behavior information.

The information in your credit report is specific, purely factual, and limited to your financial transactions. What it lacks in scope, however, it makes up for in the sheer volume of details and the length of time it covers. When I talk to high school, college, or technical school students, I tell them that if they cut one class, chances are that no one will notice, but if they fail to pay a single bill on time, the creditor notices and reports the late payment, and that info is available for all considering doing business with them to see for the next seven years!

Here's the short take on what's in your credit report:

- **Personal identification information:** This info includes your name, Social Security number, date of birth, addresses (present and past), and recent employment history.

  Be consistent with your personal information, especially how you spell your name and address. Name, address, and date of birth are the most common sources used to identify your file; Social Security number is fourth. If you're a woman and you take your husband's name when you get married, your files should be automatically updated when you get a reissued credit card or a loan in your new name.

- **Public record information:** Your credit report includes info on tax liens, judgments, bankruptcies, child-support orders, and other official information.

- **Collection activity:** If you've had accounts sent to collection agencies for handling, your credit report has that info.

- **Information about each credit account (or *trade line*), whether open or closed:** Your credit report includes details on all your credit accounts, including

  - Type of account (such as a mortgage or installment account)

  - Whether the account is *joint* (shared with another person) or just in your name

  - How much you owe

  - Who you owe

  - Your monthly payment

  - Your payment history (whether you've paid on time or been late)

  - Your credit limits

  Experian, one of the three main credit-reporting agencies, also keeps a record of rental data over the last two years.

- **A list of the companies that have requested your credit file for the purpose of granting you credit:** Requests, known as *inquiries*, are one of two types:

  - *Soft inquiries,* which are made for promotional purposes (for instance, when a credit card issuer wants to send you an offer). These don't appear on the version of your credit report that lenders see, but they do appear on the consumer's copy that you get.

  - *Hard inquiries,* which are made in response to a request from you for more or new credit. These inquiries *do* appear on the lender's copy of your credit report.

✔ **An optional message from you:** This message, which can be up to 100 words in length, explains any extenuating circumstances for any negative listings on your report. See Chapter 14 for more on adding this message to your credit report.

✔ **An optional credit score:** Your credit score is, strictly speaking, not part of your credit report but an add-on that you have to ask for. Your score is different for each credit report because the data that each bureau has may vary slightly, and each bureau may offer a proprietary score of its own. (I cover the importance of your credit score later in this chapter.)

Credit reports are easy to read, although they still have room for improvement. Each of the three major credit-reporting agencies reports your information in its own unique format. The credit-reporting agencies compete with one another for business, so they have to differentiate their products. (Chapter 7 highlights the differences in each agency's presentation.)

Among the list of items *not* included in your credit bureau report are your lifestyle choices, religion, national origin, political affiliation, sexual preferences, medical history, friends, and relatives. In addition, the three major credit-reporting agencies don't collect or transmit data on your checking or savings accounts, brokerage accounts, business accounts (unless you're on record as being personally liable for the debt), bankruptcies more than ten years old, charge-offs or debts placed for collection that are more than seven years old, and, finally, your credit score (although your credit score is generated based on information in your credit report, it's not part of the report itself).

On the CD, you can view sample credit reports from major credit-reporting bureaus.

Providing insight into your character

Many entities use your credit report to predict your potential behaviors in other areas of your life. The fact that you have a history of making credit card payments late may be a red flag for a prospective landlord that you may be late with your rent, too. A history of defaulted loans may suggest to a potential boss that you aren't someone who follows through with work commitments. A home foreclosure in your file may indicate that you take on more than you can handle or that you're just one unlucky duck. If you've declared bankruptcy because your finances are out of control, perhaps you're out of control in other ways, too.

This financial snapshot, which brings into focus the details of your spending and borrowing and even hints at your personal life patterns, also paints a *bigger* picture of two important factors that are critical to employers, landlords, lenders, and others:

✔ **Whether you keep your promises:** Your credit history is an indicator of whether you follow through with commitments, a characteristic that's important to most people, whether they're looking for a reliable worker, a responsible nanny, a dependable renter, or a faithful mate. Needless to say, a person or company that's considering extending you a commitment for a loan, apartment, insurance, or job wants to know the same.

✔ **Whether you fulfill your obligations in a timely manner:** Following through with your obligations in a timely manner is the other half of the credit reporting game. Tight lending standards make a history of past failures to pay on time harder to accept by lenders who can't afford any more defaults.

In the lending business, the more overdue the payment, the more likely it won't be paid in full — or paid at all. That's why as you get further behind in your payments, lenders become more anxious about collecting the amount you owe. In fact, if you're sufficiently delinquent, the lender may want you to pay back the entire amount at once rather than as originally scheduled. So the longer you take to do what you promised, the more it costs you and the more damage you do to your credit and credit score.

The Negatives and Positives of Credit Reporting

Whether you're new to the world of credit or you're an experienced borrower, you may be mesmerized by the amount of information on your credit report. Fortunately, it all falls into one of two categories: negative (information that makes you look like a potential financial risk) and positive (information that makes lenders want to throw money at you, or at least not turn you down for a loan). I zero in on the differences between the two in the following sections so you can focus on what matters and let go of what doesn't.

The negatives

I hate to have to be the one to tell you this, but if you aren't married, someone has to: You aren't perfect. And neither is your credit report. The good news is that you don't need a flawless credit report to qualify for the financial products and services you want at competitive rates and terms, nor do you need a financial record that entitles you to canonization for credit sainthood. Confused? Never fear. Following are the answers to some common questions about the negative data found on the vast majority of Americans' credit reports:

✔ **How long do bad marks stick around?** Most negative data stays on your credit report for seven years, although a few items are different, such as a Chapter 7 bankruptcy, which stays on your report for ten years, and student loans, which stay on until you fully repay them. Even though the negative info is out there for a long time, as the months and years roll by, this info becomes less important to your credit profile. For example, most creditors aren't concerned by the fact that you were late in paying your credit card bill one time three years ago.

✔ **Just how much does one mistake cost you when it comes to your credit report?** That depends on the rest of the items on your report that make up your credit history. Lots of positive information can lessen the impact of negative items, and the size of the mistake counts, too. A default on a credit card is less serious than a mortgage default. Along with your credit report, lenders can also access your *credit score,* a number that's calculated based on the contents of your credit report. This three-digit score comes from a mathematical equation that evaluates much of the information on your credit report at that particular credit bureau. By comparing this information to the patterns in zillions of past credit reports, the score tells the lender your level of future credit risk. (Check out the section "Cracking credit score components" later in this chapter for more info on credit scores.)

✔ **How do those who view your report interpret bad marks?** Think of it this way: Say you loan your significant other $5,000 for a very worthy cause. Your honey promises to pay you back monthly over two years but stops paying after four months, with no intention of repaying the full amount. You then decide to mention the negative experience to any friends who are thinking of floating this person a loan. In business, as in love, trust and faithful performance are keys to success. Basically, any delinquencies or charge-offs definitely count against you. However, a creditor tends to look at your bill payments in the creditor's specific area as most important. A car lender, for example, will scrutinize your car payment history more closely than a credit card issuer. Other concerns include how much credit you have available (too much is not good) and how much of what you have you've used (maxing out is not good).

Greedy lenders may use negative information from your distant past as a reason to put you into a higher-cost (and more profitable for them) loan, even though you may qualify for a less-expensive one. This is just one example of a situation in which understanding your credit score can save you money. The scenario can go something like this: You're looking for a loan for a car or some similar big-ticket item. The lender you contact for a loan reviews your credit report and offers you a loan at terms that are "a great deal considering your credit history." Translated, this means that the lender is charging you a higher-than-market rate because of your imperfect credit report.

If a lender offers you a loan at less than the best terms or if you're denied a loan, the lender must provide you with a *credit score disclosure exception notice* that includes a free copy of the credit score the lender used to make the risk-based pricing decision on your loan. The notice includes the score range and how your score compares to other U.S. consumers. You're also entitled to a free copy of the credit report that was used to obtain that credit score.

The positives

Positive information, as in the good stuff that everyone likes to see, stays on your report for quite a while. In fact, some positive data may be on your report for 10, 20, or even 30 years, depending on each bureau's policy and whether you keep your account open.

The more positive information you have in your credit files, the less effect a single negative item has on your credit score. So if you're an experienced credit user with a long credit history, that one missed payment won't affect you much. If, however, you're a young person or a new immigrant with only a few trade lines and a few months of credit history, a situation that's sometimes called a *thin file,* a negative item has a much larger effect because you have fewer positive items to balance things out. For pointers on beefing up (or just plain starting) your credit history, flip to Chapter 9.

Your Credit Report's Numerical Offspring: The Credit Score

Your credit score is a three-digit number that rules a good portion of your financial life, for better or for worse. But where did this all-important number come from? Starting back in the 1950s, some companies, including FICO (formerly known as Fair Isaac) and more recently VantageScore, began to model credit data in hopes of predicting payment behavior. (A *model* uses a series of formulas based on some basic assumptions to simulate and understand future behavior and to make predictions. A weatherperson uses models to predict the weather all the time. Usually, the credit folks are more accurate because they predict the likelihood of something bad happening in the next year or so.)

Until recently, the three major credit bureaus offered different scoring models created for them by FICO, the developers of the *FICO score.* Each one called the score by a proprietary name, and each had some differences in how it handled your data. Now, they all also offer a single credit scoring model called the VantageScore that's exactly the same across all the databases.

The following sections take a closer look at the two main types of credit scores — FICO and VantageScore — to help you understand their components and ensure that your credit score is the best it can be.

Cracking credit score components

In order to even have a credit score, you need to have at least one account open and reporting for a period of time. VantageScore requires at least one account to be open for at least three months and to have been updated in the last 24 months before generating a score. VantageScore can also develop a credit score based on rent history. FICO, on the other hand, requires the account to be open for at least six months and to have been updated in the last six months. You find out more about both main types of scores in the next sections.

Although having no credit history makes it difficult for you to get credit initially, building credit for the first time is a lot easier than repairing a bad credit history.

What makes up a FICO score?

The most widely used credit score is the FICO score, which ranges from 300 to 850. The higher the number, the better the credit rating and the better terms you get when looking for your next loan or credit card. Your particular FICO score changes over time and as your credit history changes.

FICO takes into account more than 20 factors when building your score, and the importance of each one is dependent on the other factors, the volume of data, and the length of your history. Your FICO score is made up of five components (see Figure 6-1):

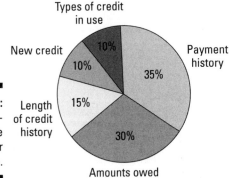

Figure 6-1: Five components make up your FICO score.

Types of credit in use — 10%
New credit — 10%
Payment history — 35%
Length of credit history — 15%
Amounts owed — 30%

Courtesy of FICO

- ✔ **Payment history (35 percent):** Payment history is the most significant factor when determining whether you're a good credit risk. This category includes the number and severity of any late payments, the amount past due, and whether you repaid the accounts as agreed. The more late payments, the lower your score.

- ✔ **Amount and type of debt (30 percent):** The amount you owe is the next most important factor in your credit score. This includes the total amount you owe, the amount you owe by account type (such as revolving or installment, which for FICO includes mortgage debt), the number of accounts on which you're carrying a balance, and the proportion of your credit lines that you're using. For example, in the case of installment credit, *proportion of balance* means the amount remaining on the loan in relation to the loan's original amount. For revolving debt, such as a credit card, proportion of balance is the amount you currently owe in relation to your credit limit. The lower amount you owe in relation to the amount of credit available, the higher your score. Having credit cards with no balances ups your limits and your score.

- ✔ **Length of time you've been using credit (15 percent):** The number of years you've been using credit and the type of accounts you have also influence your score. Accounts that you've had open for at least two years help to increase your score.

- ✔ **Variety of accounts (10 percent):** The mix of credit accounts is a part of each of the other factors. Riskier types of credit mean lower scores. For example, if most of your debt is in the form of revolving credit or finance company loans, your score will be lower than if your debt is from student loans and mortgage loans. Also, a lender is more likely to give greater weight to your performance on its type of loan, meaning a credit card issuer looks at your experience with other cards more closely and a mortgagee pays closer attention to how you pay mortgages or secured loans. An ideal mix of accounts has a positive credit history with a variety of different types of credit, such as both installment and revolving credit lines.

- ✔ **Number and types of accounts you've opened recently, generally in the last six months or so (10 percent):** When you apply for new credit or ask for a raise in your credit line, the creditor makes an inquiry into your credit report. A high number of inquiries for these actions have a negative effect on your credit score. The reasoning is that if you apply for several accounts at the same time and you get approved for them, you may not be able to afford your new debt load.

What makes up a VantageScore?

VantageScore has been around since 2006, and the score ranges from 501 to 990. As with the FICO score, the higher the number, the better the score. As you can see in Figure 6-2, your VantageScore is made up of six components (note that VantageScore reviews its scoring factors more often than FICO does, so you can expect the weighting to change as frequently as every year if large changes occur in economic conditions or consumer behavior):

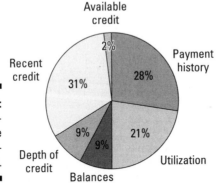

Figure 6-2: Vantage-Score components.

Courtesy of VantageScore

- ✔ **Recent credit (31 percent):** The number of recently opened credit accounts and all new inquiries. New accounts initially lower your score because creditors may be unclear on why you want more credit. However, after you use the accounts and pay on time, the accounts help raise your score by adding positive information to your credit report.

- ✔ **Payment history (28 percent):** Paying on time (satisfactory), paying late (delinquent), or never paying at all (charge-off) show up here. One of the most significant factors when determining whether an individual is a good credit risk is payment history.

- ✔ **Utilization (21 percent):** The percentage of credit available to you that you've used or that you owe on accounts. Using a large proportion of your overall available credit is a negative.

- ✔ **Balances (9 percent):** The amount of recently reported current and delinquent balances. Balances that you've increased recently can be an indication of risk and lower your score.

- ✔ **Depth of credit (9 percent):** Includes the length of your history and types of credit you've used. A long history with mixed types of credit (mortgage, car loan, credit cards, retail stores, and so on) is best.

- ✔ **Available credit (2 percent):** The amount of credit available on all your accounts. Using a low percentage of the total amount of credit available to you is a good thing.

If you're trying to build a credit history for the first time, here are two things to look for. First, seek a lender that uses a VantageScore to grant credit after you establish a credit record because the VantageScore can give you a valid score using less data (a thinner file) than FICO can. Plus, VantageScore can give you scoring credit for rent payments if that information is in your credit report. Second, consider a lender that uses the FICO Expansion score (see the next section), which uses boutique credit databases and information verified by the lender, such as utility payments, to give a one-time score.

For examples of ways to start a credit history, including using a secured card or a passbook loan, check out Chapter 9.

Examining the Expansion score

In the old days, if you didn't have much information in your credit file, you were in a pickle. Lenders had a difficult time assessing your risk because they couldn't get a score for you. Well, thank heavens for Yankee ingenuity, because just as soon as a problem shows up, so does a solution.

FICO calls it their *Expansion score.* Essentially, it's a credit-risk score based on nontraditional consumer credit data (in other words, it's not based on data from the three major national credit-reporting bureaus). The purpose of this new score is to predict the credit risk of consumers who don't have a traditional FICO score.

The use of FICO Expansion scores gives millions of new consumers without extensive credit histories an opportunity to access credit, including

- Young people just entering the credit market
- New arrivals and immigrants to the United States
- People who previously had mostly joint credit and are now widowed or divorced
- People who've used cash rather than credit most or all of their lives

VantageScore can also address thin files because its elves can come up with a score with as little as a single account. In fact, even if you've never used credit but have a track record renting from a landlord who reports to a renters database that the credit-reporting agencies use, VantageScore can get you started.

Chapter 7

Understanding Credit Reports and Scores

*W*hether you agree with the concept or not, people in your life do (and will continue to) make an increasing number of decisions about you based on your credit information. Therefore, knowing the when, what, where, why, and how of your credit information is in your best interest. In fact, I'm not sure why the need to understand your credit history and what it means for your financial life isn't included in the many instructions people receive as children. "Do your best to maintain good credit" is just as valuable a lesson to impart as "Eat your vegetables."

The majority of the credit information collected about you is contained in your credit reports from the three major credit bureaus. Getting copies of those reports and reviewing the information is important and gives you a good idea of what most persons or programs evaluating your credit see. In this chapter, I explain how to get your hands on copies of your credit report, and I walk you through the process of reviewing your reports from each bureau and making sense of all the industry jargon. I also reveal how you can dispute inaccurate information included on your reports. Of course, the three major credit bureaus aren't the only ones compiling financial information about you. I introduce you to other specialty reporting agencies in this chapter as well.

Credit scores are also a part of the credit-reporting picture, so I share how to obtain your score and how to make sense of it. By the time you're done reading this chapter, you'll be armed with the information you need to discover exactly how potential employers, lenders, landlords, and insurance agents see you when viewing you through the lenses of your credit history.

Requesting Copies of Your Credit Reports

The three main collectors of credit information in the credit industry today are Equifax, Experian, and TransUnion. These major credit bureaus are basically huge databases of information. (I reveal where all that information comes from in Chapter 6.)

Given the billions of pieces of data that flow in and out of the bureaus on a monthly basis, as you might expect, sometimes your information may be inaccurate and out of date. Getting copies of your credit reports from the three credit bureaus is therefore essential to verify that your information is correct and a true representation of your credit life. In addition, by reviewing your reports, you'll know if someone has stolen your identity to establish fraudulent credit accounts.

Any incorrect information included in your credit report has the potential to be very costly to you. For example, erroneous info could mean that you don't get the loans or terms you want or you have to pay much higher interest than you should have to pay. The trick is that the companies reporting information to the credit bureaus don't always report to all three. So checking your credit report with just one of the bureaus isn't good enough. The reality is that the information that Equifax has may be slightly different from the information that Experian has, and the information that Experian has may be slightly different from the information that TransUnion has. Also, you can have a perfectly clean Experian report while your TransUnion report has some negative items on it in error, or vice versa.

The good news is that you don't have to do much heavy lifting to get your hands on all your credit reports thanks to the Fair and Accurate Credit Transactions Act (commonly referred to as the FACT Act or FACTA). This act entitles every American to one free credit report from each of the three bureaus every twelve months. You're also entitled to an additional free report from each of the bureaus if you

- ✔ Were denied credit within the last 60 days
- ✔ Are unemployed and are planning to seek employment within the next 60 days
- ✔ Are on welfare
- ✔ Are a victim of fraud or identity theft and have reported it to the police

In the following sections, I explain how to get your reports, what kind of information you need to provide, what to watch out for, and when you should check your reports.

Where to get your reports

To obtain your one free credit report from each of the three major credit bureaus each year, simply visit the website www.annualcreditreport. com. Or if you prefer, you can request copies by phone or mail. Here's the information you need:

> Annual Credit Report Request Service
> P.O. Box 105281
> Atlanta, GA 30348-5281
> Phone 877-322-8228

Many different websites with similar-sounding names have cropped up since the central source for free credit reports was established. These sites advertise free credit reports, but the fine print of the offer is that your free report costs you something because you must purchase another product or service to receive the report. You shouldn't have to purchase anything to get your free copies. If the site requires you to provide payment information, you're on the wrong website.

Note that your credit score isn't provided with your free annual credit reports when you use www.annualcreditreport.com. If you want to know your score, you need to contact the big-three credit bureaus directly for a copy of your credit report and credit score, for a small fee. You can get things started with a phone call, a visit to the bureau's website, or through the mail. Here's the contact information for the three major credit-reporting bureaus:

- ✔ **Equifax,** P.O. Box 740241, Atlanta, GA 30374; phone 800-685-1111; website www.equifax.com

- ✔ **Experian,** P.O. Box 2104, Allen, TX 75013-2104; phone 866-200-6020; website www.experian.com

- ✔ **TransUnion,** 2 Baldwin Place, P.O. Box 1000, Chester, PA 19022; phone 800-888-4213; website www.transunion.com

I strongly suggest that you get a copy of your report from each of the three bureaus every year.

What you need to provide in order to get your reports

Whether you contact a credit bureau directly to get a copy of your report or you go through the free central source to get all three at once (see the preceding section), you need to provide information that lets the powers that be know that you are who you say you are. So be ready to give all the information you've always been told not to give to a stranger over the phone or Internet. In this one case, these strangers are okay.

The information requested varies from one bureau to the next, but the following is a list of some information you're likely to be asked for:

- ✔ Your Social Security number
- ✔ Your credit card account numbers
- ✔ Your former addresses and the dates you lived there
- ✔ Your employment history

When you order your credit report, the bureaus may try to sell you a credit score as well. See "Ordering your score," later in this chapter, for more information on this.

When to get copies of your credit reports

Because you're entitled to a free copy of your credit report from each of the big-three credit bureaus, reviewing your credit reports at least once a year makes sense.

To make it easy to remember when to reorder each year, I suggest you pick three times during the year that stand out and are roughly four months apart. Consider a birthday, anniversary, new years, and Labor Day or the like. Unless you're expecting to apply for new credit for a major purchase, get one report every four months or so to help you keep an eye out for identity theft or other problems.

You should get copies of your reports from all three bureaus at the same time when you're planning to

- ✔ Buy or lease a car
- ✔ Buy a house
- ✔ Refinance a mortgage
- ✔ Rent an apartment

✔ Apply for a job

✔ Be up for a promotion

✔ Apply for a professional license (such as a license to sell securities or insurance)

✔ Apply for a security clearance

✔ Join the military

✔ Get married

✔ Get divorced

✔ Switch insurance companies or buy new insurance

Real estate closings can be delayed, mortgage rates can go up, and job opportunities can be lost if your credit report contains incorrect negative information. So give yourself time to get your reports and correct them before going forward with your plans. I recommend getting your reports up to six months in advance of your plans so that you have time to dispute any errors on your report (like information from someone else whose Social Security number is one digit off from yours). As you get within a month or two of applying for credit, insurance, or a job, consider getting copies of your reports again in case new errors have slipped into your file.

Because you can get one free copy of each report from the three major bureaus once a year, I recommend that, every four months, you order a report from one of the three bureaus, rotating through them so that you have three separate chances, at spaced intervals, to see whether something unexpected has shown up. An exception is if you believe there may be a problem lurking on your report from an error or identity theft, or if you are going to be applying for a large credit addition. In these cases, get all three reports at once in addition to your normal free annual report rotation.

Who else has access to your report?

Anyone can get a copy of your credit report if the person has a *permissible purpose* — in other words, a valid business reason to review your report — *and* if you give that person your permission to do so. The permission part can often be lost in the fine print of a credit card application or at the bottom of an employment application.

What counts as a permissible purpose under the law? Here are some examples in alphabetical order:

✔ **Apartment rental:** It only makes sense that a landlord would like to know whether you're likely to pay your rent on time before giving you the keys to an expensive piece of real estate. For that reason, most rental applications ask for permission to access your credit file and also any tenant history information that may be available.

✔ **Credit approval:** When you apply for credit (whether that's filling out a credit card

(continued)

(continued)

application or applying for a car loan, student loan, or mortgage), creditors and lenders have the right to get a copy of your credit report. This makes sense because they need to know whether you have a history of defaulting on loans or whether you're overextended on credit already and about to miss your next payment.

✔ **Court order or subpoena:** If a court orders you to appear before the court or subpoenas information about you, the court can also get access to your credit file.

✔ **Employment:** When you apply for a job, the prospective employer can get a copy of your credit report. Why? Because your financial history says a lot about what kind of employee you might turn out to be. If you have poor judgment with money, the logic goes, you may show poor judgment at work as well.

✔ **Insurance:** Depending on the type of insurance you apply for and the state in which you live, the insurer may get a copy of your credit report and use the information in it to help predict the likelihood of your filing a claim. Insurers and their actuaries believe that a strong relationship exists between past credit performance and future claim experience. So when you apply for car, homeowners, renters, medical, or any other kind of insurance, in most states, your insurance company has the right to get a copy of your credit report.

✔ **IRS debts:** If you owe the tax man and don't pay in the time specified, the IRS looks in your credit report to find out whether you have assets to attach or sell. Some examples of things the IRS looks for are real estate, cars, bank accounts, and so on.

✔ **Professional license:** Licensing authorities take their responsibilities very seriously. Before allowing you to become licensed — or, in other words, approved to perform a specific job — they want to know all they can about your background and how you've conducted yourself in the past. If, for instance, you want a license to be a financial planner and deal with someone else's life savings, it makes sense to see how you handle your own money. Want a gambling license? Same thing applies.

✔ **Review or collection of an existing account:** If your account is overdue and sent to collections, the collector wants to know who else you owe money to and what kind of payer the collector is dealing with. If you move a lot, the collector uses the information in your credit report to find a current address or phone number. (The industry term for this is *skip tracing*.) However, even if you're current in your payments to your credit card issuers, mortgage company, or other creditors, your creditors may look at your account from time to time to determine whether your credit quality is deteriorating or, on the brighter side, whether they should increase your limits.

Tracking Down Specialty Reports: From Apartments to Casinos to Prescriptions

Specialty reporting agencies, as the name implies, gather information for specific industries. They often gather more detailed information than the big-three credit bureaus do in areas such as gambling, checking accounts, medical claims, insurance, and rental and employment history. If you're being checked out because you're applying for a loan, insuring your car, finding a new apartment, or being considered for a promotion at work, the person reviewing your application has the option to request a report from a specialty agency in addition to a traditional credit report from one of the big-three credit bureaus (Equifax, Experian, and TransUnion).

Among the better-known specialty report providers are the following:

- Insurance bureaus such as ChoiceTrust, which sells its C.L.U.E. products based on your auto and homeowners insurance claims history, as well as information for background employment and rental checks

- The Medical Information Bureau (MIB), which accumulates and sells your medical-insurance claims history report

- ChexSystems, SCAN, and TeleCheck, all of which sell various check-verification products

Many people aren't aware of these specialty reporting agencies or the fact that you have the right to request and obtain your credit reports from these agencies for free annually, just as you do with the traditional credit bureaus. Some reports contain only negative information, or they may have absolutely no information about you at all. I suggest that you get your free report annually just to make sure the information in the report is yours and accurate. You may not be aware that one of these databases is being checked because they aren't as top of mind as the three main credit bureaus.

Table 7-1 provides the contact information for the major specialty bureaus to get you started. Call the number for any bureau you want a report from and ask how to order a free copy.

Table 7-1	Specialty Credit-Reporting Bureaus	
Category	*Bureau Name*	*Contact Info*
Casinos	Central Credit Services	888-898-8021
Checking accounts	CheckRite	800-766-2748
	ChexSystems	800-428-9623
	FIS	800-237-4851
	SCAN	800-262-7771
	TeleCheck	800-835-3243
Employment	ChoiceTrust Employment Reports	866-312-8075

(continued)

Table 7-1 *(continued)*

Category	Bureau Name	Contact Info
Insurance	C.L.U.E. Auto History	866-312-8076
	C.L.U.E. Homeowners' History	866-312-8076
	ISO's A-Plus Auto and Property Databases	800-627-3487
Medical information	Medical Information Bureau (MIB)	866-692-6901
Mortgage financing	Innovis	800-540-2505
Prescription drugs	Ingenix	888-206-0335
	Milliman	877-211-4816
Rental information	Accufax	800-256-8898
	Advantage Tenant	800-894-9047
	American Tenant Screen	800-888-1287
	Resident History Report	877-448-5732
	Core Logic Safe Rent	888-333-2413
	National Tenant Network	800-228-0989
	Tenant Data Services	800-228-1837

Who's reporting you to the specialty bureaus?

Included in the growing list of companies that report on you are those that specialize in your rental history, workers' compensation claims, prescription drug purchase history, and gambling history.

Until recently, use of prescription drug use databases was unheard of. Insurers' use of these databases was first publicized when the Federal Trade Commission sued two owners of drug databases. (See www.ftc.gov/opa/2007/09/ingenixmilliman.shtm.) Like the Medical Information Bureau reports, these reports are used primarily when you're seeking private health, life, or disability insurance. Rx drug databases can go back as far as five years, detailing drugs you've used as well as dosage and refills.

Perusing Your Credit Report

When you get copies of your credit reports from Equifax, Experian, and TransUnion, you're ready to walk through what can be, at times, a very confusing landscape of codes and language that may seem as foreign as Swahili to you. Perhaps the best way to get a handle on how your credit report comes together is to take it apart, starting from the outside and working in.

Each credit report contains the following generic elements:

- ✔ Personal profile
- ✔ Accounts summary
- ✔ Public records
- ✔ Credit inquiries
- ✔ Account history
- ✔ Your 100-word statement (optional; see Chapter 14 for more information on writing a 100-word statement)
- ✔ Credit score (optional)

I cover each of these parts of your report in detail in the following sections. Bear in mind, though, that the three credit-reporting agencies use slightly different names for each of these sections.

For samples of the Equifax, Experian, and TransUnion reports, check out the CD.

Personal profile: It's all about your details

This section of your credit report may be labeled "Personal Profile" or "Personal Information," depending on which credit bureau issues the report.

Appearing first in the order of credit-report elements, your profile section contains the key components that help you verify that the report is actually about *you:* your name (and any of your previous names, like if you're married or divorced or if you use multiple spellings or short names like Steve instead of Stephen), Social Security number, address(es), and current and previous employers.

Be sure to check the personal profile section and verify that all the information is correct. Something as simple as a transposed number in an old address can cause someone else's credit history to end up on your report.

Accounts summary: An overview of your financial history

Each of the three bureau reports has a summary of your credit or accounts that shows you a broad history of what's included in your credit report. It includes summaries of open and closed accounts, credit limits, total balances of all accounts, payment history, and number of credit inquiries. The summary provides those with short attention spans a one-page snapshot of your credit history. But don't worry: If you're hungry for painstaking detail of your payment past, you're certain to find it in the Account History section of the credit report, which I describe later in this chapter.

A quick review of the summary section lets you know whether you need to scrutinize something in more detail that appears to be inaccurate or isn't related to your account at all. For example, if you don't have a mortgage, finding a mortgage account listed in your summary is an immediate red flag.

Public records: Tallying up your legal losses

Ideally, the section of your report dealing with public records is blank. Public records are only negative items that come from — you guessed it — a public record. You have a public record if you've participated in a court proceeding, filed for bankruptcy, received judgments or tax liens, or (in some states) defaulted on child support.

Credit inquiries: Tracking who has been accessing your file

Knock, knock. Who's there? The section listing inquiries into your credit file shows who's been knocking on the credit bureau's door, asking if you're home. People who are legally allowed to view your credit information and have requested your report are listed here. They may include businesses and individuals you've given permission to, such as your employer, insurance company, or lender, as well as yourself. (For more information on this topic, see the earlier "Who else has access to your report?" sidebar.)

This section also shows the date of the inquiry and how long the inquiry will remain on your report. An inquiry that you initiated to, say, shop for or obtain credit stays on your report for two years.

Your own copy of your personal credit reports has information about credit inquiries. When you're the one requesting access to your own credit file, you get some extra information in a separate section. Inquiries from creditors that looked at your credit report for the purposes of extending preapproved credit offers show up for you and only you to see. These inquiries aren't revealed to others who request your report and don't count against you.

Account history: Think of it as a payment CSI

Your Account History section, sometimes titled "Account Information," is the heart of your credit report. It shows all open and closed accounts with near forensic detail about payment history, balances, and account status over the last seven years. Each credit-reporting bureau displays these details in its own unique way, as you discover in the next sections.

Equifax's version

Equifax reports its Account History by type of account. These types include mortgages, installment accounts, revolving accounts, and so on. Under each account type, open accounts are listed first, followed by closed accounts. A short summary at the beginning of each account includes your Account Status, which indicates whether you've paid as agreed or are late (and if so, how late).

The CD contains a PDF file copy of a sample Equifax credit report.

Here's a list of all the information Equifax reports in its Account History section:

- ✔ **Account name:** A brief description of the account type and creditor. For example, 123 Mortgage Co., Address, Phone Number.

- ✔ **Account number:** That long, alphanumeric string that's unique to your card or loan. Note, though, that account numbers are shortened for the protection of your account information.

- ✔ **Account owner:** Indicates whether the account is an individual or joint account.

- ✔ **Type:** The account type. Here are the account types you may find:

  - **Mortgage account:** First mortgage loans, home equity loans, and any other loan secured by real estate.

  - **Installment account:** Loans that are for a set amount of money and often for a set period of time. Your car loan is an example of a common installment loan.

  - **Revolving account:** Accounts that have a credit limit and a minimum payment and don't have to be paid off in a set amount of time. Your credit cards fall into this category.

  - **Other account:** Includes those accounts that don't fit the set categories such as charge accounts that must be paid in full each month, like some American Express cards.

  - **Collections account:** Accounts that have been sold or turned over to a collection agency, usually when the account is more than 180 days past due.

  - **Negative account:** Past-due accounts that are less than 180 days late or debt that was written off because you couldn't pay it and it's now a collections account.

- ✔ **Term duration:** The total number of payments you're expected to make on your loan (for example, 60 payments for a five-year car loan).

- ✔ **Date open:** The date on which you opened the account.

- ✔ **Date reported:** The latest report from the lender, whether provided monthly, quarterly, or less frequently.

- ✔ **Date of last payment:** The date listed here may be different from the date reported. If you're past due, your last payment may be from September 2010, and the last date reported may be December 2010. If you had no activity on a credit card account for six months, the last payment date may be June 2010, and the last reported date may be December 2010.

- ✔ **Scheduled payment amount:** Information that applies only to installment accounts, in which a set amount of money is due at a set time every month.

- ✔ **Creditor classification:** The type of creditor.

- ✔ **Charge-off amount:** Debt or portions of debt that were written off by the creditor because of nonpayment and inability to get the money from you. For example, if you don't pay your credit card for 180 days it will be listed as charged off. You want this amount to be *zero.* Any amount — no matter how small — is not a good thing to have on your record.

- **Balloon-payment amount:** The big lump-sum payment at the end of some loans. Your loan may or may not have one.

- **Date closed:** The date you or the lender terminated an active account.

- **Date of first delinquency:** Any late payments during the seven-year reporting period.

- **Comments:** Additional information about the closed account. Some examples are "Account Transferred or Sold," "Paid," "Zero Balance," "Account Closed at Consumer's Request," and so on.

- **Current status:** The payment status that refers to whether you've paid or are paying as you said you would. You may see terms such as "Pays," "Paid as Agreed," or "X Days Past Due."

- **High credit:** The highest amount of credit used by you.

- **Credit limit:** Your maximum limit for this account.

- **Term's frequency:** How often your payment is due (weekly, monthly, and so on).

- **Balance:** The amount owed to a creditor on an account.

- **Amount past due:** The amount of money you owe that should have been paid by now but hasn't been.

- **Actual payment amount:** The amount of money that you paid.

- **Date of last activity:** The last time you used the account.

- **Months reviewed:** How many months are in the history section below (up to 81).

- **Activity designator:** A description of account activity, such as "Paid" and "Closed."

- **Deferred payment start date:** Some accounts have no payment for a year or other promotional terms.

- **Balloon-payment date:** When that big lump-sum payment at the end of some loans is due. Your loan may or may not have one.

- **Type of loan:** For example, Auto or credit card.

- **81-month payment history:** Equifax shows each month's status for the last seven years of payment history. Terms used in reporting the status include the following:

  - Pays as agreed

  - 30 (30 to 59 days past due)

  - 60 (60 to 89 days past due)

  - 90 (90 to 119 days past due)

- 120 (120 to 149 days past due)
- 150 (150 to 179 days past due)
- 180+ (180 or more days past due)
- CA (collection account)
- F (foreclosure)
- VS (voluntary surrender)
- R (repossession)
- CO (charge-off)

Experian's version

On Experian's credit report, Potentially Negative Items are listed first and include both public records and credit accounts. The remainder of your accounts in the Account History section are listed as Accounts in Good Standing. You of course want all your accounts to be listed as in good standing.

The CD has a PDF file copy of a sample Experian credit report.

Here's a list of the information that Experian reports in its Account History section:

- ✔ **Status:** Open or closed and paid or past due by X days.
- ✔ **Date open:** The date on which you opened the account.
- ✔ **Reported since:** First reported date.
- ✔ **Date of status:** Last time the status was updated.
- ✔ **Last reported:** Last time the update (which may be new or old) was reported.
- ✔ **Account type:** Specifies whether it's an installment account, a revolving account, and so on.
- ✔ **Terms:** The total number of payments you're expected to make on your loan (a 30-year mortgage would be 360 payments, for example).
- ✔ **Monthly payment:** The last reported minimum payment that you owe(d). This is typically applicable for installment loans such as auto loans or mortgages, if reported at all.
- ✔ **Responsibility:** Individual, joint, authorized user, and so forth.
- ✔ **Credit limit:** The highest dollar credit limit you've ever been approved for.
- ✔ **High balance:** The most you've ever owed on the account.

- ✔ **Recent balance:** The amount you owe. Sometimes balance information is on the report and sometimes it's not. This isn't because the credit bureau wants to save trees but because some creditors don't want their competition to know what a big spender and great customer you really are.

- ✔ **Recent payment:** Your most recent payment in dollars.

- ✔ **Account history:** Whether you've been late, and if so, how often.

- ✔ **Your statement:** This is where you tell your side of the story. For example, you may contest an account that shows you haven't paid as agreed when you contend that you didn't receive the services for which you were charged.

- ✔ **Account history for collection accounts:** Comments that the creditor may have sent to the bureau about this account, such as when the account was placed for collection.

TransUnion's version

TransUnion reports public records and collection accounts first. The Account History section for all other accounts is listed under Trades.

A PDF file copy of a sample TransUnion credit report is available on the CD.

Here's a list of the information that TransUnion reports in its Account History section:

- ✔ **Account name:** Name of the creditor with address.

- ✔ **Account number:** Only a partial account number is included.

- ✔ **Balance:** The balance owed as of date of verification or closed.

- ✔ **Date updated:** The date of the last update on the account.

- ✔ **High balance:** The highest amount ever owed on the account.

- ✔ **Credit limit:** The maximum amount of credit approved by the creditor. This isn't always reported by the creditor if your limit isn't firm (as with American Express) or if you're allowed to exceed your limit under the terms of your agreement (as with Visa signature accounts).

- ✔ **Past due:** Amount past due as of date verified or closed.

  - • **Terms:** Minimum payment amount.

  - • **Pay status:** If you are paying as agreed or not.

  - • **Account type:** Open or closed.

- ✔ **Responsibility:** A code that represents the ownership designation on the account: individual or joint.

- **Date opened:** The date the account was opened.

- **Date closed:** If the account was closed, when it was closed.

- **Date paid:** The date the account was last paid.

- **Loan type:** The type of loan and/or the collateral used for an installment loan. Includes home equity loan, mortgage, automobile.

- **Terms:** Number of payments, payment frequency, and dollar amount agreed upon.

- **Remarks:** Explanation of dispute or account credit condition, as reported by the creditor. Includes account closed by consumer.

- **Late payments:** The first number represents the number of months that are summarized, and the remaining three numbers represent the number of times the account has been 30, 60, and 90 days late.

- **Last ## months:** A graphical representation of all paid months being reported as agreed or late.

If you have an account that doesn't show a credit limit, FICO assumes your highest monthly balance reported is your max for score calculation. To increase your score, if you can afford it, for one month charge close to your real max and then pay it off the next month to avoid interest charges and minimize losing points for one month by maxing out your charges.

Your optional 100-word statement: Getting the last word

You have the right to add a statement of up to 100 words to your credit report, which can be helpful in explaining any extenuating circumstances that may have led to negative information being included in your report. For example, a statement describing a temporary job loss can explain why your accounts were 60 days late. The credit bureaus are required to include this statement whenever your credit report is accessed by anyone. On the flip side, lenders may not always pull a full credit report when ordering a score for screening, so keep in mind that your statement may not always be seen.

Use the 100-word-statement privilege with care and be sure to circle back to request that the statement be removed after any negative information that it explains is more than two to three years old. If you don't request that it be removed, your comments may stay on the report as long as the account does and may draw unwanted attention to an old credit complaint.

What's not in your credit report?

Before you get too comfortable with what's not disclosed in your credit report, be aware that the big-three credit bureaus do their best to limit *indirect disclosures* — that is, some of your personal information getting passed on inadvertently — but such disclosures can be tough to avoid. Medical information is one example. Even though credit bureaus don't report medical history, specifics on your credit report may give away information that indicates that you have some type of medical condition. Say you fall behind on a hospital or other medical bill and you're paying a collection agency under an agreement. The account noted on your credit report may read "Medical Collection." Now say that you apply for a job. As part of its background check, your prospective

employer requests a copy of your credit report. The employer can see that you have (or had) a medical condition. A week later, you get a letter saying that the position has been filled. As you can see, without disclosing medical reports or particulars about a health condition, the details on your credit report *can* reveal personal information that's legally restricted from your file.

Some other indirect disclosures that can happen include employment history you forgot to mention to a prospective employer, frequent changes of addresses (which may make you look unstable), and multiple inquiries from Central Credit Services for gambling lines of credit (which may raise a question for a lender or an employer).

Correcting Any Errors You Find

With any luck, the information on your credit reports is accurate. However, mistakes happen. After all, creditors and lenders are just as human as you and me. The good news is that those mistakes don't have to remain a part of your file.

Credit-reporting agencies are required to investigate any disputed listings. They must verify the item in question with the creditor *at no cost* to you, the consumer. The law requires the creditor to respond to and verify all disputed entries within 30 days, or else the information must be removed from your credit report. The credit-reporting agency also has to notify you of the outcome. If information in the report is changed or deleted, you also get a *free* copy of the revised report.

You have two options for fixing errors that you find on your credit reports: contacting the credit bureau or contacting the actual creditor who reported the incorrect information. I walk you through both processes in the sections that follow.

Contacting the credit bureau

If you notice incorrect information on your credit report, contact the credit bureau that reported the inaccurate information. Each of the three major bureaus allows you to dispute information in your credit report on its website, or you can call the bureau's toll-free number (I provide contact info for the big-three credit bureaus in the earlier "Where to get your reports" section). If you make your dispute online, you need to have a copy of your credit report available because information on the report allows the bureau to confirm your identity without a signature. If you opt to call the toll-free number, you're unlikely to get a live person on the other end, but you'll be told what information and documentation you need in order to submit a written request. Either way, after you properly notify the credit bureau, you can count on action.

Contacting the creditor

Another way to remove inaccurate information from your credit report is outlined under the FACT Act: Deal directly with the creditor who reported the negative information in the first place. Customer service contact information is on your latest billing statement from that creditor, and the general address and phone number is on your credit report. After you dispute the information, the reporting creditor must look into the matter and can't continue to report the negative information while it's investigating your dispute.

When contacting creditors directly, do so in writing, requesting a return receipt for everything.

For new delinquencies, the FACT Act requires that you be notified if negative information is reported to a credit bureau. That said, you may have to look closely to even see this new notice. Anyone who extends credit to you must send you a one-time notice either before or not later than 30 days after negative information — including late payments, missed payments, partial payments, or any other form of default — is furnished to a credit bureau. This includes collection agencies, as long as they report to a credit bureau. The notice may look something like this:

- ✔ **Before negative information is reported:** "We may report information about your account to credit bureaus. Late payments, missed payments, or other defaults on your account may be reflected in your credit report."

- ✔ **After negative information is reported:** "We have told a credit bureau about a late payment, missed payment, or other default on your account. This information may be reflected in your credit report."

Receiving notification about what a creditor has reported about you to the credit bureaus isn't a substitute for your own close monitoring of your credit reports, bank accounts, and credit card statements.

Getting and Understanding Your Credit Score

Getting your hands on your credit report is one thing, but getting a copy of your credit score isn't as straightforward as you may think. (And a misstep here can cost you more money and give you less-than-accurate information.) Your three-digit credit score is an additional component used in most credit reviews. When lenders order your credit report, they often also order your credit score, which summarizes your risk of default.

The two major credit scores that lenders use are the FICO score and the VantageScore. Not all the credit bureaus can offer you the trademarked FICO score that most lenders use, but they *can* all offer you the VantageScore. Four of the top five financial institutions, all credit card issuers, and two of the top five auto lenders currently use VantageScores for lending decisions. FICO scores range from 300 to 850, and VantageScores range from 501 to 990. Either way, the higher your number, the better your score.

Don't get hung up on a number. Be as good as you can be, but don't get excited and yell at the cat over a score of 820 instead of 850. The most important thing is to know what your *lenders* know about your credit score and what's in the credit report they look at. On this topic, you want to be on the same page.

The main points to keep in mind regarding credit scores are as follows:

- ✔ Your score is different for each credit bureau report, if only because each bureau has slightly different data about you in its files.
- ✔ Be sure you know which score you're getting: a FICO score, a VantageScore, or a proprietary bureau score (which may be called a *TrueScore* or a *PlusScore*).
- ✔ You improve your credit score by improving your credit history, not the other way around.
- ✔ Because credit reports commonly have errors, you're likely to have a faulty credit score. Dispute errors and outdated items to get the most accurate score possible.

With a grasp of the essentials about credit scores, you're ready to take the plunge and get your score. Of course, once you have it, you can count on me to explain what it means for you and what you can do about it. Read on!

Ordering your score

The new Fair Access to Credit Scores Act that was bundled into the massive Dodd-Frank Wall Street Reform and Consumer Protection Act (the law's wording is on the CD) allows you free access to your credit score if you've been denied credit or if some other "adverse action" (denial of insurance or utilities, for example) was taken as a result of your credit score. You don't have to make a request for your credit score if such an adverse action is taken based on your credit score; a copy of the score used to make the decision is automatically sent to you.

To get your current score, you need to order a credit report at the same time, because your score is figured based on the information in your credit report at the time you order the score. Generally, unlike your credit report, which you get for free once a year, you have to pay for a copy of your credit score.

If you want to order your FICO score, as in the trademarked FICO score that most lenders use, keep mind that you can only get it from two places:

- ✔ **myFICO.com** (phone 800-319-4433; website `www.myfico.com`)
- ✔ **Equifax** (P.O. Box 740241, Atlanta, GA 30374; phone 800-685-1111; website `www.equifax.com`)

The other credit-reporting bureaus — Experian and TransUnion — offer credit scores but not the FICO credit score. (FICO actually developed score models for them that are slightly different from the original FICO score in order to make some more cash.) Also, the credit bureaus developed the VantageScore (which is a fierce competitor of FICO), so they have an interest in you buying a VantageScore over a FICO score. Oh, and all three credit bureaus compete with one another every chance they get.

So how do you know which credit score is the right one for you? My advice is to try to get the same score that your lender uses. How do you know which one that is? Ask! Your lender will tell you. If, however, you aren't working with a specific lender and you just want the most widely used score, then FICO is the one for you.

When ordering scores, most sites try to get you to sign up for a credit-monitoring service. You should be able to get just your one-time credit report and a score without signing up for a long-term service. Just read the fine print before you hit enter. I discuss these services and their benefits and costs in Chapter 8.

Telling a good score from a bad one

Good score ranges (for example a FICO score of 760 to 850) change over time as the history of the population changes. And I don't mean history as in ancient Greek or Roman (who used credit too!) but your personal history of using credit and paying bills. Since the credit crisis in 2008, the poor economy, high unemployment, and punishing defaults have caused a lot of the population that had high scores to move much lower on the scoring ladder.

So, is your score a good one? What's a good score, anyway? Essentially, a good score is one that's good enough to get you what you want at a price you can afford. VantageScore makes it easy to figure that out because it offers you a grade of A through F. Just like school, you know what's good and what's not based on your letter grade.

FICO likes to give you a picture of where you stand in comparison to others using an eight-bar chart (see Figure 7-1). You can tell that the FICO folks were never teachers — more like statisticians! My best and simplest advice with FICO is to try and stay within the upper categories and not slip into the lower ones.

Figure 7-1: The distribution of FICO scores nationally over the period 2008 to 2010.

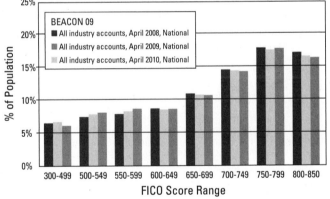

Courtesy of FICO

In the current credit environment where lending has tightened up quite a bit, the difference in loan terms between a score of 750 and a score of 800+ (the top two groups) may be small, but those with a score of 620 or lower may not be eligible for credit at all. However, not all lenders view risk the same. One lender may consider a credit score of 640 to be a high risk, while another lender may not consider such a score to be all that risky and may have a special program to take advantage of — err, accommodate — lower-scoring consumers.

What's your grade?

TransUnion recently ranked the U.S. population according to the VantageScore scale, with the shocking result that almost 20 percent of Americans have a failing grade. Under this scale, you can estimate your place in the credit pecking order like this:

✔ **A:** Formerly Super Prime — The top 15.1 percent of the population is in this category, with scores ranging from 901 to 990.

✔ **B:** Formerly Prime Plus — 26.3 percent of the population is Prime Plus. Prime Plus scores range from 801 to 900.

✔ **C:** Formerly Prime — 20.4 percent of the population is Prime. Prime scores range from 701 to 800.

✔ **D:** Formerly Non-Prime — 20.4 percent of the population is Non-Prime. Non-Prime scores range from 601 to 700.

✔ **F:** Formerly High Risk —17.7 percent of the population is High Risk. High Risk scores range from 501 to 600.

The letter grades are a nice touch and help consumers in two ways. First, they make it easy to see where you stand. And second, they help keep you from going nuts over a 950 score. True, it's not a 990, but it's Super Prime, and that's good enough for me.

A bad credit history and score can make you a target for unscrupulous lenders. If your credit is damaged, be very careful about reading the fine print on any credit agreements and understanding all fees, penalties, and interest rates before you act.

So how high is high enough? In a time of relatively easy credit, such as in 2006, the saying was that all you needed was a pulse to get a loan. Although this may not be totally true, getting a loan with a lower score in 2006 was certainly easier than it is today.

The credit market has tightened up considerably since the 2008 financial crisis and may not loosen up for some years to come. Over time, the standard for lending tends to swing like a pendulum from easy to tight and back again. So keeping your credit as clean as you can is all the more important, because today's record will be there for at least the next seven years, while tomorrow's credit market will surely change one way or the other.

Connecting pricing to your credit score

Most lending today is done on a modified version of *risk-based pricing.* Risk-based pricing used to mean that rather than saying "no" to a bad-risk customer, lenders would say "yes" and still make money on the risky loan because they'd charge a high interest rate and fees. This model allowed more people with low scores to get more loans, albeit at a higher cost. That approach ended when the subprime mortgage mess turned risky loans into huge losses at any interest rate. So though your credit score may get you a higher or lower interest rate, if it's too weak under tight credit conditions, you may get a "no, thank you" instead.

What do credit-score groupings look like in the market as of mid 2011? As an example, say you have a $300,000, 30-year, fixed-rate mortgage. (Keep in mind that I'm using numbers from mid 2011. The actual rates for your loan today will be different.) This example is meant to illustrate the magnitude of difference between scores and rates. The interest rates for each grouping for this particular loan would look like this:

FICO Score	*Rate*	*Monthly Payment*
760-850	4.258%	$1,477
700-759	4.480%	$1,516
680-699	4.657%	$1,548
660-679	4.871%	$1,587
640-659	5.301%	$1,666
620-639	5.847%	$1,769

Courtesy of Informa Research Services

Using the preceding table, for a $300,000 loan, a person with a FICO score of 620 with an interest rate of 5.847 percent pays out a total of $636,840 over the term of the mortgage, whereas a 740 FICO scorer with an interest rate of 4.480 percent pays only $545,760. That's a difference of $91,080! As you can see, maintaining the highest credit score possible can save you hundreds of dollars a month in mortgage loan payments.

Although the number of dollars you save with smaller loans may not be as high as that associated with a mortgage loan, a high credit score saves you money in interest charges for any amount of money you plan to borrow. In addition, during a tight credit market, a low credit score may mean you won't qualify for credit at any price.

Knowing the reason for reason statements

Along with your credit score, you get up to four reason statements on your credit-score report. A *reason statement* is a simple explanation of why your score is less than perfect. What's the reason for reason statements? Well, a lender can't make money turning down business, so if a poor score is keeping a lender from making a buck, knowing the reason why your credit is in a hole can help identify how to dig out and get those fees and loans flowing again!

The creditors get what's called a *reason code,* and you get the interpreted version of that, which is called the *reason statement.* For example, if a reason code reveals that your lower-than-could-have-been score is because of too many open accounts used to the max and not because you never pay on time, you can focus on reducing balances and using less of each credit line to raise your score.

Some 60 different codes give you and your lender a hint about what's causing your credit to sag. In addition, the codes may help you determine whether your credit report contains errors and where the errors exist, because the codes highlight areas that lower your score.

The bureaus generate the reason codes. Typically, on your credit report immediately following whatever section your credit score is in, both positive and negative reasons for your score are listed, with tips to help increase your score muscle.

According to FICO, the most frequently given score reasons are as follows (although the specific wording may vary):

✔ Reason code 10: "Proportion of balances to credit limits on bank/ national revolving or other revolving accounts is too high." What this tells you is that you're using more of your limits than the scoring model thinks is safe. A high percentage of usage, say 50 percent ($10,000 on a $20,000 credit line), is inherently riskier than using only 25 percent (or $5,000).

✔ Reason code 14: "Length of time accounts have been established." This code is great for senior credit users but not for first-timers. Clearly, someone with 20 years of account history has the advantage here.

VantageScore's most frequent reason statement, which shows up about 44 percent of the time, is, "Available credit across all open, recently reported accounts is too low." If you see this in your credit report, it's time to slow your charging and increase your payments. This reason statement tells you that you're using more of your credit lines than the scorers at VantageScore are comfortable with.

Chapter 8

Monitoring Your Credit Reports and Scores

In This Chapter

▶ Understanding how credit monitoring works

▶ Looking at the different types of monitoring services

▶ Deciding whether to monitor on your own or hire a company

▶ Getting your money's worth and getting help for free

*I*received my car insurance renewal recently, and for a hefty premium my insurance company offered to monitor my credit report for identity theft and fraud. What does my car insurer have to do with credit monitoring? Two things: First, bad credit (which can be caused by errors or identity theft) can raise my car insurance premium; and second, my car insurer wants to make money on a hot product add-on whether I need it or not. So I asked myself, do I need credit monitoring or don't I? To find out whether I do and you might, I created this chapter. After all, it's your credit and your money, and you want to protect them both!

Don't confuse credit monitoring with identity theft protection. Credit card fraud can be caused by the larger problem of identity theft or it can happen on its own. Credit monitoring won't stop someone from stealing your identity or using your Social Security number, but it may allow you to detect a potential problem in its earlier stages. I deal with identity theft in detail in Chapters 12 and 20.

In this chapter I discuss how credit monitoring works, what you get for your monitoring dollar, and how to decide whether you should pay someone for this service or handle it on your own.

How Does Credit Monitoring Really Work?

Hiring a company to monitor your credit means that you give the company access to your credit reports. You may wonder just how this monitoring takes place. Each service provider has a series of programs that it runs against databases that it has access to (some, like Experian, have their own credit database but also buy access to others), looking for changes, updates, or patterns that indicate something may be amiss in your world.

Some services monitor only one credit bureau, others monitor all three, and still others may monitor some of the many national, specialty, consumer-reporting bureaus (see Chapter 7) for activity or changes to your reports such as:

- The opening of new accounts
- Larger than normal charges
- Unusual account activity such as a change in the frequency, location, or type of charges appearing on your bureau reports
- A surge in balances
- Other changes to your accounts such as payments, late payment notices, credit inquiries, public records, employment, addresses, and fraud alerts

Some monitoring services produce detailed reports about your credit score and even suggest ways to make it more attractive to lenders and to improve your creditworthiness. Most also give you free credit reports and scores (they may be proprietary scores or a FICO or VantageScore; see Chapter 7 for the difference between score types). Lastly, monitoring services check your data with differing frequency. Some check your data daily, others do so weekly, and others may do so quarterly depending on their service level.

Understanding the Types of Monitoring Services Available

A universe of services is available to help you monitor or safeguard your credit.

Before I get into the details, let me add that in my experience, you can handle most of the monitoring on your own if you have the time and inclination. For instance, you're entitled to a free credit report from each of the three major bureaus annually. You get another free credit report under certain circumstances, such as if you think you've been the victim of identity theft or if you don't receive the best rates available for a loan or insurance policy based on information in your credit report. So with at least one opportunity to get a free look at your report every four months, you can do a credible job of monitoring your credit at no cost at all. You just have to remember to order your report and then examine it to see what's changed. (For more on monitoring your credit on your own, see the section "Monitoring on your own" later in the chapter.)

If you're interested in having someone else do the monitoring for you, here's a look at each type of service in more detail:

- ✔ **Credit report monitoring services:** This service notifies you about changes to your credit report(s). It often provides frequent access to your credit report upon request. Some services monitor only one credit report, while others monitor reports from the three major credit-reporting agencies (Experian, Equifax, and TransUnion) and some of the national, specialty-reporting bureaus. Credit report monitoring may provide some limited help in giving you an early warning about an identity theft, but because such services only monitor data in your credit report, an identity theft that involves noncredit or unreported areas won't be addressed.

- ✔ **Credit score monitoring services:** This service may include all or some of the credit report monitoring services, but it also includes checking your credit score. You may get access to your credit score, but which score depends on your service provider.

- ✔ **Identity theft monitoring services:** This service may offer additional monitoring areas beyond credit monitoring. The service mainly focuses on financial databases and not criminal or law enforcement data, medical billers that don't report to credit bureaus, or governmental data.

- ✔ **Credit freeze products:** This is actually a service offered by the credit bureaus. It works by freezing access to anyone who tries to view your credit report without your express permission. Typically, a lender reviews your credit file before issuing a new loan or credit card. The inability to do so may prevent issuance of new credit to criminals. A credit freeze is stronger than a fraud alert. It doesn't prevent data from being reported on your report. For more info, see the section "Setting alarms, alerts, and freezes" later in this chapter. Also, www.fight identitytheft.com/credit-freeze-laws-states.html outlines credit freeze laws by state.

- ✔ **ID theft recovery products:** By definition, recovering from an identity theft requires a process of clearing all fraudulent records and charges created by an identity thief. You can find companies that will do all the research and restoration work for you.

- ✔ **Data sweep services:** Data sweep companies monitor the Internet for listings of your personal identifying information that may expose you to identity thieves. They may also monitor specific websites known for questionable activities. If your personal data is detected, these services alert you. They may also offer insurance if they fail to perform.

✔ **Virtual account numbers or secure payment agents (SPAs):** Superman used Clark Kent, Batman had Bruce Wayne, and you have a secure payment agent to protect your identity from being discovered and misused by evil forces! An SPA allows you to better limit what personal information of yours — such as billing address, account number, or e-mail address — appears when you're online shopping, paying bills, or registering at websites. It does this by replacing your real information with anonymous data that has a very short life span and is useless after your transaction is completed. This works for most any type of purchase except for items that you pick up yourself later and may require you to match your credit card number to the receipt. Movie/game tickets fall into this category.

✔ **Identity theft insurance:** ID insurance may be a stand-alone policy or an add-on to one of your existing policies. It helps replace out-of-pocket expenses you may incur after your identity is stolen and misused. Note that ID insurance doesn't keep you safe from theft itself.

Making a Case for and against Third Party Credit Monitoring

During the housing boom of the early 2000s, people I know used to check on their home's value like it was a stock portfolio. But the reality is that a home's price is only useful information if you do something with it. Monitoring your credit or score frequently without a specific purpose is an equally empty exercise and one I don't think is worth paying much if anything for. If, however, you're trying to improve your credit or get to a certain credit score so you can make a large purchase like a home or a car, then laying out some dough for a professional monitoring service makes more sense.

Your lender's score may well be different from the one you get because it may come from another company (FICO, VantageScore, a bureau score, and so on) or because the lender applies its own algorithms based on proprietary factors that it weights based on its specific business experience.

No credit-report monitoring service can offer you complete protection. If a lender or vendor doesn't report to the credit bureaus or if it does report but not to the bureau monitored by the service you've chosen, you won't know whether a bogus account has been opened in your name until a problem arises down the road and a collector or the authorities call. Furthermore, because not all reporting creditors report daily, you're likely to experience a delay in catching fraud.

Monitoring on your own

You can monitor your credit on your own with these simple actions:

- Get a copy of your free credit reports each year from the three major credit-reporting agencies (Experian, Equifax, and TransUnion). Stagger the ordering so that you get a different report every four months. Review them and dispute any inaccuracies.

- Be sure to get a free credit report if you dispute an item on your report. You're entitled to a free report to make sure the mistake has been removed.

- Get extra free copies of your credit report directly from the bureaus (not www.annualcreditreport.com) if you live in Colorado, Georgia, Maine, Maryland, Massachusetts, New Jersey, and Vermont. These states require that you be allowed an additional free report annually. Except you lucky Georgia people, who get a total of three free reports from each bureau a year.

- Get a free report if you're turned down for credit. Anytime you get turned down for credit, you're guaranteed a free report.

- Get a free report if you're looking at a new job. Within the first six months of seeking employment you can have a freebie.

- If you apply for a mortgage, you're entitled to a copy of the credit report and score used.

- Don't forget to order your free national, specialty consumer report annually (see Chapter 7 for more information). This may give you many more free looks into your cyber files.

- Need to add a fraud alert or an extended fraud alert to your credit report? You get one or two additional free reports, respectively, over the next 12 months from each bureau.

- Every time your insurance renews, look at the disclosure language, which is usually in the front of your policy, to see whether your insurance company used a credit report to set your rates. If so, and it's very likely, then follow the instructions and get another free credit report.

- Monitor your bank and credit card accounts weekly online. If something funny is going on, you'll know about it sooner.

- Set up free alerts on your accounts that tip you off when certain types of transactions are made or if a dollar limit is exceeded.

When paid monitoring may be worth the time and money

Depending on the depth of your wallet and your degree of credit nervousness, paid monitoring may be for you. Here are some circumstances when paid monitoring makes sense:

- ✔ If your credit is damaged and you've been trying to improve it for some time. Rather than ordering your report frequently at a premium price, a service that gives you more frequent access for a low monthly or annual fee may make sense.

- ✔ If you're planning on a large purchase that requires your credit score to be in primo condition. You can take your scoring temperature often so you know when the time is right to see the man.

- ✔ If you've been the victim of an identity theft and accounts are being opened in your name. After you slap on a credit freeze (see Chapter 12), monitoring may help you sleep better at night.

- ✔ If you're slightly obsessive-compulsive about your identity or credit file, monitoring may give you a sense of security that may help you get through the night.

Credit report or score monitoring isn't done in real time. Information can be days, weeks, or months old. In addition to the fact that monitoring companies report at differing frequencies, not all credit issuers (small credit unions, medical providers, utilities, and so on) report to credit bureaus. Credit monitoring alerts you only after you have a problem.

If you decide to try a monitoring service, check to see whether it offers a free trial period. Most do. Just don't forget to cancel before the trial period ends if you're not going to stay with the service.

When paid monitoring may not make sense

Here are some circumstances when paid monitoring may not be for you:

- ✔ If your credit is in good shape and you know this for sure. But don't guess at your credit situation — find out for sure. Then decide whether you're happy with the status quo. If so, cool — no need to monitor, no need to pay.

- ✔ If your credit isn't so great but you don't care or you think that it's okay as is. Keep your cash.

> ✔ If your credit is terrible and you know it. Bad credit can't be fixed overnight. Using your three free annual reports lets you know whether you're making initial progress and can help keep you on track.

Recognizing the protection you have already

With all the marketing hype about the need to pay someone to protect you against credit card fraud, you may overlook the fact that your credit card is already protected against fraud under federal law. (See Chapter 5 for more on your legal protections.) Unless you fail to notify your credit card company about erroneous or questionable charges on your statements for at least 60 days, your total liability for fraud is a whopping $50 per card. And if you have homeowners insurance, the $50 charge is probably a covered peril that you can get reimbursement for.

Many of the major creditors have adopted a zero consumer liability policy to further limit your exposure and increase your confidence in being able to use your cards safely.

Here's an example from my own experience with one card issuer. American Express (and I'm sure this goes for some other card companies as well) monitors every transaction through a screening process. The company uses models and patterns to look for specific charges that match known fraud trigger alerts. This process allows Amex to leverage information on a real-time basis (as charges are presented for approval) so that the company can identify fraud and stop it quickly. If a certain type of fraud becomes popular, Amex can tighten up its approval for that type or group of transaction. Its system is so good that if you go on vacation overseas, you have no need to tell Amex about it. The company knows it's you and recognizes where you are to allow purchases. Other card issuers may still appreciate your help in letting them know when you're traveling away from home. Be sure to check on their policy by calling customer service and asking whether you need to notify them.

Amex also offers some optional alerts that you can set up on its website (your credit card may offer similar alerts). Amex will notify you by e-mail or on your mobile phone if

> ✔ A cash withdrawal is made
>
> ✔ A purchase exceeds a limit that you set, is made outside the United States, or is made online or over the phone
>
> ✔ Someone tries to reset your password or billing address
>
> ✔ Amex sees a questionable transaction

Getting Your Money's Worth from Monitoring Services

After you decide that monitoring is a good fit for you, you may need some help to cut through the huge volume of providers. I can't analyze each one, but I can provide tips to help you make your decision.

Asking the right questions before you buy a service is important. Here are some questions you should ask before you sign on the dotted line, or sign up online, to be sure you get the most for your credit monitoring dollar:

- What are the total costs and fees? Set a limit that you're willing to pay and stick to it. Weigh the possible $20 to $50 a month charge against your odds of suffering a credit card fraud that you'd be liable for. Any liability is likely to be low. Also, banks, insurers, and the big-three credit bureaus all offer products to detect fraud and give you a credit score. Shop around for the best price. You may get a better price from someone you already do some other business with.

- What is the monitoring company's reputation and track record? Like nearly everything else today, you can get reviews of services online. Sites like www.nextadvisor.com and www.fightidentitytheft.com offer user ratings you can compare.

- Exactly what will you get for your money? Know how comprehensive you want the monitoring to be. Be sure you're getting the type of score you want; many services offer proprietary or bureau scores that lenders don't use. These scores may be okay for reference but not if you're using them to estimate the actual loan interest rates or deal terms you'll get. Here are some common safeguards you can expect:

  - Frequent or unlimited access to your credit report

  - Frequent or unlimited access to a credit score of some type

  - Monitoring of one or more credit reports

  - Alerts when critical changes are made, including address changes

  - Alerts if your credit score deteriorates into a lower lending category

  - Alerts if your personal information like your Social Security number or your credit card number starts showing up on public Internet sites

  - Warnings if patterns of credit use change or multiple applications for credit occur in a short time span

  - A periodic statement summarizing your credit report changes, score, and alerts

  - Assistance in restoring your identity if it's stolen

✔ What is the monitoring company's cancellation and renewal policy? Avoid automatic renewals. They require storing your credit card data.

✔ Can you get help from a live customer service person when you want? Be sure to check for the hours the service reps are available. If you need help, you don't want to wait until Monday morning.

✔ What exactly will the company do to restore your identity if your identity is stolen and misused? The service should pay for and perform all the tasks needed to restore your identity. The service shouldn't push this time-consuming, expensive, and difficult process off on you.

If a company makes unrealistic claims or offers unlimited guarantees, chances are it may not be able to deliver. Be sure to check reviews by users and industry ratings.

Doing Your Own Legwork: Exploring Help for Free

If you believe that credit monitoring is right for you, before you plunk down your hard-earned and taxed cash, consider what you can do on your own.

Taking steps to monitor for identity fraud

Most of you can manage to safeguard your identity without having to pay for a monitoring service with some simple preventative actions on your part.

Here's a list of some of my favorites:

✔ Use a locked mailbox or a post office box.

✔ Don't store password, account info, or credit card info on your computer. If you do so anyway, be sure to password-protect the files. Using your safety deposit box at a bank is best.

✔ Shred any documents containing account numbers.

✔ Monitor your credit reports frequently for free.

✔ Monitor your credit card statements online weekly to catch problems quickly.

✔ Pay bills online when possible.

✔ Call 888-567-8688 to opt out of unsolicited credit card offers. Doing so reduces the chance that an identity thief pirates an application.

✔ Use virtual account numbers when shopping online. You can get these substitute account numbers from your credit card issuer. They're good for a single use when you don't want to use your credit card number to make a purchase.

See Chapter 12 for more tips on how to guard against identity theft.

Setting alarms, alerts, and freezes

In one of my favorite Three Stooges clips, the lads put a bucket of water above a partially open door. When someone comes through the door, a big crash and splash announces the intruder. You may not be able to set up buckets of water to warn you of credit or identity intrusions, but you do have access to an array of early warning tools.

✔ **Alarms:** You can set an alarm to go off with your bank or credit card company by setting certain parameters for notification. For example, if a check hits my checking account over a certain amount, I get an e-mail. You can do the same and more for your credit card accounts easily and for free. Check out your card website and look for options. You can use text or phone messages if e-mail is too slow or you don't have a smart phone.

✔ **Fraud alerts:** You can place a fraud alert on your credit file if you think someone may be trying to compromise your information. Say that you're notified that your personal information was accessed in a data breach. You may or may not have anything to worry about, but a fraud alert requires anyone using your report for new accounts or limit changes in the next 90 days to exercise extra caution and make sure you're actually the one doing the asking. You also get a free credit report from each bureau.

  • **Extended fraud alerts:** These longer-lasting alerts give you seven years for fraud alert protection and two additional free annual credit report reviews. You need to give the bureau a copy of the police fraud or identity theft report you filed earlier. See Chapter 20 for more details.

  • **Active-duty alerts:** If you're an active-duty military person, there's an alert just for you. An active-duty alert lasts for one year on your credit report.

  • **Widget alerts:** Norton, the antivirus software company, has a free widget tool, called the Norton Cybercrime Index, that sits on your desktop or phone and warns you about real-time cyber crime so you can take preventative measures. The tool also provides in-depth information on cyber crime trends and patterns. Think of it as a traffic report that alerts you to trouble spots, areas and streets to avoid, and potential hazards on the road. I expect others to follow suit and offer this type of service soon.

✔ **Credit freezes:** More serious than alerts, a freeze on your credit report locks your report. In order to review your report, a lender or other party would need to get you to unfreeze your account by asking you. This tips you off about any unauthorized inquiries right away and prevents new accounts from being opened without your permission. You may incur a small fee to unfreeze an account; it varies by state.

The Consumers Union website has state-by-state rules on freezes at www. consumersunion.org/campaigns/learn_more/003484indiv.html.

Part III
Creating Solid Credit Strategies for Every Stage in Life

The 5th Wave   By Rich Tennant

"No, Mrs. Moskowitz. There's just no way we can list the unpaid debt of gratitude your son owes you on his credit history."

In this part . . .

Credit and how you use it change as you progress through the stages of life. In this part, I help you determine the best strategies for establishing credit, taking on and paying off student loans, and recognizing the importance of building a positive credit history. I explain how your credit affects your employment, your housing, your insurance, and even your retirement rates. You also discover how to manage your credit when you have a special someone sharing your life. I show you how your credit can survive a divorce, how to manage medical debt, and what the credit implications are of losing a spouse to death.

Also in this part, you find out how to control access to your identity. I include tips for keeping your personal information safe and avoiding popular identity theft scams. Finally, I review the early warning signs you should watch for that indicate that your identity may have been compromised.

Chapter 9

Building Credit: Getting Started (or Restarted) in Life

In This Chapter

▶ Identifying credit issues for immigrants and first-time credit users

▶ Puncturing some credit myths

▶ Establishing credit when you're first starting out

▶ Avoiding common mistakes of credit newbies

▶ Knowing some special credit rules for students and military members

Credit isn't an American invention. It has been around in one form or another since ancient Roman times. Modern consumer credit, however, is as American as apple pie. Taking off after the GIs returned home from World War II, credit has been among the most prolific of financial services. Life without it is almost unimaginable today, but if you're among those just getting started or restarted in life, getting the credit you need may be easier said than done. Credit newbies such as immigrants to the United States, recent high school or college graduates, and those starting over because of divorce or death can find the process to be a stressful endeavor. You may feel like you're looking through a bakery shop window but can't find the door to get in.

This chapter is your point of entry. I help you understand why establishing a credit history and financial-services relationships is essential to getting the credit you need. Your confidence gets a boost when I show you the size and importance to lenders of the underbanked market (meaning people like you, whose financial needs aren't being met), so you know just where you stand. I also debunk some credit myths that you may have brought with you from another country or may have been taught right here at home by well-meaning but misinformed friends. I include help in this chapter for young people as well, with sections for students, grads, and military members. Credit really is as American as mom and apple pie, so take your seat at the table and help yourself to a big piece of the American dream . . . credit.

Defining the Underbanked Consumer

Just who makes up the underbanked market and what is it? The U.S. General Accounting Office says that tens of millions of adults in the United States are either unbanked or underbanked:

- ✔ Unbanked consumers have no relationship with a bank such as savings or checking accounts. They tend to use check-cashing establishments and money-order retailers for financial transactions.

- ✔ Underbanked consumers may have only basic checking or savings accounts. They don't use more advanced services like lines of credit or credit cards. For the purposes of this chapter, I refer to both unbanked and underbanked consumers as the underbanked market.

Consumers in the underbanked market have financial needs that aren't currently being fully met, and they're underserved by the credit industry. Among those included in this catchall category are

- ✔ **Immigrants:** Legal or not, to be financially successful in the United States you need to establish a U.S. credit history.

- ✔ **Consumers new to credit:** You may be generation Y or Z, or you may be a baby boomer starting life over for reasons ranging from divorce to the death of a spouse or life partner. Regardless, the longer you wait to establish a credit history, the longer you pay more for basic services like check-cashing and short-term (payday) loans.

- ✔ **Cash-paying households:** You may live in a cash economy, with many of your financial decisions driven by the realities of whatever the next day brings, be it good or bad.

- ✔ **Individuals without strong banking relationships for whatever reason:** This group includes students, rugged individualists, people who really like their privacy, and folks reentering the credit market after a long absence.

If you fall into one of these categories, you represent a fundamentally different market from your banked counterparts. Over the years, you've found ways to address your financial-service needs outside of the mainstream system — through check-cashers, payday lenders, retailers, friends, and family.

Don't confuse the underbanked with poor money managers. Just because you're new to credit in no way means that you can't handle credit. As a market segment, you collectively represent the full spectrum of credit risks that my friends at VantageScore refer to as being from high risk to super prime (see Chapter 7 for more info). You make up one of the largest untapped credit markets in the U.S., estimated at between 40 and 50 million people.

Why banks want to do business with you

Why do banks do anything? To make money, of course. With hundreds of millions of dollars in profits at stake, some of the biggest and best names in the financial-services industry would love to have you as a long-term customer. Why do they like long-term customers? You guessed it; they're more profitable. Selling something new to someone you know is much easier than selling to a stranger. So banks really do want your business, although at times you may not know it from the way they act.

Now that you know you're a valued and valuable customer in a large market segment that banks want to do business with, you should expect to be treated well, respected, and, yes, maybe even spoiled just a little. Anything less and you can just move on to the next player, who may know better how to treat a valuable customer like you.

Debunking Misinformation about Banking and Credit

Depending on your culture or what your friends and family may have told you, you may not have an accurate understanding of how credit really works. However, with a few tips, you'll find that using credit can often increase your enjoyment of life and all it has to offer. The following list spells out some commonly held misconceptions about banking and credit and debunks the myths:

- ✓ **Banks aren't safe places to put money because they can fail and go out of business, causing you to lose all your money.** Not so. All depository institutions (like banks) are insured by the full faith and credit of the U.S. government for up to $250,000 per depositor. No one has ever lost a penny of money that was in a federally insured depository account.

- ✓ **Bank accounts are unsafe because currency can decrease in value or become worthless overnight.** When you deposit money into a U.S. bank, it's deposited in dollars. The dollar, though subject to fluctuations in value, is the most stable and trusted currency in the world. So it's safe!

- ✓ **The government may nationalize your bank and your account.** If the financial crisis taught people anything, it's that the government wants to support, not own, banks.

- ✓ **You need to be rich to be well treated at a bank.** Not so. Adding new customers is a top priority for banks, and the size of your account, no matter how small your deposits may be, doesn't determine your value as a customer. Banks know that many big depositors started out small and increased their deposits over time. If a bank doesn't respect you on your terms, take your money to a competing bank.

> ✔ **Using cash is safer than credit or debit cards.** A lost or stolen card is protected against misuse by another person (most have a liability of $50 or less); lost or stolen cash is gone. Plus, purchasing with cash never builds the credit history you need for a credit score.
>
> ✔ **I have only a consular ID or a green card, not a Social Security number. I can't build a credit history.** Not true. You can establish a credit history and use credit without a Social Security number.

The following sections explain why you need credit and why it's safe. Hopefully, this information eases your potential anxiety about any misconceptions you may have.

Why you need credit

What's your definition of the good life? A good job, a safe place to live, a car, some financial security, and a good life for your kids? Sounds pretty straightforward, doesn't it? The reality of life in the U.S. is that to accomplish goals like these, having good credit is important.

For starters, let's look at that good job. Chances are that you have to compete with others for a good position. Many employers check your credit history to see whether you're reliable or you have distracting financial issues at home before making an offer. People can lie about their experience (ADP Screening and Selection Services says that about half of applicants lie on their resumes) and they can fake being nice, but a good credit history is tough to fake. As one employer put it, "When you think about it, people who have good credit keep their promises and are responsible, so it makes sense that if their credit is good, they may be more honest." So, all other things being equal, the job may go to the candidate with the best credit history.

The same thing happens when you try to rent an apartment, get a security clearance, buy insurance, apply for a college loan, or vie for a promotion at work. In all these circumstances, the person making the decision may check your credit history as part of the qualification process. Being underbanked and relying on cash may knock you out of the race. It pays to understand how to build good credit and use the banking and financial system to your best advantage.

Why credit is safe

The credit industry didn't become the huge and powerful entity that it is without addressing the question of safety. The federal government has put many regulations and safeguards in place over the last several years to ensure the safety and fair treatment of credit users. As a result, you have access to one of the fairest and most market-driven credit systems in the world. The following laws play a major role in protecting borrowers in the U.S.:

- ✔ **The Fair and Accurate Credit Transactions Act (the FACT Act or FACTA)** gives you lots of rights when it comes to how your credit is reported and what you can do to correct mistakes. It also gives you rights and remedies in the event of identity theft.

- ✔ **The Fair Debt Collection Practices Act (FDCPA)** spells out what third-party bill collectors can and can't do when they try to collect a debt. If they step over the line, you can sue them for big bucks.

- ✔ **The Equal Credit Opportunity Act (ECOA)** prohibits credit discrimination on the basis of race, color, religion, national origin, sex, marital status, age, and whether you get public assistance. Creditors may collect this information, but they can't use it to decide whether to give you credit or how to set your credit terms.

- ✔ **The Credit Card Accountability, Responsibility, and Disclosure Act (CARD Act)** protects you from unfair credit card billing practices. Major protections spell out notification requirements, grace periods, fees, interest rate changes, restrictions on student cards, and more.

- ✔ **The Dodd-Frank Wall Street Reform and Consumer Protection Act** established an independent consumer financial protection bureau within the Federal Reserve to protect borrowers against abuses in mortgage services, credit card services, payday lending, and credit counseling.

- ✔ **The Truth in Lending laws** assure you that you won't find any hidden surprises when you borrow money. All the costs of doing so must be spelled out for you before you sign a contract.

Building from checking to credit to a business

A solid credit report and a good credit score help you in employment, borrowing, and getting a credit card, a decent apartment, and insurance. They can also form the first building block in starting a new business. With good credit, savings, and the stability that savings brings, you're a prime candidate to step up to that business you may have always wanted.

Good personal credit is essential. If you want to start a new business, you can't be financially successful doing so unless you move from the underbanked to traditional banking. That big piece of the American Dream called credit is now yours to enjoy. Welcome to the table. And be sure to bring the family! For more information about starting your own business, check out *Small Business For Dummies*, 3rd Edition, by Eric Tyson and Jim Schell (John Wiley & Sons, Inc.).

Recognizing What's Not in Your Credit History

With all the information available to companies, the government, and others, you may think that a huge dossier about your every movement is housed in your credit report. To clarify: A credit history is nothing more than a snapshot of your financial life to date.

Keeping track of the information that can make or break your chances of getting credit may seem mindboggling. The good news, however, is that only information sent to the credit bureaus by people with whom you choose to do business ends up in your file. And even then, not all your information is reported. Some companies and some service providers like doctors, hospitals, and grocery stores don't report credit activity at all. Turn to Chapter 7 to read about other items that aren't in your credit report.

You have the right to dispute out-of-date or inaccurate information in your credit report. These provisions are detailed in the FACT Act, which is spelled out on the accompanying CD. Check out Chapter 7 for more specific info about what appears in your credit history.

Obtaining Credit: Starting on the Right Foot

You're ready to begin building your own credit, but you're not quite sure where to start. They say that a journey begins with a single step, which just goes to show how wrong people can be for thousands of years. The journey actually begins when you see a destination in your mind. Then, after packing your lunch and other essentials, you take that first step. You build up a credit history over a period of time. How much time depends on how active you are and which scoring model is used to rate your credit file.

Don't fret though. This section walks you through these steps to help you begin your credit journey down the right path.

Establishing credit without a Social Security number

You don't need a Social Security number to start building credit. In fact, a frequent misconception is that to establish a credit history, and thereby a credit score, you need a Social Security number, a driver's license, or a voter registration card. However, none of these items is required to establish a successful and envious credit record.

When a credit bureau receives a new data line, the bureau matches the data with the following items, in the order shown:

1. Your name

2. Your birth date

3. Your address

4. Your Social Security number

So, no number? No problem. The bureaus can use plenty of other matching points to get your information in the right file. But being consistent is important! For example, make sure you spell your name exactly the same way every time you apply for or use credit.

Setting goals before you set out

Figuring out what your goals are prior to seeking credit is an important step for anyone, but especially for the underbanked and those new to credit. Writing down your goals allows you to see what you need to do financially to achieve credit success.

To begin setting your goals, I suggest you (and your partner) follow these steps.

1. **Set aside some uninterrupted thinking time and dream about the future as you want to live it.**

   Allow at least an hour, and set an end point so you finish before you get exhausted. You can always come back to this step later after some reflection.

2. **Write down some goals that are short-term (one year or less), intermediate-term (one to five years), and long-term (more than five years).**

   Some typical goals people have shared with me include beginning to save this year, beginning to save next year, getting out of debt in the next year, and rebuilding bad credit. Others would like to receive guidance with financial matters and find out about financial topics such as bank accounts, certificates of deposit (CDs), children's college accounts, and retirement accounts.

   Writing down your goals serves two purposes:

   • It clarifies what you're talking about.

   • It makes your goals seem more real than just airy whims.

3. **Make a list of the actions you need to take to reach each goal.**

   For example, if you want to get a better apartment and a new job, how do you do this? Good credit can help. A smart first step is to get a copy of your credit report at www.annualcreditreport.com and make sure it's accurate. Dispute and remove any inaccuracies to improve your credit. Then make sure you make payments on time on all your accounts. It's simple, but it works. Chapter 4 has more suggestions and details about budgeting and goal setting.

4. **Track your progress.**

   Periodically talking about or reviewing your progress toward your goals is not only an incentive to keep up the good work but also an opportunity to celebrate your interim successes.

A real-life couple: How goals can help

I love using examples to illustrate and clarify a concept. To help me with this, I invented Roland and Carlotta, two recently engaged young people who are new to credit and want to get a head-start on their new lives. They begin by spending an hour one evening imagining what they want their futures to look like and then setting goals to make it happen.

Carlotta and Roland want to get married in a year, and they agree they want a better apartment and eventually a small house for the new

family they'd like to start as soon as they're able. Roland wants a better job than the hourly one he currently has and would really like to buy a better car. Carlotta wants to decorate their new place and buy some new furniture for it. Carlotta wants to establish credit for herself, and Roland needs to repair his credit.

Notice that you don't need to be in complete agreement on all the specifics as long as you can agree on the concept. You can make adjustments as you get closer to your goals.

Goal	Roland	Carlotta
Short term:	Get married	Plan a wedding and get married
		Establish credit
	Open savings and checking accounts	
Medium term:	Get a better apartment	Get a bigger apartment
	Repair credit	Furnish and decorate apartment
	Get a better job	
	Buy a car	
Long term:	Buy a big house	Buy a house
	Have six children	Start a family

Establishing a relationship with a financial institution

When someone says, "That's as good as money in the bank," she means that's as good as it gets. Having money in the bank is a good thing and is the situation you want to be in. If you don't have an existing relationship with a bank or credit union, I can't stress enough how important this relationship is to your ultimate success. You want to develop a relationship with a bank by setting up at least a savings or checking account, not just so you have a place to take out a loan or get a titanium credit card to impress your friends, but more important, because you need a place to put the money you earn but don't spend right away. Saving is essential to your success.

Spending what you make or using credit to supplement your income is a recipe for disaster. There's no substitute for savings when life throws you a curveball. Chapter 16 has details on what you can do when times get tough. But without savings, even life's little bumps are enough to hold you back on your journey to financial success.

Why you need to save

Everything is going along okay. The money that comes in goes out, and your debt is under control. You may be a little short at the moment and your credit card balances may be building, but you figure that will all end as soon as you get that next promotion in six months. Then, your car muffler falls off and costs $500 to repair, your tooth breaks at lunch and suddenly you need $900 for a crown, and your roommates tell you they're moving out and you have to meet the rent on your own. Where does the money come from if you have no savings?

You can use credit if you have any left. But if you do, you may be paying a high interest rate and getting close to your card limit, and your minimum payment is now huge.

Without access to credit or savings, you have fewer choices. You may have to carpool, have the tooth removed rather than crowned, and be forced to move to less-expensive housing. That's why you need savings; credit and good luck truly are never enough for you to be financially successful.

How to get started saving

Fortunately, starting to save is easy, painless, and automatic when you get going. The key is not to focus on how you're going to save six months' worth of living expenses, which could test even a saint. (For your information, St. Matthew is the patron saint of money managers.) What I want you to do is start with a small savings program but make it automatic.

To get started saving, take the following steps:

1. **Go to a bank or credit union that's near where you live and ask about automatic deposit savings and checking accounts.**

   Most likely you don't have much to put away, at least right now, but that's okay. Limited funds are no excuse for not saving. Tell the bank you don't want any fees because you'll be using automatic deposit. If the bank charges a fee, go to another bank or credit union. Banks and credit unions usually waive all fees for people who save regularly through payroll deductions.

2. **After you open two accounts, one checking and one savings, go to your human resources department or payroll person at work and say that you want your pay automatically deposited into these two accounts.**

   For example: You want all your take-home pay minus $5 (or more if you can) put into checking and the remaining $5 put into your savings account. At the end of the first pay period, you will have saved $5. Not a huge sum, but you're starting a habit that will grow and add up with time.

   If direct deposit isn't available through your employer, you can have the bank automatically transfer money monthly from your checking account into your savings account.

3. **When you get that next raise or promotion, have half the increase automatically deposited into each account.**

   Now you're making a smart financial move — increasing your savings by using the extra money from your raise before you have an opportunity to spend it! Do the same thing for IRS tax refunds and other windfalls. In no time you'll have a cushion that can get you over life's bumps without stretching your credit or causing potential damage to your credit history!

To secure your financial future, stop cashing paychecks and start automatic deposit and automatic savings. You owe it to yourself, your sweetie, and your future.

Using prepaid and reloadable cards

When trying to build your credit, you may want to consider using prepaid and reloadable cards. They're neither a credit card nor a debit card; rather, they exist somewhere in between. You deposit money onto the cards at locations throughout the nation and then use them as you would a credit or debit card. But they don't build your credit report history or score.

The following list outlines the major advantages of prepaid and reloadable cards:

✔ You can use money without getting mugged and hit over the head for the cash in your pocket.

✔ You need no credit record or credit check, just your name, address, telephone number, and the ability to pay a one-time fulfillment fee. Non-U.S. citizens can provide an alternative form of ID, such as a driver's license, passport, or alien registration. Funds may post to your account within 30 minutes.

✔ Prepaid cards offer convenience, ease of availability, guaranteed approval, and other features that can make them ideal substitutes for credit cards.

✔ You can use prepaid cards on the Internet, over the phone, and in many other places, just like a credit or debit card.

✔ Prepaid cards can help with financial discipline and the building of good financial habits.

Fattening up your credit file

You're not alone if your credit file is underweight. Today, up to 50 million U.S. adults — nearly 25 percent of the credit-eligible consumers in the country — come back from credit inquiries to the major bureaus either as no-hits or as *thin files* (files with too little data in them to receive a credit score).

If you fit this category, don't worry. You can take action to build your credit muscle. The following options work well for credit newbies and underbanked individuals:

✔ **Continue using your foreign credit card if you have one.** You may be surprised to find out that foreign credit history doesn't carry over and can't be imported into your U.S. credit file. However, you can still use your impeccable credit experience overseas to your advantage. You can either continue to use your foreign credit card here or you can get a letter from a multinational bank extolling your virtues so the local underwriters approve the issue of an American credit card that's listed with American credit bureaus.

Global scoring is expected in the future, and in fact, FICO claims a proven global score that's accurate in every country in the world except France (quelle surprise!). However, the global score isn't being used yet in any country of the world.

✔ **Ask that an expansion score be used to score your application for credit.** This is a one-time snapshot of about 90 noncredit databases that tell whether you pay your obligations as agreed. Reporting real-time information rather than keeping a warehouse full of dated material may be the future of credit reporting. (Check out Chapter 14 for more info.)

✔ **Take out a passbook loan:** A *passbook loan* is a loan the bank makes to you using your own money! It may sound strange, but if you open a passbook savings account at a bank or credit union and then borrow the money back, the bank gladly charges you interest (low, thank heavens) and reports your loan repayment history to the credit bureaus. You use your money in place of credit for the loan until you can build enough credit to get an unsecured loan. Faster than you can say "good credit," you're adding positive history to your file and improving your score.

Check with your bank or credit union to make sure that it reports the loan to at least one, and preferably all three, of the major credit-reporting bureaus. If the bank doesn't report the loan to at least one of the major bureaus, request that it do so. If the bank is unwilling to do so, take your business elsewhere.

✔ **Get a secured credit card.** These cards are a cross between a credit card and a prepaid card. After you establish a savings account and build up the balance, you can ask the bank to give you a credit card backed by your deposit in the bank. You may qualify for a credit line in excess of the amount you have on deposit.

Many credit issuers eventually move you into a traditional credit card after a period of successful payment. The best part is that, unlike most prepaid cards, many secured cards are reported to the three major credit-reporting bureaus and can help you build a history and a credit score. Shop around for the best terms; many secured credit cards have high interest rates and fees.

Here's how to get and use a secured card:

1. **Contact your bank or credit union to find out whether it offers secured credit cards or look online for an issuing bank.**

   Watch out for annual processing or maintenance fees. You can get secured credit cards for free — you just have to look around for banks or credit unions that offer them.

2. **Deposit the funds to be used as security for the card.**

   Be sure the account is FDIC- or NCUA-insured.

3. **Use the card for purchases, making sure that you can pay the balance each month.**

   You don't need to use the card a lot. Just make a few purchases each month.

4. **Make on-time payments every month.**

Avoiding scams and unnecessary fees

Unfortunately, being new to something leaves you vulnerable to abuse by people who know the rules better than you do. Abuses perpetuated on immigrants and credit newbies have been around forever and aren't about to go away. This section lists several that you're likely to run into, along with some guidelines on how to handle them.

Payday loans

When you don't have savings or credit but you have an unexpected expense, what are you to do? An entire industry has arisen to answer this question. *Payday lenders* charge a very high interest rate or fee for a short-term loan guaranteed by your next paycheck. The fee is based on the amount of your paycheck, and you must supply the lender with a signed check for the date the loan is due.

It's not unusual for the person seeking such a loan to need additional money after the lender cashes the original postdated check. This can start a vicious cycle of several high-fee, high-interest loans piling up with no practical way to pay them off. Payday lenders don't report your loan experience to the credit bureaus, so you receive no credit history-building benefit from using one of these companies. If you must use a payday lender, look for one that's a member of the Community Financial Services Association of America. Members subscribe to a code of conduct and may offer extended repayment terms if you can't pay back a loan as scheduled.

Refund anticipation loans (RALs)

Refund anticipation loans (RALs) are high-fee loans secured by your tax refund that may, and the operative word here is *may,* get you your refund a week or so earlier than having it direct-deposited after filing your return electronically with the IRS. The real downside of these loans is that the person who sells you the loan has an incentive to inflate your tax refund to get you to take out a higher loan.

If your actual refund is less than what you borrow, you owe the difference plus a hefty interest rate. A much better idea is to open a bank account and have any refund direct-deposited. You get it fast, free, and with no surprises.

Check-cashing for a high fee

Going to a check-cashing place instead of a bank or credit union is like shopping at the most expensive store in town in the worst possible neighborhood. Check cashers are often located in places that are rife with crime. Why? Because everyone coming out has a pocket full of cash. A bank or credit union with which you have an account won't charge you to cash a check, and you don't have to take all the cash with you when you leave — you can deposit it in your savings and checking accounts.

Instant credit rating

Credit-repair companies may offer you either a new identity or a repaired credit rating for only a few hundred dollars, usually upfront. Don't spend the money. The new identity is often illegal, and the instant credit repair doesn't exist.

Foreign bank accounts

Occasionally, you may receive a letter or e-mail saying that you've been chosen, lucky you, to help a rich foreign person get some money into the U.S. and that you'll receive a fat percentage of the amount for your small trouble because you're trustworthy. Most of these come from Nigeria, but they can originate anywhere. If you don't know the person, don't do it.

Overcoming Credit Fears and Mistakes

Everyone makes mistakes, even the lenders and bureaus, so a mistake needn't be a big deal if you deal with it quickly.

As a person new to credit and maybe even new to the U.S., you may be a tad scared of having to deal with credit and the problems that can potentially come along with it. Bill collectors aren't above using threats of deportation or imprisonment if they think that doing so helps collect a bill. The truth is, they can't legally do either. You won't be deported and you won't go to jail, no matter what they say. How do I know for sure? Well, these companies only get paid for collecting the money due their employers. If they were to actually deport you or put you in jail, which they legally can't, they wouldn't get their money, would they?

The CD contains complete copies of the FACT Act, the CARD Act, and the Fair Debt Collection Practices Act, all of which spell out your rights.

If you're a credit newbie, keep these basic tips in mind for dealing with mistakes:

- ✔ **Don't delay.** Credit and debt problems, unlike my wife, don't improve with age. If you're proactive and make an effort to resolve any problem before you're called, you'll get a much better reception and improve your chances of a favorable resolution.

- ✔ **Open your statements when you get them and challenge anything you don't understand or remember.** You can correct errors, but often there are time limits. Also, what may look like an error may turn out to be the beginning of an identity theft.

✔ **Do everything in writing.** You may resolve simple problems over the phone, but to protect your rights in a dispute, you need to make your case in writing. So if you really want a problem fixed, do it in writing and keep good records.

✔ **Keep track of contacts.** Keeping notes on who promised what to whom not only keeps you from making more mistakes but also tells the other person that you know what you're doing. So when the manager says this is the first time you've called, you can say, "You are mistaken, I called on these occasions and I spoke to these people who told me these things."

✔ **Keep cool and calm.** Nothing can derail your effort to resolve a mistake or error faster than raising your voice. After you escalate the volume, you'll be directed to someone who does "loud" professionally or you'll be politely ignored. Either way, you lose. Call back if you need to, but don't lose control.

✔ **Safeguard your identity.** Newbies to America or credit often come from a culture of sharing. Whether you shared with your family in Mexico or you shared with your roommate at Harvard, the time for sharing information and credit is over. Identity theft is a serious and growing crime in the U.S. that can take years to unravel and cost thousands of dollars to fix. In Chapter 20, I tell you how to safeguard your identity.

In brief, guard your personal identification information, mail, computer passwords, and bank account information. Shred financial mail. Also, if you invite people into your home, be sure to put away financial statements and your checkbook. You wouldn't leave twenty-dollar bills all over the floor and furniture. The same applies to financial information.

Chapter 7 has more information on what to do if you run afoul of the credit-reporting system. If you do end up owing more than you can pay and have to deal with collectors, Chapter 16 has what you need.

Qualifying for First-Time Cards and Loans

This section looks at how credit impacts two major and basic consumer credit instruments that most people need when they first get started on life's journey. I'm talking about credit cards and loans. You may think you know how these instruments work, but things have changed because of regulations like the CARD Act and the financial meltdown that threatened banks with failure due in large part to lax underwriting standards.

Credit cards

Getting credit for the first time used to be easy. All you had to do was drive to your nearest gas station and fill out an application for a gas card and then wait for the mail to arrive with your new plastic. If you were a city dweller who didn't drive, the trip may have been on foot to your big department store, which would often grant you credit on the spot. Both of these types of credit were relatively easy to get, and they reported your credit history to the three bureaus so that you built a credit history quickly. More and more department store and gas cards are tightening their standards to reflect tightened credit conditions. You can opt to try for cards issued by banks that use a national transaction network such as Visa. Though these cards are more versatile and powerful than their earlier counterparts, they're also harder to get. Getting that first card now requires a new approach.

To begin with, you need a credit history. But, how do you get a credit history with no credit? Two of the most popular ways: Use someone else's credit or use a secured credit card.

Using other people's credit

In most instances, when you use other people's credit, the other people are family members or a person with whom you have an emotional attachment. Why? Because using someone else's credit can be dangerous to that person if you mess up. Only someone who really likes you is willing to stick his neck out to help you get started.

You can piggyback on another person's credit in two ways. The most popular way is to be added to the person's account as an authorized user. The other way is to have the person cosign for you.

Authorized user

Being named an *authorized user* on someone's credit account allows you to have her credit history reported on your credit report while you use a card for which she's solely financially responsible. The card statement goes to the account owner, she pays the credit card company, you pay the card owner, and the card's credit history is reported in both the user's and owner's files. Problems with this approach can happen if the account owner defaults or is late with payments, because then those negative marks go on your credit history. Another more common pitfall is that you overcharge and the account owner has to ask you for more money than you have available, which can cause a rift between the two of you.

Cosigning

Cosigning on an account is more often than not a recipe for disaster, and I usually don't recommend it. The cosigner's credit history doesn't show up on your credit report. Instead, all that shows is your own payment history. The statement for a cosigned account doesn't go to the cosigner, so unless you tell him, the cosigner has no idea what's happening to the account. Often, the first the cosigner hears about a problem is when a collector calls and demands an overdue payment. Unfortunately, if you make late payments, the delinquency history appears on the cosigner's report, and negative information stays on the cosigner's credit history for a full seven years.

If you decide to go the cosigning route, I suggest that as the borrower, you commit to paying this bill before almost any other. Also, you need to have the courage to keep your cosigner informed of any changes in your financial picture, especially if you may be late on a payment.

Using secured cards

A secured card looks and works just like a credit card but is backed by a cash deposit at the bank that issues you the card. Typically, your deposit qualifies you for a credit card with a limit equal to that deposit amount. As a result, limits on secured cards tend to be low, but the real value here is to establish a credit history so you can get an unsecured card and reallocate your deposit to a better purpose, like your emergency savings account.

You can find and compare secured cards on a number of Internet sites. My favorites include www.bankrate.com and www.creditcards.com. You want to balance services, fees, and interest rates to find the best card for you.

Using savings for credit

Most banks and credit unions are happy to lend you your own money. If you accumulate some savings in a passbook account, you can use the savings to secure an installment loan of the same or a lesser amount. Needless to say, with 100 percent collateral in cash for the loan, the interest rate should be very low. Be sure the loan is reported to the bureaus so that you build your credit as you pay the money back.

One last word about credit scores and underwriting

Well, maybe more like a sentence or two! Getting a credit score takes a few months or longer of credit use. The two major credit score providers, FICO and VantageScore, each require different amounts of payment history to generate a score. See Chapter 7 for more information on credit scores. Also, you need more than a score to, well, score a card! Lenders are hyper-nervous about potential losses. New accounts are an unknown, so they look at your credit report and income information in detail to help decide whether they should grant you credit.

Considering Credit for Students and Military Members

At first blush, students and military members may not seem similar. However, as a credit grouping, they share some similarities. For example, both have relatively limited means, a high number of younger members, a susceptibility to scams, and laws designed to protect them. One last similarity is that bankruptcy doesn't work as well for students or military members as it does for the general population.

In this section I show you the protections offered under the CARD Act and Dodd-Frank legislation, as well as the impact of the Servicemembers Civil Relief Act. I also offer practical advice tuned to the unique needs of students and military members.

Giving credit to students

The reality is that most young people entering college or technical school have been brought up using their parents' credit cards. They'd sooner be without their cellphones than do without a credit card. But after they cross that credit line from authorized son or daughter user to customer, they're exposed to all the pluses and minuses of the credit industry.

Imagine new drivers getting behind the wheel with no driver's education, no insurance, no speed limit, and no police to tell them to slow down. Not a pretty picture, is it? This scenario applies to students and credit, and this section helps keep you from crashing your credit and maybe your immediate future with some insights and suggestions for students and their parents.

Checking out the CARD Act

The Credit Card Accountability, Responsibility, and Disclosure Act of 2009 (CARD Act) was aimed at bringing about more responsible lending and borrowing and fostering more accountability in debt management. For years, many credit card companies have targeted naïve kids just out of high school without regard for their basic inability to afford to repay credit used without help from their parents. The CARD Act set new rules to stem the tide of heavily indebted students who often have to drop out of school, work full-time jobs while studying to pay off credit card debts, or enter the job marketplace with damaged credit that can interfere with finding a job. Key provisions include

- **Proof of income:** Under the new law, if you're under the age of 21, you must show proof that you can repay any credit card debt you may incur.

- **Cosign requirement:** If you don't have sufficient income, you need to find someone to cosign on the account.

- **Credit limit regulations:** Card companies can no longer offer a preapproved credit limit just because you're a student. Young adults under 21 are limited to credit of the greater of $500 or 20 percent of their income or less. Also, if you have a cosigner, the cosigner has to approve limit increases in writing.

- **Fewer sign-up incentives:** Card issuers can't turn your head with free sign-up rewards such as T-shirts, pizza, or electronics. The law also prohibits credit card companies from coming onto school property and hitting you up between classes. They must now remain a specified distance away from campuses. However, they can set up shop at other locations favored by students.

- **Practical financial education:** Though not a part of the CARD Act, you may find some new financial education programs at your school. Many schools now require freshmen to attend sessions on credit and debt management.

Practicing student credit etiquette

No, you don't need white gloves or a tie to practice credit etiquette. But if you're new to having your own credit and being responsible for the consequences, here are some basic rules you can use to keep your credit neat and tidy, regardless of how messy your roommate is.

- Don't apply for every card you're offered. Every time you apply for a card, it counts against your credit score, whether you're approved or not.

✔ It's okay to leave your socks lying around on the floor but not your credit cards or billing statements. Misuse or identity theft happens to students too!

✔ Lend a shirt, your car, or your date to a friend. Never lend your credit card to a friend. You're fully responsible for anything your friend does with your card. Anything!

✔ Decide what you consider to be an emergency worthy of using your card before one happens to you.

✔ If you can wear it, eat it, or drink it, it isn't an emergency!

✔ Stick to one low interest rate-card and only charge what you can afford to pay in full each month. If you must use more than one card, pay off the card with the highest interest rate first, and make at least an on-time minimum payment on the others.

✔ Before you charge an item, reflect on whether you can pay it off at the end of the month. If you know you'll have to carry the balance over, estimate how long you need to pay it off before swiping. If the answer is more than 90 days to pay off the balance, you should seriously reconsider buying the item!

Following military credit rules

America owes a tremendous debt of gratitude to those citizens who volunteer to defend this country and way of life. Not surprisingly, Americans take a dim view of those who take advantage of soldiers and sailors during their term of service. Life is complicated enough in the service without having financial concerns distract you from your mission. This section discusses some of the rules of engagement between the military and the financial-services sector.

Student credit loopholes to watch out for

Any new law has its loopholes, and the CARD Act is no exception when it comes to protecting students from credit card schemes. The CARD Act doesn't allow credit card issuers to market their cards on campus, so they may operate just over the edge of campus. Students under 21 may need a cosigner; older students have been buying beer for younger students forever, so cosigning for them is nothing new. Students need to show income to get a card, so student loans may be counted as income. Income verification beyond filling out the application can be spotty for young adults who may not file tax returns on their own.

Enlisting with credit issues

In addition to meeting rigorous moral character standards, those seeking to join the military undergo a background check that includes a check of their credit history. Uncle Sam doesn't want to give you a loan; he wants to make sure that you don't have existing financial problems, because you're not likely to overcome those difficulties on junior enlisted pay. See Chapter 13 for ways to get your credit under control before you walk into a recruiting station and raise your hand.

Serving with credit issues

Credit problems happen in the military as well as in civilian life. Military personnel have extra protections under the law known as the Servicemembers Civil Relief Act. They're entitled to enhanced protection from eviction, auto lease cancellation penalties, high interest rates, and being brought to a court hearing while serving. For more information, see Chapter 16.

A program sponsored by the U.S. Department of Defense, Military One Source offers financial counseling if you're in financial difficulty. Military One Source also offers confidential resources and support for service members and their families on a wide range of topics, including finances. Twelve financial counseling sessions are available to service members at no cost if you're an active duty, Guard, or Reserve member or family member, as well as deployed Department of Defense civilians and their families. Financial counseling is available in-person and over-the-phone in partnership with the National Foundation for Credit Counseling (NFCC).

Counseling includes education and coaching in the areas of

- Money management and budgeting
- Housing counseling (prepurchase, foreclosure prevention, and reverse mortgage)
- Credit and active-duty alerts
- Debt management
- Debt collectors
- Security clearances
- Financial-related deployment issues
- The Servicemembers Civil Relief Act (SCRA)
- Payday loans, title loans, and rent-to-own
- The creation of a realistic action plan using specific, manageable steps

To reach Military One Source, call 800-342-9647 from inside the U.S., 800-342-6477 from outside the U.S., 484-530-5747 for an international collect call, or see www.militaryonesource.com.

Facing student loans

Student loans are critical to many people and their families as the preferred and, in some cases, only method for financing not only a college or technical-school education but also a big part of the American Dream. Most students graduate with student loan debt. Recent stats put the average debt at around $25,000, not counting any additional amount the student's parents borrow. Student loans are a powerful tool to be handled with care — often with more care than the people who grant them use when they explain the ins and outs of these debt instruments to the borrower.

Student loans are unlike most loans in their generous terms, low eligibility standards, and flexibility. They also stand out as being among a select number of bulletproof debt obligations that are nearly inviolate under the law. What this means is that neither bankruptcy nor the passage of time releases you from your obligations to pay off this debt. In this section, I help you deal with the aftermath of a student loan and its credit implications.

Managing your loan payback

Even though the price of a college education may seem high, the return on a successful graduation has always made it worthwhile. Estimates indicate that a college graduate earns $1 million more than a high school graduate over the course of his career. And the figures go up for those with a graduate-school education.

If you left school with, say $10,000 of debt, your payment is probably between $75 and $100 a month, depending on interest and the length of the loan (which can run as long as 30 years). Medical students are looking at an average of between $500 and $1,000 a month.

You usually have a good idea of when you have to start paying back your student loans (generally shortly after leaving school) and at what interest rate well before you're out of school; the lenders keep you informed about this. So the first thing I advise is to come up with a plan for payback, even socking away some of that summer job income to create a cushion in case your first real job doesn't bring in as much as you hope. Then adjust your living expenses to accommodate the loan payment.

Although student loans do offer generous terms, the danger here is that many young people just out of school don't have much experience budgeting and living on their own. You may find yourself in a real-live, "grown-up" job with a salary that may make you feel like a millionaire, and you may start spending like a millionaire, too. Without tools such as a spending plan, you may quickly lose control of credit and debt responsibility and find negative items being added to your credit report.

Financial aid: The ultimate gamble?

It all seems so worthwhile. A college or tech-school education, the promise of a good job, and the great feeling you get from doing the right/smart thing. But a student loan is really a big gamble, and I want you to understand that if anything goes wrong, you lose. Student loans are so high-risk that many have to be guaranteed by the government, and none of them are dischargeable in a bankruptcy under ordinary circumstances. If you fail to graduate for any reason, even because of illness or some other legitimate problem . . . if you can't find a job in your chosen profession and need to settle for a lower-paying job . . . if you decide that medical school isn't for you . . . no matter the reason, you still owe the money for the loan, and you may take decades to pay it off. That's a gamble that millions make every year. Some win and some lose. Look for alternative ways to pay for schooling or consider a community college before taking on the big debt of a big-name school.

Create a spending plan (see Chapter 4) so you're assured of having the money to pay your loan installments. Don't start off on the wrong foot. The majority of student loans may be guaranteed by Uncle Sam, but they're all reported to the three major credit bureaus. Missing a payment is not like cutting a class. Starting off a new life with debt is one thing, but starting off with bad credit is unnecessary.

Several repayment options are available for new grads:

- **Normal repayment:** You make principal and interest payments each month.

- **Graduated repayment:** You make lower payments at the beginning, and your payments increase at specified intervals throughout the life of your loan.

- **Income-based repayment:** Your monthly payments are set based on a percentage of your monthly gross income (for Stafford, Plus, and Smart loans and federally consolidated loans).

- **Extended repayment:** Your repayment term is lengthened.

- **Consolidation:** Your federal loans are refinanced into a single, fixed loan with a long payback period.

- **Serialization:** You consolidate only the payments into a single payment but retain the original terms and interest rates on all your loans.

Before any payment becomes past due, contact your lender and explain the situation. Ask what programs you may qualify for. All this is much better done *before* you default, because more options are available to you.

Before you call or write the loan servicer (and I suggest you begin with a call and follow up in writing), organize your thoughts. Treat this as a very important job interview. Be able to explain coherently why you weren't able to pay: medical issues, job loss, pay reductions, armed-service call-up, or family emergency. If you're calling to propose a payment alternative, have a number prepared and be able to justify it based on your budget. Call your servicer or the U.S. Department of Education information line at 800-872-5327, but be sure to do it before you miss a payment.

Reporting your loans to the credit bureaus

Student loans are reported unlike any other loan. They're similar in that a good payment history helps your credit report and credit score, and a default hurts them. But here's where student loans are different:

- **Each semester's or year's loan may be reported as a separate loan.** You could have four to ten credit lines reported on what you think of as a single loan. That's potentially four to ten negative items on your credit report, not just one.

- **Your tax refunds may be seized until the government gets its money back.**

- **You may be unable to get any additional government student aid.**

- **Your student loan stays on your credit report until you pay it off.** How long will a student-loan default stay on your credit report? Well, if you haven't paid back your loan by the time you begin to collect Social Security, payments will be taken out of your Social Security checks (along with fees and interest). No kidding.

Advice for non-English speakers

If you're new to America and new to credit, you may be new to English as well. Although many companies offer financial services in other languages and most documents are at least bilingual, the language of finance is English. Period. Doing business in the U.S. in another language limits the number of people you can do business with and thereby limits your access to competitive products and services. For example, my daughter-in-law's parents are Korean. They only do business with a financial planner who is and speaks Korean. As a result, their selection of advisors and products is severely restricted. My advice is to become fluent in English as soon as possible.

Chapter 10

Accounting for the Effect of Life's Necessities

. . . .

In This Chapter

▶ Seeing how your credit influences your job opportunities

▶ Leveraging your credit with landlords and lenders

▶ Using your credit to get the best car deal

▶ Knowing credit's role in insurance matters

. . . .

*I*n my experience working with consumers since the early 1990s, I've learned that life, happiness, and credit are intertwined. Not to say that better credit or more money makes you happy but that financial failure has a price in the rest of your life and your relationships with others. So rather than look at your life in one place and your credit in another, I invite you to look at the two as highly correlated.

Let me give you an example by using a new graduate who is going out into the world for the first time. Most of you would define a successful and fulfilling life as including a job, a place to call home, a car to get to your job and elsewhere, and, of course, insurance. In all these life scenarios, you need a good credit record. Employers often do a credit report check before making a job offer. Landlords and mortgage lenders require you to pass a credit review. To get a car you need both credit and a down payment. And insurance involves a credit check that may determine your premium.

Bad credit doesn't just deny you these things. Oh no, it can be much worse. What do you get with bad credit? Job problems, eviction or foreclosure, and debts and collections.

In this chapter, I offer you credit insights into some of what I call life's structural events and give you strategies to help you make the most of these too often credit-challenging situations. I show you ways to manage your credit for your maximum benefit as you step out in your early years. In Chapter 11, I continue this theme with credit's effects on the more personal side of your life, such as marriage, divorce, and more.

So how important is good credit to your life? Very! How can you make sure that you have the credit you need as you set up the structure of your life? That's what I show you in this chapter.

Exploring the Connection between Your Job and Your Credit Report

Most people dislike searching for a job, be it a first job or a fifteenth. I've been through the job-search process more times than I would have liked, and I understand the angst that many suffer as they take stock of their credentials and gear up to enter the job hunt. The role of credit in a job competition is sometimes overlooked, but it can be important and even critical if the competition is stiff enough.

Why? Because as part of the hiring process, employers frequently pull credit reports on candidates before making an offer. Before you get outraged at this possibility, you should know that you've probably given the potential employer permission to review your credit report thanks to some obscure language in the job application. If your report contains disturbing data, the employer can ask you to explain or simply go on to the next candidate. After all, passing on a prospect if a number of others are available is safer and less confrontational.

As you can see, keeping your credit clear when you're looking for a new job — and even when you're up for a promotion — can be a big deal. Following are two steps you can take to help you keep your credit clear, whether you're new to the job market, looking to make a change, or trying to get back into the workforce after being laid off.

✔ **Get copies of your credit reports from the three major bureaus.** The good news is that you're entitled to a free copy of your report from each of the bureaus (Equifax, Experian, and TransUnion) once per year. To find out how to order your copies, head to Chapter 7.

✔ **Read your reports to make sure no one else's negative history has been placed on your record mistakenly.** Credit bureaus get millions of pieces of data each month that they have to apply to the right file. Sooner or later, one goes to the wrong place because of an address mix-up, a misspelled last name, a suffix that was dropped, and so on. If you see anything on your report that doesn't look familiar, you need to dispute it immediately; I explain how to do so in Chapter 7.

Correcting inaccuracies in your reports can easily take a few months, so be sure to start the process well in advance of when you need your reports looking good for a potential employer's judging eye. If you ask after the errors are fixed, the credit bureau will send a copy of your shiny, updated credit report to any employer who has requested it in the last two years or even to any other business who has requested your credit report. That way those employers and businesses get the most accurate and up-to-date info in your file.

If you're new to the credit game — perhaps you're just getting ready to finish your undergraduate degree or you've emigrated from another country to the United States — flip to Chapter 9 for pointers on creating some personal credit history.

Dealing with Apartment Application Checks

Apartment living used to be a great way to start out on your way to homeownership. Today, however, more people choose apartment living over homeownership because of difficulties in selling a home and uncertainties in the long-term outlook for home prices. Others have been foreclosed on and now rent as a result. If you're looking to call an apartment home sweet home, forever or just for a while, you need to understand how credit plays into the rental process.

Credit reports figure prominently in a landlord's decision to rent to you. They show how you handle routine payments, but they generally don't include any rental-specific information (unless you've been evicted and a judgment for unpaid rent or damages was ordered). Recently, Experian has begun showing limited rental history on a small percentage of their reports. Landlords also rely on data available through some national, specialty reporting bureaus that focus exclusively on rental information.

The type of information a rental report may contain includes eviction filings from local court records and other tenant history information from landlords who report their experiences with tenants. Unlike credit reports, specialty bureau reports can pick up evictions without monetary judgments; they can even note a pending eviction. They also contain information about when you moved into or out of your rentals and can include landlord reports on lease violations and ratings. The goal of all this data? To help the landlord identify good, as well as problem, tenants.

So what happens when you finally find a great apartment, only to hear from the leasing agent that your background check has revealed problems? Is it time to move on? No way! The next sections offer some effective ways to address credit and background concerns so you can move into the apartment of your dreams.

If you're trying to rent an apartment after a mortgage foreclosure, you definitely want to be upfront about what happened, because foreclosure *will* appear on your credit report. Also, if you find yourself hitting a brick wall when dealing with large apartment complexes, which can have less-flexible renting criteria, try renting an apartment in a smaller complex (or even a house, condo, townhome, or duplex). Individuals (versus big rental companies) and owners of small complexes may be less likely to run a credit check on you; at the very least, they may be more flexible about your situation if they do run a check.

Knowing what's on your reports

First things first: Pull your credit reports (ideally, before you even begin searching for an apartment) and look them over carefully. If your reports contain negative data that's out-of-date (items over seven years old) or accounts you don't recognize, quickly dispute the inaccurate or out-of-date items with the bureau(s). Next, if you find any negative items, explain to the leasing agent that you're in the process of correcting these errors and ask the agent to repull your report. (Disputed items come off your report until they can be checked out further.)

Landlords can still say no to your application; however, if you can explain what happened, what you did about it, and why it won't happen again, many may be willing to work with you.

To find out what information is contained in the specialty bureaus' databases and whether it's correct, I suggest you ask the leasing agent or landlord which specialty bureau he or she uses and then get a copy of that bureau's report by using the contact information I provide in Chapter 7. Be sure to dispute errors just as you would for a credit report. Instructions on how to do so come with your free report.

Taking action

If clarifying that certain information on your report is incorrect isn't good enough for the landlord, you may need to take additional action. Here are some suggestions that may help you get past such a sticky credit situation:

✔ Write a letter of explanation citing the circumstances from your point of view. Submit this letter along with your application (not later), and be sure to say why the problematic situation won't happen again.

✔ Offer a larger deposit. Remember, you get the money back when you move.

✔ Offer more than one month's rent upfront.

✔ Get a letter of recommendation from your present landlord saying that you're a good tenant (you pay on time and in full each month and take good care of the apartment).

✔ Find a roommate who has good credit or who can help you with your larger deposit. Agree to have a roommate for a year, and when you renew the lease, you can go your separate ways if you like.

You could get a *cosigner* (essentially, a person who guarantees your performance), but I don't recommend doing so if you can avoid it, largely because it can put a strain on relationships, especially if you run into money problems. If you do decide to go ahead with a cosigner, family members or even friends may be willing to help.

Qualifying for a Mortgage

If you've done your homework and you come out on the buy side of the rent-versus-buy decision, then you're ready to dig into the next phase of the mortgage-qualification process. But first it helps to know what you need in order to be successful in your quest:

✔ Steady, reliable income

✔ Good credit

✔ Documentation to verify savings

✔ The savings to get through a temporary setback such as an unexpected loss of income or a home-maintenance emergency, in addition to your down payment and closing costs

If you're already having credit or financial difficulties, I strongly suggest that you do what's necessary to get these issues resolved before you start the home-buying process.

The subprime mortgage market collapse of 2007 will live in the memories of lenders for the next two decades, and it should! The upshot is that lenders are being more intelligent in their decision making. What does that mean for you? Simply that you need to adopt the same critical approach to your credit. In the sections that follow, I help you understand the essentials you want to master *before* you start looking for a home and the mortgage required to purchase it.

Ordering your credit report and score

When you apply for a mortgage, the quantity and quality of the accounts on your credit report are incredibly important. In fact, they ultimately affect your *credit score,* the three-digit number that lenders use to figure out what interest rate and other deal terms they should offer you. You're entitled to order free copies of your credit report from each of the major credit bureaus once per year, but you have to fork over some cash to find out your credit score. Of course, if you've already received a copy of your credit report from each bureau within the last 12 months, then you may have to pay for another one as you begin the mortgage application process unless you live in a state that allows you more than one free report each year (you want the most current report). Either way, I explain how to order your report and score in Chapter 7.

Because your credit score makes a big difference in the interest rate you get for your loan — and that interest rate can make a difference of literally tens of thousands of dollars to you over the course of the loan — you need to have a solid understanding of the components that make up the two main types of credit scores (FICO and VantageScore) so you can try to get the highest score possible. I reveal the breakdown of the components for both types of credit scores in Chapter 6.

So do you need a perfect FICO score (850) or a perfect VantageScore (990) to qualify for a mortgage? No way! Although lenders are certainly very hesitant to lend to people with low scores, they also understand that perfect credit is virtually a myth given all the moving parts to your score and bureau reports. What you really need to quality for a mortgage is good enough credit to get the best deals. Because what's considered "good enough credit" changes with the financial markets, I suggest you check respected sites like www.bankrate.com and www.myfico.com to see the prevailing rates for various score points.

Your credit score varies with each credit report because each bureau may have different information or errors. Chances are a mortgage lender will check all three bureau reports and your credit score, so you should too.

Looking at your credit file like a lender

When your lender looks at your credit file, he wants to see more than just your credit score. You can expect any lender to look at the following items, all of which determine whether you're a good risk:

✔ Your income, employment history, and monthly debt payments

✔ Your savings, as well as assets such as investments and properties that can be sold relatively quickly for necessary cash

Lenders love to see money in the bank, otherwise known as cash reserves. The mere fact that you have a cash reserve speaks volumes about how you manage your money and your life.

✔ Your credit history

If you believe you may come up short in any of these areas, be sure to have a plan to address this shortcoming with your lender during the loan origination process. For instance, if you have a short employment history, point out to the lender how stable your company and job are and that you just received a great performance review.

The process called *underwriting* looks at many factors and applies seasoned judgments to what's there. The term itself explains what happens. In earlier times when a risk was reviewed and approved, the person responsible would write his name below the application. Hence, underwriting.

Preparing to Purchase a Car

Car dealers, or any lender for that matter, want to know three main things about you before deciding whether to make you a loan. They call them the three C's of credit:

✔ **Your character:** To a dealer, your character boils down to whether you'll actually make the payments as agreed. Sometimes a person can have great income, low fixed expenses, and a fat down payment but just be too lazy, disorganized, or distracted to get a payment in on time. So the issue here is not *can* you make the payment but *will* you!

✔ **Your capacity:** This refers to how much of a loan you can handle. Car dealers take into account all your other obligations in addition to the monthly car payment, your income, and fixed expenses, like rent.

✔ **Your collateral:** This is something that can be taken and sold by the lender if you default on your loan, such as your car. The more equity you have in your car, the better the dealer will feel about financing you.

Although purchasing a car is a big step with lots of surprises, credit doesn't have to be a major consideration if you're prepared before you walk on the lot. The following sections detail what you should take care of before you set foot onto the lot and offer insight into what you should consider after you've picked the car you want.

Arming yourself with information

Unless you plan to buy with all cash, your credit has a lot to say about what kind of a car payment and maybe even what type of car you end up with. Naturally, you want to follow the process I describe in Chapter 7 to obtain copies of your credit reports from all three major bureaus and pore over those reports to see whether you can spot any errors. If you find any, dispute 'em (turn to Chapter 7 again for advice on correcting inaccuracies).

If you're smart, you'll also look into your credit score, a tool that helps a lender predict how risky your loan is likely to be. Here's how credit scoring works in general: Based on the information contained in your credit report (and only that), you get points on a scoring scale. The more points the better. (For more on the components that make up the credit score, flip to Chapter 6.)

In modern, politically correct America, lenders can't ask your friends or enemies if you're reliable. They can't make a decision based on anything that may be discriminatory such as how you look or sound or where you live. This is where the credit score shines. Your credit score looks at your credit history plus any public record items on your credit report, such as being taken to court for defaulting on child support or alimony payments. Using a very complex set of formulas, your score predicts the likelihood of your defaulting on your next loan. Yup, that's it. A credit score predicts defaults and nothing more. There's no magic, mystery, or sinister plot. Well, at least not in the scoring.

Find out your credit score before you approach a lender or dealer about an auto loan. Most lenders use a score developed by either FICO (a number between 300 and 850) or VantageScore (which runs between 500 and 990). If you know in advance if your credit is great or horrible, you'll be prepared to hold out for the best rate you qualify for rather than just accepting an offer that may have a higher interest rate tacked on to see whether you're paying attention.

If you're considering a specific car dealer for your purchase or a certain bank or credit union for a car loan, I suggest you find out which credit report and score the dealer or bank uses to determine eligibility. Then you can go to that site and order just what you need.

After you know your score, you can check www.bankrate.com to determine what your interest rate will be for a car loan from a traditional bank or credit union. This is good information to have before you ever set foot in a dealer's finance department. Sure, you may still want to use a dealer incentive and opt for a loan through the dealer, but at least this way you can make a valid comparison.

Reviewing what to consider when you're at the dealership

It's easy to get overexcited when you're finalizing your car deal. The thrill of a new car and the prospect of getting a bargain can lead you to miss a fine point or two in your decision-making process. To keep your passion in check, consider the following before you pick up a pen and sign anything.

- ✔ **Think about dealer financing rather than bank financing if your score isn't the best.** Dealers may have more flexibility than a bank or credit union when making a loan. Why? Because they stand to make money on the cars they have to sell. So loaning you money is worth more to them than it is to a bank, which only gets profits from the loan and not the car sale.

- ✔ **Remember that when you sign a lease, the credit aspect and its impact on your cost is the same.** With a *lease,* you work out an agreement with a leasing company or local credit union where you agree to pay the lease monthly, keep the car insured, and take good care of the vehicle for the term of the lease. From a credit perspective, you're essentially taking out a loan for the amount that the car is expected to depreciate (be reduced in value) over the lease term. Your credit report and score are big determining factors in what interest rate is applied to the term of the lease and your resulting monthly payment.

- ✔ **Don't fall into the trap of weighing monthly payments more than the overall price.** A common car dealer tactic is to talk to you about a car's cost in terms of what you're willing to pay each month instead of the actual price. Though the monthly payment amount is a very important part of your budget, don't lose sight of the total amount you'll pay over the entire term of the loan. A longer payment period (five years versus three years) costs you more overall than a shorter one.

If you're unhappy with your loan payment or interest rate for your new car purchase, don't despair. Instead, follow my advice in Chapter 14 to polish up your credit. Within six months to a year, your score may have improved enough so that you can look into refinancing your balance at a lower interest rate and a lower payment! Leases, however, can't be changed later.

Another thing you can do to help your credit in the long term is pay off your car loan early, provided the loan doesn't have a big prepayment penalty. A credit report with a good payment history and no outstanding car loan scores higher than one with a good payment history and a large balance still due.

Where to go for car info

There are a number of good places where you can find out car values, interest rates, and other critical car-buying information before you walk onto a lot to begin negotiations on a car. To find info on interest rates and the scores that track with them, check out www.bankrate.com. Kelley Blue Book, www.cars.com, and Edmunds all offer free information about car models, features, prices, and more. You can even find owner ratings, car suggestions, and reviews on sites like www.cartalk.com. *Consumer Reports* also offers a good service for a fee that helps you understand what a car costs the seller so you don't end up overpaying.

Unveiling the Relationship between Your Credit and Your Insurance Premiums

Credit plays a significant role when you're looking for insurance to cover a vehicle, apartment, or home. Thin credit, inaccuracies in your credit reports, or just plain bad credit can hurt your chances for coverage and will most likely cost you a small bundle to get coverage. Perhaps you already have blemished credit and think that charging more for insurance before a fender's ever dented or a window's ever broken is just adding insult to injury. Well, the Federal Trade Commission (FTC) agreed that this situation might be unfair (or worse, a proxy for some type of discrimination aimed at overcharging policyholders). So it did some investigating and in 2007 issued a congressionally mandated report examining credit-based insurance scores (www.ftc.gov/opa/2007/07/facta.shtm). The good news and the bad news is that these scores really do predict claim experience and often result in lower prices for people who are better risks — as in people who are smart about their credit, like you. The FTC also found that credit scores have virtually no discriminatory bias.

But just what is a credit-based insurance score? And how can you get your hands on yours? The next sections not only answer these questions but also reveal what you can do to make sure you get the best insurance rate you possibly can.

Understanding insurance scores

Understanding how your credit history affects your insurance options can be a challenge. When evaluated with other information like claims history and driving record, your credit-based insurance score (also known simply as an *insurance score*) helps insurance companies determine whether you qualify for insurance based on their underwriting guidelines and what rate you'll pay.

Your insurance score is a snapshot of your insurance risk at a particular point in time. It's a number based on the information in your credit report that shows whether you're more or less likely to have claims in the near future that result in losses for the insurance company. As with other scores, the higher your insurance score the better off you are.

Another way to look at this type of score is to contrast it with your credit score. An insurance score is a credit-based statistical analysis of a consumer's likelihood of filing an insurance claim within a given period of time in the future. A financial credit score, on the other hand, is a credit-based statistical analysis of a consumer's likelihood of a credit default within a given period of time in the future.

Note: Your insurance score (and your credit score) isn't adversely affected if you contact several insurance companies for quotes.

Getting a copy of your insurance score and insurance claim report

Fair Isaac Corporation, the provider of FICO credit scores, and ChoicePoint, owned by LexisNexis, are the most well-known developers of insurance scores. Fair Isaac insurance scores range from 300 to 900, and ChoicePoint scores range from 300 to 997. To find out where you stand on the insurance prettiness scale, you can ask your insurance company for your number. You may find when you ask that your insurance company considers this information to be proprietary, but in the land of the free, you can almost always get someone to sell you a score.

For a fee ($12.95 at the time of publication), you can get a copy of your LexisNexis Attract insurance score by going to `https://personalreports.lexisnexis.com/lexisnexis_attract_score.jsp`. While you're on the LexisNexis website, you can get a copy of your C.L.U.E. personal property and auto reports at no charge under the annual disclosure rules of the Fair and Accurate Credit Transactions Act (FACT Act or FACTA; I explain the basics of this act in Chapter 5). Consumers who don't have Internet access can order their reports by mail at C.L.U.E. Inc. Consumer Disclosure Center, P.O. Box 105295, Atlanta, GA 30348-5295, or call toll-free to 866-312-8076. LexisNexis also offers what's known as a full file disclosure that covers your insurance, employment, and tenant histories all in one swoop. Get a copy by following the instructions at `https://personalreports.lexisnexis.com/access_your_personal_information.jsp`.

Figuring out what to do with your newfound knowledge

After you have a copy of your insurance claim report, take the time to check it out. If you believe any of the information on your report is incorrect or incomplete, you can file a dispute, just like you would with one of the credit-reporting agencies, by following the instructions included with the report. All claims will be verified or removed. You can also include an explanation regarding any information that's factually correct but may warrant more discussion. Send disputes to LexisNexis Risk Solutions, LLC, P.O. Box 105295, Atlanta, GA 30348; or call 866-820-8976.

A small but still bright spot in the insurance underwriting process is that if you don't get the best rate available because of information contained in your credit report, you have to be told about it, and you can get a free copy of the credit report used (this is in addition to the free annual credit report you're automatically entitled to). Be sure to check the report carefully for the usual errors and out-of-date information. Dispute any mistakes you find and then ask for a premium recalculation by your insurer. (See Chapter 7 for more details on this.)

Taking other factors into account

Be aware that insurers and credit-scoring suppliers have no responsibility to take into account catastrophic events that may damage your credit score directly or indirectly. Consider adding a statement to your credit report and contacting your insurer for a rate review if, for example, you were unable to pay bills on time because

- ✔ You were injured or seriously ill and hospitalized
- ✔ You live in an area hit by a natural disaster such as a hurricane and were unable to mail and pay your bills on time because of the storm's effects
- ✔ Your company closes and you lose your job

Insurers may use more than your own credit history to adjust your rates or deny coverage. They may order reports and/or scores of other persons living at the same address, even if those people aren't listed on the policy. For example, insurers may consider unnamed persons' driving records at the same address. If you purchased an item or property with a former spouse and that person defaults or pays late, even if the property and debt responsibilities have been reassigned by court order, your credit history and score may be adversely affected, which in turn may affect the cost of your insurance premiums. For more on the credit impacts of divorce, see Chapter 11.

Chapter 11

Keeping Your Credit Great When Faced with Major Life Events

. . . .

In This Chapter

▶ Creating good credit as a twosome

▶ Sheltering your credit in a divorce

▶ Maintaining your credit after losing your job

▶ Handling debt incurred because of medical bills or the death of a spouse

▶ Using credit wisely in retirement

. . . .

*L*ife events often take on a life of their own. By this I mean that you may plan to get married, but few of us plan to get divorced. You may plan to get a job and end up unemployed. You plan time at the gym to be healthy but may not plan for illness and subsequent medical debts. And in the end, you may be a whiz at retirement planning, but have you planned how to handle your credit when your loved one passes on?

That's what this chapter is all about. Building on Chapter 10, which linked your life goals to your credit, here you find what you need to know to survive the twists and turns that life events surprise you with.

No matter what life throws at you, you're better able to cope if you maintain your good credit. In marriage or divorce, in employment or unemployment, in sickness or in health, knowing how to keep your finances and credit under control makes your recovery faster and stronger.

In this chapter, I offer you credit insights into some of what I call life's personal events and offer strategies to help you make the most of these too often credit-challenging situations. I show you ways to manage your credit for your maximum benefit as you journey through your own personal odyssey. So for all of you embarking on the sea of life for the first time or for the last, this chapter's for you.

Tying the Knot in Life and in Credit: A Couples' Guide to Building Good Credit

Nothing is more positive or hopeful than deciding to get married. And nothing can be as potentially dangerous to your credit and finances. Keeping your credit in its best shape can be tricky enough when you're making financial decisions on your own. Add the emotion and excitement of another person to the mix, and the process can get out of hand unless you're careful. On the positive side, marriage also offers opportunities for at least one of the partners to improve his or her credit standing if it's less than stellar initially. In the following sections, I offer you my very best hopes for the future, along with advice to match.

Engaging in premarriage financial discussions

Understanding and communicating with your spouse is critical in all aspects of married life, but especially when it comes to financial issues. I advise all engaged couples to spend significant time discussing and exploring how they plan to handle their finances, what their credit looks like, how they'll pay their bills, and what their long-term financial goals are. After all, new couples want to continue their honeymoon phase as long as possible, and arguing over finances does nothing to achieve that goal. The following sections help you begin the communication and budgeting processes.

Identifying and agreeing on your major money issues

If you're soon to be married or partnered (or even if you already are and haven't yet talked money), you need to openly discuss a range of money issues, including your current credit and financial status. If you could live on love, the conversation would be unnecessary, but if you two pool your resources, you need to determine together how your credit and your money plans will affect your lives as a married couple.

Here's a list of ten things you need to do with your betrothed before the wedding day. If you're already married and you haven't yet discussed these issues, the sooner you do so, the better:

- ✔ **Show each other your credit reports and credit scores.** Discuss what you see, but don't judge.

- ✔ **Discuss your current annual income and your income hopes for the future.** This is a chance to show support, not to criticize.

- ✔ **Determine your financial style — are you a saver or a spender?** Find out the same about your spouse.

✔ **Talk about your debts and how you plan to handle them.** Will you each pay your own debts? Will you pool them together and split them 50-50? Or will the bigger earner pay more?

✔ **Tell each other about any major negative financial events in your past.** For some this may be outstanding (or defaulted) student loans; for others in second marriages, a bankruptcy will be around longer than the kids, and you wouldn't forget to talk about *them*.

✔ **Discuss your spending and budgeting habits (whether you're frugal, indulgent, or don't even know how to budget).** The frugal one may be the best choice to handle your bill paying.

✔ **Talk about whether you've cosigned any loans.** Cosigning for an old flame may be forgiven, but hiding it won't.

✔ **Discuss your personal budgeting approaches.** Will you count every penny or go for estimates instead? Yes, you need a budget!

✔ **Discuss your financial goals for the next five years.** Make this fun. After all this is all about dreams and hopes. No wet blankets allowed!

✔ **Talk about your long-term financial goals and how you'll fund them.** Will you retire at 50? Sail around the world? Give all your worldly possessions to charity?

Looking ahead to "dessert"

When my wife, Barbara, and I go out to dinner, she always looks at the dessert menu first. In the beginning of our courtship, this behavior baffled me. As a typical linear-thinking man, I approached my meal choices in the order I planned to consume them — starter, salad, entrée. In fact, I typically wouldn't even think about dessert until I was sopping up the last of the marinara sauce from my plate.

Finally, I got up the nerve to ask her about this display of, in my view, backward behavior. She explained that dessert, for her, was the most important part of the meal, and she wanted to plan ahead to accommodate what for her was a priority. If she saw bread pudding (her favorite) on the menu, she'd go for a light entrée or salad and skip the bread. If the dessert choices were just so-so, she'd order a heartier main course and perhaps take an extra piece of bread.

Although my wife's logic, as always, is different from my own (and usually right), her approach to dining out is a great way to look at household budgeting. Focus on the goal (like traveling to an exotic destination or buying your dream home) instead of zeroing in on all the mundane bills and expenses of everyday life. This approach has served our relationship well.

Oh, and just in case you were wondering, over the years, I've adjusted to my wife's ordering style in restaurants. I'm no longer a bemused bystander but often an active participant. If, for example, she's saving up for that decadent chocolate cheesecake but is tempted by the featured entrée, I offer to order the fat main course and give her a few bites, and she settles for a salad. But, of course, she has to share her dessert!

I strongly advise that you each get copies of your credit report when your relationship turns serious. Credit is a critical relationship factor, and bad credit can be a deal breaker. You may have bared your heart and soul to your sweetie, but until you bare your credit, the job's not done. Flip to Chapter 7 to discover how to get copies of your credit report.

Building a budget for your new life together

I strongly recommend that you and your partner sit down and make out a budget for your new household. Budgeting is among the most important first steps you can take together to strengthen your relationship and reduce the risk of a split due to financial stress and spending incompatibility.

Explore together and agree on what you want to save for, such as a family, a house, a cat or two (my wife made me put that in), or early retirement. This discussion paves the way for all the saving steps you want to establish in order to reach your goal. You also need to budget for the everyday stuff (think utilities, transportation, food, housing, and the like). If you find that you just aren't able to get the numbers to add up, you can always consider a credit counselor. Good credit counselors aren't just for credit, debts, or problems — they can help you plan a budget before disaster strikes. (See Chapter 15 for more on credit counseling.)

Chapter 4 includes suggestions on how to budget. The CD also has a number of resources that can get you going.

When working with your budget, always start with the fun part: your future goals. What could be more inspiring than describing all the things you're going to do and the adventures you'll share together over the years? For example, my wife and I are planning an extended road trip looking for the perfect piece of blueberry pie.

Through a commitment to maintaining communication, establishing common goals, and working together for mutual benefit, couples can achieve financial bliss.

Considering joint accounts

If your sweetheart has a less-than-glowing credit history, it will affect *you* as soon as you apply for credit together and open joint accounts. Why? Because the bank reviews both of your credit histories. You each keep your own original history, but in addition, your new joint accounts appear on both of your credit reports. So if you're concerned that your spouse may not be as diligent as you are in paying bills on time, paying the bills yourself is a good idea.

Many couples decide to merge their financial accounts because consolidated accounts often make for easier record keeping and enhance that feeling of togetherness. But beware: Both of you are equally responsible for all debt incurred in any joint credit accounts. Regardless of which one of you takes the credit card out for a joy ride, if you miss a payment on a joint account, that missed payment negatively affects both of your credit records. Also, if you miss a payment on an individual account, that missed payment may affect your ability to open joint accounts because both credit histories are considered.

In those states with community-property laws, you may be responsible for your spouse's debts even if you aren't on the account. As long as the debt is incurred during the marriage, you're liable, even if you receive no benefit from it or don't even know about it. Currently, 9¾ states fall into this category: Arizona, California, Idaho, Louisiana, Nevada, New Mexico, Texas, Washington, and Wisconsin. Alaska has an opt-in provision (so I count it as half), and Puerto Rico has community-property laws but isn't a state (so I count it as a quarter).

Even if you decide to consolidate your accounts with your spouse, always keep at least one credit account in your own name as a safeguard in the event of an emergency. Keeping an individual account can also be a good thing in the event of divorce or the untimely death of a spouse; having your own account can help you reestablish an individual credit history.

Keeping separate accounts

If you have a credit-challenged spouse or partner or if you're merely cautious and want to take the credit-sharing slowly, you can always keep separate accounts and allow each other to be authorized users on your accounts. Both of you can charge on the account, both of you get the credit history reported on your credit reports, but only one of you is responsible for the bill.

Although this strategy can safeguard your credit score from a late payment, it also exposes you to the *potential* of at least one bigger-than-expected bill (if your spouse or partner is a dangerous shopaholic, this setup won't protect you from his or her spending). But if you can trust your sweetheart not to go crazy with the credit card, this method allows him or her to add additional credit history while you keep responsibility for and overall control of the account in your hands. (And, of course, if your sweetie gets out of control with the credit card, you can always remove him or her from the account.)

Provided you don't live in a community-property state (see the nearby "Considering joint accounts" section for a list of these), separate accounts can really make sense, especially if you and your spouse or partner have come together later in life and each of you has substantial assets of your own. As long as you both agree, this sort of financial independence can keep you looking attractive to your sweetie long after your personal charms have become less charming. It can also help each of you to feel that youthful independence and financial vigor that only money of your own can provide. For my birthday one year, my fab wife took me, at her exclusive expense, to Walt Disney World. If we had merged all our finances, she couldn't have done this without spending at least some of my money. Happy Birthday to me!

Managing joint debt

Talking to your creditors is hard, but talking to your sweetie about money may be even more daunting. Dealing with joint debt isn't necessarily twice as difficult as dealing with debt alone — it can easily be 20 times harder! If you're trying to keep your bad credit from getting worse and you have some joint debt involved, you may well feel as though your situation is out of control. And it may be.

The most helpful tool at your disposal is communication. Here's what you and your partner need to discuss:

- ✔ **Agreeing on goals:** Starting here is important. This conversation is about the future, and setting goals gives you a shared positive future that you both buy into as the impetus to make some changes in your lives. Goals may include saving for college tuition, retirement, or vacations. In the goal-setting process, you don't have to be specific the first time around. After you get through all the steps that follow, I suggest you go back to the goals and put a price tag and date on each. Then rework the savings and spending plan to see how many goals you can fit in and what needs to be cut or delayed. Keep in mind that your goals will change over time. Refer back to these shared goals as you continue talking.

- ✔ **Eliminating debt:** Remember that you're trying to keep bad credit from getting worse, so determining the best way to eliminate debt is a priority. How much can you allot each month for paying off debt? While paying down debt, agree that neither one of you will add to credit card balances.

- ✔ **Paying bills:** If possible, pay bills together so you both know how much you owe each month and where your money is going. Decisions that need to be made, such as how much to pay on a particular credit card balance, can be determined together.

- ✔ **Keeping track of check-writing:** Make sure that you both record any checks you write in one place so that you can keep up with your balance. The same goes for using your ATM or debit card; you both need to record expenses. If you have separate accounts, decide who pays what and let each other know how things go with your respective bills.

- ✔ **Saving:** Come to an agreement as to how much you can afford to put aside in savings each month. At an early point in your financial life, you may save only $5 or $10 a paycheck. But the key is to start a habit; the savings *will* add up over time.

Now that you have the good feelings flowing and a plan in place, make a commitment with your significant other to track your progress, communicate regularly about your finances, and avoid making large purchases without discussing them with each other first.

Avoiding money conflicts

The moose on the table. The elephant in the room. These are just a couple of the euphemisms I've heard to describe those huge, looming issues that couples or families pretend don't exist. But ignoring credit and money conflicts is done at great peril to a marriage. As in the case of the elephant, you can pretend it's not there, but it will still wreck your home.

Too often, couples who thought they were in perfect — though unspoken or assumed — agreement find out after the nuptials that they're polar opposites when it comes to spending, borrowing, and saving. If you talk with your spouse about your finances, you shouldn't run into credit conflicts — certainly not any that destroy your marriage. But money seems to be a taboo topic, even among married couples. Couples often don't discover money conflicts until that bounced check, late payment notice, or mammoth-sized credit card balance shows up, and by then, the discussion may not be pretty.

Lack of careful and constant communication about money can lead to irreconcilable differences that result in divorce. When divorce is on the horizon, you see how the fighting can escalate. Here are some of the pitfalls I hope you can avoid:

- **Not being open with each other about how you see and value savings, money, and credit:** Silence is your enemy. The list in the "Identifying and agreeing on your major money issues" section earlier in the chapter can help you start a money-focused discussion you might otherwise put off.

- **Pooling all your funds, earnings, and credit:** Keeping some credit in your own name is important. The same goes for money. How much? Enough so that you feel comfortable!

- **Surprising your partner with a big expenditure (a car, boat, home theater, designer shoes, large donation to the cat-rescue fund, and so on):** Spending joint money without consulting your spouse is a big no-no. Determine together an amount over which you need consultation to purchase an item, such as more than $100. You'll both be looking at any household purchases for a long time, so before you buy that great moose head to hang over the bed, talk about it.

- **Criticizing your partner's money style in front of others:** No one wants to be ridiculed in front of others, even in good humor. If you're uncomfortable with your mate's spending behavior, talk about it when the two of you are alone.

- **Failing to set mutual goals:** Discuss your goals and agree on a plan for achieving them. (Turn to Chapter 4 for budgeting advice.)

- **Not meeting your financial obligations:** If you're unable to pay a bill that's your responsibility, let your spouse or partner know as soon as possible.

✔ **Letting kids set the rules:** Kids know how to play one of you against the other to get what they want. This time-tested kid strategy can lead to discipline issues and fights between Mom and Dad. If you have a blended household (kids from different marriages), establishing the rules and standing together as a united front are especially important.

Protecting Your Finances in a Divorce

Marriage is to me the ultimate expression of hope for the future. When that hope goes unfulfilled, you may be faced with the prospect of a divorce, which can impact your credit and finances. If your financial and credit life was challenging as a married couple sharing a common future, in divorce it may become even more so. To add to the stress of the moment, you may find that some of your expenses are greater as you separate into two households (for example, you may have two mortgage or rent payments every month). The financial fallout from divorce can also include difficulties in opening new accounts and obtaining new loans in your name. The sections that follow outline the steps you can take to protect and, if need be, restore your good credit in the event of a divorce.

Taking precautions when a split-up looms

If you suspect that a divorce may be in your future, I suggest you consider the following. (Even if things end up working out for the better, these strategies are still worth considering.)

✔ **Keep good credit in your own name.** A couple of different types of accounts — such as revolving (credit card), installment (car loan), and retail (department store card) — should be sufficient.

✔ **Build your own credit while you're married.** Remember that your credit score is made up mostly of the amount you owe and whether you pay on time. (For the scoop on all the components that make up your credit score, turn to Chapter 6.)

✔ **Open your own bank account with checking and savings features.** Overdraft protection is a plus.

✔ **Keep track of your joint credit accounts by checking your credit report frequently or by enrolling in a credit-monitoring service.** Doing so may provide you with an early warning that your partner is having some issues. At a minimum, check one of your three credit reports every four months. (Chapter 7 explains how to obtain copies of your credit report from Equifax, Experian, and TransUnion — the three major credit bureaus.)

Preparing your credit before heading to court

If the possibility of divorce becomes a reality, you want to ratchet up your credit-protection action. At this point, quickly separating your financial selves to the best of your ability is important. Here's how:

- ✔ **Inform your other half that you're closing joint accounts, and then send a letter to each joint creditor asking that the account be closed to any new activity.** Closing the accounts protects you. Telling the other person in advance allows your partner to make other plans and is the decent thing to do. Just don't wait too long to send the letters.

- ✔ **Attempt to agree on how joint or community property accounts will be paid and who'll be responsible for making the payments.** If you can't reach an agreement, make the minimum payments yourself so that your credit doesn't deteriorate. You can always recoup the money in a reconciliation or divorce settlement; just keep track of what you pay.

- ✔ **Transfer joint balances to individual accounts, if at all possible.** Also, include a division of joint debts as a stipulation in your divorce decree, with specific amounts assigned to each person.

- ✔ **Build individual credit as soon as possible.** Start small and build up gradually if you have to. If your credit is damaged already, start with a credit card that has a small credit limit — perhaps a card from a local department store, gas station, or credit union. After paying your bills on time for six months or so, apply for another card and continue paying bills consistently. (Check out the section "Getting new credit in your own name" later in the chapter for more info.)

- ✔ **Check your credit more frequently than normal.** Consider subscribing to a credit-monitoring service or freezing your credit to avoid any new accounts being added.

Even if your prospective ex is uncooperative, keep paying at least the minimums on all joint bills on time. Don't listen to uninformed but well-meaning friends and relatives who may tell you to ignore making payments or to run up debts to spite your ex. Missed payments generally stay on your credit profile for seven years, making it hard or more costly to obtain new credit, employment, insurance, and maybe even a new spouse.

If you change your name, be sure to write to all your creditors and the three bureaus to let them know. Doing so helps keep errors based on name mix-ups from affecting your credit history.

Your joint credit history may outlast your marriage

From the time you open your first joint account, you and your mate link your credit futures together. Your personal credit history and credit score are now influenced by the behavior of your spouse or partner. A blemish on his or her part is a blemish on yours, too.

How long do you have to suffer from your ex's joint-account misdeeds? Conventional wisdom says seven years, but what if I told you it could be longer? Maybe *much* longer. Just look at the numbers: Negative credit items are reported for seven years in most cases. Your ex's credit may be part of your credit report for seven years from whichever event happened last:

✔ Your honey first forgot to pay the credit card bill.

✔ You got that notice saying that your ex was 60 days late.

✔ Your ex's loan charged off after going six months past due.

If the bill goes to court after the six months of charging off, and if the creditor goes for a wage garnishment (which precipitates a bankruptcy filing), the original account is reported for seven years, as is the public record of the court action. The bankruptcy overlaying that, however, is reported for up to ten years.

It can get even worse in certain situations, but I think the point is made. 'Till debt do you part — but your spouse's debts may be with you for a long, long time after you go your separate ways.

Protecting your credit in a divorce decree and beyond

When the judge rules in your divorce decree, be sure that all joint debts are clearly and specifically assigned and that both you and your ex understand that these debts must be paid on time. Close all remaining joint accounts by the date on which the divorce is granted. In the case of joint real estate that will eventually be disposed of, the party living on the property has the most interest in making sure that the payments are made and should ask the judge to rule that the person in the house will send in the payments, even if the money to make the payments has to come from the other party.

A divorce decree doesn't end either party's responsibility for joint debts incurred while married, including individual debts in community-property states (see the section "Considering joint accounts," earlier in the chapter, for a list of these states). After all, you both promised the lender that you'd repay the loan. The fact that the judge says that only one of you has to make the payment from now on doesn't change your contract with your lender. Each person is fully responsible for the entire balance of joint accounts, from credit cards to car loans to home mortgages.

The following sections help you figure out your next steps after your divorce is finalized.

Overcoming your ex's defaults on your joint accounts

Given the stress associated with divorce, the fact that your ex may miss a payment or two is almost understandable. I said *almost*. Although you may be understanding of such a mishap, keeping your credit record as clean as possible is critical in order to rebuild a positive credit history as a single person.

Because you want to address any missed payments as soon as possible, you need to stay up-to-the-minute on payment status. You may find out about a delinquency in a number of ways: a letter, a phone call, a duplicate billing statement (you can request one), a website visit, or a credit-monitoring service. As soon as you know that a payment wasn't made, take action.

- ✔ **If your relationship allows, contact your ex to find out whether the bill has been paid.** If trust is a concern or if your relationship precludes such direct communication, let the lawyers handle it. Instruct your attorney to notify your ex's attorney that the court order has been violated, and ask for a response.

- ✔ **If the situation isn't resolved, you can always go back to court.** You can ask the judge to reorder your ex to pay as agreed or face the not-so-pleasant legal consequences of contempt of court, which can include jail time. Returning to court to enforce the paying of assigned accounts is a lengthy and expensive course of action, so you may consider making the payments yourself if you think the two of you can resolve the issue. Making the payments costs you money but perhaps less than bad credit (not to mention attorney fees) costs you.

By now you've probably figured out two things: Life isn't fair, and paying a bill yourself may be a lot easier than having to deal with your ex and can be beneficial to you in the long run.

Controlling the damages

Credit damage from divorce or its aftermath isn't unusual, but you can take the following steps to lessen the negative impact to your credit report and score:

- ✔ **Pay your bills on time.** Paying on time adds positive credit history on top of any negative history. Over time, your credit score gives a large number of new and positive reports more weight than older negatives. As your credit report ages, older items count for less, so make the most of new credit going forward.

- ✔ **Add a 100-word statement to your credit report.** Through this statement you can explain mitigating circumstances that a prospective lender or employer may not know about when considering your application.

Be careful not to leave this statement on your report longer than you need to because it may draw attention to a past problem that's no longer a factor in your credit score.

✔ **Review your credit report frequently.** Getting copies of your credit reports may be a good investment in controlling unexpected negatives, especially if your ex is still paying off joint or community-property debts. If your ex winds up not paying on a joint account, you'll probably be subject to collection activity and have to pay, or you may end up in a different court. (The rationale here is that creditors shouldn't be made to suffer just because your marriage failed. Poor babies, huh?)

You can pay for monitoring services that alert you to any negative credit-reporting entries as soon as they occur, allowing you to take immediate action to reduce your credit damage. Flip to Chapter 8 for the scoop on credit monitoring.

Getting new credit in your own name

The first step in successfully getting credit in your own name is to find out where your credit stands. Begin by obtaining your credit report and your FICO score or VantageScore (I tell you how to get both in Chapter 7). A good FICO score is between 660 and 725. If you're at 760 or above, you're a FICO High Achiever!

If you have a good credit score

If your FICO score is 660 or above or your VantageScore is in the A to B range, you probably have a good chance of getting new credit in a normal credit environment.

Credit tightens or loosens from time to time. In loose credit periods, a good score gets the job done. In a tight credit environment, a good score may not be enough to get the terms or even the credit you want. I suggest you apply for the following in your own name (this diversity of credit helps you respond to most financial situations that may arise and helps build your credit score with on-time payments):

✔ Checking account

✔ Savings account

✔ Small installment loan (use the savings account for collateral, if you must)

✔ Retail store credit card

✔ Major bank credit card

✔ Library card (because it saves you money on books and videos)

If you have a borderline credit score

If your FICO score is around 660 or less or if your VantageScore is a C or below, your journey toward establishing credit in your own name may be a bit slower. But when you eventually do reestablish credit on your own, you'll most certainly feel better. Begin with the following:

- Checking account
- Savings account
- Passbook loan (secured by your savings account)
- Major bank credit card (if you qualify)
- Secured credit card (if you don't qualify for a credit card). Secured cards give you a line of credit based on a savings deposit to secure the credit line. These show up on your credit report just like an unsecured card; no one but you and the issuing bank will know!
- Retail store credit card (you're likely to qualify if you qualify for the bank credit card)
- Library card (no kidding)

If you apply for a credit card from your credit union or bank and you aren't sure whether you'll qualify, bring your credit report into a branch and have the bank employee look at it rather than the employee pulling your report himself. Why? If the bank declines you, a credit report inquiry won't show up on your credit report and lower your credit score unnecessarily.

If you have a sympathetic parent or relative with decent credit, you may be able to speed up the process of reestablishing credit by having that person cosign for you, but I don't recommend it. Too often this arrangement fails, and relationships are damaged along with credit.

Keeping Credit under Control while Unemployed

Unfortunately, the U.S. job market fluctuates just as the stock market does. The economy has good years and bad years. During bad years you may find yourself laid off or downsized. During good years you may decide the time is right to make a job change on your own volition and for good reasons (getting a new job at higher pay, for example).

The reality is that you can expect that your *employer* will make the decision to say farewell at least once in your career. I can tell you from experience that the event will arrive at the least advantageous time possible. In the following sections, I help you through this almost inevitable fact of modern-day life — temporary unemployment.

Employment information isn't regularly reported as part of your credit report. The credit bureaus don't keep track of where you work or what you earn. So unemployment doesn't show up on your credit record unless you fail to make your payments on time, go over your credit limits, or do something silly, like opening a lot of credit lines just in case you need them.

Preparing your credit for the worst-case scenario

The following suggestions help you protect your credit in case of unemployment.

- ✓ **Start an emergency savings account if you don't have one already.** Fund it regularly so it grows to somewhere between six months' to a year's worth of living expenses (not income — your expenses are supposed to be less than your income). This is a good number to work toward, because six months to a year is how long you're likely to be unemployed if you're caught by surprise.

- ✓ **Keep one or two credit cards or lines of credit open.** Many employers view your credit report when hiring, so you want your report to look its best even if you're unemployed. To do so, make sure you continue to pay your bills on time and keep your credit card balance at less than 50 percent of available credit if possible. (See Chapter 7 for more on what you can do to look "normal" and not raise any red flags on your credit report.)

Using credit when you don't have a job

If you're already unemployed, don't beat yourself up. You're in good company. Many people lose their job, often more than once. But if you've established savings, regardless of the amount, and you have some available credit lines, you have two tools that are a big help to get you through this time without damaging your credit. You can put together a new plan that includes finding that new job and a budget that works while you do so. This section tells you how.

Stay away from using cash advances on your credit cards! Spending money this way is much more costly than simply using the credit card to pay for items. Cash advances incur an extra fee, usually have a much higher interest rate than purchases, and often have a lower limit than your credit limit.

Looking at credit differently

When you're unemployed, you move from spending resources to *conserving* them, a situation that calls for you to change your credit-use priorities and really start looking at credit differently. While you were employed and making a regular income, you may have used credit in a different way from cash. You may also have used it for larger purchases that you needed some time to pay off.

When you're unemployed, possibly for longer than you anticipate, you don't have those earnings coming in (you may have funds from a severance package or unemployment benefits, but they're only temporary, and they may not last as long as your unemployment does). At the point when you have little to no funds coming in, you may need to use credit for basic living and job-hunting expenses only. This is just about the opposite of what most people will tell you, but you'll do this only for a limited period of time and for a specific, worthy purpose. If it helps, think of this approach as borrowing money to invest in a surefire investment: yourself and your future.

Preserve your cash for as long as possible by using credit first. You want to keep your cash because you can't replace it after it's gone. This advice may contradict what you've heard in the past. Conventional wisdom says to control expenses by paying cash for as many things as possible. But when you're unemployed, the opposite is the case. Pay with credit *for essentials* as much as possible and save the cash. You can limit your overall spending to just the essentials by closely following a budget (see the following section).

Refiguring the family budget

With your reduced resources, cutting back spending to only the basic needs is essential. Begin by sitting down with your family and discussing the situation and the need to temporarily reduce expenses. Don't be embarrassed in front of the kids. This situation is an important lesson in reality for them. And you can show them how adults face difficult issues and win.

The CD includes worksheets that are helpful in putting together a spending plan/budget. For additional budgeting pointers, whether you need to start a budget from scratch or revise a budget that you've already created, turn to Chapter 4.

If your severance is being paid out over time or you haven't yet received it, ask your employer or human resources department to raise your deductions to the maximum allowed. The IRS wants a report of anyone with more than ten deductions, so you should generally ask for ten (after all, you don't want the IRS looking at you if you can avoid it). This strategy results in more cash flowing through to you for the present, when you need it. Yes, you may owe some taxes on this money in April (though your deductible job-hunting expenses and reduced earnings for the year may offset that). But you want to maximize today's income at the possible expense of tomorrow's demands.

Getting credit counseling to help

If you're overwhelmed and think you can benefit from some professional perspective or guidance, go to an accredited credit counselor. You can get more information on credit counselors and where to find them in Chapter 15.

Protecting your credit lines

The downside to using your lines of credit for your basic living expenses while unemployed (a strategy I recommend) is that you *may* do some damage to your credit. Here are some tips for protecting your credit status while you leverage your available credit to help you get through this challenging time:

- **Keep balances at less than 50 percent of your available credit limit.** If it becomes necessary, spread your credit use over several accounts to keep your balance on each credit card at less than 50 percent. For example, rather than have a $2,000 balance on one card and a zero balance on three other cards, consider spreading the amount over all four cards equally, with each balance at $500.

- **Make all payments on time.** Remember that 35 percent of your credit score has to do with whether you make payments on time. (For the full scoop on the various components that go into your credit score, see Chapter 6.)

- **Pay the car loan first.** A car can get repossessed in as little as two weeks. Then how will you get to work when you do find a job to earn the money to pay the mortgage?

- **Pay your mortgage a very close second.** Not all bills are created equal, and your mortgage is among the most unequal of them all. Partial payments don't work, and falling behind 90 days begins a very difficult-to-stop foreclosure process.

Don't contact your creditors unless you *know* you're going to default. If you just *think* you may miss a payment, it's none of their business. If, however, you know you're going to miss the current month's payment, telling them before it happens is important. Why? Because you'll have more options if you do.

If you have any income, ask for a *hardship program* (a special repayment arrangement that may be offered to a good customer in need of some extra help). Such programs tend to last for no more than three to six months. Most credit grantors have them, but the hardship has to be real and imminent, and you have to ask for it.

What to do when you run out of credit and options

If you aren't able to make any payments on maxed-out credit cards or credit lines and you still have no job on the horizon, something has to give. This triangle has only three sides: income, expenses, and credit. If credit isn't an option, income and expenses are the only things you can alter.

Take out that budget you prepared when your unemployment started and consider some extreme moves to cut expenses. Can you move to a smaller home? Can you move in with a friend? Can you sell things to raise some cash? On the income side, have you considered taking a job to tide you over until something in your field opens up? The goal here is to generate some income, not move a career forward. *Remember:* Given time and perseverance, you *will* come out of unemployment stronger than you went in.

If the hardship program isn't sufficient to bridge the gap between what you can afford to pay and what the creditors insist you pay, send a letter stating that you can't make any payments but that you intend to in the future, as soon as you find employment. An example "Unemployment Letter" of this type appears on the CD.

Curing Medical Debt

Little in life can seem more unfair than medical debt. You didn't ask for it, you got no pleasure from it, but you owe it just the same. Medical debt isn't much different from any other type of unsecured debt except that it tends to come quickly and in large amounts. The key to curing medical debts is to be proactive by negotiating discounts before a service is provided or, in the case of overwhelming debt, to cut your losses early.

If you have health insurance coverage, your approach to maintaining your credit is different from the approach you'd take if you didn't have insurance, at least initially. Even if you're insured, dealing with health insurance and how it covers your medical bills can be a complicated and stressful issue. Not to worry though. The sections that follow cover the relevant issues concerning medical debt and your credit report.

Reviewing your options for paying medical bills

When faced with a pile of medical bills, you have five main options:

- ✔ You can work with the healthcare provider to pay them off over time.
- ✔ You can seek assistance from a patient advocate resource
- ✔ You can seek medical debt consolidation.
- ✔ You can attempt to negotiate your bills down (this works just like when you settle credit card debt).
- ✔ You can file for bankruptcy.

If you know in advance that you'll be incurring uninsured medical expenses and don't know whether you can afford them, I suggest that you speak to your service providers as soon as possible. Ask if discounts are available for under/uninsured patients. (Note that you may have to provide financial disclosures to qualify for these discounts.) Be sure to get all agreements in writing so there's no misunderstanding about what everyone agrees to.

Applying for medical financial aid

Many hospitals provide charitable or financial aid to people who qualify. Many clinics and doctors' offices also consider helping those who can prove they're under unusual financial duress because of escalating medical bills or decreasing incomes. However, if you decide to apply for assistance, you may be better off doing so as soon as possible because many providers have time limits on aid applications (usually 6 to 12 months).

Although you have to complete a substantial amount of paperwork and supply a lot of information, you may wipe thousands of dollars off your financial ledger.

Getting professional help

Help is available to the consumer in the form of advocates. A number of organizations, some nonprofit, help you negotiate fees and payments or just get through the process of filling out the forms you're likely to encounter in the bill negotiation process.

Some advantages to using intermediaries are

✔ They know the industry, the laws, and the regulations.

✔ They're not emotionally involved.

✔ They've done this before, and you may not have.

✔ They may help identify benefits, grants, and entitlements.

✔ They may have developed existing relationships that can be helpful in resolving issues more quickly.

The Patient Advocate Foundation is a nonprofit organization that for 14 years has provided mediation and arbitration services nationally. It offers assistance to patients dealing with the effects of chronic, debilitating, or life-threatening illnesses. Some of its free services include resolving insurance access issues, helping with employment issues for patients, and assisting with medical debt crisis. Reach the organization at 800-532-5274 or www.patientadvocate.org.

You can find fee-for-service advocate organizations on the Internet but you may want to check out:

✔ Healthcare Advocates, Inc. They know the industry, the laws, and the regulations to help you get the best healthcare: http://healthcare advocates.com/index.html

✔ Medical Billing Advocates of America. They help you cut your medical costs by manually reviewing each charge to verify that your insurance payments are not shorted: http://billadvocates.com/findanadvocate/tabid/69/Default.aspx

Financing your medical debt

Having one bill to deal with may be easier for some than keeping track of many service provider payments. Here are the two ways you can consolidate your medical debts:

✔ **Paying with credit cards:** Putting your medical debt on a credit card may seem like a way to just make the problem go away, if only for a billing cycle. But what you're really doing is borrowing money from a lender to pay a medical provider. You may be better off dealing with an individual provider than with a lender if you have a hardship.

If you opt to use plastic to cover your bills, be sure that you can afford your payments, that you know what interest rate your card charges, and that you're aware of any possible issues this may cause, such as affecting your eligibility for Medicaid (medical debt on a credit card may no longer qualify as a medical expense).

> Be sure to consider a new card or one that has a balance transfer option with a long, low introductory interest rate to keep payments affordable.

✓ **Paying with installment loans:** Another option is to get an installment loan from your bank or credit union. This type of loan has a fixed interest rate, term, and payment. Under the Fair and Accurate Credit Transactions Act (FACT Act or FACTA), lenders can't use your medical condition against you when they decide whether to give you credit and when they establish terms. To help ensure enforcement of this requirement, your consumer copy of your credit report shows the name of the creditor so you can identify the debt. To protect your privacy, others ordering your report would see only the generic descriptor "medical payment data."

Negotiating your debt down

Believe it or not, you can actually negotiate medical expenses. Most providers have more than one rate for the same service or product — the insured price and the uninsured price. Because they negotiate prices in advance, many insurers get much lower pricing than you do. Asking for a discount is nothing new, and asking for at least the insurance company pricing shouldn't cause any heart rates to rise at your provider's office.

If you're not comfortable attempting to negotiate medical charges yourself, try working with a patient advocate group that has experience in this area. To find one, refer to the "Getting professional help" section earlier in the chapter.

Filing for medical bankruptcy

You may hear the term *medical bankruptcy* touted as though it's something different from a regular bankruptcy, but technically the two are the same. Personal bankruptcies are generally either a Chapter 7 or a Chapter 13. A Chapter 7 eliminates many but not all debts, and to qualify you have to pass a means test based on your state's median income. A Chapter 13 bankruptcy allows you to repay what you can, from current earnings typically over a five-year period, and is not income restricted.

A medical bankruptcy is a bankruptcy brought on by medical bills that are either so large or owed to such aggressive providers or collectors that they can't be satisfied. No one I know of is happy when forced to consider bankruptcy. However, in the case of overwhelming medical debts, you need to be

✓ Realistic in assessing whether you'll ever be able to repay what you owe.

✓ Certain you know the full extent of what you owe and to whom you owe it.

What to do when your insurance company denies payment

If your insurance covers only a portion of a bill and you can't afford the balance, rather than letting the bill go to collections, which damages your credit, you have a couple of alternatives:

✔ **You can ask for a discount.** The big insurance companies ask for discounts all the time, and the hospitals grant them. Don't be afraid to ask.

✔ **You can ask the doctor to accept the insurance payment amount as payment in full.** Doctors do this all the time. Doctors in a network get whatever the insurer pays. The doctor agrees to this arrangement upfront in order to be a member of the network and get referrals. You may be able to get the same deal if you ask.

After you know that your bills are insurmountable and providers won't accept reduced payments that you can afford, see an attorney to assess and plan your best legal options. To be sure that a bankruptcy is in your best interest, use an attorney that specializes in debt problems. A nonspecialist may leave debts out of a filing or expose your assets to claims. Factors like income, recency of debt acquisition, and homestead exemptions are examples of items that can be overlooked.

Going without medical treatment isn't an option just because you can't afford to pay for it.

Discovering how insurers get your medical information

Whether you like it or not, insurers have access to your medical records and prescription drug records, thanks to the MIB and the newer prescription drug databases. When I say MIB, I'm not referring to the Men In Black but to the even more mysterious Medical Information Bureau, that maintains a database that's home to health-related information on more than 15 million people. Insurance companies use and share the MIB's information to supplement their underwriting before pricing their services or issuing you life, disability, or individual health insurance products. And that information isn't always accurate.

Settling medical debts

You or your attorney may be able to settle your medical debts rather than declare bankruptcy. In a settlement, a partial repayment that you can afford is negotiated and agreed to. Upon payment of the less-than-full balance, the remainder of the debt is forgiven. I recommend using an attorney for the negotiations and to handle the payments. Using a legal professional can be much cheaper and faster in the end. The forgiven portion of debts may be considered taxable income, so be sure to consider this in a decision whether to settle or file bankruptcy. Tax debts aren't usually dischargeable in bankruptcy.

Not everyone has an MIB file. You need to have applied for life, disability, or individual (not group) insurance from an MIB member company previously. Information about your health or longevity is sent to MIB by the Member company in a coded, encrypted format. The data identifies medical conditions or medical tests and a few codes that are non-medical. Those codes report potentially hazardous avocations or hobbies, or results of a motor vehicle report showing a poor driving history.

Insurers also rely on prescription drug databases, such as those operated by Ingenix and Milliman, primarily when you're seeking private health, life, or disability insurance. Prescription drug databases can go back as far as five years, detailing drugs used as well as dosage and refills — and they aren't always error-free either.

You're entitled to copies of the information in your file at the MIB and both prescription drug databases. Simply call the organizations (I provide contact information in Chapter 7) and ask how to obtain your free copy of your records. If you want to dispute any inaccurate information, just follow the instructions on your report. Should the dispute not be resolved to your satisfaction you can submit a statement of dispute which will then become part of your MIB file. From that point forward, any MIB Member that receives your MIB file will also receive a copy of your statement of dispute.

Monitoring insurance claims for errors

You may be tempted to ignore the whole medical-payment process and assume that the insurance company and the doctors will handle everything satisfactorily. But you know better — what can go wrong often does. Claims payments and treatment-authorization communication between doctors and insurance companies are coded, and one misplaced digit can make a big difference in what medical care is paid for or allowed. Catching those small errors early is important, and you, as the party responsible for the bill, have the most at stake.

Between the insurance companies — which have a better day when they don't pay a lot of claims than when they do — and the underpaid help in medical offices and hospitals that must code all your procedures, errors are common, and legitimate claims are sometimes rejected. If your claim is rejected, always ask for the bill to be resubmitted and for an explanation of why it was rejected.

You don't have to be a claims whiz to keep track of your insurance process. Familiarizing yourself with your coverage limits is worth your time. Read through your insurance contracts (sorry, it's not the most scintillating reading). Get a copy of your coverage if you don't already have one. It may be a policy, a booklet, or something called a *summary plan description.* (The insurance policy itself is the best and most complete source.) The health plan description is 20 to 30 pages or more. The devil is in the definitions, so terms you want to pay attention to include the following:

- ✔ **Schedule of benefits:** This explains what the insurance company pays and what you pay — deductibles, percentages, co-pays, and so on.

- ✔ **Covered benefits:** Often separate from the schedule of benefits, this section is a laundry list of what's covered.

- ✔ **Exclusions and limitations:** This section tells you what isn't covered, as well as items covered but with limits.

- ✔ **Claims procedures:** These procedures explain the steps for filing claims and appealing denials. You may want to read all the way through this part, as it usually has some important time limits and details.

Reviewing these key components should give you a good idea of your coverage. If the bills and statements start showing up and you find that keeping track of medical expenses and reimbursements is just too stressful, consider a *daily money manager* (DMM). Relatively new on the scene, a DMM is similar to a personal financial advisor — someone who can provide a wide range of services depending on your needs. This individual can also keep track of medical bills and insurance forms. The best way to find a good DMM is through a referral. If no one you know can direct you to a good DMM, contact the American Association of Daily Money Managers (AADMM) at www.aadmm.com or 877-326-5991.

Dealing with denied medical claims

Most doctors and hospitals don't report payment histories to credit bureaus. They don't like to pay the fees, and some of them don't like to think they're in the credit business. However, if a debt moves from a medical provider to an outside collection agency, odds are it will hit your credit report. The message here is that you have more wiggle room with a medical provider, but be sure to ask whether the provider reports your payment history to one of the credit-reporting agencies.

Managing expenses to avoid credit repercussions

If, when all is said and done, you're still left with medical expenses that you're responsible for paying, you have some options:

✔ **Suggest a reduced repayment amount either in a lump sum (ask the service provider to consider an ease-of-handling discount for cash) or a set payment every month.** Do this before you get billed. When third-party billers get hold of a debt, they're tenacious, and the doctors generally don't want to get in the middle. Deal with the doctor first, if you can.

✔ **Find out whether your hospital is covered under the federal Hill-Burton Act, which prohibits discrimination in providing services.** In 1975, Congress amended the Hill-Burton program, which established federal grants, loan guarantees, and interest subsidies for certain health facilities to require that they must provide uncompensated services forever. The U.S. Department of Health and Human Services at the Health Resources and Services Administration has information about where to find the 190 facilities covered under Hill-Burton. Check out `www.hrsa.gov/gethealth care/affordable/hillburton/ facilities.html`. There are no such facilities in Alaska, Indiana, Minnesota, Nebraska, Nevada, North Dakota, Rhode Island, Utah, or Wyoming.

Keep in touch with the hospital and billing people. They assume that if the insurance company denies the claim, you'll pay the difference. Communicating that you don't consider the claim settled and that you need their help to resubmit or appeal a decision makes them a part of the process and keeps their expectations in line with yours. Just as you take an active role in your healthcare and treatment as a patient, you also have to take an active role in the payment of your medical costs.

If you have a hard time getting your bills covered and you think the insurance company is wrong, take the following steps:

1. **Complain.**

   Most insurance carriers, believe it or not, don't like complaints. Here's a list of people to complain to, starting with the lowest one on the totem pole:

   • Claims adjuster

   • Supervisor

   • Unit manager (over several supervisors by line of business)

   • Assistant manager (over unit managers, but not in all offices)

   • Claims manager or claims vice president (in charge of a local office)

   • Regional claims vice president (in charge of several offices in a region)

   • Home office claims, senior vice president

2. **Maintain detailed records.**

When dealing with insurers, keep records of conversations (times, dates, and what was said), as well as copies of any documents you receive. If you write to an adjuster, copy his supervisor and request a written response in a set time frame.

Despite how frustrated you may be feeling, always be polite and direct. Nasty complaints are easily dismissed or sent to a lawyer.

3. **File a written complaint.**

If you reach an impasse, write to your state insurance regulatory agency. Don't go into great detail; just explain the very basic issues that are in dispute. To find your state regulator online, go to www.naic.org. Complaining to your state regulator is likely to motivate the insurer to pay better attention to resolving your claim.

If you have no insurance, definitely let the doctor or hospital know this fact early on in the process. Then ask about discounts and payment plans, but be sure you can afford the payment plan before you agree to it. (You may want to follow the same process I recommend in the "Keeping Credit under Control while Unemployed" section, earlier in this chapter, which involves resetting your spending priorities until you have the new bills under control.) Being willing to pay a reasonable bill over time is the best course of action to keep any collection activity off your credit record. Communicating with your doctor and hospital is the key.

Resolving Credit Issues after Death

If you've lost a spouse or partner, you're already going through one of the most emotionally draining experiences possible. Unfortunately, in the midst of the often debilitating experience of losing a loved one, numerous financial matters surface, including credit and debt issues.

For one thing, thieves may use the deceased's Social Security number and identity to open fraudulent credit accounts. Promptly sending a copy of the death certificate to the bureaus can help deter this crime: **Equifax,** P.O. Box 105069, Atlanta, GA 30348; **Experian,** P.O. Box 9530, Allen, TX 75013; **TransUnion,** P.O. Box 6790, Fullerton, CA 92634.

Stabilizing your credit in the event of a death can be difficult, especially if your spouse held all or most of the credit in his or her name. A creditor wants a copy of the death certificate and typically asks the estate to pay the bill. As a rule, you aren't personally responsible for credit held in the deceased's name alone, unless the two of you lived in a community-property state.

In community-property states — Arizona, California, Idaho, Louisiana, Nevada, New Mexico, Texas, Washington, and Wisconsin — credit accounts opened during marriage are automatically considered joint. That means that you're responsible for any debt that your deceased spouse incurred during the marriage. This may also be true in Alaska if you opted for community-property status when you moved there. Although Puerto Rico is an American territory and not a state, it has community-property laws too.

The following sections tell you how to protect your credit when the debts belong to a deceased spouse.

Understanding what happens to joint credit when you're single again

By law, a creditor can't automatically close a joint account or change the terms because of the death of one spouse. Generally, the creditor asks you to fill out a new credit application in your own name. If your creditor doesn't approach you with this option, close the joint account and open a new individual account in your name alone. The creditor then decides whether to continue to extend credit or alter the credit limit. ***Remember:*** You don't have to deal with this the day after your spouse's death, but sooner is better than later because there has been a major change to your account.

Knowing exactly what your liability is

If you're a joint account holder on a credit card or if you live in one of the community-property states noted in the earlier "Resolving Credit Issues after Death" section, you may owe the debts of the deceased. In a community-property state, as long as the debt was incurred during the marriage, even if you received no benefit from it or didn't even know about it, you are still liable.

Terminating the deceased's preapproved credit offers

Credit bureaus automatically update records with periodic reports from the Social Security Administration. When the update is made, your spouse's credit history will be flagged, and his or her name will be removed from any preapproved credit-offer mailing lists. This reduces the mail you get in your spouse's name. You can speed this process up if you notify the three major credit bureaus — Equifax, Experian, and TransUnion (I provide complete contact information for each bureau in Chapter 7).

In states other than the community-property states, credit card debts and other debts that are solely in the name of the deceased aren't passed on to surviving spouses or children. However, notifying creditors is a good idea, even if you aren't liable. They'll ask for proof of death and generally request that a certified copy of the death certificate be forwarded to them to close the account. If the estate has assets, creditors may try to collect any balance due from the estate's executor. If the estate doesn't have enough cash and the assets that can be sold are few, that will generally end the issue.

Some people feel that they should pay their deceased spouse's debts, whether out of a sense of obligation or honor or just to set the record straight. Paying the debt of your deceased spouse isn't necessary unless you're required to do so by law. The creditors understand risk very well and factor it into fees and interest rates. In that regard, they've already been paid. If creditors try to pressure you to pay a debt that you aren't obligated to pay, I recommend telling them to go to *<insert your choice of venues>* and ask there.

Building your credit record on your own

If the deceased was your spouse or life partner and you shared financial matters, you need to reestablish yourself as an individual once again. Your first task is to come up with a budget or spending plan that covers your expenses as a single person. This budget helps you understand how your financial situation has changed, for better or worse. I offer pointers on creating a spending plan in Chapter 4. When setting goals, I suggest you stick to short- and intermediate-term goals until your life has settled down.

When you know where you stand financially, you can begin deciding how you want to use credit. Because your credit score determines what you pay for credit and under what terms it may be available, I suggest you get your FICO score from www.myfico.com, along with your credit report. The better your score, the less you have to pay to borrow or use credit. (For guidance on reviewing your report, flip to Chapter 7.)

Don't close old accounts with positive credit histories unless you have to. The length of time an account is open counts in your favor for credit-scoring purposes. A variety of accounts also helps your score. If you have a mortgage or a car payment and you can afford to pay it off, you may want to consider keeping it open for a short while instead of paying it off, just to keep new positive information flowing into your credit file.

Fitting Credit into Retirement

Up until a certain point in their lives, most people think of their kids or their home as the most expensive part of their financial environment. Then they hit retirement. Retirement may not last as long as your kids or your home, but it does require more saving and planning to be successful. The sooner you begin to plan, save, and invest for your exit from the workforce the better.

Credit can be a help or a hindrance in retirement. On the help side of things, using credit rather than cash can be a great convenience and can add value to your later years if done wisely. But because credit essentially allows you to use tomorrow's income today, when you stop getting raises and find that your income is more or less fixed, you may wind up overusing credit, which can be very difficult to rebound from. To avoid falling into a credit crunch in retirement, make sure you have a solid budget. To do so, you need to know what you're spending and what you have coming in each month. In this section, I present the basics on creating a budget that can set you up well for retirement, and I help you understand how the use of credit changes in this phase of life.

Budgeting on a fixed income

Following are the essential ingredients for successful budgeting (I go into detail about how to construct a budget that works for you, not against you, in Chapter 4):

- ✔ **Set short- and long-term goals.** Whether you're 55 or 95, you need a reason to get up in the morning. Goals provide this and more. Although they may be different from those you had earlier in life, goals, especially around spending, keep you looking forward to tomorrow. They may include traveling to places you've always wanted to see, making a difference in your community, or just seeing more of family.

  Short-term goals for your stage of life should be in the 6 to 12 month range, while longer-term ones may go out to 5 years.

- ✔ **Know your monthly income and expenses.** After you settle on your goals, you need to fund them. Don't guess; know what you can afford. Make sure that you can cover basic recurring monthly expenses, and don't forget to keep an emergency fund. You don't need the standard 12 months of expenses because you won't have to fund a period of unemployment. But you will need to meet any unexpected out-of-pocket expenses like home repairs, a major car repair, or insurance deductibles. Know what your exposure is and set funds aside for it.

- ✔ **Protect your cash.** When your cash is gone, it's gone! Be sure that you control your urge to spend for items not in your budget. Don't use tax-deferred retirement funds to pay off debt if you have any other choice. Although you may be beyond the age of early withdrawal penalties, taxes take a big chunk out of any withdrawals. Use excess cash flow to gradually pay down debt whenever possible. Home equity loans or reverse mortgages may be sources for interest-deductible or tax exempt funds if they fit your goals and plan.

✔ **Control debt payments.** Any new debt payments must fit into your budget. Try to match the time it takes you to pay off a debt with the time you'll be using an item. For example, the debt you incur by paying for a meal out with a credit card should be paid off at the end of the month. The debt you incur for a car should be paid off over the useful life of the car or before you plan to buy a replacement. The debt you incur in buying a home that you intend to live in for the rest of your life need not be paid off until you die.

Using credit for convenience

Although your income may decrease when you hit retirement, your credit history keeps on growing. Great reasons to use credit rather than cash include reward points and easier tracking of expenses. These conveniences add value to the money you spend.

With some simple caveats credit can be as big a boon to seniors as it is to the population as a whole. Here are three easy and simple safeguards for you to consider:

✔ **Never lend your good credit to someone else.** Adding authorized users to your account — to help a friend with bad credit or by cosigning on a loan — usually ends in disaster. Allowing someone else access to your credit gives that person access to your cash and your future well-being; it's absolutely not worth it.

✔ **Don't put yourself in a position to become a victim of credit card fraud.** To avoid becoming just another statistic, be on guard when you use your credit. When shopping online, look for the padlock icon in the address bar or *https* in the URL (website address); both indicate that you have a secure connection. Also, never give credit card information to anyone who contacts you first.

✔ **Check one of your free credit reports every four months, alternating them among the three credit bureaus.** Staying on top of your credit reports is one of the most effective ways to catch credit card fraud early. Be sure to dispute any accounts you don't recognize. They could mean identity theft! For guidance on scoring free copies of your credit reports from the three major credit bureaus, head to Chapter 7.

Chapter 12

Controlling Access to Your Identity

In This Chapter

▶ Using technology safely

▶ Keeping your financial documents secure

▶ Watching for signs of identity theft

*I*dentity theft doesn't involve someone dressing like you and copying your hairstyle. It's much simpler than that. The thief simply acquires and uses the myriad numbers that are associated with your name to become you, electronically and financially. But how does an identity thief get this valuable data about you? Often by stealing your mail, hacking into your computer, breaking into your home, or sifting through receipts and personal information from your trash can.

Depending on what information the thief steals from you, he can use your favorite credit card or open new credit card accounts in your name. He can buy a car in your name, rent an apartment and leave you to pay the damages, order designer furniture, and stay a week at the Ritz in Buenos Aires — all while posing as *you*. And, of course, the thief makes no payments on any of the debts. The negative credit activity is reported on your credit report, and if the thief is lucky — and you aren't — you may not discover him living it up and wrecking your credit rating for months (or maybe longer!). You may only discover your identity has been stolen when you apply for a line of credit and are rejected or when you receive a flurry of aggressive calls from collection agencies for not paying bills of which you aren't even aware.

After you discover the ID theft, you do get to defend yourself and prove the fraudulent accounts aren't yours, but the process can be expensive and may take a long time to resolve. Worse yet, while you're dealing with the mess the thief has made of your finances, you may suffer harassing phone calls and be denied credit or a job because your credit report includes negative information. In this chapter, I tell you the important steps you need to take to protect yourself, your identity, and your credit from identity theft.

Keeping Thieves at Bay

Identity theft was the number one source of consumer complaints in 2010, according to the Federal Trade Commission (FTC). Estimates are that up to 9 million people were victimized in 2010, although only about 200,000 complained to the FTC. Credit card fraud is much less likely.

Your identity may be stolen by a stranger. Then again, as often happens, it may be, and most frequently is, stolen by people whom you know and willingly let into your life, such as friends, relatives, or co-workers. To reduce your chances of falling victim to identity theft, make sure you protect your personal information at home and at work by keeping it secure. In short, don't leave financial or confidential documents out in the open where someone has easy access to them.

In the following sections, I walk you through some simple steps you can take to reduce the chances of your identity being stolen.

Getting on the technology train

One of the easiest ways to protect yourself is to simplify bill-paying, information transfers, and financial transactions by performing them all securely and electronically. Having bills and statements delivered to your password-protected computer is much better than having them delivered to your mailbox outside your home. The stats tell me that the more information you send and receive electronically, the lower your chances of identity theft.

Using a computer has other benefits as well: When you get your information online, as in the case of your bank statement, you can check up on it anytime you want. No need to wait until the end of the month for a statement to arrive. In fact, I recommend that you do a quick once-over of your checking account activity weekly or have preset dollar-level alerts e-mailed or texted to you. For example, you can arrange for transactions that are over $1,000 to generate an e-mail automatically. Set your alert level so that it doesn't result in dozens of notices but does catch transactions you're most concerned about. That way, you can spot a problem early.

Take precautions when conducting business via the Net. As long as you only use secure websites and ensure you're protected by a firewall, you're much better protected than you are with snail mail. (See the next section for info on determining whether a website is secure, and see the section "Safeguarding your computer data" for a few words on firewalls.)

Looking out for phishing scams

Phishing is when a stranger pretending to be someone you trust (for example, a Facebook friend, a credit card company, or a representative of your bank) e-mails you and asks you to confirm critical information about your account (for example, by replying with your password, Social Security number, or other personal information). Phishing can also be perpetrated via a spyware program that you unwittingly download to your computer by clicking a link or opening a file; the program then records your personal information and sends it to the thief.

Phishing scams are increasing and becoming more sophisticated. Bottom line: Think twice before replying to unsolicited requests or giving out your personal information over the Internet. As with phone solicitation, don't give out your personal information unless you initiate the transaction. You can find out more about preventing Internet fraud, securing your computer, and protecting your personal information by visiting www.onguardonline.gov.

Here are some do's and don'ts that can help keep you and your personal info safe:

- ✔ **Do be suspicious of any e-mail with urgent, exciting, or upsetting requests for personal financial info or money.** The sender is using your emotions to stimulate an immediate, illogical response to the request.

- ✔ **Don't give out personal or financial info unless you're certain of the source and you can confirm that the link is secure.** You can tell you're on a secure website if the site's address begins with https:// rather than http://.

    Your e-mails are almost *never* secure, which means you should never e-mail your credit card number, Social Security number, or other personal info to anyone, even someone you're sure you can trust.

- ✔ **Don't ever respond to e-mails that aren't personalized or that have your name misspelled.** If the message has your name wrong or doesn't have your name at all, chances are high it's a fraud.

- ✔ **Don't ever click links in e-mail messages to find out what the great offer is unless it's a service you know you signed up for.** If you click the link, you may end up downloading spyware onto your computer, and your security may be compromised.

- ✔ **Don't unsubscribe to e-mails unless you know you've subscribed in the first place.** Some phishers send you e-mails hoping that you'll respond or unsubscribe, thereby confirming that your e-mail address is valid.

- ✔ **Be careful of e-mails pretending to be from companies you do business with.** I periodically get e-mails that look like they're from banks I use, but the e-mails lack the detailed logo or look and feel of the real companies, or the e-mails ask me to update information that I know the banks already have.

✔ **If you suspect that you're being phished, do forward the e-mail to the Federal Trade Commission at spam@uce.gov and file a complaint with the Internet Crime Complaint Center (IC3) by going to www.ic3.gov.** The IC3 is a partnership among the FBI, the National White Collar Crime Center (NW3C), and the Bureau of Justice Assistance (BJA). The IC3 website not only lets you report suspected Internet fraud but also provides disturbing statistics about this growing crime.

Safeguarding your computer data

You need to safeguard your computer so it doesn't give up its secrets without a fight. Here are some computer-safety rules to consider:

✔ **Don't leave your laptop out where it can be picked up.** Whether at home, in a hotel, or at work, when you're not in the same room as your laptop, put it away and out of sight. Would you leave a $100 bill lying around? The same consideration applies here.

✔ **Don't walk away from your computer and leave files with personal information open, particularly if you're online.** If you're offline, anyone in the room can see your information. If you're online, especially with a broadband connection, your computer can be hacked easily and your data can be stolen, or you can be observed for sensitive information like passwords.

✔ **Come up with a user name and personal identification number (PIN) or password that isn't obvious and set your computer so that this information is required in order to log on to your computer.** You can also use a screensaver that has a password so that if you walk away from your desk for a certain period of time and the screensaver comes on, you need to enter a password to get back to your desktop.

✔ **Include at least one number, capital letter, or special character in your password as a minimum precaution.** A good example is Steve@1. Don't use birth dates or Social Security numbers; they're too easy for hackers to guess.

✔ **Don't use your kid's or pet's name or birthday for your password.** These are easy things for someone who knows you to guess.

✔ **Don't keep a list of your passwords under your keyboard or near the computer.** That's the computer equivalent of leaving your house key under the mat.

✔ **Install a firewall.** A *firewall* is a program or hardware device that filters Internet information before it gets to your computer. If you use a wireless network, make sure the network and firewall are encrypted. (You can get firewalls for your home computer at most office supply stores.)

✔ **Use an antivirus and spyware protection program to keep key loggers off your computer.** *Key loggers* are programs that send out to the crook any information that you type while on your computer, including your credit card numbers, user names, passwords, Social Security number, and so on.

✔ **Make sure to thoroughly delete all personal information on your computer if you decide to get rid of it.** Your best bet is to completely reformat your hard drive, which wipes it clean and gets rid of everything. You may want to format your drive more than once to do a thorough job of permanently erasing data. (Check with your computer manufacturer to find out how to scrub your hard drive.)

Keeping passwords secret

A testament to the trusting nature of Americans is that if you want to know something personal or secret about them, all you have to do is ask. But you'd be wise to keep your computer password secret because it protects you from others — even trusted co-workers — accessing your personal information. To make sure you don't get taken advantage of, follow these suggestions:

✔ **Don't give anyone your password.** If the guy in the next cube wants to be helpful, you can enter your password for him.

✔ **If you have to give out your password, be sure you trust the source, and then change your password immediately.** And by immediately, I mean right after you give out your password. Don't wait until the next day or the next week.

Avoid giving out confidential information to friends, acquaintances, or even your kids. They may not be identity thieves, but they sure are great, naive sources of information.

Protecting your mail

The fact that tampering with the U.S. mail is a federal crime doesn't seem to deter identity thieves from helping themselves to the contents of your mailbox. And your mail often contains sensitive information. For example, although some credit card issuers don't include your full account number on your monthly statement, others still do. And you don't want a thief to have access to your bank account numbers. Unless you use a Uni-ball Gel Pen, which uses the only type of ink that thieves can't acid-wash, an enterprising identity thief can also easily convert that check you sent off for the heating bill into ready cash by acid-washing the original recipient off the check and replacing the name.

Following are some easy ways you can reduce your exposure to mail fraud:

✔ **Convert as much of your financial business to online transactions as you can.** Doing so helps you avoid delivering information to the waiting hands of the criminal scouting your unattended mailbox.

✔ **Explore alternatives to your unlocked, end-of-the-driveway mailbox.** Consider using a post office box or a locked mailbox that accepts mail (not unlike the old slot in the door).

✔ **Don't mail checks or financial information from your home mailbox.** Use your local post office mailbox or bring your mail to work with you. (Don't forget the stamps, or the boss may cancel your work identity.)

✔ **Ask your bank to hold new check orders and pick them up at the bank.** Check reorder boxes are easy to spot with a trained eye. You wouldn't send cash through the mail; don't send checks, either.

✔ **If you're away for a day or more, have someone pick up your mail or, better, have the post office hold it until you return.** Don't let it sit in your mailbox overnight.

Storing financial data in your home

You may believe that your financial information is safe inside the sanctuary of your home, no matter where it's located. Unfortunately, even in your home, keeping your documents and personal information protected and secured by keeping them out of sight is best. Your information is still accessible to anyone who may gain access to your inner sanctum, friend or foe. The following sections describe ways to protect your information and yourself in your home.

Securing confidential documents and information

Keep all financial, confidential, and legal documents and information in a secure place — a strong box, a locked desk drawer, or a locked file cabinet. Doing so ensures that your valuable data is safe from prying eyes and sticky fingers, and you also benefit from having all critical information in one place in case you need to access it quickly.

Sometimes, a simple thing can save the day. Making and securely storing a photocopy of your account numbers and your wallet's contents is one of them. If you haven't already done so, empty the contents of your wallet or purse and photocopy everything, front and back. Write the contact phone numbers next to each item and file the paper in a locked cabinet. Voilà! You're now better prepared to deal with an identity theft crisis.

Destroying information

Your mailbox isn't the only place that identity thieves look for useful information. Your garbage can is also ripe with potential. A determined thief doesn't mind sifting through your detritus if it means snagging a credit card number from those coffee grounds–covered receipts. A fishing expedition in the backyards and trash cans of suburbia can yield a good return.

Purchase a good crosscut shredder and shred all financial documents that contain account numbers (including savings, checking, and credit card statements) before you discard them. Don't overlook all those preapproved offers for credit you receive either; a thief can send them in with a change of address and get new credit that you won't know about until it's too late. Look for a shredder that takes multiple sheets of paper, is easy to use, and can be emptied without making a mess. Why? Because you're more likely to use it if it meets these criteria.

Putting your credit information on ice

Frozen margaritas, frozen yogurt, frozen credit? The option to freeze your credit to keep it from identity thieves is available to everyone. The concept is simple: You can freeze or lock up your credit information at the major credit bureaus (meaning your credit report won't be available for new creditors to view) so that anyone who's looking to extend credit has to ask you to *thaw out* (unlock) your file. Freezing your credit information seriously hampers an identity thief from opening credit in your name without your knowledge because few lenders extend credit without a credit report in hand.

The main consideration surrounding to-freeze-or-not-to-freeze your credit information is whether you value access to instant credit more than you fear your personal information being compromised. Only you know the answer to that question.

Of course, the freeze-your-credit-info strategy isn't foolproof. Thieves can still pirate, use, and abuse existing accounts by such tactics as simply swiping your mail, changing your address from Peoria to Las Vegas, and getting replacement cards issued. So a freeze may help protect your *information* but it may not protect your *money,* although hopefully you'd notice a problem before it gets too far out of hand. Given the low personal level of liability on credit cards, however, your monetary losses shouldn't be significant.

The bottom line of freezes is as follows:

- ✔ All the bureaus allow you to freeze your credit files regardless of the laws in your state.
- ✔ Freezing doesn't prevent abuse of existing accounts.

✔ Thawing an account takes a few days and may keep impulse or sale purchases from happening — which can be a good thing or a bad thing, depending on how you look at it.

If a freeze seems extreme to you, consider a *fraud alert*. It's like an account "chill" rather than a hard freeze in that it only requires enhanced verification of identity. To place an alert, contact any one of the three bureaus using the information in Chapter 7. The bureau you contact will automatically forward your request to the other two bureaus for action.

Safeguarding active-duty military personnel

While on duty outside the country, military personnel — as well as their families at home in the United States — may lack the time or means to monitor their credit activity. After all, calling TransUnion about an error isn't exactly a high priority when someone is trying to blow you up, and military families back home can understandably get distracted and let their guard down when a loved one is serving overseas. So it seems only fair that while soldiers are protecting their country, their country should protect them from credit problems. Fortunately, thanks to the FACT Act, active-duty military personnel can place an *active-duty alert* on their credit reports as a way to notify potential creditors to possible fraud.

If you're in the military and away from your usual base or deployed, place an active-duty alert on your credit report by contacting any one of the three major credit-reporting bureaus (don't bother calling all three bureaus, because the one you contact will notify the other two; see Chapter 7 for the bureaus' contact info). You'll be required to provide appropriate proof of identity, which may include your Social Security number, name, address, and other personal information in order to place the alert.

The active-duty alert stays on your credit report for at least one year. It helps minimize the risk of identity theft by requiring that a business take "reasonable" care to verify your identity before issuing you credit. However, if you're in some distant land trying to keep the peace, verifying your identity may not be feasible. So before you leave your base or home for active duty, be sure to appoint a personal representative and provide that person's contact information to the credit bureau. If you don't, a creditor only has to "utilize reasonable policies and procedures to form a reasonable belief" before granting credit to someone who claims to be you. This is way too *reasonable* for my comfort level. Be sure to appoint someone you trust!

After the alert is in place, lenders have to take additional steps before issuing additional credit cards or changing your limits. When the alert is placed, you can get an additional free credit report in addition to the annual report you're already entitled to (see Chapters 6 and 7 for more on this). Plus, your name is removed from preapproved offer lists for credit cards, insurance, and loans. To lessen the chances of an identity theft, you can place additional alerts if your deployment lasts longer than a year. (To delete an alert, just contact one of the bureaus; it will notify the others of your desire to deactivate the alert.)

Remember: If your contact information changes before your alert expires, update it or have your representative do so.

Shielding your credit card number

One of the easiest ways you can guard your identity is to ensure thieves don't have access to your credit card numbers. Luckily for you, the Fair and Accurate Credit Transactions Act (the FACT Act or FACTA) has made this task a tad easier for you. Electronically generated receipts for credit- and debit-card transactions may not include the card's expiration date or more than the last five digits of the card number. If you receive a receipt that has your full account number on it, bring it to the attention of the business and insist that it gets with the program — now! Some credit card issuers print only partial account numbers on statements as well.

You can find out more about the FACT Act in Chapter 5, on the CD, and at the Federal Trade Commission website (www.ftc.gov/os/statutes/fcrajump.shtm).

Catching Identity Theft in the Act

If your identity is stolen, you may not notice it for days, weeks, or even months. If a thief sets up a phony identity at another address and you don't get the bills, you may not know about the crime until the debts go bad and a collector finds you. Called *skip tracers,* these collectors look for people who don't pay their bills and then move — which is what they'll consider you until you straighten matters out.

That said, by being vigilant, you can spot signs of identity theft. Vigilance on your part can make all the difference between a minor or a major crime. In the following sections, I introduce you to some key indications of identity theft so you can be on the lookout for them.

Watching for early-warning notices

To help spot identity theft early on, the FACT Act requires that creditors give you what may be called an *early-warning notice* (and it may be your first sign of a problem). Whenever credit is extended within 30 days of a missed payment, late payment, partial payment, or other type of default, you must be sent a one-time notice letting you know that this information is being sent to the credit bureau. This notice has to be sent by collection agencies too, as long as they report to a credit bureau.

The FACT Act doesn't dictate how *big* of a notice you get. You may have to look closely to even see it, so be sure you do your part by closely monitoring your credit reports, bank accounts, and credit card statements.

Predicting identity theft before it happens

The FACT Act demands that financial institutions establish procedures to attempt to spot identity theft *before* it occurs. To predict an identity theft before it happens may seem as far-fetched as calling in a psychic on a missing person's case. But like our trusty weather forecasters who look to the skies for clues to tomorrow's weather, financial prognosticators are writing programs to look for specific activity in your financial records that may indicate a problem. In fact, several credit card companies now tout their own programs to fight identity theft. In Chapter 8 I go into some detail about the efforts that American Express is making to

spot fraud and theft as quickly as possible. A change in pattern or type of spending can trigger an alert to your phone or e-mail if you have an alert in place. Alerts are free and easy to set up; see Chapter 8 for more information.

Certain events — such as a change of address, a request for a replacement credit card, or efforts to reactivate a dormant credit card account — may trigger a fraud alert. That said, you can only do so much to protect yourself from identity theft, so even with prevention programs in place, in most cases you won't know about a problem until after the fact.

An early-warning notice means something bad is in your account history, and if it's reported to the credit bureau, it has a negative effect on your credit and score. Whether it's reported or not, it's lurking out there. Before negative information is reported, the early-warning notice may look something like this:

> *We may report information about your account to credit bureaus. Late payments, missed payments, or other defaults on your account may be reflected in your credit report.*

After negative information has been reported, the early-warning notice may look like this:

> *We have told a credit bureau about a late payment, missed payment, or other default on your account. This information may be reflected in your credit report.*

The wording makes it sound as though the bad information may not show up. It will, and probably already has.

So what do you do if you get a notice? Immediately contact the issuer and find out what's going on. The issuer will be as interested as you are in shutting down a thief early, so you can expect cooperation and maybe even a thank-you for acting quickly.

Handling a collections call

If you're the victim of identity theft, you may receive a collections call, likely a demanding and unpleasant one, from a collector insisting on payment for an overdue account — as in, an account that the collector is certain you owe but that you've never heard of. What should you do? The FACT Act, designed to address identity-theft issues, states that you need to tell the collector very clearly that you didn't make the purchase and that you believe that your identity may have been stolen.

After you tell the collector you believe your identity may have been stolen, the collection agency is required by law to inform the creditor. You're also entitled to get a copy of all the info the collection agency or creditor has about this debt, including applications, statements, and the like, as though this really were your account or bill. I suggest you do this before the collector gets off the phone or in your written response if the collection activity is in the form of a letter.

The best part is that, under the FACT Act, as soon as you notify the creditor or collector that the debt is the work of an identity thief, the debt can't be placed for collection or sold to another collector.

Detecting unauthorized charges

Are you among the many people who just look at the amount due on your monthly statement and make a payment? Or does your credit card bill automatically get paid from your bank account and you check the details later? In either case, you may be paying for purchases you didn't make, and more important, you may be missing an opportunity to stop a thief!

Take the time to thoroughly review your statements to ensure all the charges are legitimate. Set a reminder to alert you that your busy schedule must be interrupted to check your statement in detail and on a regular basis. Remember, you only have a limited time to dispute an error. Plus, an identity thief is faster than the proverbial speeding bullet! I recently had a card stolen from me while on vacation. In a matter of hours, the thief racked up over $9,000 in bogus charges — even a lunch a McDonald's! So don't delay checking your statements or else you may be in for quite a surprise.

 Don't rely on your memory as you review your statement. My memory isn't the greatest in the world (or so my wife says, although I can't remember why). So I make sure to keep all my credit card receipts in a file, and I pull them out when reviewing my monthly statement. Keep all credit card receipts in a convenient place, at least until you receive, verify, and pay your bill.

If you see any unauthorized charges on your statement, call the customer service number for the card issuer and get the details. You may have to dispute the charge, but that's no big deal. Also, the representative may see some indication of an identity theft. That happened to me — I saw a stray charge, called the credit card company, and the customer service rep recognized it as fraud right away. Make the call.

Being denied credit or account access

Rejection is always a painful thing, but it's especially painful when you're rejected because of something you didn't do. If you get rejections for credit, you may want to ask why, but your best bet is to order a copy of your credit report and look for evidence of identity theft (accounts you never opened and/or activity you don't recognize). You can get a free copy of the credit report used to deny your application in addition to the free annual reports you get normally. (I tell you how to order those in Chapter 7.)

Another sign of identity theft is receiving a notice that you've been rejected for credit that you never asked for. Take this seriously. Someone who shouldn't be may be applying for credit in your name.

You may try to access an ATM and get a denial message. If this happens to you, contact your bank immediately to determine whether it's the result of identity theft.

Noticing missing account statements

Your monthly statement is really late. Hmm . . . now that you think of it, you didn't receive a statement last month, either. Yes, I know this was one of your birthday wishes, but the real reason you're not hearing from your creditors may be more sinister. It could mean an identity thief has changed your address in order to use your bank accounts, hoping you won't notice for a few months.

Create a system by which you remind yourself when statements are due and bills must be paid. This way, you're more likely to stay on top of your payment schedule and be alerted when something is amiss. If you pay bills and get statements online instead of by snail mail, you make it harder on the thieves (and easier on yourself).

Part IV
Navigating Negative Credit

The 5th Wave
By Rich Tennant

"Coming out of bankruptcy, I can say I learned my lesson—don't spend what your relatives don't have."

In this part . . .

This part helps you move from ugly to attractive credit in the shortest time possible. I help you clean up your credit by explaining how to dispute inaccurate information on, and add positive information to, your credit report. You discover that good help for bad credit is available and that the very best help is free if you know where to find it!

I show you how to take charge of the collections process with tips on effectively communicating with your creditors and ideas on how to get back on track using money you already have in your own budget. You discover the best strategies for handling a mortgage foreclosure and ways to minimize the damage to your credit from a bankruptcy. Finally, I give you practical advice on controlling and managing the damage to your credit from identity theft.

Chapter 13

Turning Your Credit Around

· ·

In This Chapter

▶ Identifying what you want most out of life

▶ Cleaning up your credit with some credit tools

▶ Improving your credit with both small and big purchases

▶ Using debt to build good credit

▶ Deciding whether to use a cosigner on a loan

· ·

*E*verybody makes a wrong turn or gets lost from time to time. Sometimes you misunderstand a sign, other times you get bad directions, and then there may be times when you just don't know how to get where you're going but decide to try anyway and figure it out along the journey. Credit works the same way. The big difference is that a lot of people watch and keep score of how you find your way. If you're not sure how you got where you are or if your credit isn't in a great place, you want to get back on track as quickly as possible.

Like a road trip that takes you to new and interesting places, building and improving your credit helps you attain your life goals. You're more likely to enjoy your journey if you have specific, self-serving, and enjoyable goals in mind when you begin your trip to get into better credit shape. Identifying those goals is your first step. You don't have to lay out your whole future in financial terms, but taking a peek at least five years ahead is an excellent place to start, and it's easy and fun to boot! Credit, like your car, is a means to an end, a tool and nothing more. Building up your credit for no purpose is dull. Credit with a destination is exciting!

This chapter is dedicated to helping you improve your credit and boost your credit score. Consider it your own fiscal fitness plan, designed to help you prevent those unwanted credit negatives from adding up. Allow me to serve as your navigator and guide. Time to gas up the car and hit the road!

Setting Your Life's Financial Goals

Some people think of credit as a way to spend money on the stuff they want when they want it, regardless of whether they actually have the money. Well, they're right *and* they're wrong. Credit doesn't give you any more money. Having a credit card with a $5,000 limit doesn't mean that you have $5,000 more to spend. It *does* mean that you can spend $5,000 that you haven't yet earned with the promise that you'll pay it back tomorrow. Credit is borrowing against the future or, as I'm fond of saying, "spending tomorrow's money today."

Problems often arise, however, when you spend *more* of tomorrow's money today than you're able to repay. Spending *some* of tomorrow's money today can actually help you lead a better life now, as long as you spend those future dollars on things you've decided *you* want rather than things *someone else* wants to sell you.

A good example is buying a home. If you had to wait until you saved up, say, $300,000 to purchase your dream house in cash, you might be ready for assisted living before you moved into your first home. Borrowing on future income to move in today makes sense and may well improve the quality of your life for years to come. On the other hand, buying a $300,000 Ferrari on borrowed money may be a mistake. Chances are you're buying the Ferrari because you were sold on the idea by some clever marketing campaign or you're looking for an image makeover, but you're not buying it as a sound expenditure.

This leads me to the concept of your goals. Everyone I know who sells a product has a plan to get you to buy it. In a grocery store, milk is always at the opposite end of the store from the door, requiring you to pass by numerous other products to get to it, because of a *plan*. Candy at a checkout counter is placed low where kids will see it (and ask parents to buy it for them) because of a *plan*.

What are your financial plans? If you don't have plans or goals, then like it or not, believe it or not, you'll end up following someone else's.

Setting some goals is easy. Just keep these steps in mind:

1. **Do a little prep work.**

   Set aside an evening or a weekend afternoon, sit down alone or with your partner and without distraction, and look into the future. No need to pull out the crystal ball. Simply describe what you want your future to look like. Consider the short term (generally from a few months up to a year), intermediate term (two to five years), and long term (five years and beyond). Your goals may include such things as getting a car, buying a home, having a family, saving for college or weddings, and going on a fabulous vacation. In no time, you'll be imagining all those things you've always wanted to do.

2. **As you identify your goals, write them down.**

   Documenting your dreams is important because doing so makes them more real. Better yet, cut out or print out pictures that illustrate your goals. Maybe a picture of a big cruise ship or a tropical island surrounded by blue waters or, yes, you just relaxing without financial worries.

Now you've taken the first critical step toward creating a successful plan for yourself: You've established a powerful reason to save some portion of your income. And you now have the motivation to get your credit standing back on track to help you achieve those goals. Believe it or not, achieving your goals is generally not the problem. Knowing where you're going — and, for couples, agreeing on mutual goals — is the trickiest part.

 Take the list you made to create your plan and keep it for reference when things get a little rocky. It's a big help in getting through difficult periods (for example, when something *not* on your list of goals is calling your name).

Your next step is to get to work building your financial goals. The following sections focus on what I've found to be the three essential credit tools you need:

- ✔ A plan for spending, saving, and credit building
- ✔ Copies of your credit reports
- ✔ Your credit score

Selecting the Best Tools for Building Your Credit

I've learned over time that using the right tools makes any job go faster and gives me better results. The tools for mending your credit are readily available, and I show you how to find and use them in this section. I begin with essential job preparation by walking you through a spending plan, and then I discuss how to tweak your credit report. Finally, I tell you how to determine when the job is done by using your credit score.

Spending your way to better credit with a spending plan

Unless you have a trust fund or you make a huge amount of money and just can't seem to spend it all, you need a spending plan. A spending plan, which helps you take care of today's responsibilities and tomorrow's goals, has four components:

- ✔ **Household income:** This includes all the money coming into the house from salaries, tips, overtime, bonuses, royalties, and so on. Be sure to consider your payroll deductions (such as money you put into a retirement plan) as income.

- ✔ **Living expenses:** Your present outlay — from groceries and lunch money to rent or mortgage — make up your expenses. Also consider those nonessential frivolities that crop up, like your daily dose of designer coffee or the occasional trip to the movies.

- ✔ **Savings for financial goals:** In this category you account for vacations, college education, and retirement.

- ✔ **Emergency fund:** Without an emergency fund to cover unexpected (and usually unpleasant) life events, such as a medical expense or job loss, you won't succeed. Saving for that unexpected emergency is critical. You need between six to twelve months of living expenses; otherwise, when the emergency comes along, you have to get the money from one of two sources: the future (as in spending tomorrow's money today) or your savings for your goals (as in the money you were setting aside for that Ferrari).

Adding up your income

Here's how a spending plan works: You start by identifying all your household income — that's your regular salary or wage, plus overtime, bonuses, and predictable windfalls like an IRS refund if you're pretty sure you'll get one. If you're self-employed, your net income from your business or practice is what I'm talking about here.

Saving in your company retirement account makes sense, especially if your employer contributes a matching amount to the fund. Plus, saving for retirement probably ties into one of your goals (unless you plan to die at your desk).

Adding up all your expenses

After you have the income part down on paper or in your computer, do the same with your expenses. Make sure to include a savings category as an expense for each of the financial goals you list. The best way to manage this goal-based savings is to estimate how far in the future the goal is, what the goal costs, and what you have to put aside each month to cover the expense in time.

For example, say you want to take a cruise on your wedding anniversary three years from now. The cost is $3,600 for the two of you. That's 36 months at $100 a month. If you can't afford the $100 a month, postpone the cruise for a year and save $75 a month instead, or take a cheaper cruise and still go in three years. The next time you find yourself standing before the 3-D flat-screen HDTV at the mall, your picture of the future will be in clear focus: the cruise or the TV, but not both.

Paying your existing debts

Don't forget to set aside money to pay your existing debts, such as outstanding credit cards and car loans. You may need to tweak your plan a time or two so that the numbers and the time frame for your goals reconcile. But you're now more firmly in control of your financial future. From here on, you make the decisions about what money goes to what categories — not those marketing guys.

On the CD included with this book are forms that help with setting up a spending plan. In Chapter 4, I get into more detail on budgeting for your future.

Tracking your credit progress: Paying attention to your credit report and score

Knowing where you and your credit stand is important so you can gauge your progress and make adjustments if necessary. You don't need to check your credit every day, but you should take advantage of all the opportunities you have for free peeks that come your way. You get a free report annually, another if you apply for credit and don't get the top rate, another when a credit report is used to set your insurance cost, and yet another when you're out of work.

The Fair and Accurate Credit Transactions Act (also known as the FACT Act or FACTA) now requires all three major credit-reporting bureaus to provide you with a free copy of your credit report once each year. Some states require that you be given two reports annually. Stagger getting a copy of your report from *each* of the three bureaus, because they often contain differing information. (See Chapter 7 for information on how to get your reports.)

When you get your credit reports, read them over and make sure that the information is accurate, complete, and up-to-date. Chapter 7 provides information on how to scrutinize your credit report and fix any errors that you find.

Generally, negative items stay on your credit report for seven years. The main exceptions are:

- ✔ Student loan defaults, which remain until they're paid
- ✔ Overdue tax debts, which stay until resolved
- ✔ Child support defaults, which stay posted until cleared up
- ✔ Bankruptcy, which remains on your report for up to ten years

Positive account information stays on your credit report for much longer. Some positive trade lines continue to be reported for 10, 20, or even 30 years.

Steve Bucci's theory of good-enough credit

I often advocate the concept of *good-enough credit* as opposed to *perfect credit.* Your credit standing, which is represented by your credit score, is a reflection of your life in financial terms. Lose your job, get a divorce, suffer an illness — the fallout from all these life events shows up on your credit report and affects your credit score one way or another. Late payments and too much borrowing activity are some of the symptoms that may appear in your credit data. Although these events may lower your score to a degree, you shouldn't be driven to aspire to a perfect FICO score of 850 (or 990 if you're using VantageScore). Your life isn't perfect (just ask your mother-in-law), so don't

expect your credit history to be perfect either. Again, credit is only a means to an end. As long as your credit score remains good enough to get what you need and want, you're in good shape to achieve your financial goals. No use staying up nights worrying if your credit score has dropped from 775 to 774.

A bad credit score can cost a lot in extra payments. For example, say you buy a house for $360,000 at a 30-year fixed rate with a down payment of $60,000. If your credit score is 639 instead of 760, you'd have to pay about $105,840 more in interest over the life of your loan!

Turning Small Purchases into Big Credit

Because a lot of your credit score is based on using credit and making payments on time (see Chapter 6), I recommend using small purchases to get back in good standing quickly. Why does making small purchases work so well? Because each item costs less, so more purchases are reported to the credit bureaus faster. My rule of thumb is if it's over $10, charge it (and pay it off each month).

Major bank cards certainly report your activity to the credit bureaus. Some store cards may report to only one bureau or they may not report at all. To know whether your credit purchases are being reported and scored, call your card's customer service number and ask.

Pick up some extra points on your credit score by following a simple plan when you pay down balances. Scoring models look at how much of your limit you use. The more you use, the higher risk they believe you to be. To maximize your credit score, spread purchases over more than one card to keep your balance on each card as small a percentage of your maximum limit as possible. Say you have two cards, one with a $10,000 limit and one with a $20,000 limit. Simply charge twice as much on the higher-limit card to maximize your score. When your balance exceeds 50 percent of your max, you begin to lose points.

If you're less concerned about your score than paying down your balances, here's some advice. Some experts suggest that you pay down balances based on the interest rate (that is to say, pay them in descending order starting with the highest interest rate) to save more money on overall payments. Others say that paying off smaller accounts gives you a feeling of accomplishment, and, therefore, you're more likely to achieve your overall goal. My suggestion is that you make your choice about what approach you take based on which one you find most satisfying. Just be sure that *you* make the choice and don't let the first bill that shows up get the extra payment by chance.

Make a list of each credit card, its balance, and its credit limit. Then allocate your payments to reduce your percentage of your maximum limit used to 45 percent of the credit limit or less on as many accounts as possible. Doing so creates some great positive data in your credit report. The big balances take an extended amount of time to pay down to about 45 percent of the credit limit. This approach not only allows you to regain control of your accounts but also helps you maximize your credit score, because accounts that exceed 50 percent of the limit count more heavily against you. When all your cards are at 45 percent of your limits or below, you may want to allocate more money to the highest-interest-rate cards.

If you don't have a major bank credit card, you may want to try a secured card. You can get one without a fee if you shop around. A secured card differs from a regular Visa or MasterCard in that you maintain a balance in a savings account equal to your credit limit (some cards may allow you more credit than you have on deposit) to guarantee your payment. Secured-card activity is reported just as any other credit-card activity is reported, and it affects your credit score in the same way, so it can be a great option if you're trying to build credit.

You can find great card comparisons at www.bankrate.com or www.credit cards.com. The latter website has two sections to help you find the right card, depending on your circumstance. One section (www.creditcards.com/no-credit-history.php) is for those who have little or no experience with credit or who have recently come to the United States and need to start a U.S. credit history (credit from overseas doesn't follow you). The other section (www.creditcards.com/bad-credit.php) is helpful for those with bad or damaged credit.

Generally, if you make all your payments on time for a year, you should have enough of a positive payment history to get an unsecured credit card.

Creditors who don't report to the bureaus

Why doesn't every creditor report your history to all three credit bureaus? Because every time your creditors send data on you to a bureau, they have to pay a fee. Some lenders don't think this is worth the expense. Others don't see themselves as lenders. They may still order a credit report before approving your loan or credit card, but they want to save as much profit as they can. Typically, these nonreporters may include

✔ Credit unions: They look to save money where they can, so some report to only one bureau and not all three.

✔ Utilities: They don't see themselves as lenders, so they don't use credit reports to hook you up. They also usually don't report unless you pay very late.

✔ Tradesmen: They aren't lenders, but liens or suits for old bills show on your credit reports because they can be found in public records.

✔ Doctors: If they send a bill to collections, their collectors report you to the bureaus.

✔ Hospitals: They don't see themselves as lenders and they are really cheap, so they usually don't pay to report until outside collectors take over.

✔ Local finance companies: They may not report to a bureau, but they may come visit you if you're late.

✔ Landlords: They don't report to credit bureaus but may report to a rent bureau (see Chapter 7). Experian has begun to report some rental history on their credit reports.

✔ Insurance companies: They don't report to the bureaus but may report to specialized bureaus like the Medical Information Bureau.

Maximizing Your Credit Score with Major Credit Expenditures

Big-ticket creditors — those that specialize in expensive products or services — typically report to the credit bureaus. The reasoning is simple: They have a lot more to lose if they lend based on inaccurate information, so they want to see as complete and accurate a file as possible.

Examples of big-ticket items that may enhance your credit activity are a home mortgage, a car or boat, a student loan, furniture, and appliances. Such major credit purchases may give your credit score a boost for two reasons:

✔ **Major purchases are more likely to be in the form of a secured installment loan.** *Secured* means you pledge collateral on the item you purchase as security for the loan. If you default on the loan, the lender repossesses the security you pledged — in other words, you don't get to keep it. Adding some secured credit to the variety of other types of credit you use, such as revolving credit (cards), helps raise your credit score.

✔ **Making the same payment each month.** When it comes to credit scoring, making set monthly payments allows the people who figure your score to discover more about your creditworthiness. Making a set monthly payment is a measure of your stability. This is different from paying on a credit card, where you can vary your payment depending on your cash flow. Adhering to a regular payment schedule also indicates that you can handle a higher limit than you may have on a store, gas, or credit card account.

Leveraging your mortgage for good credit history

Owning a home and paying your mortgage can help build your credit in a few different ways. Credit grantors look at your credit report and credit score in order to rate your lendability, but they ultimately rely on you to be responsible for making the payments. Here's where the three Cs of credit really show up: Character, collateral, and capacity are what credit scoring and lending are all about.

A mortgage on your report tells the reader and the scorer that you have all three of the Cs and that at least one lender was so sure about you that it was willing to lend you a huge amount of money. The report indicates a large installment loan with fixed payments for a long period of time. All these factors favorably affect your credit score. The opposite is also true: Because of the huge amount of money involved and the seriousness of a long-term commitment, a mortgage default counts for a large negative on your credit history. A foreclosure is an even bigger negative.

A mortgage is secured by the house, so if you default, the lender forecloses and takes the house back to pay off the loan. A foreclosure ends up costing the lender an average of tens of thousands of dollars when all is said and done. But don't feel too bad for the lender: *You're* held responsible in one way or another for any loss on the loan.

Home-equity lines of credit and home-equity loans are a popular subset of traditional mortgages. They're good ways to access money at a low interest rate. They also represent new and additional borrowing on your credit report. For example, you can take out a big mortgage and have only one lender report one loan to the bureaus. If you use a home-equity loan or line of credit in addition to your mortgage, you use the same collateral (your home) and you borrow the same amount as you would with a bigger mortgage but you do so with more than one loan. Thus, more than one item gets reported to the credit bureau each month, building more positive information in the same time period. (See the nearby "Lines versus loans" sidebar for more.)

This scenario has a hitch, however: As you stack more debt on your home or your home decreases in value, you may reach the point where you and your castle are *upside-down* (that is, you owe more on your home than it's worth). I've seen some homes so far upside down that their owners think they'll never get their money back and question whether continuing to pay good money into a bad investment makes sense. You may think that because you have a 30-year mortgage you can just wait until prices rise to clear up your debt-to-value problem. But what if your boss offers you the general manager's job in a city too far away to commute to? Or what if the company lays you off and you either have to move to find work or downsize to reduce your mortgage commitment? Or what if your adjustable rate mortgage resets and you can't afford the payment anymore? You'd then be in the position of needing to sell the house but not at a price that would satisfy the loans attached to your home. If you don't have the money to make up the difference, you could face a potential foreclosure or lost opportunity. (See Chapter 9 for more information about how to avoid a foreclosure.)

Lines versus loans

What's the difference between a home-equity loan and a home-equity line of credit? Here's the scoop: A *home-equity loan* is for a specified lump sum or single payment of cash — say, $10,000. When you get the home-equity loan, you get the ten big ones to put down on that car (or whatever else you want to buy), and you have an installment payment due every month, usually at a set interest rate for a set amount of time. In the old days, these loans were called *second mortgages,* and they were a sure sign you were on the path to ruin. Today, they're called *equity products,* and it seems that too many of us have more than one. And yes, they're still a sign that you could be on the road to ruin!

With a *home-equity line of credit,* you get a line of credit, maybe for $10,000 or $20,000, depending on how much you want to have available just in case you need it. You don't have to take any money out of the line at all, unless you have a use for it. The money just sits there like a wallflower at a dance, waiting for you to ask it for a tango. Generally, you have a set period of time (called a *draw period*) when you can access the line of credit and a set period before which you have to pay it back. So until you use it all, the money is available and just sits there through the remainder of the draw period for free (or sometimes for a small annual fee).

When you do draw money from the line, you generally have the option of paying it off anytime without a prepayment penalty. The loan terms often allow you to pay only the interest and not the principal (an interest-only loan); the principal is due at the end of a time set in the loan agreement. Or you can choose to pay both interest and principal until the debt is paid off. Some loans allow you to decide what you're going to pay on a month-by-month basis, such as paying the principal and interest one month but only the interest the next. Lines of credit are subject to review, and unused portions may be reduced or eliminated if conditions warrant.

Financing your car

Because of the very large price tags on most cars, most of us require some financing in order to purchase one. Such financing typically comes in the form of a two- to five-year installment loan. Anyone lending you the money to buy a car receives and reports credit bureau data. When lenders go on the hook for that much money, they want to be sure that you'll make your payments, even if you get in a cash squeeze. Most car loans are secured by the car.

If you're debating using equity in your home to purchase a car, be careful. Using a home-equity loan to buy a car may offer a tax advantage (with tax-deductible interest), but it may increase the risk of a home default and subsequent foreclosure if you can't make the extra payment. If you default on that home-equity loan, your car won't be repossessed; instead, and much worse, your home may be foreclosed on. Plus, any mortgage debt forgiven in a short sale or foreclosure may be subject to income taxes. Although the Mortgage Forgiveness Debt Relief Act eliminates taxes due on forgiven mortgage debts, it excludes non–house-related debt. (See Chapter 17.)

Be sure to pay off the loan you used to buy your old car before you buy your next new one! Some people keep old car loans on their home-equity lines long after the cars are gone and just keep adding new balances without paying off the old ones. This can lead to an unpleasant surprise when interest rates go up or you need to sell your home.

Weighing the pluses and minuses of leases

Leasing is a popular way to get a car. Please note, I didn't say *buy* a car, because you don't own the car in a lease arrangement. Consider a lease a long-term rental. Leases are popular because they generally require only a small down payment or perhaps none at all. Plus, they're a tax write-off if you're a business-person. Signing the lease commits you to a stream of payments for an extended period of time, so this activity is normally reported to the credit bureaus.

Leases are very difficult and costly to terminate. Unlike with a car loan, you can't sell the car and pay off the loan. With a lease, you owe all the payments and you can't terminate the lease without making all the payments first.

An active-duty serviceperson who is called away for military service can break a car lease. Chapter 16 covers this in more detail. For the law itself, check out the Servicemembers Civil Relief Act (SCRA) on the CD.

Steering clear of upside-down loans

The term sounds as uncomfortable as it is. Basically, in an *upside-down loan*, you owe more than the value of the item securing the loan. Avoid being upside down in a car loan, or any secured loan (upside-down house mortgages work similarly) if you can help it. Any repossession or default shows negatively on your credit report, and your score will fall — hard!

An upside-down loan can hurt you when you want or need to sell the car and stop making payments. Say you owe $10,000 on a car loan, and the value of the car is $7,000. You have to come up with the $3,000 difference or you can't sell the car. If you're in a car accident and the car is totaled, the insurance company only pays what the car is worth; you have to pay the upside-down part.

This situation gets worse if your financial situation changes, you can't make the payments on the car, and the creditor repossesses the car. The car is worth $7,000, but that's the retail value. The lender likely sells the car at auction, where the creditor only gets $5,000. The fees on the repossession are $2,000 among the towing guy, the sales commission to the auctioneer, and the attorney's fees. So you get credited with $3,000 against the $10,000 you owe. Now you owe $7,000 in a lump sum to settle your account, and you have no car, plus you have bad credit in the bargain.

Paying student loans to rebuild your credit

Because of the increasingly unaffordable price tag on higher education, many people have student loans. Student loans make a lot of sense to lenders: Although the person responsible for repayment may have no income at the time of the loan, the lender expects that good income is just around the corner, and the person will soon pay the loan back. But what really makes these loans attractive to lenders is that the lenders can't lose. Almost no student loans are dischargeable in bankruptcy, except in extreme situations, meaning you have to pay them back sooner or later.

If you have a student loan, chances are it appears on your credit report. It may also be reported more than once. Why? Each loan is usually for a semester's or year's worth of school expenses. Each is reported as a separate loan for each enrollment period. So four years' worth of loans add either four or eight loans to your credit report. If you make payments and/or file for benefits on time, your credit report reflects a positive history and adds to your credit score. This can be a lot of good news for your credit report!

Conversely, if you end up in default on your student loans, you'll see a lot of negative marks on your credit report and credit score from all those individual loan entries. Any missed payments are reported to the bureaus, and you're subject to the full range of collection activity, just like you would be with any other loan.

If you consolidate your loans after graduation, they show up on your report as one loan. *Consolidating* is the process of refinancing all your individual loans into a single loan. The original loans are marked *paid in full,* and the interest rate is often lower and the repayment term is typically longer for the consolidated loan than for the individual loans. The net result is the convenience of a single, lower monthly payment. With consolidated loans, you typically have a number of different repayment options, including paying the same amount each month, paying less now and more later, and changing your payment plan based on your income.

Student loans aren't secured with collateral in the normal sense of the word. When you're in default on a student loan, you can't defer payment of the loan. In fact, you may have to pay it all at once unless you come up with an acceptable repayment scheme. Additionally, you're not eligible for further student aid, your school may withhold your transcripts, state and federal income tax refunds may be used to offset the loan amounts, and your wages (when you get that job) may be attached or garnished. Finally, if you don't pay long enough, your Social Security may be garnished.

Understanding How Good Debt Builds Good Credit

No doubt about it: Getting into debt *can* get you into trouble. And if you're reading this section, chances are you've had some experience with debt trouble or you're being proactive and hoping to avert potential credit problems. Although debt certainly has a downside, borrowing money can also do a great deal of good for your credit record. In the following sections, I tell you how.

Achieving goals with the help of credit

Debt allows you to take advantage of those opportunities and experiences that enhance your life and create joy and fulfillment: that dream home with the white picket fence, the around-the-world cruise, the Ivy League school, and more. When you can train your sights on your life goals and develop a spending plan that allows you to get there in the time frame you set, you've found the secret to the true value of credit.

Sending a message to potential lenders

If you had no debt — ever — then you'd never have used credit and you wouldn't likely have a credit report or credit score. But let's face it: In today's world, living without credit is hard. Most people need credit to buy those big-ticket items — vehicles, homes, higher education — and they rely on credit in the case of life's emergencies. Creating a positive credit history — a credit reputation, of sorts — says to prospective lenders that you're a good credit risk. Showing that you can handle debt puts you in a position to receive the best rates and terms.

Using credit wisely not only is a good thing for your lifestyle but also gives prospective creditors the opportunity to show you the respect you deserve based on your past performance. Lenders prefer to loan money to individuals who've borrowed before, who can show that they understand the commitment of credit, and who have a history of prompt payment and reliable follow-through. In fact, given the choice between lending to someone who's *never* borrowed before and someone with a history of debt — even with a couple of blips on the report — my guess is that most creditors would favor the credit veteran over the rookie.

Think of it this way: Say your two 20-year-old nephews ask to borrow your car. One has never driven before and the other has a four-year driving history, but with a parking ticket last year. Who would you pick?

Giving nonlenders a sense of how you handle responsibility

If you've had no debt and therefore have no credit history, you may find yourself disadvantaged in other ways. Many prospective employers check your credit record as part of the hiring process. If you have no record, they can't confirm their good opinion of you. Plus, they can't use your credit history as a positive factor when trying to decide whether to hire you. Without that credit record, they lack an additional tool when comparing your application to those of other applicants.

The same holds true when it comes to renting an apartment, applying for insurance, and so on. When you have no track record, you're an untested risk.

To Use a Cosigner or Not? That's the Question

Getting a loan by having someone cosign for you is very much a triple-edged sword. *Cosigning* means that you have another party (usually one with better credit) sign alongside you to guarantee future payments if you default, drop dead, or are abducted by aliens. As long as your lender reports to the bureaus, each time you make a payment on time and for the right amount, you and your cosigner both accumulate more positive items. As time goes by, this helps offset earlier negative items on your report. Like snow falling on the ground, the good stuff covers all the muck underneath.

Although a cosigned loan can help you get positive info on your credit report, I call it a triple-edged sword because

- ✔ **You may be borrowing when you shouldn't.** If a professional lender is reluctant to give you a loan, the lender has a good reason. So now the cosigner, who's not a professional and who likely has emotional ties clouding her judgment, decides that guaranteeing your loan is okay.

- ✔ **The cosigner is at risk if you default.** The cosigner is fully responsible for the payment. If it takes 60 days for the cosigner to be informed that you haven't paid on time, the cosigner's credit gets dinged, as does yours.

- ✔ **A default could destroy a relationship.** If your ability to pay off the loan is compromised and you incur late fees/penalties or you default on the loan, your cosigner is fully liable, and her credit score may be damaged. This scenario — no surprise — just may be the end of your relationship, but not the end of the loan obligation.

My advice: If you ask a friend or relative to cosign a loan, make sure the life of the loan is for as short a period of time as possible. The longer the loan is outstanding, the greater the chance a problem will arise or a relationship will strain. Also, put your agreement in writing to make it official and to make sure that you both clearly understand what you're agreeing to and that there are no miscommunications.

A final word of caution to the good-credit partner: The lender probably has a good reason not to make this loan. You need to understand that reason and then decide whether you want to guarantee the debt. The worst of all possibilities: You end up on the loan but not as a co-owner of the property. In my counseling days, I had a client who had cosigned on a car loan for his sweetie. After she got the wheels, she hit the road, and the collectors were all over him for payment. He had no girlfriend or car, just a big bill. *Remember:* Love may be blind, but it doesn't have to be stupid.

Chapter 14

Polishing Your Credit Reports

· ·

· ·

*F*acebook, YouTube, Internet tracking cookies, webcams, traffic cameras, credit reporting . . . all are different ways that you expose yourself to others. People form impressions of you, and their perceptions aren't always correct. This is particularly worrisome where credit and financial matters are concerned, because in these cases, much of your appearance is influenced by others. Yes, you have a say in how you run your financial life and pay your bills, and such data should be reported accurately. But increasingly, with billions of pieces of data floating around, errors do happen. Errors, misinformation, and other people's negative behaviors can all affect your credit report from time to time.

Despite a natural desire to restrict access to the more intimate details of your personal financial history, your credit report and score are accessible to much of the world. More and more decisions are being made from long distances by people who only know you from your credit file. In this environment where your credit report can make the difference between a job, an apartment, or access to credit, the best you can hope for is that your credit profile is as accurate as possible.

That's where knowing what's in your credit report and polishing it to its highest luster is vitally important. The tools are yours to use; you just need to know what and where they are. That's what this chapter is all about: helping you to look your very best by burnishing your credit.

Understanding the True Value of Good Credit

You may think that banks are the main entities that review your credit profile and that they use the information largely to decide whether to approve you for a loan or to determine what interest rate to grant you. Though that's still certainly the case, banks, employers, landlords, insurance companies, and others are increasingly using the data in your credit report to make all kinds of decisions, including whether to

- Extend credit to you and on what terms
- Hire you for a new job
- Rent you an apartment
- Give you a promotion at work
- Grant you insurance coverage
- Award you a professional license in your line of work
- Qualify you for security clearance for your job or in the military

The bosses and landlords who make such decisions know that they're in an increasingly litigious society. Discrimination on any basis other than hard fact can cost them massive court awards. Consequently, they look for independent data — void of discrimination, favoritism, or prejudice — to support and justify their decision making. What does this mean to you? If you have negative items on your credit report, you may pay more for an apartment, insurance, or a loan, or you may not be able to access them at any price. That's why having a good credit report is important.

The information in your credit report is a good predictor of future financial and nonfinancial behavior in your life. So if you're borrowing, looking for work or a place to live, seeking career advancement, renewing insurance, or getting licensed, you want to make sure that your credit information is accurate, current, and, yes, about you and not someone else.

Reviewing Your Credit Report for Problems

The task of knowing what's in your credit report is a lot easier than some people may lead you to believe. But it does take some time, patience, and persistence. You don't need to pay anyone to monitor your credit or send you hourly updates on what's happening in your credit universe. You can do this on your own and for free in most cases. You want to keep a close eye on your credit report for any potential problems, because with the large number of items reported daily, errors are fairly common. (The U.S. Government Accountability Office has found that about 25 percent of reports have serious errors.) In addition, your credit history is used to make an increasingly large number of decisions about your future, financial and otherwise, from lending to insurance to employment.

To begin your review, arm yourself with the information in your credit reports (one from each of the three major bureaus), as well as your credit score from either FICO, VantageScore, or a bureau score. (Chapter 7 shows you how to get these reports and your score.) If you have to pick one, the FICO score is the most widely used by lenders. If you're going to apply for a loan in the near future, ask your lender which report and score it uses, and then get that one. Otherwise, any score will do for your purposes here, to establish a benchmark to see where your credit report ranks and then to be able to track improvement.

As you study your credit reports, you may be surprised by how many accounts you find. Because your report lists negative information for seven years (longer exceptions, such as government debts and bankruptcy, also exist) and positive information for much longer, you're likely to see accounts, referred to as *trade lines,* that you've forgotten about and perhaps even some you didn't realize you still had. Some creditors, like retail stores, don't close accounts, even if you haven't used them in years. Your task is to wade through the trade lines — current and ancient alike — and identify errors and inaccuracies. (For a rundown on all the different sections of your credit report, turn to Chapter 7.)

Here's what you should look for in particular:

- ✔ **Verify that your name, address, birthday, and Social Security number are correct.** Although variations on your name are okay (for example, my report shows both Stephen and Steve), make sure that your address, date of birth, and Social Security number are also correct. With all the data moving through the financial reporting system, a Jr. or Sr. can easily be missed, or confusion over a II or III designation may occur.

- ✔ **Check to see whether all your accounts are shown on your credit report.** Remember that your credit report may not show all your accounts. Why? Because creditors may only supply information to one (or none) of the three major credit bureaus, particularly if they only use one bureau's report to make credit decisions.

- ✔ **Look to see whether account activity is being reported correctly.** If you see accounts that are familiar but activity that isn't — such as a late-payment notation when you don't recall being late — you want to report that error to the credit bureau. Also, if you see accounts you don't recognize, they may be a simple misposting of data from someone else's report, or they may be something more serious, like signs of identity theft. Here, too, contact the bureau and find out.

✔ **Look out for accounts from a bank or store with which you've never done business.** Someone else's account information may have been added to your credit report because of a misspelled name, wrong address, or incorrect Social Security number.

✔ **Identify and verify any accounts that show negative activity.** *Negative activity* can include anything from a missed or late payment to a charge-off (see Chapter 18 for more on delinquencies) or bankruptcy notation. Making sure this negative information is really yours and is really accurate is very important. Remember, 25 percent of reports have errors. Also, some negatives are much more serious than others. For example, an unpaid charge-off is more serious than a paid charge-off, even though both are negative.

✔ **Be sure that an account that moved from one source to another is listed as open only once.** Bank and store mergers can result in multiple entries for the same account. Multiple entries can make it look like you have excessive amounts of credit available.

✔ **Look for any overdraft protection lines of credit.** These lines of credit may be reported to the bureaus even after you close the accounts that the lines were meant to support. Closing these lines of credit can be helpful if you have a lot of credit available.

If you make a correction to your file, keep in mind that the change may not be updated if the creditor doesn't generally report to that credit bureau every month. If you're in the loan application process, ask whether your lender offers a rapid rescore product for sale. Developed by the three national bureaus, *rapid rescore* is essentially an unscheduled update to the information on your credit report. If a recent change (such as paying down a balance or closing a card) helps your credit score, then as soon as it's made, the lender can order a rapid rescore within 72 hours.

Using the Law to Get Your Credit Record Clean and to Keep It That Way

Nowadays, you have expanded rights regarding access to your credit report, granting you more empowerment than perhaps at any time in the modern history of credit. The Fair and Accurate Credit Transactions Act (the FACT Act or FACTA), an update to the old Fair Credit Reporting Act (FCRA), is legislation that helps you get the facts about you straight. This law can help you with new tools to fight the growing crime of identity theft. Additionally, the Dodd-Frank Wall Street Reform and Consumer Protection Act brings new safeguards to consumers.

In addition to requiring lenders and credit bureaus to play a greater role in protecting you, these laws promote consumer rights by allowing you to

✔ **Receive your credit report for free.** You're entitled to a free copy of your credit information once a year (see Chapter 7 for information on how to get a copy of each of your reports). You can get additional free reports if you believe that your identity has been stolen or if you've been on the receiving end of bad news caused by information in your credit file. The credit business refers to this as *adverse action.* Some actions by lenders and some state laws enable you to get multiple free reports each year. Check with your state's attorney general's office to find out the laws in your state. You can also check out this bureau site for more free reports: `https://aa.econsumer.equifax.com/aad/landing.ehtml`.

✔ **Limit access to your credit report.** Only people and institutions with a need recognized by the FACT Act — usually generated by an application with a creditor, insurer, employer, landlord, or other business — may access your credit report.

✔ **Require your consent before anyone is provided with your credit reports or specialty reports that contain medical information.** Your employer, prospective employer, creditors, insurers — anyone — needs your permission or an existing business relationship with you before being able to access your private information.

✔ **Have access to all information in your file.** Ask and you shall receive. You must be given the information in your file, as well as a list of everyone who has recently requested access to it. Creditors are also required to give you an early-warning notice and a free credit report or score if any negative information is placed on your credit report.

✔ **Be informed if your report has been used against you.** People who use information in your credit file and take action against you — such as denying you credit or making an unfavorable rate decision for credit, insurance, or employment — must reveal that they used the information in your credit report to make the decision. They must also reveal

- The name, date, and actual numerical credit score they used in the adverse decision

- The range of possible scores under the model they used

- All key factors that adversely affected the credit score

✔ **Dispute and have removed any inaccurate or outdated information.** After you file a dispute saying that your report contains inaccurate information, the credit bureau must investigate the items — usually within 30 days — and give you a written report of the investigation and a free copy of your credit report with the revisions made if the investigation results in any change. If the reported information is later found to be valid, it can be reinserted into your report, in which case you must be given a written notice telling you of the reinsertion. The notice must include the name, address, and phone number of the information source. As for outdated info, in most cases, information more than seven years old — ten years for some bankruptcies — should be deleted from your credit report. If it isn't, you may demand that it be dropped.

✔ **Place a statement on your report.** You may include a 100-word statement in your report to explain extenuating circumstances or to note your disagreement with items on your report. For more about this statement, see the section "Adding a 100-word statement" at the end of this chapter.

✔ **Exclude your name from lists for unsolicited credit and insurance offers.** Although creditors and insurers may use file information as the basis for sending you unsolicited offers of credit or insurance, they must also include a toll-free phone number for you to call if you want your name and address removed from future lists.

The opt-out toll-free number for all national credit-reporting agencies is 888-567-8688.

✔ **Initiate a fraud alert by calling one of the three credit bureaus.** If you believe your identity may have been stolen, you just have to make one phone call or visit one credit bureau website (as opposed to having to contact each of the three credit bureaus individually) to initiate an alert. A *fraud alert* requires the credit grantor to exercise enhanced levels of protection, such as taking additional steps to verify you are who you claim to be.

✔ **Freeze access to your credit report.** You can *freeze* your credit report for any reason. This allows you to lock the door on any unauthorized review or use of your credit information. The only exception is, of course, if Uncle Sam wants to see your credit record. Generally, you can freeze, and then unfreeze or thaw, your information as your needs warrant. You may be charged a small fee, but the process is effective.

✔ **Receive damages from violators.** If anyone violates the law, you can sue the person in state or federal court. Some people have, and they've collected millions of dollars!

✔ **Place an active-duty alert to protect military personnel's credit access.** Businesses that see an active-duty alert on your credit report must verify your identity before issuing credit in your name. The business may try to contact you directly, but if you're on deployment, doing so may be impossible. Therefore, the law allows you to use a personal representative to place or remove an alert. Active-duty alerts are effective for one year and may be renewed. The alert also cuts down on your junk mail. Your name is removed from the nationwide consumer-reporting companies' marketing lists for prescreened offers of credit and insurance for two years. Sweet!

For the complete story on the FACT Act . . .

If you just can't get enough of this stuff, the complete text of the FACT Act and Dodd-Frank is on the Federal Trade Commission's website (www.ftc.gov) and on the CD. You can also contact the FTC at:

If that doesn't satisfy you, contact your state or local consumer-protection agency or your state attorney general to find out more about your rights.

> Federal Trade Commission
> Consumer Response Center, FCRA
> Washington, DC 20580
> Phone 877-382-4367

Identifying and Disputing Inaccurate Information

You can't legally remove accurate and timely info from your credit report, whether it's good or bad. But the law does allow you to request an investigation of any information in your file that you believe is outdated, inaccurate, or incomplete. You're not charged for this, and you can do it yourself at little or no cost.

Inaccurate data serves no purpose for anyone in the credit-report chain. The credit bureaus, the lenders, and you all want the information in your report to be accurate.

In the following sections, I show you how to file a dispute with the credit bureaus as well as with the creditor in question.

Understanding the dispute process

The process for disputing and correcting inaccurate information is easy. Your role is to check your reports at least once a year, and if you see information that looks unfamiliar or wrong, you file a dispute with the bureau in question. Dispute procedures come with your credit report.

After you notify a bureau of a disputed item, the bureau contacts the source that placed the data in your report. That source has 30 days in which to respond. If the source can't verify the data within the time allowed — whether because the information never existed, the info can't be found, or

Helen (the data retriever) is on vacation — the bureau must remove the information from your report. If, on the other hand, the information is verified, it stays on your report. In either case, you're notified in writing of any actions or nonactions that occur as a result of your dispute.

If you disagree with the findings, you can contact the company that placed the erroneous report yourself and try to get it to change the info. Be sure to ask how the investigation was conducted and who was contacted. You also have the right to add a statement to your report or a specific trade line saying why you disagree.

If you place a statement on your report, be sure to keep track of the time that it's on the report so that it doesn't outlast the negative data it explains and cause you further problems.

Correcting all your credit bureau reports

Not all the bureaus have the same information in their files. So, for example, if you look at your Experian credit report, see an inaccuracy, follow the dispute process, and have it corrected, you may not be out of the woods. TransUnion or Equifax may have *different* inaccurate information. Therefore, you need to get all three reports to see which reports contain *which* false data.

If the exact same error appears on two or all three reports, you only need to dispute it once; if the information is inaccurate, the credit bureau reports this finding to the other two bureaus on your behalf. But, being a cautious person by nature, I suggest that you double-check.

Contacting the bureaus

Correcting all three reports is important, because some lenders and businesspeople purchase the three-in-one report that includes a credit score and credit-history information from each of the three bureaus. Each bureau has slightly different procedures for consumers to file disputes, but all three allow you to dispute inaccurate or out-of-date information by phone, online, or by mail:

- ✔ **Equifax:** Call the phone number provided for disputes on your credit report and be sure to have your ten-digit credit-report confirmation number (on your report) available. You can also dispute by mail at Equifax Information Services LLC, P.O. Box 740241, Atlanta, GA 30374 (no confirmation number is required on written correspondence) or online at www.equifax.com.

✔ **Experian:** You can dispute by phone by using the toll-free number on your credit report; online at www.experian.com; or by mail at Experian, P.O. Box 9701, Allen, TX 75013.

✔ **TransUnion:** You can dispute any information by phone; online at www.transunion.com; or by mail at TransUnion Consumer Solutions, P.O. Box 2000, Chester, PA 19022-2000 (be sure to include the completed request for investigation form found on the website).

Though initiating a dispute by phone or via the Internet may be the easiest route, most experts suggest that you keep written records of everything you do (names, times, dates, and so on) to create a trail of documentation you can point to if things go wrong or get lost.

If you choose to dispute items on your credit report via mail, write a letter stating which item(s) you're disputing. Include any facts that support and explain your case, and include copies (not originals) of documents that support your position. Enclose a copy of your credit report with the items in question circled or highlighted. Be sure to provide your complete name and address and to tell the company what your desired action is (correction or deletion). Also, if you contact the credit bureau by mail, send your letter by certified mail, return-receipt requested, so you can document the fact that your dispute letter was mailed and received. Keep copies of your dispute letter and enclosures.

The CD includes a sample letter to a credit bureau called "Request To Remove Error" that disputes information on a credit report.

Avoiding a frivolous dispute

Credit bureaus must investigate any disputed items in question — usually within 30 days — unless they consider your dispute frivolous, in which case they're required to notify you within five business days. The bureau must tell you why it considers your dispute frivolous and explain what you must do to convert the dispute into one that will start the dispute process.

So what is frivolous? If you send a long list of disputes — for example, you list all the negative information on your credit report — you may give the appearance of trying to overwhelm the agency with requests just to get items taken off your report while you apply for a loan. In this situation, the agency may refuse to honor your request. For this reason, you're better off sending only a few disputes in a single letter.

Following through with the creditors and bureaus

The credit-reporting agency must forward all relevant data you provide to the company that originally provided the information. When the company receives the request for verification from the credit bureau, it must investigate, review all relevant information, and report the results to the credit bureau.

- ✔ **If the information is found to be inaccurate,** all nationwide bureaus are notified so they can correct this information in your file.

- ✔ **If the company can't verify the accuracy of the information you're disputing,** the information must be deleted from your file.

- ✔ **If the disputed information is incomplete,** the credit bureau must update it. For example, if you were once late in making payments but your file doesn't show that you've caught up, the bureau must show that you're now current in your payments.

- ✔ **If the disputed information in your file shows an account that belongs to another person,** the bureau must delete it.

When the investigation is complete, the credit bureau must give you the written results and a free copy of your updated credit report if the dispute results in a change of information. (The bureau may refer to your request for an investigation as a *reinvestigation;* they're the same thing.) If an item is changed or removed, the bureau can't put the disputed information back in your report unless the company providing that information subsequently verifies its accuracy and completeness. Then the credit bureau must give you written notice that includes the name, address, and phone number of the company that provided the verification.

You can request that the bureau send notices of corrections to anyone who received your report in the past six months. If you've applied for a job, you can have a corrected copy of your report sent to anyone who received a copy during the past *two years* for employment purposes.

If you aren't satisfied with the results of your dispute, you can dispute the item directly with the creditor (see the "Contacting the creditor" section later in the chapter). Be sure to include copies of all the information you have. You also have the right to include a 100-word statement of the dispute in your report and in future reports. Submit the written statement to the credit-reporting agencies, which are required to include it in your report (see the "Adding a 100-word statement" section later in the chapter). Depending on each bureau's rules, this statement can stay on your report indefinitely, so don't forget about it!

Knowing the rules on negative information

When the negative information in your report is accurate, only the passage of time can assure its removal. Most accurate negative information stays on your report for seven years, but certain exceptions to the seven-year rule exist:

- ✔ Criminal convictions may be reported without any time limitation.

- ✔ Chapter 7 bankruptcy information may be reported for ten years.

- ✔ IRS liens remain on your credit report indefinitely, until removed by the IRS.

- ✔ Unpaid student loans are reported indefinitely as long as they remain unpaid. After they're paid, they remain on your credit report for an additional seven years before dropping off.

- ✔ An inquiry due to an application for more than $150,000 worth of credit or life insurance or a job paying a salary of more than $75,000 has no time limit.

- ✔ A lawsuit or an unpaid judgment against you can be reported for seven years or until the statute of limitations runs out, whichever is longer.

If you're unhappy with the results of your dispute or think you've been treated unfairly or haven't been taken seriously, contact the Federal Trade Commission (FTC). The FTC works to prevent fraudulent, deceptive, and unfair business practices in the marketplace and to provide information to help consumers spot, stop, and avoid these practices. To file a complaint or to get free information on consumer issues, visit www.ftc.gov or call 877-382-4357 (TTY 866-653-4261).

What to do if you're not sure about your data

The dispute process is protected from abuse by the law, so you don't want to dispute information that you know is accurate or claim that an account listing is the result of identity theft when you know that's not the case. However, you can dispute any listing in good faith if you're uncertain of its validity — in other words, if you can't find records that confirm the item, you don't recall the status, or you're simply uncertain that the information has been reported correctly.

Follow the dispute processes outlined in this chapter and explain why you believe the item is questionable. Just as you might challenge a word that you aren't familiar with in a game of Scrabble with friends, disputing information about which you aren't completely sure is okay. Disputing information that you know is correct is *not* okay.

Contacting the creditor

Any financial institution that submits negative information about you to a national credit-reporting agency has to tell you so. This gives you a heads-up to jump on errors earlier than under the old laws.

You have a right to directly contact the furnisher of the disputed information. The actual contact process varies and can be as simple as walking into the credit department and explaining the problem, calling the company's toll-free number, or visiting its website (many companies' websites also have information on reporting fraud).

After you contact the creditor, it must investigate the dispute and report the results back to you following the same guidelines that the credit bureaus have to follow (see the preceding section), including responding in the same time frame as the bureaus.

Best of all, the creditor can't continue to report the negative information without noting that the info is in dispute. And if the information that's been disputed was reported as the result of a possible identity theft, then it can't be reported at all while the investigation is pending.

Again, as with the credit bureaus, the creditor must respond to your request within 30 days. If the creditor doesn't respond, the item in dispute is removed or corrected. If the creditor finds the information to be inaccurate, it must be corrected. If the information is outdated or someone else's, it must be removed. The result must be submitted to each credit-reporting agency with which the creditor has shared the incorrect information. If your dispute isn't found to be valid, you can add a 100-word statement to your report explaining why you dispute the item.

Be sure to keep good records such as names, dates of contact, and copies of letters and e-mails. Any company can experience what I call *bureaucratic memory loss.* So if you get a response like, "We've never heard of this before; who were you speaking to?" you'll have the answer handy. Good record keeping keeps these delays and irritations to a minimum.

Adding Positive Info to Your Credit Report

Just as negative information on your credit report can be a problem, insufficient information can also cause trouble. The best way to get positive information inserted into your credit report is to make payments to your creditors on time and in the full amount each month. Do so for a year or more and you'll have made great strides in improving your credit history and your credit score.

Called a *thin file* in the industry, a file with very little information in it may not be able to be scored. To get around this problem you can request that an expansion score be used. An *expansion score* uses information from alternative databases (such as cell phone records) to get enough data to form a valid score. Expect an extra charge for this service. The major supplier of this type of data is a company named MicroBilt. See `www.microbilt.com/fico-expansion-score.aspx` for more information.

Opening new credit accounts

Another way to get positive information into your data file is to open new credit accounts. Opening types of accounts that aren't already on your credit report is particularly helpful. For example, you may have several credit cards, so you could add an installment account, which can increase your "type of credit used" profile (see Chapter 7 for more information).

Be careful when using this tactic to improve your credit score. You may do more harm than good if you open an account with a large amount of available credit. This is likely to push your available credit over the limit of what's acceptable by lenders. Also, do this well in advance of applying for a loan because opening a new account may have a short-term negative impact on your score.

Adding a 100-word statement

Don't like what others are saying about you? You can add a 100-word statement to explain certain items on your credit report. Although a statement doesn't change your credit score, it may help answer questions that a lender or employer has when reviewing your report. Yes, the score is important, but so is the analysis by the person looking at your record. This statement can be used to accomplish several things:

- ✔ **Explain your side of the story for a series of past late payments, collections, or charge-offs.** These may be due to a life event such as a job loss, divorce, or illness.

- ✔ **Document your dispute information that you believe is incorrect but that the credit-reporting agency won't remove from your report.**

- ✔ **Tell your side of a dispute.** For example, you may have ordered a product that wasn't delivered on time or was unsatisfactory to you and you refused to pay for it. Although the situation wasn't resolved in your favor, you may be able to explain it more clearly in your 100-word note.

The CD contains a sample 100-word statement. Just plug in your personal info and you're ready to go!

Do these 100-word statements really help? It depends on who reviews your credit report and what you say. The statement stays on your report at least as long as the disputed item does, and at least one credit-reporting agency — TransUnion — thinks the statement is important enough to offer you help in writing it (call 800-916-8800 for help from TransUnion).

If you decide to put a statement on your report, be sure not to forget about it. In a year or two, old information becomes less of a factor in your score or eventually drops off your report. Statements can highlight past payment problems better forgotten, especially if the credit report shows no recent delinquencies. Your outdated statement could call attention to past situations that no longer apply, and it could hurt more than it helps. To remove an outdated statement from your credit report, send your request to the three major credit-reporting agencies at the addresses listed in the "Contacting the bureaus" section earlier in the chapter.

Chapter 15

Getting the Best Help for Bad Credit for Free

・・・

In This Chapter

▶ Figuring out whether you need credit assistance

▶ Taking care of some credit problems yourself

▶ Finding free mortgage help, credit counseling, and legal advice

・・・

*W*here does bad credit come from? The credit fairy? Bad credit karma? No, it comes from overextending your finances and falling behind on your debt payments. Yes, other factors make up a credit score, such as the length of your credit history and whether you've shown that you can handle a variety of types of credit. But nothing whacks your credit score and report like being delinquent on payments and overusing your lines of credit. FICO, the company known as Fair Isaac that produces one of the most widely used credit scores, counts these two factors as 65 percent of your score, and lenders are very hesitant to lend money to people with too much debt or too many late payments, regardless of their credit score. So the only legitimate way to get rid of bad credit is to get your spending and income in sync and then make sure you make all your debt payments on time, as agreed.

Doing so can be easier said than done, so you may need some help. Getting help from someone with lots of experience is a smart thing to do. Getting it for free is even better. Yet when it comes to seeking help for money or credit problems, many people avoid it. Why? Because getting the wrong help can just make matters worse. After all, haven't you been taught that when an offer is too good to be true, it usually is?

In this chapter, I help you sort through the conflicting and overblown claims for help that you find in the media. I also include valuable insights to help you decide which problems you can handle on your own, when to turn to others for assistance, and where to get the help you need.

Knowing Whether You Need Help

If you're asking yourself whether you need to get some outside advice or help, you're no doubt feeling some pressure, even if it's only a squeeze. This is a very personal decision with one or two exceptions, which I cover in the following sections.

Gauging your need for outside assistance

To help decide whether outside assistance is right for you, ask yourself — and include your partner if you're not in this alone — a few simple questions.

- ✔ **Are you stressed out to the point where you need assistance?** You know you need to get some game-changing help when

    - You screen your calls to avoid creditors (see Chapter 18 for more info).

    - You argue with your partner about money or credit.

    - Your sleep is interrupted because of financial worries, and you don't look forward to getting up in the morning and greeting the day.

- ✔ **Are you (or you and your partner) being pulled in multiple directions regarding possible solutions?** You may be unsure about which approach to use:

    - Increasing income to support your current bills and future goals (refer to Chapter 4).

    - Decreasing expenses to bring your lifestyle in line with your present income (check out Chapter 2).

    - Getting a loan to pay off debt or reduce payments (flip to Chapter 5 for more).

    - Filing for bankruptcy (see Chapter 18).

- ✔ **Are you dealing with multiple creditors or multiple problems at the same time?** You probably can use outside help if

    - More than two or three collectors or creditors have you on speed dial (check out Chapter 18).

    - You have many problems at the same time (for example, financial, medical, and marital) creating stress in your life.

✔ **Are you more than one month late on your mortgage payment?** No matter what else is going on, or even if nothing else is going on, you need to see a counselor now! A delay or runaround from a servicer can cost you

- Thousands of dollars.

- Your credit.

- Your home (see Chapter 17 to avoid a foreclosure).

✔ **Are you thinking that bankruptcy may not be so bad for your credit?** Getting professional, nonprofit counseling before you decide is smart; otherwise, you may not know

- Whether bankruptcy will solve your problems or add to them.

- Whether other alternatives exist that may be less damaging to your credit.

✔ **Are you new to credit or new to this country and don't like your current credit situation but don't know what to do next?** You'll benefit from help if

- You don't understand how credit works.

- You need to establish credit.

- You want to get started on your own version of the American Dream as soon as possible (refer to Chapter 9 for more info).

Handling situations on your own

In the following sections, I outline three credit situations that you can probably resolve without much help.

To solve any credit/debt problem, you need to

✔ Identify the cause of the problem and resolve to fix it.

✔ Know how much money you have available to work with.

✔ Act quickly.

Credit cards

If you can't make this month's credit card payment or if you've missed a payment already, you need to take action on your own. As long as you know what you can afford and you don't mind explaining your situation over the phone, you can get quick results. Here's what to do: Call the toll-free customer service number and explain who you are, what happened, and how you'd like to handle the situation. If you need a break from having to make payments, say so. If you can make up the missed payments over the next month or two, make an offer. Just make sure that you can make good on the offer. Be sure to ask the customer service representative not to report your account as late to the bureaus. This decision is up to the credit card company; often, the company will go along with your request as long as you keep your end of the bargain.

Usually, if you're polite and proactive and you contact the credit card company before the company contacts you, this approach establishes you as a good customer who needs and deserves some special consideration — much better than a customer who's behind in payments, doesn't call, and may be a collection risk.

Be careful about asking that a payment be stretched out for more than a month or two. If you need three months to catch up, you may get it — or even qualify for a longer hardship program — but the creditor may close your account, which hurts your credit. Also, don't be surprised if the company asks you to do more than you think you can. The company doesn't know the details of your situation. Do *not* agree to anything you don't think you can deliver. Saying that something isn't possible and explaining why is much better than caving in but not being able to follow through. Ask to talk to a supervisor — he or she may have more authority to bend the rules.

Mortgages

If you're behind on your mortgage payment but you're within the grace period allowed in your loan documents (typically 10 to 15 days from your contractual due date) and you have the money to make up the shortfall, just send it in. If you're past the grace period, what you need to do to catch up depends on the state in which you live. Say you're behind on your monthly payment of $1,000 from last month. This month you can only send in $500 extra with your $1,000 payment, so then you'll be short $500, right? Wrong. You may be behind the full $2,000 if the bank doesn't accept either payment because you didn't catch up in full. Or the bank may apply the extra $500 to this month's principal payment rather than to last month's deficit. So the gist is, if you aren't far behind and you can catch up in one shot, do it. Otherwise, don't delay — see the section "Considering credit counseling" later in this chapter and get help.

Mortgage lenders count delinquency occurrences differently from credit card issuers. As soon as you're one day beyond the grace period, mortgage lenders consider you late, back to the original, contractual, nongrace due date. After you're 90 days late from the contractual due date (not the grace period), all the rules change, and you're in serious danger of a foreclosure! (Check out Chapter 17 to find out what a foreclosure can do to your credit and how to avoid it.) Also, be mindful that some banks have shorter grace periods for mortgage holders who don't have a bank account with them.

Student loans

Getting some breathing room on a student loan isn't difficult if you have a qualifying reason for not being able to pay. Unemployment, a low-paying job, illness, a return to school — any of these reasons may qualify you for a short-term waiver, but only if you give the lender a call before you get into a default situation. The student loan people usually cooperate as long as they think you're playing it straight with them.

If you don't think you have enough money to catch up on your payments, you may have an alternative: The money may be hidden in your financial budget clutter. The first step in addressing a financial problem is to maximize your sources of income and minimize your expenses. A spending plan (or budget) helps you with that. Only a real spending plan that accounts for at least 90 percent of all your income and expenses will help. Rough guesses don't yield the results you need. Turn to Chapter 4 for more on budgeting.

Identifying Help You Can Really Get for Free

Many sources of financial advice and help charge one way or another, including debt settlement firms, debt reduction companies, debt erasing lawyers, for-profit credit counselors, credit monitoring services, and credit repair companies. And despite TV and radio ads that seem to promise better credit and relief from debts, collectors, and even the IRS, only three sources provide truly helpful, truly free assistance for those whose credit is overextended:

- ✔ **A mortgage counselor:** Mortgage counselors can obviously help you with mortgage issues. They're expert at helping you make the decision whether to stay in your home and then making your decision work in the best way possible for you. See the next section for help in finding a mortgage counselor.

- ✔ **A nonprofit credit counseling agency:** I'm a big fan of good credit counselors for a number of reasons: They're free, they take the time necessary to tailor solutions to your situation, they're well trained, and their mission in life is to help you, pure and simple. The main things they deal with are goal setting, identifying the sources of your problem and a solution, and budgeting (the foundation of everything financial). For tips on locating a good credit counselor, see the "Finding a great credit-counseling agency" section later in the chapter.

✔ **A pro bono lawyer:** Because credit and collections are governed by laws and because life isn't always fair, the time may come when you need an attorney. But if you're broke or quickly getting there, paying for an attorney may not be possible. Pro bono lawyers work for little or nothing. See the "Working with an attorney" section later in the chapter for advice on how to find a pro bono lawyer.

In the following sections, I cover these sources of free assistance in more detail.

The financial guru media celebrity can't take the time to understand your situation, so although he or she may give you some useful general information, getting help that's useful to your specific situation is unlikely. Plus, you can't get important follow-up advice to fine-tune your options and actions. Magazines offer still more generic help that may give you ideas but rarely solutions.

Getting help with your mortgage

Home mortgage debt is different from all other types of debt and can be very complicated. I strongly urge you to use a professional to be sure you don't make costly and damaging credit mistakes. Here are a few places to look for professionals:

✔ **Hope Now:** This organization is an alliance among counselors, mortgage companies, investors, and other mortgage players. It helps distressed homeowners work out mortgage problems so they can stay in their homes. The folks at Hope Now know the ropes, have access to decision makers, and can help you with the necessary paperwork for free. The U.S. Department of the Treasury and the U.S. Department of Housing and Urban Development back this alliance. For help, call 888-995-4673 or see www.hopenow.com.

✔ **State housing authorities:** Every state has a housing authority. These organizations offer help to first-time homebuyers and homeowners in crisis, referrals to counseling, and sometimes funds to cure a delinquency. You can find one in your state or community at www.phada.org/ha_list.php and www.ncsha.org/housing-help.

✔ **Legal/document review:** One of your last resorts is to see an attorney to review your loan documents. Some documents may have been drawn or executed incorrectly and may be challenged in court. A pro bono attorney may be able to help you for free. See the "Working with an attorney" section later in this chapter.

Considering credit counseling

A legitimate, certified credit counselor may be just the help you need to get a handle on your financial problems. A nonprofit credit-counseling agency serves as an objective party to help you see your financial situation without emotion and fear clouding your vision. In addition, a trained and certified counselor may be able to offer you some credit education, personalized budgeting advice, and a custom-tailored plan to get you out of debt — all for nothing or next to nothing.

Recognizing debts credit counseling can help with

Although credit counseling can help in a variety of circumstances, I believe it's essential in five situations. So if you find yourself dealing with any of the following scenarios, I suggest you get some outside advice pronto, before matters get further out of hand.

- ✔ **Mortgage default:** The rules are complex, the dates are often inflexible, and the servicers are often paper pushers who waste your time until a foreclosure is imminent. Many credit counselors, but not all, are certified as mortgage counselors and can get to the right people faster than you and can lead you through a complex process based on a lot of experience and special access to decision makers.

- ✔ **Multiple bill collectors:** You can handle one or two collectors, but when you get to five, ten, or even more, conflicting demands can be impossible to balance.

- ✔ **Joint credit problems:** Credit problems are exacerbated when you share them with someone who doesn't see things the way you do. An outside, dispassionate point of view can make all the difference.

- ✔ **Debts that are backed by assets:** Loans for cars, houses, and boats are all secured by an asset. If you don't or can't pay, the lender can repossess and sell your car, your home, or your yacht. If you don't pay your credit card bill, the lender doesn't have any collateral it can take, because it has no security beyond your word and your willingness to pay as agreed. As a general rule, the more security lenders have, the less willing they are to work with you to solve what they see as your problem.

- ✔ **Bankruptcy:** You must get credit counseling before you can file for bankruptcy. Be sure to pick a good agency that does a lot of this stuff. The agency should be fast, efficient, and cost-effective. Otherwise, you may run into problems and delays later on. See Chapter 19 on bankruptcy for more info.

In all these situations, you stand to benefit from talking to a professional who can help you with his or her experience, resources, and a clear and unbiased outside view of your situation that you can't get when you're stuck in the middle of things.

Knowing what a credit-counseling agency can offer you

Although no magic wand exists to make all your financial problems disappear, a good, certified credit counselor can offer thoughtful and useful solutions. Expect more than one option for resolving things, including some options you won't like. Your counselor can give you a balanced perspective of what you need to do, how long it will take, and what resources are available to help you along the way. Your counselor will probably discuss bankruptcy, as well as other solutions.

Goal-setting for the future

A good credit counselor offers solutions with your future goals in focus. A solution that works best for you is one that not only deals with current issues but also takes into account how you see your future. For example, if you're planning to buy a house, get a security clearance at work, or send your triplets to college in five years, that future goal affects which courses of action best fit your needs.

Improved communication with your family

For about 75 percent of the approximately 2 million people who bare their souls to credit counselors each year, advice and direction are all they need. One unexpected byproduct of credit counseling is improved financial and other communication. For many couples and families, the credit counseling session is the first time that they openly communicate about goals, spending priorities, and even some secrets such as hidden debts.

A plan that works for you

Expect to have a customized *action plan* when you're finished with your credit counselor. To be useful, an action plan has to fit the way you live. If it doesn't, you won't follow it. You don't wear clothes that are too tight, and you won't follow a poorly fitted financial plan. A comfortable budget designed with your spending and saving style in mind is more likely to be effective.

An often overlooked aspect of using nonprofit credit-counseling agencies is that they know a lot about other community resources that may be able to help. Doing due diligence before making referrals to other resources, whether community, legal, or otherwise, is part of a good agency's service.

The credit-counseling process isn't something you can breeze through in 15 minutes, because the plan you walk away with is tailor-made for you and your financial situation.

Periodic checkups

Expect some fine-tuning to adjust to changes down the road after counseling. Although your counselor anticipates bumps in the road as much as possible when developing your plan, the counselor can't foresee the future. Murphy's Law applies to financial and credit problems in spades. Not only can things go wrong, but with limited financial resources, every bump in the road feels much worse. Ongoing involvement with your credit-counseling agency as you navigate this credit-repair journey helps you stay the course. Expect the agency to make this easier for you by giving you names, e-mail addresses, and phone numbers of people to contact beyond the agency for more help. You should be able to go back to your counselor for additional suggestions and referrals as you go along, although most people, when they have a workable plan in hand, are off on their own.

Finding a great credit-counseling agency

Here are some things to look for in a quality credit-counseling organization:

✔ Nonprofit status.

✔ Accreditation by an independent third party, especially the Council on Accreditation.

✔ A willingness to spend at least 45 to 60 minutes with you, and more if needed. And for free.

✔ An agency that has been around for at least ten years.

✔ An agency that offers help the way you're most comfortable receiving it — in person, by phone, or via the Internet.

Here are a couple of organizations that can help you with your credit-counseling needs:

✔ **The National Foundation for Credit Counseling:** www.nfcc.org; 800-388-2227.

✔ **The Association of Independent Consumer Credit Counseling Agencies:** www.aiccca.com; 866-703-8787.

Deciding on debt-management plans

For about 25 percent of those who turn to credit counselors, more than advice is prescribed. In these cases, in addition to the action plan (see the section "A plan that works for you" earlier in this chapter), a debt-management plan is recommended. A *debt-management plan* (sometimes called a *debt-repayment plan*) involves the agency as an intermediary, meaning that for a small monthly fee, the agency handles both communications and payments on your behalf. A debt-management plan includes revised payments that

✔ Are acceptable to all your creditors.

✔ Leave you enough money to handle your living expenses.

✔ Generally get you out of debt in two to five years.

Debt-management plans are an alternative to bankruptcy and often go by other names, such as a *workout plan, debt consolidation,* or an *interest-rate-reduction plan.* Debt-management plans offer all these benefits and perhaps a lot more. Here's how they work: When creditors realize that you can't meet the original terms of your credit cards or other loan agreements, they also realize that they're better off working with you through your credit counselor. Under a debt-management plan, your creditors are likely to be open to a number of solutions that are to your advantage, including

✔ Stretching out your payments so that the combination of *principal* (the amount you originally borrowed) and interest pays off your balance in 60 months or less.

✔ Changing your monthly payments to an amount you can afford to pay.

✔ Reducing your interest rate and/or any fees associated with your loan.

✔ Refraining from hounding you day and night.

Why would creditors be willing to do all these things for you? Because if they don't do some or all of them, and if you really can't make the payments, they'll spend a lot more money on collections than they'd give you in concessions. Plus, maybe you'll file bankruptcy, and then your creditors may *never* get their money.

The critical point here is that the creditor has to believe that you can't make the payments as agreed. But how does the creditor believe that without staking out your house or apartment? The creditor generally takes the word of the nonprofit credit-counseling agency you go to for help. Still, being lenders, creditors will check your credit report from time to time while you're on a debt-management plan to make sure you haven't opened new lines of credit.

The value of an intermediary

You may wonder why a credit-counseling agency has to serve as an intermediary as part of a debt-management plan. Why can't the agency just set up the plan and leave you to follow it on your own, without paying the agency a monthly fee?

The answer is twofold:

✔ **Most people hit a bump or two in the repayment road.** Through its ongoing involvement, your credit-counseling agency can explain your situation to the creditor, dispassionately and professionally. Many plans would blow up at the first misstep without the trusted intermediary to smooth strained communications.

✔ **The creditors want the credit-counseling agencies involved.** Creditors can easily reach agencies for questions, the agencies' checks don't bounce, and the agencies don't get excited and yell over the phone the way consumers have been known to do.

Steering clear of debt-settlement plans

Debt settlement isn't the same as credit counseling or a debt-management plan. It's sometimes advertised as a way to save money, but it can be one of the most expensive methods of all! In a *debt-settlement plan,* you pay money to a company that holds your money without making any payments, until the creditor gives up hounding you and is supposedly ready to take less than the face value of the debt.

This course of action *severely* damages your credit for years to come. If that's not enough to scare you off, consider this: Often, if you actually get to a settlement, the amount that

the creditor forgives actually becomes taxable income to you! You guessed it: The IRS wants taxes on the forgiven amount, which can, in some cases, add up to thousands of dollars due on April 15 to Uncle Sam. And those agents at the IRS don't go away! Even if you later decide to go the bankruptcy route, the IRS still gets its money.

Debt settlement is an unsavory, confrontational business. My advice: Don't do it! If you must, use a qualified attorney whom you know to negotiate settlements on your behalf.

Sounds like a good deal: lower interest rates, smaller payments, and all. Well, the debt-management plan isn't a free lunch. The minuses may include

- ✔ A possible negative impact on your credit report, depending on how your creditors report your credit-counseling account (although just being in a debt-management plan doesn't affect your credit score).
- ✔ Restricted access to credit during the term of the plan.
- ✔ Difficulty in changing credit-counseling agencies after you begin a debt-management plan.

The bottom line is this: If you're in debt crisis or you're concerned you may be getting close to it, a debt-management plan from a good credit-counseling agency may be a solution. If you're just shopping for an interest-rate reduction or a consolidation-loan alternative, a debt-management plan may *not* be in your best interest.

Working with an attorney

You may be asking yourself whether an attorney can possibly be free or low-cost. The answer is yes, if that's what you need. I said *need,* not *want.* If you can't afford an attorney, free or very low-cost services are available if you know where to find them, and that's what this section is all about.

The words *pro bono* come from the Latin and mean "for the public good." Pro bono lawyers exist in most firms and can be the very same lawyers who charge hundreds of dollars an hour to well-heeled clients but will help you for little to nothing. The trick is to find one.

Here are some suggestions on finding free legal help:

- ✔ **Legal Services Corporation (LSC):** LSC is the single largest provider in the country of civil legal aid for those who can't afford it. LSC is a nonprofit corporation that supports 136 legal aid programs through more than 900 offices throughout the United States. LSC offers a variety of help, including cases involving family law, housing and foreclosure issues, and consumer issues such as protection from lenders, debt management, and bankruptcy. LSC serves consumers at or below 125 percent of the poverty level, an income of $27,563 a year for a family of four at the time of this book's publication. See www.lsc.gov.

- ✔ **Local bar association:** Your local bar association can help you find the help you need for what you can afford to pay. The American Bar Association has a consumers' guide to legal help on its website to help you find such resources in your state; see http://apps.americanbar. org/legalservices/findlegalhelp/home.cfm.

- ✔ **LawHelp:** LawHelp (www.lawhelp.org) helps low- and moderate-income consumers find free legal aid programs in their communities and provides links to other social service agencies.

- ✔ **Pro Bono Lawyers:** This website (http://probonolawyers.org) has nearly 200 links covering all 50 states, with info about lawyers who may be willing to work for free or for a reduced rate depending on your circumstances.

- ✔ **Armed Forces Legal Assistance (AFLA):** All branches of the military can find legal assistance at a central routing site: http://legalassistance. law.af.mil/content/locator.php.

A qualified attorney can handle anything that a mortgage counselor or a credit counselor can. The big difference is that most attorneys don't deal with credit situations every day. As a result, they'll probably take longer to get to the same place as someone who deals with hundreds or thousands of these cases every month. So though you can make a versatile tool fit most situations, sometimes you're better off with one designed specifically for the job at hand — especially when it comes to mortgage issues.

Chapter 16

Coping with Bad Credit and Debts

. . . .

In This Chapter

▶ Controlling your spending and paying your bills

▶ Opening a dialogue with your creditors

▶ Being proactive with creditors and collectors

▶ Knowing the collection rules

▶ Finding someone who can help you when a collector can't (or won't)

. . . .

Chances are that you opened to this chapter because you're feeling anxious about debts. You may be behind on your bills and wondering what to do. You may be getting calls from collectors and don't know how to possibly meet their demands for payment. Well, you've come to the right place to relieve your anxiety. Relax, take a calming breath, and read on.

When it comes to coping with debt and bad credit, an important ally is the Fair Debt Collection Practices Act (FDCPA). Congress enacted this federal law to amend the Consumer Credit Protection Act in order to prohibit abusive practices by debt collectors. That's right, laws exist to protect you from overzealous collectors who can be prosecuted if they threaten you, harass you, or lie to you. I bet you feel a little bit better already just knowing that specific rules govern how far a collector may go and that you have rights — legally enforceable rights! Knowing your rights under the FDCPA gives you some much-needed confidence when you must communicate with those who attempt to collect from you. I cover in detail your rights and protections in this chapter.

You can read the text of the FDCPA on the CD or on the Federal Trade Commission (FTC) website (www.ftc.gov).

Hopefully, your heart rate has decreased and you're feeling more comfortable about dealing with your debts. Let's get started!

Reducing Expenses to Clear Credit Woes

You owe, you owe, you owe. Where are you going to come up with the money to pay what you owe? In this section I explore ways to reduce expenses and free up some funds to satisfy those creditors and collectors. I'm not going to lie to you: Cutting expenses is no fun! But after you've done it successfully and have money to make payments, you feel much better. The short-term sacrifice of retooling your spending and changing some old habits turns out to be well worth the effort when you're able to reduce or even eliminate your credit or debt challenge.

Utilizing a spending plan

The best way I know to get the most out of every dollar you earn and set yourself on the road to credit recovery is to develop a detailed spending plan. I'm not proposing anything that leaves scars or hurts you permanently. A *spending plan* puts you in control of your finances, allowing you to decide how much money you spend on the stuff you want. A spending plan tells you just how much available cash you have to meet your obligations and allows you to set some aside to have fun, too. More important for this chapter, your spending plan lets you know how much you can afford to offer a collector or creditor to rid yourself of unwanted problem debt. For more on developing such a plan, turn to Chapter 4.

Creating a spending plan is easy, but putting it in writing is critical in determining what you need to change! The CD includes forms to help you. If you still feel overwhelmed, Chapter 15 offers advice on choosing a good credit counselor who can help you with this process for free. (Believe it or not, there *are* people who love putting together spending plans.)

Cutting the fat from your monthly spending

The simplest way to cut expenses is much like cutting calories when you're on a diet. When slimming down, you eat the stuff that's lower in calories and you skip the cake. When cutting expenses, do things that cost less (use more coupons at the grocery store and plan meals to match what's on sale) and lay off the expensive stuff (cancel that reservation to your town's hot new restaurant).

Speaking of calories and entertainment, one of the biggest entertainment expenses for American families is eating out. If you add up your monthly expense for restaurant food, you may be shocked. Even that $4-a-day latte on the way to work adds up to a more than $1,000-a-year expense. Instead of eating out, eat in more often, and pack a lunch for work or school. Make eating at home fun by involving the entire family in preparing some of the dishes you'd order at that fancy restaurant. You'll be surprised to see your monthly spending on food shrink by as much as 25 to 50 percent.

Some other entertainment cutbacks to consider are

- ✔ **Shopping as entertainment:** Cruising the mall often leads to purchases of nonessential items. You and I know that most entertainment shopping is for *wants* or stuff you didn't know existed until you saw it in the mall, not *needs*.

- ✔ **Movies, theater, sports events, and concerts:** You know how much a night at the movies can cost, especially after you add the cost of popcorn and drink. Don't even talk about season tickets for a major sports team. If by denying yourself these leisure activities you're afraid you'll become uncultured or uncool, look for free concerts and community plays in your town. Watch sports on TV instead of going to the games, and rent movies instead of going to the cineplex. Many local libraries allow you to check out movies and music for free.

- ✔ **Hobbies:** If your favorite pastimes come with a high price tag — golf or gambling, for example — consider switching to something that demands a little less of an investment, such as bike-riding (if you already own a bike) or bird-watching (as long as it doesn't entail a canoe trip down the Amazon).

You're not giving up doing something you love forever; you're only giving up these things until you resolve your current financial situation.

Finally, take a look at your monthly expenses and determine whether you can trim back anywhere. Some places to look are

- ✔ **Cellphone expenses:** Perhaps you can switch providers, combine several phones onto one plan, or switch to a less-expensive plan.

- ✔ **Cable TV:** Cut back on cable and spend more time reading, talking, or otherwise enjoying different pursuits.

- ✔ **Utilities:** Get energy-efficient lights, turn up or down your thermostat (depending on the time of year), and lower the temperature on your water heater. Check to see whether your utility offers free or low-cost energy audits to identify more opportunities to save money.

The savings from cutting back on expenses may not seem like much at first, but they add up quicker than you realize. And before you believe you can't go another day without a grande triple latte, you'll have reached your goal of regaining control of your finances and stabilizing your credit situation.

Paying Your Bills on Time and in Full

I recognize that if you're reading this chapter, there's at least a chance that not paying your bills on time may be what got you into a bad-credit situation in the first place. But making on-time payments for the amount agreed is the most important thing you can do to keep bad credit from getting worse. This section lays out specific ideas to help you pay your bills on time and keep creditors off your back.

Getting organized

Nothing is quite as frustrating as getting hit with a $25 or $35 late-payment fee on your credit card statement when you're trying to cut expenses. The good news is that a late payment on your account doesn't necessarily cost you any more than the fee. Thanks to the Credit Card Accountability, Responsibility, and Disclosure Act of 2009 (CARD Act), you no longer have to worry about getting hit with a penalty on your account for being one day late with your payment. New rules require 60 days past due for the penalty rate. Find out more about how the CARD Act benefits you in Chapter 5. Don't get me wrong, I still don't want you paying late and getting hit with large fees, but at least the punishment now better fits the crime.

Getting organized is a surefire way to avoid unnecessary late payments. Here are some options for getting organized:

✔ **Pay bills as soon as you receive them.** Make a pact with yourself to get the mail, sit down immediately, and write checks or go online to pay any bills *that day*.

✔ **Mark a calendar with due dates for all bills.** Allow at least a week for bills that you mail and a few days for bills that you pay online. Place the calendar where you'll see it every day so you don't miss any due dates.

✔ **Set up a filing system.** Place bills in folders or in due date order, marked with the day of the month that they need to be paid. The trick is remembering to place the bills in the folders or organizer and to check the folders on a daily or weekly basis.

Experiment, find a solution that works for you, and get those bills paid!

Stopping the paycheck-to-paycheck cycle

If you live paycheck to paycheck, you may find it difficult to pay all bills on time and in full every month because money is so tight, especially when an emergency crops up and you have to pay for it out of money allocated for another bill. Consider these tips:

✔ **Start a savings account.** Wait, what does starting a savings account have to do with living paycheck to paycheck? Plenty. Without emergency savings, you won't be able to stop living paycheck to paycheck. How else do you have money to replace the muffler or pay that doctor bill for your child? Find out more about the importance of savings in Chapter 4.

✔ **Ask your creditor to change your due date.** You can request that your due date fall when you have the money to pay the bill in full and on time.

✔ **Look to your job to free up extra cash.** If you want to increase your cash flow and can't get a second (or third) job, you may not have to look far. A couple of things you can do regarding your current job include

- **Check your payroll deductions.** If you get a hefty tax refund each year, see your employer and add withholding allowances on Form W-4 to increase your take-home pay. But if you'll end up writing a check to the IRS, don't do it.

For assistance in figuring out the right number of withholding exemptions you should take, see the IRS withholding calculator: `www.irs.gov/individuals/article/0,,id=96196,00.html?portlet=4`.

- **Free up some money in your retirement plan.** I'm not suggesting that you take money out of the plan; doing so would result in some ugly penalties! But you can temporarily reduce or suspend your contributions if that helps to close the gap. You can always make it up later.

✔ **Follow the advice in the "Reducing Expenses to Clear Credit Woes" section, earlier in this chapter.** Doing so can help you loosen up the money flow so you have more flexibility making payments.

Communicating with Your Creditors

Communicating effectively isn't always easy, and many people don't even know where to begin. If you're one of those people, keep reading. When dealing with creditors, communication can be even more difficult because of the associated emotion, guilt, and anger; basically, you have a recipe for conflict and communication breakdown.

From your end of the phone line, the situation looks like this: You're a responsible adult who has been a good customer for a long time. A series of unfortunate, unexpected, and undeserved events has descended upon you like a flock of unwanted relatives. You've tried for months to overcome your payment problems before asking for help. You can't seem to catch up. You're at the end of your rope, dangling at the edge of a cliff. But with some help, you know you can pull yourself out.

Collecting on a mortgage

An overdue mortgage payment is definitely a different animal from other types of overdue accounts. The rules for mortgages are very different because the debt is secured by a complex piece of collateral — namely, your home. Never allow your mortgage payment to be 90 days past due. Why? After your payment is 90 days overdue, you have to pay all the money past due — three months, plus the regular payment — or the foreclosure process begins. Send in less and you'll get it back.

Remember, after you're late on the first payment, the 15-day grace period no longer applies. Be careful not to cross the 90-day mark by mistake, thinking you still have 15 days to go.

Contact a good HUD-certified counseling agency and get help before you miss your second payment. You can find listings of approved housing counseling agencies by state at www.hud.gov or by calling 800-569-4287. I also recommend contacting the Homeownership Preservation Foundation (888-995-4673; www.995hope.org), a national network of nonprofit housing counselors funded by HUD who have a strong working relationship with most of the big mortgage servicers.

For more information on managing credit in a mortgage crisis, see Chapter 17.

From the creditor's point of view, the scenario looks like this: You made an agreement and broke it. Everyone else is required to pay his bills on time, including the collector, so why shouldn't you? You may be overspending and living it up beyond your means. You need to catch up on payments as fast as possible. If you don't come through with your payments, the mortgage servicers' business and job performance will be hurt, and when they get fired, they'll be unable to pay their bills.

See how different people can see the same scenario so differently? And before you accuse me of being soft on the creditor, let me just reassure you — I *am* on your side! I just know that you'll be more successful in getting the outcome you want if you're able to see the situation from your creditor's perspective. For whatever reason, you haven't been able to keep all the promises you made to your creditors. Although this doesn't mean you're a bad person, it does indicate that doing business with you may be more risky than doing business with someone who pays as agreed.

So now it's *your* job to explain why this isn't the case and why the creditor should accommodate you. Is resolution possible here? Yes — if you do your homework, offer a solution, and follow through on your promises. Where do you start? What do you say? To minimize negative perceptions, be proactive from the start and follow the steps in this section.

Contacting your creditor promptly

It's human nature to put off unpleasant tasks. However, when it comes to requesting assistance from your creditors, the earlier you make the request the better. From the creditor's point of view, three types of customers exist:

✔ Good customers who pay as agreed

✔ Good customers with a temporary problem who are willing to work things out

✔ Bad customers who have to be chased

You'd like to be the first type of customer, but sometimes, life pushes you into the second category. What's really important, however, is not to be classed in the third group.

The best time to let your creditors know you're in trouble is as soon as you *know* and have a solution to offer. Don't wait until you've missed a payment — or more than one — on that credit card or auto loan. Don't wait for the phone to ring or the letter to come and *then* give your story. Get in touch *before* the payment is late. By preempting the bad-news announcement, you increase the odds that your negative event won't show up on your credit report! Read on to find out what you need to say.

Explaining your situation

Depending on your preference, you may choose to contact the creditor by phone, in writing, via e-mail, or through the creditor's website. In some cases, you can even communicate through intermediaries like an attorney or credit counselor. Whatever method you use, you need to explain your situation as clearly and effectively as possible, assuring the creditor that, despite your temporary difficulties, you intend to get back on financial track as quickly as possible.

But what do you want to say? What can you do to increase the chances that you get the help you need and deserve? Here are some elements you want to communicate (using a phone conversation as an example):

✔ **Get the person's name.** Use it. Why? Because doing so adds a human dimension to the dialogue and may help personalize your call. Don't say "you" or "you people." I suggest you write the name down, because you're probably stressed out and may easily forget it. Plus, when you call the creditor again, you'll have a name to refer to.

✔ **Begin the conversation on a positive note.** Say something nice about the company and your relationship to it. For example, "I've been a customer for years and always had great products/service from you."

- ✔ **Briefly (in a minute or so) explain your circumstances.** For example, you lost your job, you have no savings, and you have only unemployment insurance for income.

- ✔ **Stick to the facts.** Skip all the gory details that may bias the listener in ways you can't anticipate. For example, you can simply say, "I experienced a serious illness and was off work for three months." Such circumstances are all too common — and understandable. Don't digress into details or emotional commentary such as, "I would never have gotten sick if I hadn't gone to that dirty Indian restaurant. Those people can't cook anything properly." After all, you may be speaking to a person in or from India!

Offering a solution

After you've succinctly laid out the situation, you're still not finished. Before you turn control of the conversation over to the customer service representative, I want you to propose a solution that works for you. Your goal is to make getting what you need as easy as possible for the creditor to agree to, and the best way is to just ask for what you need! Yes, this is a critical and very positive step in the communication process. Your lender may actually be relieved that you've taken the responsibility to come up with a workable plan. Doing so not only increases the chance that you'll get what you want but may also shorten the call if the rep can agree to your request, thereby making the rep look like a very productive employee to his or her boss. Plus, by keeping *more* control over the outcome, you have a much better chance to get a repayment plan that actually works for you. (You may even be able to negotiate a concession or two in your favor; see the section "Negotiating a payback arrangement" later in this chapter.)

Whatever your proposed plan, be sure to cover these bases:

- ✔ **Assure the creditor that you're already taking steps to resolve the problem** *now.*

- ✔ **Offer an estimate of how long you realistically need to rectify the situation.** Not "soon" or "I don't know."

- ✔ **Propose a specific payment figure and plan that you can manage.** Don't ask the creditor to suggest a payment. You won't like the answer.

- ✔ **Offer specifics.** Avoid saying, "I can't afford the $300-a-month payment right now. You're going to have to accept less." That's not a plan. "I need to reduce the monthly payment to $150 for the next four months. I could even pay $75 twice a month. Then, in four months, I believe I can return to $300, which only extends the length of the loan by two months." Now *that's* a plan. It shows that you're sensitive to the creditor's situation and that you're making a fair effort to make good.

✔ **Don't overpromise.** You may feel intimidated or embarrassed, and it's only natural to want to give the creditor what the creditor wants. Don't be surprised if the creditor pushes back and asks for more. Stick to your offer if possible. In the end, though, remember that the creditor won't be happy if you promise a certain payment and fail to deliver. If you get stuck, ask to speak to a manager, who may be able to approve your offer.

If you prefer to handle things in writing, check out the "Partial Payment Hardship Letter Current" document on the CD, along with other letters you may find useful as starting points.

Covering all the bases

After you propose your plan and the terms have been agreed on, ask for a letter with the new agreement to be mailed or e-mailed to you so there's no misunderstanding. If that doesn't seem to be forthcoming from your contact or if you don't receive written documentation of the new terms in a few days, follow up yourself, stating the agreement in writing.

Handling Those Collection Phone Calls

You have some late bills, but you put off dealing with them, and now you're getting calls from collectors. You may find yourself in the middle of a recurring nightmare of insatiable callers who won't go away and who seem to draw strength from your inability to give them what they want.

This scenario doesn't have to be the case. The Fair Debt Collection Practices Act (FDCPA) protects debtors from harassment from collectors, particularly if the harassment is via telephone. Armed with your knowledge of the rules and a plan of action, as I describe in this section, you can handle those calls before they handle you.

Deciding whether to answer the phone

After you know a collector is calling, you may find yourself reluctant to answer the phone for any number of reasons. You may have had a hard day at work, you may be overtired, or you may not be feeling in control of your emotions at the moment. Or if you've been contacted by the collector and you've already explained that you're doing your best and that's all you can do, having the same conversation again and again may feel frustrating and unproductive, especially if the collector is on the overbearing side. Don't answer the phone if you know you won't be able to have an effective conversation. (For tips on what to say, see the following section.)

You don't have to pick up the phone. Keep in mind, however, that although answering machines and caller ID can help you screen calls (and may help you with your sanity), they won't help you avoid or solve your debt problems. If collectors can't reach you by phone, they'll try to find another way to contact you.

Preparing to answer collection calls

When you decide it's time to bite the bullet and answer the phone to talk to the collector, you need to make sure you're prepared. The best way to be prepared is to write down the key points you want to cover in your conversation with the collector. Having a plan in mind helps you keep on track and in control of the call. It also helps you to not over-promise and under-deliver, to avoid losing your temper, and to know when to terminate the call if it gets abusive. Lastly, if you start to feel overwhelmed or backed into a corner by the collector, get outside professional help. You can find out about getting help in Chapter 15.

Even though you may feel nervous, guilty, or angry, you aren't the first or only person to have gone through debt collections. It happens all the time, and you *will* get through it.

If you're late on some bills, expect that sooner or later (typically when you're 30 to 90 days late or more) you'll get a call from a collector. If you decide to pick up the phone, here's what you need to do:

- ✓ **Get the caller's name and contact information.**

- ✓ **Use the collector's name.**

- ✓ **Ask for proof of the debt.** Mistakes happen, and crooks call to get money from people all the time. (See "Asking for proof the debt is yours," later in this chapter, for more information.)

- ✓ **Explain what happened.** Provide a very short story of why you're behind and what you're able to do, if anything, about the debt.

- ✓ **Make a payment offer.** You can make an offer for a period of time. Say you owe $1,000. If you offer to pay $50 per pay period for the next 20 weeks, that may be acceptable. Or you can offer to pay $25 per pay period until your next raise in three months, at which time you'll pay $75 per pay period. Offering the amount you're able to pay is always better than waiting for the collector to demand a certain amount. (See "Negotiating a payback arrangement" later in this chapter.)

- ✓ **Don't agree to a payment schedule you can't keep.** Be realistic or you may find yourself agreeing to something you know you can't follow through on. (See "Keeping your promise" later in this chapter.)

✔ **Get it in writing.** If you come to an agreement, ask for it to be put in writing so it's clear to both parties. If the collector won't do that, write the letter yourself (keeping a copy for your records) and send it to the collector by certified mail (return receipt) so you have proof that the collector received it.

Knowing what not to say

Saying the *wrong* thing in a conversation with a collector may be unproductive and can also push the conversation into a hostile confrontation that could end up causing you more harm. No matter how adversarial your caller seems, here are some definite don'ts:

✔ Don't let yourself get drawn into a shouting match.

✔ Don't make threats.

✔ Don't say you're getting a lawyer if you don't intend to.

✔ Don't say you're going to file bankruptcy if you don't plan to.

✔ Don't lie for sympathy (for example, "My mother's in the hospital," when your mother's on a celebrity cruise in the South Pacific). When you're caught stretching the truth, even once, people have a hard time believing you again.

Keeping Collectors in Check

Let me begin by demystifying the power of collectors. I'm told that collectors are people just like you and me but with a tough job to do. My personal experience over some 20 years of helping people who are dealing with debt is that this is sometimes, but not always, the case. Although some professionals in the debt-collection field see collections as no more than an extension of customer service to customers in trouble, others see collections as a power trip and an excuse to use unfair and abusive collection practices on people they think are vulnerable.

Some collections people work as employees of the company to which you owe the debt. They're termed *in-house collectors*. The FDCPA doesn't apply to them. In-house collectors are governed by individual state laws. Most, however, use the federal law as a benchmark to be sure they're on the safe side in case they're called to task for their actions.

The FDCPA sets the rules for outside or third-party collection agencies and prevents abuse and intimidation of individuals in debt. Very strict regulations exist that govern what a collector *may* and *may not do,* as well as what a collector *must do.*

Knowing what collectors can do

First, the *must do* rules: If a collector contacts you about a debt by phone, the collector has five working days to send you a written notification of the amount of debt you owe and the name of the creditor who referred the debt to the collector. The notice has to say that this is an attempt to collect a debt and that any information obtained will be used for that purpose. The written notice also must disclose that you have the right to dispute the debt within 30 days of receiving the notice.

The debt collector *may*

- **Contact you directly, unless you tell the collector not to call again or to contact your attorney instead and give the collector the attorney's contact information.** In this case, the file usually goes straight to a collection attorney.

- **Contact you by phone between 8 a.m. and 9 p.m., unless you agree to other times.** The collector can only contact you outside those hours if you offer permission to do so.

- **Call you at work.** However, if you tell the collector that your employer prohibits such contact, the collector must not call you at work.

- **Contact you by mail.** Although the collector can contact you by mail, the collector can't put information on the outside of the envelope that indicates a collection attempt or send information in a postcard.

- **Contact others to get information on where you live and work.** The collector can only request contact information. The collector can't say that he's calling in regards to an owed debt. The sticky part is that if the collector calls your wife or sweetie and *she* asks who the collector is, the collector can state his name and the name of his employer.

- **Super-size your statement.** Only charges that you agreed to under the original terms of your loan may be added to your bill. You'll find a list of them in the account terms, in the fine print that few people read. These charges include endless fees, huge interest rate hikes, and the costs of collection.

✔ **Ask for a postdated check.** Depending on the state in which you live, the collector may be entitled to ask for postdated checks. Look into your state guidelines. Although your state may permit collectors to ask for postdated checks, providing one is not in your best interest (see the nearby sidebar "Postdated checks: Good for the collector, bad for you" for more information).

✔ **Tell the credit bureaus that you're behind on your payments.** Remember, a delinquency that shows up on your credit report stays there for seven years and lowers your credit score.

✔ **Hike your interest rate.** You may be hit with a penalty rate. You can't pay the current bill, so why would creditors increase your interest rate to 20 or 30 percent? Because you're a higher risk than they thought, and because they can.

✔ **Repossess your purchase.** This is almost always a bad deal for you because the creditor determines the value of the repossessed item, and the creditor can charge you for costs incurred in reselling it, too.

✔ **Sue you in court.** The collector may ask a judge for a judgment against you in a court of law. Depending on your state laws, this can be a prelude to garnishing your wages or placing a lien on your home. A court action further damages your credit report.

✔ **Change the terms of your agreement.** Some collectors may allow you to make up what you owe over time by adding an additional amount to future payments. Some, to their credit, offer hardship programs, but usually only if you ask. Be sure to get any agreement or changes to existing agreements in writing, particularly if communications are, at best, strained. You need documentation to ensure the agreement is honored.

✔ **Accept or offer a debt-settlement option for less than the full amount.** If a lower amount is agreed on, the collector usually wants the settlement at once and in a single payment. The debt is reported negatively on your credit report as "settled." Depending on the amount of the debt forgiven (usually a $600 threshold), you may get a Form 1099C from the creditor in the mail at tax time. The IRS considers the forgiven portion of the debt as income to you and requires that you pay taxes on it. (Check out Chapter 18 for more on settlements.)

Knowing what collectors can't do

A debt collector is *not* allowed to

✔ **Threaten you.** Whether in writing or over the phone, a collector must use businesslike language. Any threatening, abusive, or obscene language is not allowed.

✔ **Be annoying.** An annoying collector — isn't that redundant? This rule means that the collector isn't allowed to make repetitive or excessively frequent phone calls to annoy or harass you.

✔ **Be deceptive.** No trick or treat, smell my feet! Collectors can't pretend to be anything other than what they are in order to get you on the phone.

✔ **Lie about the consequences.** Collectors can't claim that you've committed a crime or that you'll be arrested if you don't send payment. America doesn't have debtors prison.

✔ **Make idle threats.** Collectors can't threaten you with illegal actions or actions that they have no intention of carrying out. If they don't intend to take you to court, they can't threaten to.

Fighting harassment

Getting harassed by a collections agency? You're not alone. If you complain to the Federal Trade Commission (FTC), which watches over the collection industry, you'll be among the more than 80,000 people who lodge collection complaints annually. Some consumers have even taken collectors who overstep the law to court, and some of them have won very large settlements.

To file a complaint against a collector who is harassing you, contact the FTC at www.ftc.gov or 877-382-4357. The FTC won't follow up on your specific case, but your complaint helps others by allowing for patterns of possible law violations to surface. Enough complaints against the same collector and the FTC may act.

Other things you can do about harassment or abuse include the following:

✔ **Keep cool.** Always be professional and as calm as you can manage, and never raise your voice. Take notes during each call. Be prepared with facts and dates, and know what you're going to say before you say it. After all, the collectors do!

✔ **Get a name.** Always get the name of the person calling you, and ask for full contact information, including the name of the company and the manager of the office. Do this *before* things get out of hand.

✔ **Just say no.** If the collector goes over the top or breaks a rule (threatens, yells, uses obscene language, and so on), you can tell him to stop it and call back when he can act in a businesslike manner. Keep a record of the call and behavior.

✔ **Complain to the original creditor.** Even though you aren't in good graces at the moment, a complaint here can result in action. No business wants past or future customers scared away by an abusive collector. The original debt holder may take the debt back and deal with you directly if you make a good case.

✔ **Complain to the boss.** Remember, you were smart enough to ask for the manager's name when you were first contacted, so use it. Your complaint may be the one that gets the abuser canned. No collection agency wants to be sued because of a bully who can't be professional.

✔ **Tell the collector to deal with your lawyer.** This is a double-edged sword. After you tell a collector to contact your attorney, all contact with you ends. Usually, the collection agency sends the debt to its own lawyer.

Taking Charge of the Collection Process

The best way to deal with the collection process is to face your debts head on and as quickly as possible. Debts don't improve with age, and they certainly don't go away if you ignore them. In fact, as debts age, they get bigger, uglier, and harder to satisfy. Unresolved debts also have an uncanny knack for resurfacing when you're least prepared to deal with them.

Accounts that are 30 to 90 days *delinquent* (overdue) are usually handled by people who work for the company from which you bought your product or service. If you're contacted by a third-party collector early in the process, chances are the company hired the collection agency because of its tact and effectiveness rather than its skill for offending people. Outside or third-party collectors are covered by the FDCPA and must abide by those rules (see the "Keeping Collectors in Check" section earlier in the chapter). The biggest difference between an inside and an outside collector is that the inside collector may want to keep you as a customer in addition to collecting the money due. However, if the business determines that you're unlikely to make your payments, your customer status becomes less and less of a factor in working things out.

Calling your creditors before they call you is always better because it places you in a much different category from the category you'd find yourself in if they do the dialing. Good faith is on your side, but even that fades if you don't deliver on your commitments. Plus, you're prepared and ready for business instead of having to respond to an unexpected call.

This section walks you through what to do to give you the greatest chance of success when dealing with collectors.

Postdated checks: Good for the collector, bad for you

At some point in the collection process, you may be asked to send postdated checks to the creditor. The logic here is that, with the postdated checks in hand, you show a firm intent to honor your payment agreement, and the collector doesn't have to call you to remind you to send in any payments you may have agreed to. This scenario also covers the collector who has accepted your promise to pay in case you "forget" to send a check at the appointed time.

This practice is akin to putting a piece of bacon on your dog's nose and telling him not to eat it.

Giving a collector a postdated check is almost always a bad idea because she'll likely be very tempted to cash the check too early, even though she isn't supposed to. If she cashes the check early and the money isn't in the account yet, the check will bounce, and the collector will be upset. If she cashes the check early and the money is there but the collector gets it sooner than you planned, all your other checks may start to bounce.

Asking for proof the debt is yours

When you get a call or a letter claiming you have a past-due financial obligation, make sure you verify its accuracy. Even if you're sure you owe the money, ask for details: which account, what the bill was for, how old the debt is, when the statement was mailed to you, and so on. Doing so never hurts. Why? Here are two good reasons:

- ✔ **Mistakes happen.** Creditors make mistakes, so asking for a little proof is reasonable. You're not denying you owe the debt; you're just making sure that you owe this particular debt and that they have the right customer and the right account.

- ✔ **Some callers are scammers.** People will call, e-mail, or write and say you owe money. Maybe you do, but not to them. They may even have proprietary information that persuades you that they must be legitimate, but they may not be. Get the facts in writing through the U.S. mail before you act. Having the information mailed to you opens scammers up to mail fraud charges.

The FDCPA rules say that you have 30 days to respond to a collection attempt, and you're both smart and well within your rights to dispute a debt. Here's how you do it: Send the collector a letter via certified mail with a return receipt. In the letter, ask the collector to provide proof of the debt. Keep copies of everything you send. When you dispute the debt, the collector must stop all activity and provide you with proof of your obligation before reinitiating contact.

Disputing a bill stops collection activity, but it doesn't stop the clock. Your bill continues aging during the process. So try to resolve matters as quickly as possible when you're sure the debt is yours and the collector is legit.

Knowing when debts fade away: Statutes of limitations

The United States is the land of the present, the here and now. As a result, people tend to let the past, well, be history. This applies to old debts, too, when they become ancient history. Each of the 50 states has a *statute of limitations* (SOL) that limits how long the courts can be used for collecting a debt. After a debt is anywhere between 2 and 15 years old (depending on your state of residence) without a payment having been made, it becomes history as far as the law is concerned.

I don't have enough room here to give you every state's SOL rules, but you can check out www.bankrate.com/finance/credit-cards/state-statutes-of-limitations-for-old-debts-2.aspx to help you find out where you stand. Overage debts can't be enforced in a court of law. This turns even the fiercest collector into all bark and no bite.

Here's what to do if you think you may have an old debt that qualifies for SOL treatment:

- ✔ **Verify the last time you made a payment.** Use your credit report or, if you keep checking account records for seven years like I do, find your old check registers. Depending on your bank, you may be able to access checking payments from long ago. You don't want to see any recent payments here. Making a payment resets the clock on the SOL all over again. Say it has been 6 years and 51 weeks since your last payment, and the SOL is 7 years. If you make a payment, the 7-year period starts again. So expect some pressure from the collector to get you to send in anything as the SOL date approaches.

- ✔ **Check the CD to see what your state's age limit is for SOL status.** The info on the CD isn't a legal guarantee, but it is grounds for you to see a lawyer if you believe your debt may qualify.

- ✔ **Get a real legal opinion.** Yes, I suggest that you see a lawyer even though it may cost you some cash. Don't trust your friends or cousins. This is a legal matter, and only a lawyer can drive a stake through the heart of a dead debt.

> ✔ **Have the attorney write a letter.** So you look like a champ, the letter should include documentation of the debt's age, proof that it's over the SOL limit, a statement that you don't intend to pay a penny, and, here's the crusher, a note that all future contact must go through the attorney. No collector I know of will bother to try to collect an uncollectible debt from a lawyer who knows better. And collectors can't go around the attorney after you notify them that you have a lawyer or they can be sued. Oh, yes indeed, sued by your attorney!

Negotiating a payback arrangement

When you and the collector agree that all the particulars of the debt are legitimate, it's time for you to make an offer to resolve the obligation, whether the cause of the delinquency was an unintended error or unfortunate circumstances. For tips on devising a payback plan, see the earlier section, "Offering a solution."

You want to convey your concern and reassure the collector that you're sincere in your commitment to pay. But that doesn't mean you shouldn't try to negotiate some concessions. For example, you may want the creditor to

> ✔ **Keep the matter between the two of you.** If, for example, you're able to pay off your obligation and you're only 30 to 60 days past due, ask the creditor not to report your oversight to the credit bureau.

> ✔ **Lighten the late fees.** It doesn't hurt to ask creditors if they'll waive any fees. Be sure to tell them that, if they do, you'll be happy to get off the phone so you can run to the post office to mail your check. Most — but not all — creditors will agree if they're getting the actual balance due without delay.

> ✔ **Reduce your interest rate.** Not the ideal time to try to get a better interest rate? Actually, it is. The lender wants to get what's called a *promise to pay* from you to resolve your situation. So ask for a break on the interest rate in order to help you resolve the debt situation faster. On a delinquent credit card account, for example, you may be looking at a 30 percent default interest rate. The lender knows that adding this much to a strained budget increases the chances of a longer and more costly default or even a bankruptcy if you feel you have no way out. The bottom line is that lenders often help if you're sincere.

 If you're under extreme financial duress, go a step further and ask if the creditor has a hardship program. You may have to meet some qualifications, but if you do, the lender may drop your interest rate dramatically, perhaps even to zero, and may lower your payments for six months to a year.

If you're in the military: Special help for special people

In Chapter 9, I discuss the rules of engagement between the financial system and military personnel. Generally speaking, some significant safeguards are built into the Fair and Accurate Credit Transactions Act (also known as the FACT Act or FACTA), the National Defense Authorization Act for Fiscal Year 2007, and a rewrite of the Soldiers' and Sailors' Civil Relief Act (SSCRA). Here's what you need to know about your rights when it comes to debt collection:

✔ **Delayed court hearings:** If a creditor summons you to court for a hearing, you can request for the date to be held off by at least a 90-day stay. The judge can grant additional delays as the case warrants.

✔ **Interest rate reductions:** The interest rates on preservice loans and obligations can't exceed 6 percent; interest due in excess of 6 percent per year must be forgiven, not just deferred. But you have to ask the lender for the reduction in writing and include a copy of your military orders.

✔ **Interest rate caps:** Interest rates are capped at 36 percent for payday loans and refund anticipation loans. This cap includes all fees and charges.

✔ **Eviction protection:** You can't be evicted from rental property for not paying the rent (if the monthly rent is $1,200 or less) without proper court action. The law gives you other special protections if the rent is between $1,200 and $2,400.

✔ **Lease termination:** You may terminate without penalty a housing lease that you enter into before you start active duty if you're under orders for a permanent change of station or deployed for at least 90 days. You don't need a military termination clause in your lease.

✔ **Auto lease cancellations:** You can cancel automobile leases if your orders are for 180 days or more, even if the auto is for a family member.

✔ **Vehicle title loans:** Military personnel can no longer be asked to secure loans with their vehicle titles except as part of receiving an installment loan to purchase a vehicle.

If collectors attempt to contact you to collect a debt, let them know your situation and ask for their cooperation in accordance with the SSCRA. If you have a spouse at home, you may have him or her follow up on your behalf; be sure to mention that in your initial letter.

Most military units have a financial specialist who may be able to help further. If that fails, contact a lawyer or an accredited credit-counseling agency and ask the lawyer or agency to act on your behalf. The lawyer may be expensive but should be worth it. The credit counselors are free or low-cost, and most try to help you by e-mail or through their websites. See Chapter 15 to find a credit counselor.

Keeping your promise

Following through with whatever payment promise you make is essential. From the collector's perspective, you've already broken your original agreement to make payments. Breaking a second agreement places you squarely in the not-to-be-trusted category.

To make sure you and the collector are clear on what you promised, put everything you agreed to in writing. Keep a copy of the names, addresses, and phone numbers of everyone you talked to and include a written copy of your agreement with the payment. Asking for an e-mail confirming the arrangement is a reasonable request. A letter is a little more challenging because the delivery time may cause you to delay acting on your promise for another five days or so. It's important to the collector that you act quickly, so confirm all the agreements in a quick note with names and times (don't forget to keep your copy) and send it off with your payment. Certified mail, return receipt requested of course!

If you feel any payment plan is unrealistic and may push you over the financial edge, work on a *spending plan* (see Chapter 4 for more information). After you've established your goals, identified your sources of income, and tackled your living expenses, you'll discover what you can actually afford for debt service.

If working out a repayment plan is too intimidating, if you're dealing with multiple creditors, if you just can't seem to communicate on money matters, or if you just want help getting started, a reputable credit-counseling agency can help you with a spending plan. (See Chapter 15 for help finding an agency.)

Identifying Escalation Options That Help

When you're dealing with a debt collector, you may arrive at a sticking point and recognize that the person you're speaking with doesn't have the authority to do what you're asking. Instead of stopping at that frustrating dead end, you're better off tactfully suggesting that you'd like to take your situation to a higher authority, one who's empowered to make decisions. This is known as *escalating* the issue. In this section, I show you how to do this, as well as how to contact other people who may be able to help you when the manager doesn't do the trick.

Asking to speak to the manager

Collection representatives may have several reasons for not warming to your proposed payment plan. They may

✔ Not believe you're offering your best effort to repay

✔ Have a quota to fill, and your offer won't do it

✔ Have strict rules regarding permissible payment options

✔ Be having a bad day and just not feel like being helpful

✔ Have just been yelled at for coming in late

A manager has more flexibility and may even see the bigger picture of a best offer. By asking to speak to the manager, you take the pressure off the little guy and free him to move on to another customer while you and the boss work things out. If you look at the situation as though you're helping every-one, you may have an easier time escalating the problem to management.

You can say something like this:

> I understand that you've done your best to try to resolve this issue satis-factorily. Thank you for helping. But I'd like to speak to someone who has the authority to make exceptions/waive policy/take my offer to a higher level. It's not fair of me to ask you to go against company policy and take the payment I'm offering, so please let me speak to a manager.

If the collector refuses to let you speak to a manager, tell her you'll call back on your own and ask someone else. Thank her for trying and say good-bye, nicely. Going over the same ground with the same person quickly wears thin on one of you.

Approaching the creditor

My wife tells me that she doesn't like to revisit the past. Believing that what's done is done may be a good way to handle many things, but credit may be an exception. Your original creditor may be willing to cut a deal with you even after sending your bill to an outside collector. Much depends on how you left things with the creditor. If you left with bad feelings or you lost it with a customer service representative, you may not be welcomed back. But if the transition from inside collections to an outside agency was just a migration and not a stampede, the creditor may still be willing to talk with you.

So why would you want to approach the creditor directly? If you're not get-ting anywhere with the debt collector, the creditor may be willing to work something out with you. After all, the creditor just wants his money.

Creditors either place a debt for collection (and pay a commission based on results) or they sell the debt outright. The former is more common, unless your debt is really old. If your debt has been sold, calling the original creditor won't do any good. But this bit of bad news has a silver lining. You may well have more room to negotiate in a debt-sale situation because debts aren't sold at full value. So a smaller-than-owed payment may still be very profitable for the collector.

Calling in a credit counselor

On your own, you can get to a manager, but the manager can't get around policy that is set by corporate headquarters. Very often, the powers that be set a special collection policy that applies only to the legitimate credit-counseling agencies with which they've established a working relationship. Thus, when a credit counselor gets involved, she may be able to deal with a special department that handles only credit-counseling accounts and is much more sympathetic than the line collector or manager. So in one leap, you escalate to high-level corporate policymakers.

Talk to a credit counselor from a nonprofit, independently accredited agency. Chapter 15 explains how to pick one from a crowded field. The cost to find out what these agencies can do for you is zero, free, nada. The professional analysis of your financial dilemma and your options is valuable. As an intermediary, the credit counselor can deal with your creditors on your behalf and may be able to administer a favorable workout plan (often referred to as a *debt-management plan*) while you follow a fairly strict budget.

Fair Isaac's FICO score doesn't take points away for using a credit-counseling agency.

Referring the matter to your lawyer

A good lawyer can work wonders with the more complex legal situations people face from time to time. Like showing up to a gunfight with the second-fastest gun, hiring a so-so lawyer isn't worth the effort. The best attorney for you is one who specializes in debt law. The drawbacks: Lawyers are expensive, and after *you* start down a legal path, so do the collectors.

Get an attorney who specializes in representing debtors. He knows the routine, has the letters on file, and may even know the collection agency or company. Besides sheltering you from having to deal directly with the collectors, the attorney helps slow down the freight train of events heading your way. He knows what is acceptable to the collector, collection lawyer, and judge (if things get that far). Plus, in today's complex debt sale and resale environment, an attorney can review your loan documents to make sure that your debt is enforceable.

Chapter 17

Managing Credit in a Mortgage Crisis

*L*ittle has changed more over the last two years than homeownership. What used to be a no-brainer decision has become more complicated than any of us could have imagined. Is buying a home a good idea? What about staying in a home that's worth less than what's owed on the mortgage? And what does a home loan default do to my credit?

Millions are asking these questions today. This chapter helps you make these decisions with the best information available. Here I cover legal obligations, taxes, credit, and the long arm of the credit score.

This chapter is an important one for every homeowner who's under financial stress. Money, credit, self-esteem, and the very roof over your family's head are at stake when a mortgage crisis looms. This chapter provides you with the advice you need to make the best decision for your situation. The need to get help and get it early is critical. Fortunately, help *is* available, and this chapter guides you through the process of getting what you need.

Understanding How Mortgages Are Different from Other Loans

Mortgages differ from other consumer loans partly because of their huge size — a lot of money is on the line — and partly because they're backed by what historically has been the gold standard in collateral, your home. With more at risk, the stakes of failure are greater. Furthermore, mortgages are not only underwritten differently from other types of credit but also have a different collection process, generally called the *foreclosure process.* When you default on a mortgage, the lender *forecloses,* or terminates the mortgage, and your house is consequently taken away from you.

From a credit score and credit reporting standpoint, mortgage defaults and foreclosures are among the most serious negatives out there with the exception of bankruptcy.

Obviously, foreclosures put a serious hit on your credit score and history. To ensure you minimize this hit, this section gives you an overview on how mortgages differ from typical credit and how mortgages and your credit go hand in hand. Here you can find valuable information to help you understand when a late mortgage payment can quickly cause you problems and what you can do to get help.

Assessing the damage from a mortgage meltdown

Credit score misinformation is everywhere today. What you don't know can and will hurt you if what you don't know is that your credit report and score have been seriously damaged. If you're trying to assess the damage to your score from a mortgage meltdown or even just mild mortgage sunburn, having the best information available is important. That's what this section is all about.

Figure 17-1 illustrates the effects of various types of mortgage defaults on your FICO credit score. The chart shows the relative damage from mortgage problems, underscoring how important it is to resolve any problems as quickly and amicably as possible.

People with great credit, like Consumer C, who go into a default are penalized more than those whose credit isn't so great, like Consumer A. The relatively greater credit-score point drop is because a good score has to fall farther in order to end up at the lower point level that indicates someone with serious credit problems.

A few items stand out in the list of credit and loan negatives in Figure 17-1. Delinquencies and some actions that result in your home being taken back by the lender *(deed-in-lieu)* or sold under distress (as in a *short sale*) cost you big points. However, there's no significant difference in score impact between a short sale, a deed-in-lieu, and a settlement. Mega drops in your score points tend to occur when the lender loses money in addition to your being in default. A short sale or a foreclosure, both of which cost the bank money, costs you extra penalties on your credit score. But the worst and longest lasting of all injury to your credit occurs when you file for bankruptcy. Unlike the other, lesser defaults, a bankruptcy can stay on your credit report for up to ten years, not just the usual seven years.

Impact to FICO Score

	Consumer A	Consumer B	Consumer C
Starting FICO® Score	~680	~720	~780
FICO® Score after these events:			
30 days late on mortgage	600-620	630-650	670-690
90 days late on mortgage	600-620	610-630	650-670
Short sale / deed-in-lieu / settlement (no deficiency balance)	610-630	605-625	655-675
Short sale (with deficiency balance)	575-595	570-590	620-640
Foreclosure	575-595	570-590	620-640
Bankruptcy	530-550	525-545	540-560

Estimated Time for FICO Score to Fully Recover

	Consumer A	Consumer B	Consumer C
Starting FICO® Score	~680	~720	~780
Time for FICO® Score to recover after these events:			
30 days late on mortgage	~9 months	~2.5 years	~3 years
90 days late on mortgage	~9 months	~3 years	~7 years
Short sale / deed-in-lieu / settlement (no deficiency balance)	~3 years	~7 years	~7 years
Short sale (with deficiency balance)	~3 years	~7 years	~7 years
Foreclosure	~3 years	~7 years	~7 years
Bankruptcy	~5 years	~7-10 years	~7-10 years

Figure 17-1:
Credit score
damage.

Note: Estimates assume all else held constant over time (e.g., no new account openings, no new delinquency, similar outstanding debt).

Courtesy of FICO

In addition to credit score penalties, you need to take collateral damage into consideration.

✔ Though a score may *begin* to improve sooner, it can take up to seven to ten years to *fully* recover.

✔ Fannie Mae (Federal National Mortgage Association) is the nation's largest mortgage buyer. It buys and then resells mortgages on Wall Street, helping to keep mortgage interest rates low. Fannie excludes borrowers who've gone through a foreclosure from obtaining a Fannie-backed loan for seven years.

✔ If you can't get a Fannie Mae loan, you may have to take a nonconforming loan from the Federal Housing Administration, which requires expensive mortgage insurance premiums and, for those with low credit scores, higher interest rates and a steeper down payment.

✔ In general, the higher your starting score, the longer it takes for your score to fully recover.

✔ You may find a significant difference in the time required for your score to fully recover even if there's minimal impact between moderate and severe delinquencies. For example, a person with a 720 FICO score loses an average of only 5 additional points for a short sale if that person makes a payment to the bank to cover the resulting mortgage deficiency versus a 90-day delinquency that is cured. But rebuilding the credit score takes up to seven years for the short sale versus only three years for the 90-day delinquency.

Spotting a foreclosure on the horizon

A lender has a lot of money on the line with your mortgage, and the longer you're delinquent, the greater the risk that the lender will lose money on a defaulted loan. The result is that a mortgage lender has a much lower tolerance for your delinquency than, say, a credit card issuer. For example, as long as you're less than 180 days past due on a credit card, it's not the end of the world. Generally, you can just pay the minimum due along with a late fee and pick up where you left off. If you're really lucky, you may get the lender to waive the late fee and not report the delinquency. For a mortgage, however, when you're just 60 days late, you're well on your way to the edge of a cliff, and you may not even be aware of it.

The key number to avoid in a mortgage delinquency is 90 days late, not 180. After 90 days, unless you get some help or work out an arrangement, the servicer generally requires the entire arrearage to be paid at once and may not accept partial payments. A 90-day mortgage delinquency on a credit report is very serious. To make matters worse, many people don't understand when the 90 days is up. The time frame isn't as simple as you may think, so I cover it in detail in the next section.

Mortgagees don't call you at work or at night, and they don't yell or threaten you over the phone. On the contrary, the tone of their messages, often letters, is concerned, low-key, and polite. If you ignore these messages, you could lose your home. But if you know where to get help, what to ask for, and what to avoid, your situation can change for the better.

Counting to 90

A major difference between mortgages and credit cards (or other types of consumer loans) is the amount of time you're allowed to be late. What's the magic number? After you're 90 days late on a mortgage, unless you take action, the servicer requires you to pay the entire overdue balance at once. If you fail to do so, the servicer may proceed to foreclosure.

Up until then, you may be able to make partial payments on your own. If you're 30 or 60 days late and you make a partial payment, the servicer usually credits your account with the payment. After you cross the 90-day mark and then send in a month or two's worth of overdue payments rather than the entire amount due, the servicer may send the money back, and the foreclosure clock keeps ticking.

After you're late on your first payment, your grace period disappears. (A *grace period* is a period of time that's specified in your mortgage loan agreement during which a default can't occur, even though the payment is technically past due.) The grace period only applies to loans that are up-to-date, or current. The following example illustrates how this works.

Say your loan papers state that your due date is March 1. Assuming you have a typical two-week grace period, your payment actually has to be in by March 15. If you don't submit your payment by March 15, you miss that window of opportunity and lose your grace period. Your April payment is now due April 1. April 15 is no longer an option. In other words, no more grace period in April. If you pay April's payment on or before April 1, you get your grace period back for May and, thereafter, as long as your payments stay on time.

If you lose your grace period, the counting of the number of days you're late begins on the first of the month rather than the fifteenth. So if you don't send in a payment on March 15, April 1, or May 1, then on May 2, you need to catch up all the payments for March 1, April 1, and May 1, plus any fees and penalties (which can be hundreds of dollars or more), all at once. This sum is a huge amount for someone in financial difficulty. If you don't pay, then on May 2, the formal foreclosure process can start, and you may incur fees for collection costs, attorneys, title searches, filings, and more. After the foreclosure process begins, and it's up to the mortgage servicer when this process actually begins, the loan servicer can *accelerate* the loan, meaning that the servicer can ask for the loan's entire balance — not just the late part — to stop the foreclosure.

Knowing Where to Turn for Help

If you're having trouble making your mortgage payment, time is of the essence. Getting your mortgage issue resolved quickly is critical. Remember, the mortgage company doesn't want your house; it just wants to keep your loan *performing/up-to-date/current* (different terms for the same thing). But also remember, the mortgage company doesn't care whether it has to take your home. If the rules say foreclose, the mortgage company will, without hesitation and without remorse.

Following are a few ideas on who to turn to for help (along with some tips on who *not* to turn to!). The essential point, however, is not to wait but to take action. You can work directly with your servicer, but the servicer may only offer you what it thinks is the easiest solution, not the one you need, because the servicer doesn't know your situation in detail.

Finding good help for free

A number of housing counseling agencies are available to help you work out a solution. I strongly recommend that you use a third-party intermediary that's approved by the U.S. Department of Housing and Urban Development (HUD). These intermediaries are cheap, experienced, knowledgeable, and can help guide you through what can seem like an insurmountable problem. They're expert at getting the right information on the right forms and to the right person at the mortgage servicers — no easy task!

Although the contact information may change over time and new players are continually offering this service, you can look for resources through HUD's website, www.hud.gov, or contact the Hope Now Alliance at 888-995-4673 or www.hopenow.com. For the fastest service, I suggest you call before you e-mail or visit an office. You can also get good help by contacting the National Foundation for Credit Counseling at www.housinghelpnow.org or 866-557-2227. Many credit counselors are also HUD-certified housing counselors.

See Chapter 15 for additional sources of help.

Working with your mortgage servicer

If you're unable to make your mortgage payment on time, you can contact your mortgage company for help. If you believe this may the beginning of a serious problem that needs serious attention, ask for the *loss mitigation department,* which may also be referred to as the *workout department* or the *homeownership retention department.* This department is able to go the extra mile to help you and can deal with complex issues better than the standard collection department, which usually only offers to make catch-up payment arrangements. To find the contact information for these departments, you can look in your loan documents, on your monthly statement, or in correspondence you've received from your mortgage servicer. When you call, get names and extension numbers so you can try to keep a single point of contact and continuity. This may not be possible, but knowing who you talked to, when, and what was agreed on is important in case matters get really serious. And keep good notes!

Keeping the call simple is a blessing to everyone concerned, so I suggest you do some homework before you call and have a written, well thought out proposal prepared that meets your needs and helps solve your problem. Be sure to include what concessions you need and for how long. I also suggest that you write down what happened, what changed, and how to contact you or your counselor if you're working with one. Putting the facts and options in writing before you call helps you keep from drifting during the conversation and keeps everyone focused on the task at hand. When you ask for what you need, be sure to also ask what other options may be available beyond the one that's offered.

If you can't resolve your mortgage issue quickly or if you get transferred to multiple people, get expert help quickly. Time is precious, and servicers can easily pass the buck until you find yourself in a foreclosure situation. See the preceding section for information on where to find free experts.

Avoiding help that hurts

Some people make a living, and a good one, on the backs of folks in trouble. People who offer to help you with a mortgage problem for a fee are only trying to help themselves. So proceed with caution and consider the following tips as you evaluate any prospective source of help:

- ✔ Don't decide anything while in a panic.
- ✔ Be sure you're dealing with a HUD-qualified nonprofit organization. Look them up at www.hud.gov.
- ✔ Don't make payments to anyone other than your servicer or its designee.
- ✔ Be wary of any organization other than your servicer that contacts you to help.
- ✔ Never sign a contract under pressure.
- ✔ Never sign away ownership of your property.
- ✔ Don't sign anything with blank lines or spaces.
- ✔ If English isn't your first language and a translator isn't provided, use your own.
- ✔ Get a second opinion from a person or an organization that you know and trust.

If you're having trouble paying your mortgage, a high-risk, expensive second mortgage won't help. It will only keep you from finding real solutions by wasting critical time and money.

If you receive an offer saying that you've been preapproved for a loan, don't get too excited. It only means that you've been preapproved on a very cursory level and only for the offer, not the actual loan. Don't waste too much time chasing preapproved offers.

Alternatives to Going Down with the Ship

If you're having trouble making your mortgage payments, you may have a host of options that can help you avoid the expense and upset of losing your home through a foreclosure. Even if you can't or don't want to keep your house, you can still lessen the damage to yourself, your family, and your credit by taking positive action.

Before you take any action, assess your situation as dispassionately as you can. If stress and anxiety make that impossible, I suggest you get a third-party professional such as a nonprofit HUD agency (see "Finding good help for free" earlier in this chapter) or an attorney to help you do this. Your situation may not be as bad as you think, or it may be worse. What's important is to know for sure where you stand. You need what's called loss mitigation counseling help. *Loss mitigation counseling* is help to develop a solution that allows you to afford to keep your home or lessen the damage caused by a foreclosure.

This section gives you some loss mitigation alternatives to protect your credit history.

What to do first

If you already have a plan to resolve your problem, catch up, or at least resume payments in three to six months, consider the following suggestions:

- ✔ **Find a good nonprofit housing counseling agency.** I recommend the Hope Now Alliance (888-995-4673 or www.hopenow.com) or a credit counseling agency that has a HUD-approved housing counseling program. Expect an assessment of your overall financial picture and whether you can realistically afford your mortgage payments.

- ✔ **Ask your mortgage servicer about mortgage repayment plans.** These entail the servicer setting up a structured payment plan (sometimes called a *special forbearance plan*) that gets the mortgage back on track in three to six months by making up past due amounts in addition to your regular payment. Get all the terms in writing so you're both clear on the terms. The sooner you do this, the less damage to your credit report and score.

- ✔ **Check the HUD website at www.hud.gov for resources and help.** Don't forget to talk to your lender about your need for assistance, and do it soon. Some servicers have programs that are only for those who are not yet delinquent and other programs for borrowers who already are. To get the greatest number of options, get started as soon as you know you have a problem making mortgage payments as agreed, and be sure to ask for all the options your servicer may have for you.

What to do for more serious problems

For problems that take longer than three to six months to remedy, ask for mortgage loan forbearance or loan modifications.

A *forbearance* temporarily modifies or eliminates payments that are made up at the end of the forbearance period. This also prevents your credit from being damaged by a string of late payments.

A *loan modification* changes one or more terms of the original mortgage permanently in a way that addresses your specific needs. If this seems intimidating, use a HUD agency to deal with the servicer and offer solutions on your behalf. Clear communication is key here.

Modifications need to be in writing and approved by both the servicer and borrower. Don't be surprised if the servicer asks for a fee of around 1 percent to cover the costs of processing a loan modification.

What to do to end matters

Even when you can't solve your problem or just can't stand it anymore, you're better off if you stay in control of the process. This can lessen credit damage and expenses and keep your dignity — and maybe your sanity — intact.

Here are some of the many options available. And don't forget that another reason to use a free professional mortgage counselor is that you may have newer options as well. Be sure to check out the resources mentioned in the section "Knowing Where to Turn for Help," earlier in this chapter.

- ✔ **Sell your home:** You may be able to sell your home in a short sale if you have no equity left or a pre-foreclosure sale if the value of the house still exceeds the remainder of the mortgage.

    - **Short sale:** You get your lender to allow selling your home for less than the mortgage value. This is generally cheaper for the bank and less stressing for the homeowner than a foreclosure. Because this is good for the investor, you can negotiate a bit. Ask that the loan deficiency be reported to the credit bureau as a zero balance rather than a charge-off.

        The Mortgage Forgiveness Debt Relief Act exempts up to $2 million of forgiven mortgage debt, subject to certain conditions, from federal taxes. Normally, you have to pay income tax on that amount. I suggest that you check to see whether you may have state taxes due, as they aren't covered in this federal law. The full text of the law is on the CD.

    - **Pre-foreclosure sale:** A pre-foreclosure sale arrangement allows you to defer mortgage payments that you can't afford while you sell your house. This also keeps late payments off your credit report.

- ✔ **Deed-in-lieu of foreclosure:** If the home can't be sold, you sign the home's title over to the lender and move out. Usually, to qualify for this option, you can't have a second mortgage, a home equity loan, or another lien on the property.

Managing a foreclosure

If you're being foreclosed on, you may still have the option to talk to the servicer and try to work things out, buy more time to come up with a solution, or at least make a more dignified exit from the home. But again, timing is very important, so don't wait!

- ✔ **Get a HUD-approved counselor involved and review loss mitigation options with your servicer.** Most want to help. (Check out "Knowing Where to Turn for Help" earlier in this chapter.)

- ✔ **Contact and keep contacting the servicer's loss mitigation staff until you get a solution you can live with.** If they don't offer workable suggestions, ask to speak to managers and vice presidents or higher. This is not a time to stand on protocol or accept "I'm sorry" for an answer.

- ✔ **See an attorney.** Ask for options. Review all the mortgage and foreclosure documents to be sure they were properly drawn and executed. The technical phrase used here is *truth in lending compliance*. Ask about bankruptcy options and timing so you know all options available to you.

Strategic default: Walking away

A *strategic default* is an intentional mortgage default based on a strategy. Here's an example: A person has a home whose value has fallen so far below what is owed on the mortgage that he'll never realistically recover enough equity to break even on the home. The person stops paying the expensive mortgage on a home that will never be worth what is being paid. This is especially popular in states with *nonrecourse mortgages* (meaning the property is the sole security for the mortgage loan and you aren't responsible for any shortage beyond what the property value brings at sale).

The "Summary of State Foreclosure Laws" chart on the CD shows each state's recourse classification, as well as the typical timeline for foreclosure in that state.

According to the Federal Reserve (www.federalreserve.gov/pubs/feds/2010/201035/201035pap.pdf), strategic default is fairly common among deeply underwater borrowers (those whose home values are way below what's owed on the mortgage). About half of strategic defaults are from homes where the equity is below 50 percent of the home's market value. In addition, negative equity of more than 10 percent (a mortgage of $110,000 on a home with a value of $100,000) in combination with other financial setbacks or life events can drive a strategic default.

Another consideration is that homestead exemptions make collecting deficiencies unlikely in some states.

Strategic default is a high credit-damage strategy but one that may be cost-effective depending on your situation and plans that involve loans or credit use for the future. Refer to Figure 17-1, earlier in the chapter, for details on the damage to your credit score from a foreclosure.

Strategic default is happening more frequently than ever before. Thousands of home purchasers are walking away from their homes rather than making any more payments on an underwater asset. The argument goes: Why continue to pay more for something than it's worth? Why throw good money after bad? After all, this is business, and businesses routinely stop paying on debts that are worth less than they owe. Most of you have been told that you have to pay your bills, honor your obligations, and keep your promises. Many home buyers take a business rather than a personal approach to their homes and finances.

Most mortgages detail what happens to you if you don't pay. Either you pay or your home is taken away. So the question arises: If you tell the bank to go ahead and take the house, are you meeting your obligations or not? Clearly, from the bank's perspective, you're not.

Further complicating the ethics of walking away is the fact that some states require all mortgages to be *nonrecourse,* meaning that the state agrees that the lender should only have recourse to the defaulted property and nothing else. Also consider that the federal government passed the Mortgage Forgiveness Debt Relief Act, which, until at least 2012, prohibits the IRS from taxing any forgiven mortgage debt up to $1 million from a foreclosure, short sale, or deed-in-lieu action as income.

Staying in a home you can't afford can deprive your family of your precious savings, empty your retirement accounts, and eventually ruin your credit when you finally default. The price of shame and guilt is something that many are willing to put up with to ensure a faster recovery with more money in their accounts.

Dealing with Deficiencies

When all is said and done, you may still owe some money. If your home sells for less than the amount still owed on the mortgage plus fees, then you may have what's called a *deficiency balance.* For example, say a borrower borrows $500,000 from a lender to purchase a home, but the borrower falls behind in payments or walks away from the home, and the bank forecloses. The home is ultimately sold for $400,000. The $100,000 that the lender lost on the deal is called a *deficiency.* Current practice is to forgive this amount. There was a time when this wasn't always the case, and the situation may change again in the future. It's not always the case for second mortgage holders who more often do go after the borrower for deficiencies. The most important thing is to realize that your problems may not be over when you leave the home. You may need to deal with the IRS if you don't qualify for mortgage debt forgiveness under its rules.

The following are some potential, and I stress *potential,* deficiencies you may face and what you can do to deal with them:

- ✓ **The lender may ask for a note.** Though this practice isn't current among first mortgage holders, I want you to be aware of it for the future or if your second mortgage holder loses money on your loan. This note isn't written on monogrammed stationery; it's a promise to pay an unsecured amount to cover the mortgage deficiency after the sale. Use an attorney if your lender mentions this to you.

- ✓ **The lender may send a demand letter.** Like asking for a note, this practice isn't current among first mortgage holders. However, a second mortgage lender may send a demand for payment of any deficiency following the sale of a home. The lender uses a *demand letter* if it doesn't want to give you an unsecured loan for the balance due. In essence, the problem is all yours, and you need to work out a way to pay the balance. Here again, if this ever happens, get an attorney to advise you.

- ✓ **The lender may forgive what you owe.** This is a current practice among first mortgage holders but isn't required. Forgiving your debt is nice as far as it goes, but the IRS counts forgiven debt as income. Forms 1099 A and C, which are normally used to document unreported income, are used to report forgiven debt. The amount of the forgiven debt becomes taxable income in most cases, unless you're covered by the Mortgage Forgiveness Debt Relief Act. Remember, the law is federal and may not forgive state tax obligations.

  The law applies to debt forgiven in 2007 through 2012 only. Debt reduced through mortgage restructuring, as well as mortgage debt forgiven in connection with a foreclosure, may qualify for this relief. If you spent the forgiven debt money to pay a car loan, credit card bills, or for any non–real estate purpose, it's not covered, and you'll get a tax bill for it. Debt on second homes, rental property, and business property doesn't qualify.

  A foreclosed borrower faced with a sizable 1099 still has hope. If you file IRS Form 982, named "Avoid Taxes on Forgiven Debt" on the CD, and you're insolvent at the time of the forgiven debt, the IRS may forgive the liability. Again, see your attorney for the details.

- ✓ **The state you live in makes mortgages nonrecourse.** If you live in certain states, you may get a break relating to personal mortgage deficiencies. Some states have passed laws saying that you're not responsible for any mortgage deficiencies.

Chapter 18

Working with Collectors, Lawyers, and the Courts to Manage Debt Obligations

. . . .

In This Chapter

▶ Understanding charge-offs

▶ Settling a debt for less than you owe

▶ Handling judgments and wage garnishments

▶ Telling your story in court

▶ Dealing with undischargeable debts

. . . .

I'm a jazz fan, and I write about credit. If I were to combine my enjoyment of music with my writing, I might come up with a tune called "Take the A+ Credit Train" or "Kind Of Blue: Credit." Jazz is very much about the human condition and emotions we all feel. Credit gone bad can be an emotional roller coaster for those trapped on that train. If the world of credit has you singing the blues, this chapter shows you how to deal with the most stubborn of debt obligations — charge-offs, judgments, garnishments, student loans, child support, and IRS debt.

 Because these debts are so troublesome, they attract hustlers and scam artists who promise to bring you relief for just a fraction of what you owe. Claims of settling an IRS debt for pennies or removing valid charge-offs from your credit report are as bogus as those claims made by the endless stream of Nigerian millionaires who ask for your bank account information and promise to share their millions in return.

In this chapter I give you the skinny on charge-offs, judgments, and debts that can't be wiped out, even by a bankruptcy. I tell you how to minimize damage to your credit (yes, you'll probably have some) and give you strategies for controlling and even eliminating those sour credit notes before they make your credit score sound flat. So have a seat and listen up — the music is about to begin, and you don't want to miss a beat.

Getting a Handle on Charge-Offs

During the collections process, you come to some significant stopping points where unresolved matters take a turn for the worse. It's important for you to know when you've reached these points, how important they are, and what comes next. In this section I discuss unpaid charge-offs and paid charge-offs. Understanding how these actions work and what you can do about them may save you credit score points and money in the long run.

So what is a charge-off?

When a collector or creditor *charges off* your account, the lender's accountants, regulators, or audit firm have decided that your debt is very unlikely to be collected so they don't allow it to remain on the books as an asset. For accounting and tax purposes, the creditor considers your account a loss, and your account is charged off the company's books.

Some generalizations hold true for many types of unsecured debts like credit cards or personal loans. Specifically:

- ✔ If you pay a bill after its due date, it's technically late.
- ✔ Paying up to 30 days late is usually no big deal.
- ✔ After you get to 60 days late, you may face some fees and maybe an interest-rate raise.
- ✔ Being 90 days late can cost you more and often brings on the serious players in the collection department.
- ✔ If your account is between 120 and 180 days past due, your debt enters a new phase known as the *charge-off*.

A creditor charging off a debt in no way means the debt is canceled, nor does any interest associated with the account stop accruing. If you imagine that no one is happy about this turn of events, you're correct. And among those who should be the least happy is you. Why? Because you still owe the bill while fees and interest continue to accrue and your credit damage grows.

The rest of this section covers the credit reporting difference between unpaid and paid charge-offs and why paying a charge-off is worthwhile even though it stays on your credit report. I also explain the role a spending plan plays in getting debts and collectors under control.

Making sense of unpaid charge-offs

A debt charges off when it gets so old (typically 180 days past due) that its value is called into question (as is your sincerity in paying it). If your creditor reports account histories to the credit bureaus, and most major ones do, the charge-off is considered a very serious negative.

When a debt charges off, you still owe the debt, and the creditor or collector will still attempt to collect it. The charge-off only means that the creditor doesn't count the debt as an asset. An unpaid charge-off causes more damage to your credit report than a paid one.

Until you pay what's owed, the debt is labeled an *unpaid charge-off* on your credit report. When an account first charges off, you may experience a lull in collection attempts. The reason is that the debt is probably changing hands from the collectors who were unsuccessful trying to save the account to those who want to save at least some part of it.

The most-experienced, longest-serving collectors typically deal with charge-offs. These collectors have heard it all a thousand times before and have lasted in this business because they're efficient and effective. Make no mistake, collectors will try to collect the money due; however, after they determine that you either can't or won't pay, your account may be sold many times for decreasing dollars to increasingly aggressive collectors or lawyers whom you really don't want to deal with.

Making charge-off payments

Collectors try to make you promise to pay your debt either in full or in a series of agreed-upon payments. They take promises very seriously, so you don't want to make and then break one. I suggest that you know for sure how much you can afford to pay monthly or in a lump-sum amount before you make any promises. The best way to do that is to prepare a budget (see Chapter 4) that takes into account all your income and all your expenses. Using this spending plan, you can identify areas to trim and put more money toward paying off your debt. Without a plan, you'll only be guessing.

The key steps to making and carrying out a plan (see the "Household Monthly Budget Plan" form on the CD for a sample of a spending plan outline) are as follows:

- ✔ List all your income.
- ✔ List all your expenses.
- ✔ Cut out or decrease as many of the expenses as you can.
- ✔ Increase your income if possible.

✔ Repeat this process until you have enough money to pay the bill in a reasonable amount of time.

Be sure you don't promise more than your plan says you can afford to pay just to get off the phone. Be sincere, explain how you arrived at your payment amount, and request that the collector send you a written agreement for this amount. When you receive the agreement, send the payment in, and do so on time, every time. You can ask for a reduction in fees and interest when you negotiate the payment agreement, but a reduction in the amount owed is harder to get (see the next section).

A delinquent debt that hasn't reached charge-off status and is paid becomes current on your credit report, but a charge-off never does. An unpaid charge-off becomes a paid charge-off. A paid charge-off is much better for your credit than an unpaid charge-off because it indicates that you had a problem — perhaps a serious one — but that you eventually paid the bill. Hallelujah! Now you can get a little boost on your credit report (check out Figure 18-1), and you're on the way to obtaining credit at a more reasonable rate. Why? Simple: You've established that, although you may be a high-risk borrower, you do pay your bills in the end.

Equifax Credit Report for **Melissa Carson**
As of: 08/07/2007
Available until:
Confirmation #: 123456789

Report Does Not Update
Print Report

Negative Accounts Show All Account Details

Accounts that contain a negative account status. Accounts not paid as agreed generally remain on your credit file for 7 years from the date the account first became past due leading to the current not paid status. Late Payment History generally remains on your credit file for 7 years from the date of the late payment.

Open Accounts

Account Name	Account Number	Date Opened	Balance	Date Reported	Past Due	Account Status	Credit Limit
XYZ BANKCARD Show Details	4873664803 16XXXX	08/2001	$0	07/2007	$287	PAYS 91-120 DAYS	$8,000

Closed Accounts

Account Name	Account Number	Date Opened	Balance	Date Reported	Past Due	Account Status	Credit Limit
ABC LOANS Show Details	31667XXXX	09/1997	$0	09/2003	$0	CHARGE-OFF	$0

Figure 18-1: An example of a paid charge-off trade line on a credit report.

Coming to a Debt-Settlement Agreement

When your creditor allows you to pay off your debt for less than you originally borrowed, you're *settling a debt*. And because no one likes to lose money, settling a debt is rarely easy. Although you may not have stiffed the lender completely, your actions did result in at least a loss of profit for the company, which isn't a positive incentive to do business with you in the future. Settling a debt also has a negative impact on your credit report, so you may want to consider what's more important to you, the money or your credit history. This section focuses on what happens if you agree to a debt settlement.

Considering a debt settlement offer

Some businesses may offer you a debt settlement option if they believe that they may never recover what you owe them, or continuing collections becomes uneconomical, or they think they can recover more by settling than by selling the debt to a third-party collection agency. Although a settled debt is considered paid, the settlement shows on your credit report for seven years from the date of the delinquency leading to the account charging off, and you may have a tax liability if the creditor forgives more than $600 of the debt.

The IRS considers the difference between the amount you owe and the amount you pay as income. I know; this thinking defies logic. But if your settlement amount allows for more than $600 to go unpaid, you're responsible for paying income taxes on that amount. For example, if you owe $5,000 and you work out a settlement where you pay only $3,000, the $2,000 that was forgiven becomes taxable income on your next tax return. As the saying goes, only two things in life are certain — and one of them is taxes!

If you decide on debt settlement as a payment resolution, I strongly advise you to get the settlement terms in writing and read them carefully before you send in a penny. You need to be on your guard if you're negotiating a settlement or if you've been offered one. You're dealing with people who know settlements better than you do and who don't mind that you're making a mistake that's to their advantage and may result in more of what you owe being collected. After you send in the money, you have no leverage with the collector, and any promises that aren't in the written agreement are unlikely to be kept.

Hiring a debt settlement firm

You're likely to see and hear advertisements for debt settlement firms and may even be contacted by one. These companies have recently come to the attention of the Federal Trade Commission (FTC) because most charge large fees and provide few results for consumers. New regulations from the FTC have curbed some of the abuses in this industry, but I still recommend that you try to settle on your own or use an attorney rather than using a debt settlement firm. However, if you want to hire a settlement company, keep these points in mind:

✔ Make sure the company is a member of The Association of Settlement Companies (TASC).

✔ Don't pay an upfront fee. Companies are required to settle at least one account before charging consumers.

✔ Don't sign anything if you feel pressured to do so.

 Consider running any offer by an attorney. Doing so will cost money but may save you big if you avoid making a mistake or if only a bankruptcy can solve your problem. A consumer debt goes away in a bankruptcy; an IRS debt from a settlement doesn't.

Reaching expiration dates on debts

Sometimes, procrastination has a silver lining. When a debt reaches a certain age (as defined by the statutes of your state of residence), it's no longer collectible in a court of law. Each state has its own statute of limitations rules. Check out Chapter 16 for more on expired debts and statutes of limitations.

Finding Out about Judgments and What They Mean to You

An unpaid charge-off often makes its way to a lawyer sooner or later. A collection attorney may take your case to court, you may have a judgment entered against you, you'll lose a day to court and incur additional legal expenses, and maybe — if it's just not your day — your wages will be garnished for up to 25 percent of your take-home pay. This is about as much fun as a legal colonoscopy. If you get a court summons for a hearing on a debt issue, don't ignore it, answer it! Read on for all the details.

The legal side of the collection process typically begins with a letter, not a phone call. After so many months of phone assaults, a simple mute letter is easy to ignore. Don't! The letter is a summons telling you that a court hearing will be held on a certain day in a certain place (see Figure 18-2). I strongly suggest you show up with a plan and, if possible, an attorney. A good plan includes

✔ A short explanation of why you haven't paid.

✔ Any disputes about the bill or collection process so far.

✔ A plan to repay the debt on terms you can afford.

✔ Documentation that shows why you can't afford more.

SUM-120

ATTORNEY OR PARTY WITHOUT ATTORNEY *(Name, State Bar number, and address):*	FOR COURT USE ONLY *(SOLO PARA USO DE LA CORTE)*

TELEPHONE NO.:   FAX NO. *(Optional):*
E-MAIL ADDRESS *(Optional):*
ATTORNEY FOR *(Name):*

SUPERIOR COURT OF CALIFORNIA, COUNTY OF
   STREET ADDRESS:
   MAILING ADDRESS:
   CITY AND ZIP CODE:
   BRANCH NAME:

    PLAINTIFF:
   DEFENDANT:

SUMMONS (JOINT DEBTOR) *(CITACIÓN (DEUDOR CONJUNTO))*	CASE NUMBER: *(Número del Caso):*

NOTICE! You have been sued. The court may decide against you without your being heard unless you respond within 30 days. Read the information below.

You have 30 CALENDAR DAYS after this summons and legal papers are served on you to file a written response at this court and have a copy served on the plaintiff. A letter or phone call will not protect you. Your written response must be in proper legal form if you want the court to hear your case. There may be a court form that you can use for your response. You can find these court forms and more information at the California Courts Online Self-Help Center *(www.courtinfo.ca.gov/selfhelp),* your county law library, or the courthouse nearest you. If you cannot pay the filing fee, ask the court clerk for a fee waiver form. If you do not file your response on time, you may lose the case by default, and your wages, money, and property may be taken without further warning from the court.

There are other legal requirements. You may want to call an attorney right away. If you do not know an attorney, you may want to call an attorney referral service. If you cannot afford an attorney, you may be eligible for free legal services from a nonprofit legal services program. You can locate these nonprofit groups at the California Legal Services Web site *(www.lawhelpcalifornia.org),* the California Courts Online Self-Help Center *(www.courtinfo.ca.gov/selfhelp),* or by contacting your local court or county bar association. **NOTE:** The court has a statutory lien for waived fees and costs on any settlement or arbitration award of $10,000 or more in a civil case. The court's lien must be paid before the court will dismiss the case.

¡AVISO! Lo han demandado. Si no responde dentro de 30 días, la corte puede decidir en su contra sin escuchar su versión. Lea la información a continuación.

Tiene 30 DÍAS DE CALENDARIO después de que le entreguen esta citación y papeles legales para presentar una respuesta por escrito en esta corte y hacer que se entregue una copia al demandante. Una carta o una llamada telefónica no lo protegen. Su respuesta por escrito tiene que estar en formato legal correcto si desea que procesen su caso en la corte. Es posible que haya un formulario que usted pueda usar para su respuesta. Puede encontrar estos formularios de la corte y más información en el Centro de Ayuda de las Cortes de California (www.sucorte.ca.gov), en la biblioteca de leyes de su condado o en la corte que le quede más cerca. Si no puede pagar la cuota de presentación, pida al secretario de la corte que le dé un formulario de exención de pago de cuotas. Si no presenta su respuesta a tiempo, puede perder el caso por incumplimiento y la corte le podrá quitar su sueldo, dinero y bienes sin más advertencia.

Hay otros requisitos legales. Es recomendable que llame a un abogado inmediatamente. Si no conoce a un abogado, puede llamar a un servicio de remisión a abogados. Si no puede pagar a un abogado, es posible que cumpla con los requisitos para obtener servicios legales gratuitos de un programa de servicios legales sin fines de lucro. Puede encontrar estos grupos sin fines de lucro en el sitio web de California Legal Services, (www.lawhelpcalifornia.org), en el Centro de Ayuda de las Cortes de California, (www.sucorte.ca.gov) o poniéndose en contacto con la corte o el colegio de abogados locales. AVISO: Por ley, la corte tiene derecho a reclamar las cuotas y los costos exentos por imponer un gravamen sobre cualquier recuperación de $10,000 ó más de valor recibida mediante un acuerdo o una concesión de arbitraje en un caso de derecho civil. Tiene que pagar el gravamen de la corte antes de que la corte pueda desechar el caso.

1. TO THE DEFENDANT *(name):*
    (AL DEMANDADO):
        You are hereby directed to file in this court, within **30** days after this summons is served on you, a written response to the Declaration or Affidavit accompanying this summons, giving any legal reason why you should not be required to pay the unpaid amount of: $ on the judgment rendered by this court on *(date):*
        against *(name each):*

Date: Clerk, by   , Deputy
(Fecha)   *(Secretario)*   *(Adjunto)*

(For proof of service of this summons, use Proof of Service of Summons (form POS-010).)
(Para prueba de entrega de esta citación use el formulario Proof of Service of Summons, (POS-010)).

2. **NOTICE TO THE PERSON SERVED:** You are served
  a. ☐ as an individual defendant.
  b. ☐ as the person sued under the fictitious name of *(specify):*

  c. ☐ on behalf of *(specify):*
    under: ☐ CCP 416.10 (corporation)   ☐ CCP 416.60 (minor)
          ☐ CCP 416.20 (defunct corporation) ☐ CCP 416.70 (conservatee)
          ☐ CCP 416.40 (association or partnership) ☐ CCP 416.90 (authorized person)
          ☐ other *(specify):*

  d. ☐ by personal delivery on *(date):*   Page 1 of 1

(SEAL)

Form Adopted for Mandatory Use Judicial Council of California SUM-120 [Rev. July 1, 2009]	**SUMMONS (JOINT DEBTOR)**	Code of Civil Procedure § 989 www.courtinfo.ca.gov

Figure 18-2: A sample court summons letter.

REMEMBER

If the debt is valid (not in dispute or belonging to someone else) and hasn't been collected, the court generally issues an order confirming that you owe money and commanding you to pay it. This is called a *judgment,* and it involves legal fees, public-record information on your credit report, and dealing with a system that doesn't fool around. Figure 18-3 shows a copy of a typical judgment from a hearing on a debt issue. If you get one of these, you need to wake up and get a repayment plan going. If you *dishonor,* or ignore, a judgment, the next step could be wage garnishment. (Check out the section "Understanding Wage Garnishments" later in this chapter for more info.)

CIV-130

ATTORNEY OR PARTY WITHOUT ATTORNEY (Name, State Bar number, and address):

FOR COURT USE ONLY

TELEPHONE NO.:   FAX NO. (Optional):
E-MAIL ADDRESS (Optional):
ATTORNEY FOR (Name):

SUPERIOR COURT OF CALIFORNIA, COUNTY OF
STREET ADDRESS:
MAILING ADDRESS:
CITY AND ZIP CODE:
BRANCH NAME:

PLAINTIFF/PETITIONER:

DEFENDANT/RESPONDENT:

NOTICE OF ENTRY OF JUDGMENT
OR ORDER

CASE NUMBER:

(Check one): ☐ **UNLIMITED CASE**   ☐ **LIMITED CASE**
(Amount demanded   (Amount demanded was
exceeded $25,000) $25,000 or less)

TO ALL PARTIES :

1. A judgment, decree, or order was entered in this action on *(date)*:

2. A copy of the judgment, decree, or order is attached to this notice.

Date:

▶

(TYPE OR PRINT NAME OF ☐ ATTORNEY ☐ PARTY WITHOUT ATTORNEY)   (SIGNATURE)

Page 1 of 2

Form Approved for Optional Use
Judicial Council of California
CIV-130 [New January 1, 2010]   **NOTICE OF ENTRY OF JUDGMENT OR ORDER**   www.courtinfo.ca.gov

---

Figure 18-3:
A sample court judgment letter.

Why some lenders don't care about your judgments — and why you should

Some lenders won't consider you for a loan unless you have great credit. Others don't care if you have judgments or a bankruptcy against you. You may consider such lenders saints to overlook a proven risk. Fact is, they probably don't mind the risk because they charge enough interest to still make money. Or they expect you to default and are prepared to take aggressive collection actions when you do.

Groucho Marx said it best when he quipped, "I don't care to belong to a club that accepts people like me as members." You really don't want a loan from a company that would lend money to a person with active unpaid judgments against him.

The judgment itself doesn't force you to pay the debt. It does, however, set you up for execution — not execution as in the electric chair, but a *judgment execution.* If you receive a judgment and you still don't pay, the lender can go back to the judge and get an execution order. Depending on the laws in your state, the order allows the creditor to

- ✔ Garnish your wages, up to 25 percent. (See the next section for more on wage garnishments.)

- ✔ Place a lien on your home or other real property for the amount owed. The lien is like having another mortgage on the property. Before the property can be sold or mortgaged, the lien has to be paid off.

- ✔ Repossess any property involved with the debt you owe (for example, your furniture if it's a furniture loan).

A judgment is a very serious development in the collection process. At this point, many people seriously consider bankruptcy to wipe out their debts. Unfortunately, for many people who earn above the median income in their states, bankruptcy is no longer an attractive option (see Chapter 19). This is one of the reasons why I think consulting a professional early on in the game makes a lot of sense. If you don't have the option to file bankruptcy, you want to know as soon as possible.

Understanding Wage Garnishments

If you receive a judgment (see the preceding section) and still don't or can't pay the debt, your employer may be court-ordered to garnish part of your paycheck to pay off your creditors. After the court orders a wage garnishment, certain rules must be followed as defined in the Consumer Credit Protection Act

(CCPA). This section focuses on the main points, including how you can avoid wage garnishments. Remember, however, that state law can take precedence over federal law but only if the amounts allowed for garnishment are lower.

Dodging wage garnishments

Before anyone can garnish your wages, a judgment from a court of law is necessary. You get a summons to appear in court to defend yourself against a suit for payment brought by the owner of your debt. If a judgment is issued and the debt remains unpaid, the lender can go back to court and execute the judgment to push matters to the next stage, which may include having your wages garnished. You receive another summons if this happens.

Each state has its own debt-collection laws. Some states permit a lender to garnish your wages; others don't. Some states exempt large amounts or categories of assets from attachment or seizure by a creditor to pay your debt. Others may force you to sell possessions to satisfy a judgment. The best source for up-to-date information is your state's consumer-protection office. You can find a list of these offices at http://consumeraction.gov/state.shtml.

In many cases, you can avoid wage garnishments by doing the following:

✔ **Keep complete records of the collection process.** Be sure to keep a record of names, dates, copies of correspondence, summaries of conversations, and any agreements or disputes.

✔ **Show up in court when you're supposed to.** Go to the hearings and speak up! If you have a reasonable story to tell the judge and a reasonable offer to make, you may be surprised at the result. The judge won't be happy that a collector is wasting his valuable time with a case that should have already been settled out of court.

Your state law may set garnishment limits lower than the federal maximum. In that case, the state law supersedes the federal law. The CCPA says that your boss can't fire you for having a garnishment. However, the CCPA doesn't provide this protection for multiple wage garnishments. You can find much more information on minimum wages and wage garnishments by contacting the U.S. Department of Labor by phone at 866-487-9243 or by visiting www.dol.gov/dol/topic/wages/index.htm.

CCPA protections don't apply to the following types of nondischargeable debts:

✔ **Child support and alimony:** The court has little sympathy in matters of back support payments. The garnishment law allows up to 50 percent of your disposable earnings to be garnished for child support and alimony if you're supporting another spouse or child and up to 60 percent if you're not. An additional 5 percent may be garnished for support payments more than 12 weeks in arrears.

✔ **Government-owed debts:** The garnishment restrictions don't apply to certain bankruptcy court orders or to debts due for federal or state taxes. A consumer debt such as a credit card or personal loan can be garnished up to 15 percent and a student loan up to 10 percent. If you're being garnished for more than one debt, you're subject to a 25 percent maximum. If a state wage garnishment law differs from the CCPA, the law that results in the smaller garnishment must be observed.

Figuring out how much can be garnished

After your creditor is granted a judgment, you may wonder how much the court can order your employer to garnish from your wages. The court uses *disposable earnings* (the amount left after legally required deductions like taxes, FICA, mandatory retirement withholding, and unemployment insurance) to figure your garnishment amount.

Whether you have one or more garnishments, the law sets the maximum amount that your employer may garnish in any workweek or pay period. Exceptions are made for court-ordered support, bankruptcy, or any state or federal tax. The amount may not exceed the lesser of two figures: 25 percent of your disposable earnings or the amount by which your disposable earnings are greater than 30 times the federal minimum wage (currently $7.25 an hour). See Table 18-1 for calculations of the latter.

Table 18-1	Maximum Garnishment of Disposable Earnings under Normal Circumstances* for the $7.25 Federal Minimum Wage		
Weekly	**Biweekly**	**Semimonthly**	**Monthly**
$217.50 or less: None	$435.00 or less: None	$471.25 or less: None	$942.50 or less: None
More than $217.50 but less than $290.00: Amount above $217.50	More than $435.00 but less than $580.00: Amount above $435.00	More than $471.25 but less than $628.33: Amount above $471.25	More than $942.50 but less than $1,256.67: Amount above $942.50
$290.00 or more: Maximum 25%	$580.00 or more: Maximum 25%	$628.33 or more: Maximum 25%	$1,256.67 or more: Maximum 25%

*These restrictions don't apply to garnishments for child and/or spousal support, bankruptcy, or actions to recover state or federal taxes. Source: U.S. Department of Labor

Stating Your Case in Court

Asking for time off from work to go to the courthouse can be intimidating, embarrassing, and expensive. Most creditors count on this and are very happy if you don't show up. Why? Because they'll get just about anything they want from the judge without you there to object. I strongly suggest you show up and tell your side of the story to the judge. Be sure to bring

- ✔ Statements from the account in question to make sure the document filed with the court has no mistakes or unwarranted additions.
- ✔ Records of phone calls and written correspondence with the creditor to document that you've been trying to come to an agreement.
- ✔ A budget of your expenses and income to support a payment plan you can afford so the judge can see that your offer is serious.

You can represent yourself, but you're at a disadvantage if you do. Trust me: Your creditor is intimate with the ins and outs of the court process. If you can afford it, get an attorney. If you can't, go to court anyway; your presence and your genuine commitment to coming up with a workable way to repay your debt may be all that you need.

Show the court that you've made a good-faith effort to propose the best settlement you can afford using your records. Show that you've offered a reasonable repayment plan based on your means but that it was refused. If you went to a credit counselor along the way, mention it; if you can say that the counselor thought your proposed settlement was reasonable, all the better. Of course, none of this reasonable stuff applies to overdue child support; unless your income has changed for the worse, you have to pay as agreed.

The following list shows the progression of the process for collections that have gone to an attorney for legal action.

1. **You receive a demand letter from an attorney demanding payment.**

   This letter comes in addition to all the letters you may have received from the creditor or collector. The demand letter gives you one last chance to try to resolve the problem before court action begins.

2. **A suit is filed in court, often within 10 to 30 days of the date of the demand letter.**

   This suit alerts the court of the situation and again demands payment.

3. **You get served with a summons.**

   You get a summons from the court to respond by a certain date and time.

4. **If you don't answer the summons, the attorney can file for a default judgment.** If the court enters a default judgment in the matter, the creditor wins.

5. **If you do file an answer, the discovery process begins, and a trial date is later set.**

When you respond to the suit, be sure to explain any discrepancies in the creditor's claims. If you can't, then be sure to show up at the court on the hearing date with all your documentation and your own lawyer if possible.

6. **If a judgment is awarded and not paid by the due date, the attorney attempts to locate and verify any of your assets.**

The attorney initiates court-ordered bank levies, garnishment orders, liens, and so on to satisfy the judgment.

Understanding what happens may just help demystify the process and remove one more obstacle that may keep you from reacting until it's too late.

Managing IRS Debts, Student Loans, and Unpaid Child Support

IRS debts, student loans, and unpaid child support are among a class of debts that aren't in most cases dischargeable in a bankruptcy and must be paid. That puts them in a special category, and I cover them in the following sections.

Handling IRS debts

An IRS debt can be one of the easiest debt situations to deal with. First, the IRS knows that *you* know who's in control, so the IRS doesn't need to intimidate you with high-pressure, strong-arm tactics to get your attention. Second, the IRS isn't chasing down its own money — it's chasing down taxpayer money. And third, IRS employees don't get a bonus for collecting a debt. Dealing with the IRS, you can probably negotiate a reasonable repayment plan that you can manage over time.

Figure 18-4 shows a sample of an IRS repayment form that covers repayment plans. The full version of Form 9465 is on the CD. As you can see, it's not scary, so don't wait too long before you act.

If you have an accountant, I suggest you bring him or her along when you meet with the IRS. The accountant may be able to calmly explain why you shouldn't owe taxes on some income or why you should get certain deductions.

WARNING!

IRS debts just keep growing with age. In fact, if you delay too long, the IRS pulls any tax refunds you have coming and directs the money straight into the treasury until the debt is paid. Just what you wanted to hear, huh?

Form **9465**
(Rev. December 2009)
Department of the Treasury
Internal Revenue Service

Installment Agreement Request

▶ **If you are filing this form with your tax return, attach it to the front of the return. Otherwise, see instructions.**

OMB No. 1545-0074

Caution: *Do not file this form if you are currently making payments on an installment agreement or can pay your balance due in full within 120 days. Instead, call 1-800-829-1040. If you are in bankruptcy or we have accepted your offer-in-compromise, see* **Bankruptcy or offer-in-compromise** *on page 2.*

This request is for Form(s) (for example, Form 1040) ▶ _____ and for tax year(s) (for example, 2008 and 2009) ▶

1 | Your first name and initial | Last name | Your social security number

If a joint return, spouse's first name and initial | Last name | Spouse's social security number

Current address (number and street). If you have a P.O. box and no home delivery, enter your box number. | Apt. number

City, town or post office, state, and ZIP code. If a foreign address, enter city, province or state, and country. Follow the country's practice for entering the postal code.

2 If this address is new since you filed your last tax return, check here . . . . ▶ ☐

3 | Your home phone number | Best time for us to call | 4 | Your work phone number | Ext. | Best time for us to call

5 Name of your bank or other financial institution:

Address

City, state, and ZIP code

6 Your employer's name:

Address

City, state, and ZIP code

7 Enter the total amount you owe as shown on your tax return(s) (or notice(s)) . . . . | 7

8 Enter the amount of any payment you are making with your tax return(s) (or notice(s)). See instructions | 8

9 Enter the amount you can pay each month. **Make your payments as large as possible to limit interest and penalty charges.** The charges will continue until you pay in full . . . . | 9

10 Enter the day you want to make your payment each month. **Do not** enter a day later than the 28th ▶

11 If you want to make your payments by electronic funds withdrawal from your checking account, see the instructions and fill in lines 11a and 11b. This is the most convenient way to make your payments and it will ensure that they are made on time.

▶ a Routing number

▶ b Account number

I authorize the U.S. Treasury and its designated Financial Agent to initiate a monthly ACH electronic funds withdrawal entry to the financial institution account indicated for payments of my federal taxes owed, and the financial institution to debit the entry to this account. This authorization is to remain in full force and effect until I notify the U.S. Treasury Financial Agent to terminate the authorization. To revoke payment, I must contact the U.S. Treasury Financial Agent at **1-800-829-1040** no later than 10 business days prior to the payment (settlement) date. I also authorize the financial institutions involved in the processing of the electronic payments of taxes to receive confidential information necessary to answer inquiries and resolve issues related to the payments.

Your signature | Date | Spouse's signature. If a joint return, **both** must sign. | Date

Figure 18-4:
A sample
IRS repay-
ment form.

TIP

It's not unusual for the IRS to be very slow in notifying the credit bureaus or in clearing any liens on your town property records when you've paid your bill. Keep good records of payments and discharges, and follow up by checking your credit report and, if appropriate, the property records at your local town hall. Make sure that the records are updated or you may miss an opportunity to sell your home because it has a big fat lien on it that shouldn't be there.

Teaching yourself about student loans

Student loan collections used to be a joke, but no one is laughing anymore. The bankruptcy law has granted student loans nondischargeable status, and lenders pursue delinquencies forever. Depending on how many loans are involved — and you may have as many as one for each semester you were in school — the effect on your credit of being in default (*default* is defined differently for different types of loans; check with your lender to determine when your loan enters into default) varies from bad to nuclear meltdown. A lot of people ask me if they owe the money even if they didn't graduate or finish a semester. The answer is yes. You borrowed and spent the money, and you need to repay it regardless. What you did with it is of no interest (no pun intended) to the lenders. In fact, if you die while attending school, your estate (or your parents' estate if they cosigned the loan) still owes the debt.

A student loan isn't secured with collateral in the normal sense of the word. When you leave school, whether you graduate or not, certain situations, such as economic hardship or unemployment, may allow you to defer the payment of your loans for a period of time. However, after your student loan is in default, you lose your opportunity to defer payment. To make matters worse, you may have to pay the loan all at once unless you come up with an acceptable repayment scheme. You're also unable to receive any further student aid, your school may withhold your transcripts, your state and federal income tax refunds may be taken to offset the loan amounts, and your wages (if and when you get a job) may be *attached* or *garnished.* (See the "Understanding Wage Garnishments" section earlier in this chapter.)

If you can't pay back your loans as originally hoped, use all options available to you to defer your loans as long as possible. However, after you've exhausted your deferments, you'll be in default if you don't agree on a new repayment plan. Depending on how your loans were issued, what may seem like a single loan to you may be as many as eight or ten individual loans (one per semester) because each loan is reported separately. So the loans may show up as eight or ten separate trade lines in your credit report. If you end up in default, you may get ten times the negative information on your credit report you expect, and your credit score may crash from all those negative individual loan entries.

For multiple student loans, consider the Direct Consolidation Loans program. The program provides borrowers who have at least one up-to-date federal student loan the opportunity to consolidate into a single monthly payment. You may also extend the repayment term on a student loan, which can reduce your monthly payment. Eligible loans include the Stafford, PLUS, Perkins, Health Profession, Health Education, and Nursing student loans. You may also be able to consolidate most defaulted education loans if you can make satisfactory repayment arrangements with the current holders or agree to repay the new Direct Consolidation Loan under an Income Contingent Repayment (ICR) plan. For information on the Direct Consolidation Loans program, see `www.loanconsolidation.ed.gov`.

Delinquent student loans can be a big hiring issue. Getting a job with bad credit is a lot harder if your employer pulls a credit report to see whether you're reliable and stable. If you have any unpaid loans, explain early in the hiring process why you haven't paid them and that you'll make good on a loan repayment plan as soon as you get a paycheck.

Working with a student loan creditor is essential to moving on with a normal life. Dealing with these folks is very much like dealing with the IRS: You need to get in contact, have a plan, make an offer to repay the loan, and follow through.

Putting your kids first: Child support

Unpaid child support is another category of debt that lives as long as you do. Under the bankruptcy law, child-support obligations can't be discharged. And now the courts provide custodial parents the names of collection agencies that specialize in child-support debt, so your ex can easily work with a collection agency to come after you for what you owe.

Child-support debt can result in a criminal charge and jail time if you continue not to pay it. The decision of whether to seek prosecution in nonsupport cases rests with your state's attorney general. Courts have absolutely no sense of humor when it comes to child-support debt. You really don't want such a debt hanging over you. Plus, these debts make a very bad impression on any new employers. Make paying off such a debt your number-one priority.

Chapter 19

Minimizing Credit Damage in a Bankruptcy

In This Chapter

▶ Getting the inside scoop on bankruptcy

▶ Establishing the pros and cons of bankruptcy

▶ Discovering the eligibility requirements for filing bankruptcy

▶ Rebuilding your credit after bankruptcy

*B*ankruptcy used to be easy. You decided that you were too far over your head in debt, and you went to see an attorney, who made your debts disappear. Presto chango! Not anymore. Today's bankruptcy is less likely to rid you of all your debts than previous versions. Plus, some chapters of bankruptcy leave you on a bare-bones, IRS-sanctioned spending plan for the next five years. Ouch.

Still, bankruptcy can be a cure for over-indebtedness that threatens to deprive you and your family of the hope of a prosperous financial future. A fresh start is the intent of the law, and when done correctly and for the right reasons, that's just what you get.

Equally important is assessing the role bankruptcy plays in your life for years to come as a result of damaged credit and long waiting periods before you can file again, should you need to. With credit playing an increasingly important role in most Americans' financial life these days, the damage a bankruptcy can do to your future had better be worth it. But how do you know whether bankruptcy is right for you and your situation? How do you know which type or chapter of bankruptcy you qualify for, and what bills you'll still be responsible for going forward?

In this chapter, I give you an accurate, unbiased, and unprejudiced picture of how bankruptcy law works. I help you figure out whether bankruptcy makes sense for you, which type of bankruptcy is best for your situation, and how you can minimize bankruptcy's effects on your credit. I've seen too many people use bankruptcy for the wrong reasons, and instead of providing them with a fresh start, it placed them squarely behind the financial and credit eight balls. So if you're thinking about bankruptcy or know someone who is, this chapter helps you see past the legal fine print to consider what may be the most important financial decision you'll make in your next ten years.

Understanding Bankruptcy, Chapter and Verse

Filing for bankruptcy is a very serious decision, one for which you need to be armed with all the information you can find. Why? Because for all the problems a bankruptcy solves, it can create many more if you make a mistake. As with many laws, the bankruptcy laws in this country may seem like a secret code. Besides being long and written in legalese that's hard to understand, these laws contain all those mysterious chapters with numbers — 7, 11, and 13 — rather than names. What do the chapters really mean, and which one is right for you? That's what this chapter is all about! But before you pick which chapter may be best for you, I suggest that you first determine whether bankruptcy itself is right for you.

Both financial and quality-of-life components may factor into your decision to file bankruptcy, as well as the benefits gained versus the damage to your credit. If your wages are about to be garnished because of your inability to pay a bill — perhaps a totally unexpected medical bill — do you allow your family to suffer the financial consequences? Do you do so for years, or seemingly forever? More than half of those who file bankruptcy have large uninsured or underinsured medical expenses.

In basic terms, the reason for filing bankruptcy is to seek the protection of the court from your creditors. It's that simple. If you can't pay what you owe on your own, now or in the foreseeable future, call in the judge and he'll handle your collectors.

The courts allow many different types of bankruptcy, identified as chapters with numbers. The variety of options reflects the variety of solutions needed for different situations. One size doesn't fit all. A farmer's problems and needs differ significantly from a corporation's or an average individual's. A Chapter 9 bankruptcy, for example, is reserved for municipalities (cities and such). Chapter 12 allows farmers to reorganize their debt and keep their farms. Most people are familiar with Chapter 11 bankruptcy because of the high-profile companies that take advantage of it to reorganize, reduce obligations, and keep creditors at bay until they can turn their companies around. Actually, individuals sometimes file for Chapter 11 bankruptcy, too. As long as no creditor objects to the plan, a Chapter 11 bankruptcy may not require all of a filer's disposable income to be committed to the plan.

But among all the various chapters, two are most commonly used by consumers who find themselves unable to come to an agreement with or to meet contractual payments with their creditors:

- ✔ **Chapter 7:** Also known as *liquidation,* this is the most popular form of bankruptcy. It may require you to give up some assets (the liquidation part), but it gets you out of almost all your liabilities.

- ✔ **Chapter 13:** Often referred to as *wage-earner bankruptcy,* this form of bankruptcy allows you to keep most of your assets and pay back what the judge rules you can over a period of time, usually three to five years, under court supervision and protection.

Regardless of which chapter you file, you need to get counseling before filing and some financial education at discharge. This is actually a good thing and not just another hoop to jump through. Counseling can help assure you that a bankruptcy will solve your problem, and the education afterward may help you avoid financial trouble in the future.

Deciding whether Bankruptcy Makes Sense for You

Declaring bankruptcy is a big decision that affects your life for up to ten years. It's a decision that may affect your self-image and confidence for even longer. It's a condition that redefines your credit report, certainly lowers your credit score, and remains an issue for future credit and employment.

In other words, bankruptcy is a major life event, so it's something you want to consider very seriously. Don't get me wrong — bankruptcy may just be the best alternative if you've suffered some serious financial setbacks. But you need to invest time in carefully weighing all your options in this section before you take the plunge.

Deliberating the bankruptcy decision

As you consider bankruptcy, take this into account: Can you do anything more to help meet your obligations? Do you have hope of finding a solution to this mess that's acceptable to both you and your creditors? If you answered no to both questions, I think you're on the right track in considering bankruptcy.

Before you make the final decision to throw your credit and creditors off a financial cliff, I suggest you review the following:

- ✔ **Decide whether bankruptcy will solve your financial crisis.** Getting rid of all your debts and making collectors go away may solve one problem, but will it solve *the* problem? If the problem is too much spending and not enough income, declaring bankruptcy won't help you for very long. Likewise, bankruptcy won't help if you've been using credit to supplement your income for basic living expenses.

- ✔ **Understand bankruptcy's effects on your goals.** Bankruptcy is a big step, and its consequences will affect you for years. To make the decision based only on immediate events without considering the future impact would be a mistake. How will this decision affect your chances of buying a home, getting married, getting divorced, or getting a job? Describe your world as you'd like to see it in the next five years, and ask yourself what impact a bankruptcy has on that goal.

- ✔ **Consider all your options.** Make a list of other ways to deal with your debts. Can you increase your income? Reduce your expenses? Stretch out your payments? Sell some possessions on eBay to pay your bills for a while until things improve?

- ✔ **Seek out a professional nonlegal opinion.** Talk to a good credit counselor. You have to meet with a credit counselor anyway within six months before filing for bankruptcy. Expect this visit to give you options, an analysis of your spending and income including a written budget, and an action plan. This consultation goes a long way toward answering the question of whether bankruptcy will help you. See Chapter 15 for more on credit counselors.

- ✔ **Get a professional legal opinion.** Find a lawyer who does a lot of bankruptcies. Find out whether you qualify for bankruptcy and, if so, which chapter. Make sure you understand what bankruptcy will and won't do for you. Ask about alternatives, including settlements, statutes of limitations, and other options. Also ask about the pluses and minuses of filing for bankruptcy on your own. Called *pro se,* the law allows you to represent yourself, and in some courts with sympathetic judges, doing so can be a money saver (in other courts, it can be a disaster). Your lawyer is the best one to guide you here.

- ✔ **Talk to your creditors.** Seriously. If you're considering a bankruptcy, let your lenders know and ask whether they can offer a repayment plan. Keep in mind that you have to be able to afford this plan. Don't expect too much, but talking to your creditors is always worth a shot.

✔ **Consider the stiffer consumer rules in the Bankruptcy Abuse Prevention and Consumer Protection Act of 2005.** This act had a wide-ranging impact on bankruptcy in the United States. It was enacted because lenders convinced Congress (yes, the people you voted for) that a significant number of consumers had abused bankruptcy protection over the years. The act established restrictions to try to cut down on any such abuse in the future. Here's a brief summary of the main provisions that may help you decide whether a bankruptcy is worth pursuing in your situation:

- **Passing a means test is required to be eligible for Chapter 7.** Except in limited circumstances (check out the later "Qualifying for and Filing for Bankruptcy" section to see if you qualify), your net income has to be below the median income in your state of residence to file for liquidation of your debts in a Chapter 7.

- **You're required to get credit counseling from an "approved nonprofit budget and credit-counseling agency" before you can file.** The Executive Office of the U.S. Trustee provides a master list of approved agencies from which you may choose. You can find out who's on the list by contacting the clerk of the court where your bankruptcy is to be filed; by going to the U.S. Department of Justice website (www.justice.gov/ust/eo/bapcpa/ccde/cc_approved.htm); or by talking to your attorney.

- **After you file, you must complete a course in financial management before you're discharged from bankruptcy.** You may contact the same provider for this requirement as for the credit counseling requirement or you can use a different provider. You can find a list of approved providers at www.justice.gov/ust/eo/bapcpa/ccde/de_approved.htm.

- **You're limited in what you can buy immediately before filing.** Having made the decision to file, you're prevented from going out and spending up a storm or taking cash advances and then not having to pay. Generally, the limits apply to the 90 days preceding your filing.

- **You have to wait a long time after filing for bankruptcy before you can file again.** The law requires eight years between Chapter 7 bankruptcies, two years between Chapter 13 bankruptcies, and four years between Chapter 7 and Chapter 13 bankruptcies.

- **Your *homestead exemption* (how much equity in your home you can keep out of your filing and keep for yourself) is limited by state law.** In addition, if you acquired your home less than 40 months before filing, you're allowed a maximum exemption of $125,000, regardless of your state's exemption allowance.

- **Under Chapter 13 bankruptcy, you're allowed to spend only what the IRS guidelines allow.** The rest of your disposable income must be included in the plan, and every year you have to document your income and expenses to see whether you can pay more (or less).

- **Your attorney must certify that what you say in the documents you submit to the court is true.**

- **You still owe some past and future debts.** These debts include taxes (incurred in the last three years, unfiled, or filed late), domestic support, restitution and fines for drunk-driving injuries and other criminal offenses, and student loans. Courts are extremely reluctant to discharge student loans, and the general policy is not to discharge them. Rarely, some older student loans can be discharged, if an "undue" hardship condition exists, you file a separate motion with the bankruptcy court, and then appear before the judge to explain your hardship.

- **Domestic-support obligations are a priority debt that you must pay.** A *priority debt* takes precedence over other debt payments you owe and is paid completely. However, the *bankruptcy trustee* (the person appointed by the court to administer your Chapter 13 plan) gets his administrative fees before your spouse, ex-spouse, or kids get their money.

- **You may be evicted if you don't pay your rent after you've filed for bankruptcy.**

- **You must provide your latest tax return to your creditors if they ask for it.** Before you can finalize your bankruptcy, you need to give information about your financial status to your creditors so they can see that you can't afford to pay what you owe. If you're filing for Chapter 13, you must provide your tax returns for the last four years.

✔ **Visit with someone who cares about you.** Although this person may not be a professional, he or she knows you and may offer an important perspective. Avoid visiting with someone who would be personally affected by your choice (such as a person you owe money to, someone who owes you money, or a dependent).

✔ **Look in the mirror.** Given your current financial state, how do you see yourself? Consider your goals; weigh the options offered by your creditors, your credit counselor, and your lawyer; and be sure to consider the advice of others who care about you. Now you're ready to decide what's best for your future and your peace of mind. If you don't like what you see, go through the process until you do, and then do what you think is in your best interest.

TIP

Locating a bankruptcy attorney

A qualified attorney is essential if you're considering filing bankruptcy. I always consider friends, family, or co-workers who've had a satisfying experience with an attorney as a good source of reference. I'm not suggesting that you put a note up on the company bulletin board, but someone who has already been through the bankruptcy process may be a good referral source.

The Internet also has some very good resources. A few that you may want to check out are

✔ The American Bankruptcy Institute (www. abiworld.org). You can also find a

listing of pro bono bankruptcy attorneys at http://probono.abiworld.org.

✔ The National Association of Consumer Bankruptcy Attorneys (www.nacba. org).

✔ The American Bar Association (www. abanet.org).

✔ Lawyers.com (www.lawyers.com).

If you've used a lawyer who handles other issues for you, ask for a referral to someone who specializes in bankruptcy. Don't use your cousin, the real-estate lawyer. Get a pro. You have to live with any mistakes made here for years.

Adding up the pluses and minuses

Like anything in life, bankruptcy is neither all good nor all bad. In the following sections, I explain bankruptcy's benefits as well as the harsh reality of bankruptcy's consequences.

The silver lining of filing bankruptcy

I'm always in favor of hearing the good news first. With bankruptcy, it's no different. Here are some of the positives that bankruptcy can do for you:

✔ **You get a fresh start.** The silver lining in a bankruptcy is that you get to begin again. The collection activity stops. The fees, penalty rates, and calls from bill collectors stop. In fact, in a Chapter 7 bankruptcy, virtually your entire debt may go away. Without the ability to call a stop to the madness of credit gone awry, some people would never — and I mean *never* — be able to live a normal life again. Bankruptcy can allow that to happen.

✔ **You get credit education.** Another plus of bankruptcy: The bankruptcy law says that anyone who files is required to get some credit education. This is an opportunity to look back at what happened and to reset your financial and credit course going forward. If you take full advantage of this opportunity, you'll walk away with a much better sense of how to manage your financial life, which means you'll be less likely to end up back where you started.

The darker side of filing bankruptcy

As you can probably guess, filing bankruptcy comes with some pretty heavy consequences. Here are the major ones:

✔ **You may still owe money.** Bankruptcy may not wipe out *all* your debt. Some debts don't go away, even though you'd like them to, and you must pay them in full. The debts that don't disappear are

- • Federal, state, and local taxes

- • Child support

- • Alimony

- • Student loans from the government or a lender (except in very limited circumstances)

- • Money owed as a result of drunk driving and other criminal offenses such as willful injury or damage to people and property

✔ **Your credit score will be affected for years.** Bankruptcy is a major negative on your credit report that appears as a public record in your file as well as in your account history for up to ten years. Worse, it causes your credit score to stay depressed longer than a normal delinquency does. Good credit can plunge by 200 points. Declare bankruptcy and you're likely to see your score drop to the lowest 20 percent of all credit scores. Ouch! See Chapter 17 for more info.

✔ **Borrowing money becomes more difficult.** When a lender sees a score in the lowest percentile, your interest rates and terms escalate. In a tight credit market, lenders may decline to give you credit at any price.

Some lenders, however, specialize in loaning to people with bad credit. They're delighted to see you; the fact that you've just gone bankrupt is a big plus in their eyes. Why? Because under the law, you can't file a Chapter 7 bankruptcy again for eight long years. So although lenders get to charge you high interest rates as a risky borrower, you can't avoid repaying them by playing the bankruptcy card. If you fall behind, you can run, but you can't hide. Usually, these lenders are very good at collecting overdue accounts. The bottom line: Avoid these lenders at all costs. If you must borrow shortly after a bankruptcy, only use a reputable lender.

✔ **Renting an apartment may become more complicated.** Many landlords use credit reports to approve tenant applicants. They may refuse to rent to you, require a cosigner, or increase your deposit if they see a bankruptcy.

✔ **Insurance costs rise.** A bankruptcy may cost you more in insurance premiums, particularly for homeowners and auto insurance. The insurance mavens and their actuarial elves love credit reports. All those dispassionate numbers lend themselves to justifying rate increases much more than real claims do. So even if you have no losses, expect your premiums to go up. Credit reports are used mostly by homeowner and auto insurers; some states don't allow credit to be a factor in setting rates, but most do.

✔ **Employment searches may be more difficult.** Even under ideal circumstances, job hunting is extremely competitive and can be very stressful.
When you consider the fact that many employers run a credit check before
making a job offer, your stress level can increase as your opportunities
decrease. As a practical matter, some licenses can't be given to people
who've filed for bankruptcy, and security clearances can be denied.

The things that resulted in your bankruptcy — outside events or your
behavior or judgments — are all concerns for prospective employers.
These are the silent killers, because although you can't legally be denied
employment because you filed a bankruptcy, the prospective employer
rarely asks the questions to find out the reasons. Going on to the next
candidate is just easier and legally safer.

✔ **Your self-image and confidence may suffer.** Bankruptcy can take its
toll, because like it or not, a great deal of the way many people view
themselves is wrapped up in their financial persona. Most people think
of themselves as responsible adults, and they've been taught that
responsible adults pay their bills and keep their promises. Even though
you know that filing for bankruptcy is okay and that you have no choice
in the matter from a practical standpoint, you may find that you have an
internal conflict to deal with that you didn't expect.

Considering a debt-management plan first

One of the stops you're required to make on the road to getting help from the
bankruptcy courts is a credit-counseling agency. The court has recognized
the value of the work done by these agencies by requiring that your financial
circumstances be reviewed by them (*before* filing). The idea is that you'll get
an unbiased assessment of your financial condition, and that you may, upon
reflection, find other alternatives to handle your debt.

Understanding what a debt-management plan is

One of the services provided by the credit-counseling industry is the debt-
management plan. You begin with an individually tailored spending plan that
you create with the help of a credit counselor. A *debt-management plan* uses
the equivalent of your disposable income after actual expenses and real-
locates some or all of your income to pay your creditors. The average debt-
management plan is set up for three to five years but in practice tends to be
completed in about two years. (For more on debt-management plans, turn to
Chapter 15.)

Seeing how a debt-management plan differs from bankruptcy

Under a debt-management plan, the money left (if any) after you've paid your
living expenses and your creditors is yours to use as you see fit. If you file
Chapter 13 bankruptcy, however, all your disposable income goes toward

paying off your creditors. The amount you get to use for living expenses with minor adjustments comes from less-than-generous IRS guidelines.

Unlike the terms of a Chapter 7 or a Chapter 13 bankruptcy, a debt-management plan is a voluntary arrangement between you and your creditors, using the credit-counseling agency as an intermediary. You can walk away from a debt-management plan at any time and still file for bankruptcy. Or, if you're on the receiving end of a windfall, you can pay off your creditors in one payment and be done with it.

Of course, your creditors don't have to accept the terms of the debt-management plan, whereas they *have* to accept a court-ordered repayment plan if you file bankruptcy. That said, most creditors do accept debt-management plans because they know you'll be off to the courthouse to file bankruptcy if they say no. Additionally, if a creditor refuses to negotiate with a credit counselor, the court can order that the uncooperative creditor's debt get a 20-percent haircut.

Whereas a Chapter 7 bankruptcy liquidates many debts, a Chapter 13 bankruptcy forces creditors to accept a lower payment over a set period of time that may not cover all that you originally owed. The difference between what you owe and what you've paid under Chapter 13 is what the creditors lose. They also can't charge interest or fees under Chapter 13. A debt-management plan allows the creditors to collect interest charges, although many creditors reduce the rate to one that's more affordable and reflects your circumstances and your desire to repay the debt.

Perhaps one of the biggest differences between a Chapter 7 or Chapter 13 bankruptcy and a debt-management plan is the effect on your credit score. Bankruptcy has a large negative impact on your score, which affects your ability to do lots of the things I mention earlier in this chapter for years after the *end* of your bankruptcy.

A debt-management plan, on the other hand, doesn't have the same negative impact on your credit score. In fact, many creditors don't report to the credit bureaus that your account is being handled by a credit-counseling agency at all. Those that do report it to the bureaus report it as a description of the account (for example, credit card, real estate mortgage, or credit counseling), not as a payment history item (such as "pays as agreed" or "X days late"). Payment history items are included in calculating your credit score but account descriptions are not. Further, your credit report shows the credit-counseling account description only until you pay off the account or decide to discontinue the plan, at which point the notation is removed, which means the description isn't reported for the next seven years.

More good news: Even while you're enrolled in a debt-management plan, the FICO scoring system doesn't subtract any points. That's right — your credit score isn't affected. A credit-counseling notation on your file is perceived as a neutral item, not a negative or public-record item.

If you decide to try the debt-management-plan route rather than a Chapter 13 and the debt-management plan doesn't work out for you, you can always file for bankruptcy without any waiting period.

A debt-management plan may be less restrictive and damaging to your credit report and score than bankruptcy. I suggest that when you get your mandatory counseling on the road to bankruptcy, you explore making a debt-management plan work for you. Your credit and score will be glad you did.

Qualifying for and Filing for Bankruptcy

After reviewing the previous sections, you may determine that bankruptcy remains your best or only viable solution for your financial situation. But you still need to see whether you qualify for bankruptcy. Both Chapter 7 and Chapter 13 bankruptcies have eligibility requirements, which I cover in the following sections.

For a look at the new rules, refer to the document "Bankruptcy Code Filing Procedures Chart" on the CD.

Qualifying for Chapter 7

Access to Chapter 7, the most popular form of personal bankruptcy in recent years, is restricted by the Bankruptcy Abuse Prevention and Consumer Protection Act of 2005. Chapter 7 has been so popular because of its ability to get rid of debts and collectors. Under a Chapter 7, you receive relief from virtually all your debts, with a few exceptions, and you get it fast — like the same day (unlike a Chapter 13, which may take years before you get a discharge). I cover the major hurdles to a Chapter 7 in the following sections.

Passing the means test

The first hurdle in moving forward with Chapter 7 bankruptcy is meeting the *means test*. If you have too many means (that is, too much money), you can't declare Chapter 7. And sorry, but the courts won't take your word for it. You have to *prove* that your income really is as you said by handing in your most recent tax return. If your income is above the applicable median for your state of residence, you can't file for Chapter 7.

Do you have family income above the median for your family size in your state of residence? To find out, go to the census website: `www.census.gov/hhes/ www/income/data/statemedian/index.html`.

If your income is above the median, don't give up just yet. Next, you want to determine whether you have *excess monthly income* of more than $166.66 to pay $10,000 of debt over five years. So what counts as excess income? To find out, you have to use the spending guidelines approved by the IRS to discover whether you spent according to IRS guidelines. Allowable expenses are shown here: `www.justice.gov/ust/eo/bapcpa/20110315/meanstesting. htm`. The IRS guidelines may be very tight for you. (I know from personal experience: My dad was an IRS agent, and his idea of a reasonable allowance was $5 a week, even through college!)

Using the IRS allowable expenses as a guide, if you *can* squeak the $166.66 a month out of your budget, the best you can do is to file under Chapter 13.

If you have less excess monthly income than the magic number of $166.66 after IRS expense allowances, you may proceed to the next hurdle: Do you have an extra $100 a month over the next 60 months? And will that $6,000 account for at least 25 percent of your debt? If the answer to both questions is no, you can pass go and file for Chapter 7. If not, go directly to Chapter 13.

Tithing — giving money to your church — is allowed in both Chapter 7 and Chapter 13 bankruptcies. You may donate up to 15 percent of your gross income and have it count as an expense that may lower your income. Donating to your church may just help you make the numbers work to become eligible for a Chapter 7 rather than a Chapter 13.

Receiving required counseling

At some point during the six months before you file for bankruptcy, you have to receive counseling and get a certificate from a court-approved credit counselor. The law leaves these requirements to the court (actually the Executive Office of the U.S. Trustee) to define. However, Congress has set certain minimum criteria. To be approved, a credit-counseling agency must

- ✔ Be nonprofit.
- ✔ Have an independent board of directors, the majority of whom are neither employed by the agency nor directly or indirectly benefit financially from the outcome of a credit-counseling session.
- ✔ Charge "reasonable" fees and provide services for free if you can't afford to pay the reasonable fee.
- ✔ Disclose its funding sources, counselor qualifications, possible impact on your credit history, any cost imposed on you, and how those costs will be paid.

✔ Offer adequate counseling encompassing an analysis of your current situation, what brought you to your current situation, and options to solve your problem without incurring *negative amortization* of your debts. Negative amortization happens when you make payments on a debt but the payments are too small to offset interest and fees on the account, so the debt grows instead of getting paid off.

✔ Train its counselors adequately but not pay them based on the outcome of the counseling.

The law also spells out minimum requirements for the personal financial-management course you must attend as part of the bankruptcy discharge process. The course may or may not be given by a credit-counseling agency; others are allowed to offer it if they qualify with the court, but all must

✔ Provide experienced and trained personnel

✔ Incorporate relevant teaching methodologies and learning materials

✔ Offer the course in an adequate facility or over the phone or Internet

Just because the court has approved the counseling agency doesn't make it the right one for you, so exercise caution when selecting. (See Chapter 15 for guidance in choosing a credit counselor.) You want someone who has a good track record and has electronic-certificate-issuing capability. Why? Because if the counselor makes a mistake or if the certificate is delayed in getting to you, you could face costly delays in getting this matter successfully concluded.

Qualifying for Chapter 13

The strict guidelines to qualify for filing a Chapter 7 bankruptcy mean that some people only qualify to file Chapter 13. The requirements for counseling and proof of income are the same for both types of bankruptcy, and although you must take the same means test, the outcome leads to different results.

Chapter 13 differs from Chapter 7 in that, after your income has been established and allowable expenses have been deducted, you must use the remainder of your disposable income toward the repayment of debt. *Disposable* is defined by taking your income and subtracting the IRS allowable expenses (see the earlier "Passing the means test" section).

Just as with Chapter 7, those filing for Chapter 13 bankruptcy must establish that their family income is either below or above the median for their state. If your income is above the state median, your disposable income gets disposed of (paid to your bankruptcy trustee, who forwards it to your creditors) for the next five years, unless you can show that you can pay off 100 percent of the debt in less than 60 months. If your income is below the state median, your disposable income may be paid to your creditors over the next three years. The rest of the debt that you owe to the creditor goes unpaid, and there's no interest on any of the accounts involved. (To find out what the median income is for your state, see the "Passing the means test" section earlier in the chapter.)

The current bankruptcy law is intended to require those who can afford to make payments toward their debt to do so.

Filing, then backing out

If you decide that bankruptcy isn't for you *after* you file your court papers, you can ask the court to voluntarily dismiss your case before you get your discharge. For example, say you file a Chapter 7 and then find out that you have to give back that 3-carat diamond ring your sweetie gave you recently. Or in the case of a Chapter 13, maybe you've been making payments and eating peanut butter for a month and can't go on. Or looking on the bright side, perhaps you get a windfall inheritance from a rich uncle and can pay off the Chapter 13 in one fell swoop.

No matter what the reason, you can call the whole thing off and get a dismissal. Keep in mind, however, that the credit-reporting bureaus pick up the record of your bankruptcy filing and report it, even if you stop the process without getting out of any debts. The bureaus must also report that the filing was dismissed, but the record of your filing a bankruptcy stays on your credit report, and continues to lower your score, for the remainder of the reporting period (up to ten years). Both you and the creditor have the same rights and remedies as you had before you filed your bankruptcy case.

If you ask for a dismissal of your bankruptcy filing, you won't be the first to do so. In fact, the law has a specific section that deals with people who not only change their minds but

also change them back again. Perhaps after you back out of the bankruptcy to save the diamond ring, your creditors turn up the collection heat to the point where you'd gladly give them the ring and your grandfather's watch if they'd just leave you alone.

Here's how the change works the second time around: In your first filing, after you file the paperwork with the courts, you receive an automatic *stay* (or suspension) of collection activity on the part of your creditors. The length of time for the collection stay depends on the type of debt or action pending and can vary in time allowed. But generally, it's in place until you discharge your debts (that is, get rid of them). But if you change your mind and ask for a dismissal and then change your mind and refile a second time within one year of the original filing, the automatic stay (the stopping of all collection activity) is for only 30 days. So you have to get all your testing, counseling, and paperwork done in the 30-day time period or the collectors and foreclosers return in force. If this is the third such filing in a year, you don't get *any* stay unless the court orders it.

What this means is this: When you file for bankruptcy, do your best to make sure it's a decision you can live with for the long haul.

Managing Your Credit after a Bankruptcy

Declaring bankruptcy is more of a hassle than it used to be, and qualifying for relief is definitely harder. But if you qualify and take the bankruptcy plunge, don't think you're out of the woods. You still have to live with the effects of bankruptcy on your credit report and your credit score, as well as the barriers that your new status creates. You're likely to discover that bankruptcy has an impact on your insurance rates and your ability to get hired or promoted.

Your bankruptcy isn't something you want to let take care of itself. Your bankruptcy status remains on your credit report as the mother of all credit negatives for up to ten years, and that's a long time.

So just how do you get a handle on your credit future, post-bankruptcy? You rebuild your credit as quickly as possible, and you use credit carefully as you go forward. This section shows you how to do so.

Preparing your side of the story

Now that your credit report shows a bankruptcy and will continue to show it for a long time, expect the matter to come up from time to time in a number of life's future scenarios. You need to be ready with an explanation of what happened, what you did about it, and why it won't happen again. To begin with, work on a short statement that describes your valid reasons for filing for bankruptcy. Businesspeople and potential lenders who have access to your credit report want to know your reasons to help them decide whether to extend you credit or do business with you in general.

Note: This statement *isn't* the 100-word statement I discuss in Chapter 14 that you can attach to your credit report. This is an actual verbal statement that you make when you're doing anything that requires other parties to see your credit report (applying for a loan, applying for a job, and so on). Be proactive and tell them about this before they see your credit report, but only if you're sure they'll be looking at it. (Why raise the issue if they'll never know about it otherwise?)

Like the statement you use explaining why you left your last employer, a tight and targeted statement explaining your bankruptcy is important. Whatever your parting circumstances were, your explanation is always a positive spin on the truth. It's short, sweet, and rehearsed. Having it at the ready allows you to convey yourself as confident, professional, and reliable.

Beware of solicitations generated by your bankruptcy filing

After you declare bankruptcy, you'll likely face a flurry of solicitations and telemarketing calls from companies that receive notices of your filing. Many businesses use these bankruptcy notices as mailing lists for the high-cost credit products or scams they sell.

Read all the fine print on any solicitations and be suspicious of a company anxious to give you a new start. You're very vulnerable, both from a personal and a financial perspective. This may be a good time to opt out of the credit bureau and direct-marketing mailing programs that a lot of solicitors use to send you those preapproved offers. If you want your name and address removed from mailing lists obtained from the main consumer credit-reporting agencies, go to www.optoutprescreen.com or call 888-567-8688. The Direct Marketing Association can provide information about opting out of lists produced by companies that subscribe to their mail and telephone preference services. Contact the DMA at the following addresses:

- ✔ Direct Marketing Association
  Mail Preference Service
  P.O. Box 643
  Carmel, NY 10512

- ✔ Direct Marketing Association
  Telephone Preference Service
  P.O. Box 1559
  Carmel, NY 10512

You can also contact the DMA at www.dmaconsumers.org/consumer assistance.html. Include the following information with your request:

- ✔ The date

- ✔ Your first, middle, and last name (including Jr., Sr., III, and so forth)

- ✔ Your current address

- ✔ Your home phone number (only for the telephone preference service)

On The CD: Check out the "Credit Bureau's Sample Opt-Out Letter" on the CD, which is recommended by the Federal Trade Commission. Be sure to send your letter to all three credit bureaus.

It wouldn't hurt to make sure you're in the Federal Trade Commission's National Do Not Call Registry as well: www.donotcall.gov.

Although it's rare for one debt to push you over the edge, a single traumatic event is more easily accepted by a lender, employer, or landlord. The event may be a divorce, a layoff, or an illness. Something that's beyond your control is a plus. Your efforts to pay the debts or deal with collectors are only of interest to you. All you need to convey is that you reviewed all other solutions. End the short statement with some words of wisdom, like, "I've learned a lot from this experience" or "I've become better at saving money as a result." Here's an example of a tight little speech that takes less than two minutes to share:

When you look at my credit report, I want you to know that you'll see a bankruptcy there. It's not something I'm proud of, but because of an illness, I ended up with $100,000 in medical bills. I felt terrible about having to declare bankruptcy, but I had no choice. I've increased my insurance coverage and savings so that this will never happen again. I certainly learned a painful lesson, but that's all behind me now.

Reaffirming some debt: How it helps and hurts

As part of your bankruptcy rights, you can request to keep some of your debt if you can show the court that you can afford to pay it. After all that trouble to relieve yourself of the terrible burden, isn't keeping some of your debt sort of like going through a knock-down divorce and remarrying your spouse? Well, people do both, and here's why.

Believe it or not, keeping some debt (and its associated credit lines) has some benefits. This is technically called *reaffirmation*. For starters, having some ready credit available when you walk out of the courthouse may be a good idea. Also, a chunk of your credit score is based on longevity of accounts. Keeping an old account with a positive credit history may help with rebuilding your credit score.

 If you decide to keep some of your debt, make sure that you really *can* afford to pay. And more important, if the debt is in the form of a credit card, be sure that the terms of the card, including your original unused credit limit and interest rate, don't change going forward because of the bankruptcy.

Working on repairing your credit score

Your credit score is likely to suffer dramatically from a bankruptcy. The better your score originally, the more it drops. If you had terrible credit before, a filing may not cause such a big drop. Either way, you'll likely have a very low credit score for a very long time unless you take positive action to correct it.

Now that your credit score has been slammed by bankruptcy, you want to take steps to repair it as best you can. In Chapter 7, I explain what factors influence your credit score. Here's how those factors are influenced by a bankruptcy:

✔ **Timeliness of payments:** This category may be heavily affected. I say *may be* because nearly half of all bankruptcies happen with no prior delinquencies. After you get new credit, be sure to make all your payments on time, every time.

✔ **Amount and proportion of credit used:** In a bankruptcy, you or your lenders close most of your accounts. Your available credit drops to $0 in most cases. As you reestablish credit, expect low limits at first and try not to carry balances over 50 percent of your limit for best results.

✔ **Length of time you've been using credit:** Here again, your score is damaged, because the history on your open accounts stops at your filing. Negative accounts drop off your record in seven years, although the bankruptcy record may remain for up to ten years. Positive accounts are reported for at least ten years and sometimes longer.

✔ **Variety of accounts:** Chances are you're left with only secured debt such as mortgages, student loans, or car loans. All your revolving and retail accounts may be gone, which means you don't have the variety of accounts that helps to boost your credit score. Consider a secured credit card or a passbook loan to restart your revolving or installment credit history.

✔ **Number and types of accounts you've opened recently:** After the bankruptcy, you may have more activity here than usual as you attempt to reestablish your credit. And your score will fall. (The more inquiries you have for new accounts or changes, the lower your score.) To minimize damage, don't apply for more accounts than you actually need.

Keeping this in mind, a helpful tactic is to take steps to improve your credit in these five areas. And don't forget that creditors don't necessarily report to all three of the credit bureaus. Now more than ever, you want to make sure that your good creditor experiences get on *all* the credit reports. Ask a potential creditor whether it reports all your information to all three bureaus. If it doesn't, try to get credit from a creditor that does.

Follow the tips below, as well, to increase your credit score as much as you can during the aftermath of your bankruptcy:

✔ **Keep one or two of your older and lower-balance cards or lines open by reaffirming them.** See the preceding section for more information.

✔ **Apply for a secured credit card.** This type of account uses a deposit of yours to secure or guarantee that you make the payment. Most report to the credit bureaus as any other credit card would, but be sure to ask the issuer whether the card you choose is reported.

✔ **Open a passbook savings account, and then borrow against it to demonstrate that you can make those fixed payments on time every month.** And again, be sure the lender reports the loan to the credit bureaus.

Establishing new credit

Yes, you can probably get new credit soon after you come out of bankruptcy. In fact, establishing some new lines of credit could be the first step in improving your credit score. You'll face some new challenges as you pursue new credit opportunities. For example, you'll discover that the best loans at the most attractive terms and interest rates may not be available to you. Instead, you may find that you're being pursued by loan-shark types that make Jaws look like a guppy (see the earlier sidebar, "Beware of solicitations generated by your bankruptcy filing").

I caution you to be extra careful about committing to new lines of credit. Not only are you a target for unscrupulous lenders who specialize in post-bankruptcy loans, but also — now more than ever — you're vulnerable to slipping back into an out-of-control borrowing situation. You don't want to get trapped in debt again. New credit is okay as long as it's part of your plan to rebuild your rating, you're 100 percent confident that you can handle the payments, and it fits your spending plan.

Moving forward with a game plan

Moving forward with a plan is very different from moving forward *without* one. Although plans may not always work exactly as you want, they help you realize when you're drifting, and they give you direction, motivation, and the tools to achieve your financial ends.

Begin by paying close attention to the post-bankruptcy education class you must attend as the springboard for your future. You may feel shell-shocked or that this class is a waste of time, but it isn't. Then, if you didn't create a spending plan the first time you went to the credit-counseling agency (as you were required to do before filing for bankruptcy), work with your counselor to develop a detailed spending plan, complete with saving for financial goals.

A credit counselor will work with you to craft a spending plan that not only fits your current needs but also allows you to set aside money for emergency savings and savings for those goals you want to achieve in the future. This tells you how much money you can comfortably spend each month and helps you make sure that you're spending only on those things that you've consciously decided to spend your money on. No impulse buying for you. That money will be allocated to other choices you make — like a college fund, a vacation fund, or a retirement account.

Chapter 20

Repairing Identity Theft Credit Damage

*R*ecovering from identity theft is almost always more difficult and takes longer than most people think. If you're a victim of identity theft, you need to act quickly and comprehensively. Don't rely on others to resolve this mess. You have the biggest interest in getting this situation stopped, fixed, and behind you, and you need to assume all responsibility for doing so. In this chapter you find out who to contact, what to do, and, most important, how to minimize the damage and move on.

Taking Fast Action When Identity Theft Happens to You

If your identity has been stolen or you believe it has (you don't need a smoking gun, videotapes, or a ransacked room to act), do everything I recommend in the following sections as soon as possible. Most of the places you need to contact are open 24 hours every day, so a late-night call won't bother anyone.

Communicating with the right people

You may read different advice on who to call *first* when you believe your identity has been compromised or stolen. Some sources say to begin by reporting the crime to the police to establish a formal record, others suggest you call your creditors, and still others say to notify the credit bureaus. My advice is to begin in one of two places, depending on your circumstances:

> ✔ If your existing bank or credit accounts have been compromised, call your bank or creditors first.
>
> ✔ If you find out about accounts you've never heard of and didn't open, call the credit bureaus first.

Either way, don't wait long between the two calls.

Before you pick up the phone, do one more thing: Start recording everything that happens from now on. You want dates, times, names, badge numbers, phone numbers, and so on. Documentation is critical because, unfortunately, this situation may go on for a long time and require a lot of calling and writing to resolve. Don't trust your memory or count on people to call you back when they say they will. You'll help yourself out by being responsible and in charge of writing down the facts and promises.

On the CD, I include a handy worksheet, courtesy of the Federal Trade Commission, called "Chart Your Course of Action" that you may find useful. You can use it as is or use it to generate ideas for creating a customized chart of your own.

Canceling your credit cards

If your credit or debit cards have been compromised, call the card issuers, ask for the fraud department, and have the cards in question cancelled immediately. You can find the phone number on your monthly statements, in your terms-and-conditions brochure, or on the card issuer's website. If you're away from home when you find out the bad news, use a business center computer — don't wait until you get home to call. If you have the card, look for the toll-free customer service number on the card itself.

A small comfort: Your liability on stolen credit card accounts is relatively low — just $50 maximum per card. Even so, you need to contact all your creditors as quickly as possible so that the thief doesn't continue to rack up charges in your name or open new accounts.

For ATM and debit cards, your maximum liability is $50 if you report the loss within 48 hours of noticing it, but the liability can be $500 or even the full amount of your accounts (including any overdraft protection) if you delay too long.

Getting in touch with the credit bureaus

If you call just one of the three major credit bureaus (Equifax, Experian, or TransUnion) to report identity theft, a 90-day fraud alert is placed on all three of your credit files within 24 hours. A *fraud alert* can make it more difficult for a thief to get credit in your name because it tells creditors to follow certain procedures to protect you. (See the section "Sending out a fraud alert" later in this chapter for more info.)

Fraud alerts aren't foolproof, and compliance by lenders can be spotty at times. Therefore, I prefer to lock a door rather than just close it. So consider putting a *credit freeze* on your credit reports until you know how severe the identity theft damage is (see Chapter 12 for info on how to place a freeze). A frozen credit report can't be pulled to issue new credit without your express permission. You can always remove or thaw your accounts later, and a freeze shuts off access to your information much more completely than a fraud alert.

You can also add a *victim's statement* to your credit report. This statement informs people who view your report that the information in your file has a potential problem and that they should be very wary of making any decisions using the information. Most creditors take strong notice of this fact and won't issue new credit in your name.

Adding a victim's statement to your report may motivate creditors to close existing accounts that weren't affected until they can determine that you're safe again, which may keep you from using your accounts until you can speak with the creditors.

After you notify the credit bureau of your situation, you'll receive a free credit report from each of the bureaus. Be sure to keep a copy of all reports (store them with those copious notes you're taking).

Contacting the Federal Trade Commission

The Federal Trade Commission (FTC) is the nation's number one consumer protection agency and supports an entire department that handles identity theft issues. The folks in the identity theft clearinghouse don't follow up on individual cases, but they play an important role in looking for patterns and accumulating statistics that help everyone concerned with stopping identity theft.

Call the FTC's Identity Theft Hotline at 877-438-4338. From a purely self-serving perspective, contacting the FTC bolsters your claims regarding unauthorized credit card charges or accounts opened by thieves in your name. Go to www.ftc.gov/bcp/edu/microsites/idtheft/instructions1. htm to fill out the Identity Theft Complaint Form (www.ftc.gov/bcp/edu/resources/forms/affidavit.pdf). The site gives you detailed instructions on how to fill out the form and how to print the form to use when disputing accounts or charges with creditors or filing a police report.

Notifying the police

If you call the local sheriff, will he flip on his blue and red lights and tear around town to find the thief? Not exactly. But you do have a crime on your hands, so you need to call the police and report it. Plus, some of the people you'll be dealing with may require a police report to take action.

The police report is also a way for others in the process to get a straight, consistent story from a third party about what happened and when. You'll have less difficulty convincing a collector if you can send an official police report to bolster your story. Be sure to get a copy of the report as soon as it's available, or at least get the police report number for reference.

Here's how the police reporting process works:

1. **Contact your local police station if you suspect someone is using your identity.**

   You don't need legal proof or a smoking gun to prove your claim; it's your identity, and your suspicion is enough to file a police report.

2. **File the report, providing all the facts and circumstances.**

   You need all account numbers and other relevant information (see the preceding section regarding the FTC Identity Theft Complaint Form). No standard form or procedure exists; each police department has its own.

3. **Make sure you get the police report number with the date, time, police department, location, and name of the officer writing the report.**

   You'll likely need to provide this info if you deal with insurance claims, credit card companies, or lenders or collectors to clear your account.

4. **Be persistent if the police seem reluctant to take your statement, but be polite.**

   Most states require police departments to file reports for identity theft victims, but some police departments may not be required to do so. If your local police are reluctant to file a report, you can remind them that, without a police report, credit bureaus may not block fraudulent items on your credit report, and lack of a formal report may inadvertently help a crook.

   If your police department still doesn't want to file a report, contact your state's Attorney General's office (you can find contact info at www.naag.org) for assistance.

Alerting the post office

Many identity theft cases result from unauthorized and illegal access to your information via the U.S. mail. Tampering with the U.S. mail is a federal crime. If you're a victim of identity theft and think your mail may have played a role, contact the U.S. Postal Inspection Service and report your concerns. Call 877-876-2455 or see https://postalinspectors.uspis.gov/forms/IDTheft.aspx.

Taking advantage of the FACT Act

The Fair and Accurate Credit Transactions Act (the FACT Act or FACTA) has numerous provisions for businesses, credit bureaus, and you. An entire book could easily be written on the topic, but in essence, the FACT Act was designed to bolster the Fair Credit Reporting Act (FCRA) and address issues surrounding incomplete or inaccurate credit reporting, including new safeguards for identity theft. The following list highlights the consumer-oriented, identity theft–related provisions of the act that I believe are most informative or useful:

- ✔ **You're entitled to at least one free credit report each year from each of the three credit bureaus.** In reality, you can often get more than one report if you file a fraud alert (see the next section) or an active duty alert. Specialty reporting agencies, such as insurance and landlord reporting services, must also give you a free report if you ask. (See Chapter 6 for more info on specialty bureaus.)

- ✔ **Information based on an account that you've reported as fraudulent or that you've shown to be inaccurate or incomplete is not allowed to be reported to a bureau.**

- ✔ **Businesses must cooperate with you to help clear your name in the case of identity theft.** They must provide copies of records about goods or services they provided to the thief. Businesses may require a police report and may take up to 30 days to comply.

- ✔ **You may place a 90-day fraud alert, a 7-year extended fraud alert, and a 1-year military active-duty alert on your credit file.**

- ✔ **You may have fraudulent trade lines on your credit report blocked if you've reported the crime to a police department or law enforcement agency.**

- ✔ **You may request that your Social Security number be *truncated* (shortened) on your credit report and communications in case it falls into the wrong hands.** And credit report users can't just throw your used reports in a trash bin. They have to dispose of the report in a legally sanctioned manner.

- ✔ **Businesses must truncate your credit card number on credit card receipts.** In other words, your restaurant receipt shouldn't show your entire credit card number — just the last four or five digits.

Sending out a fraud alert

As I mention earlier in this chapter, contacting the credit bureaus is one of your first steps when you discover an identity theft. When you contact them, you have the opportunity to place a fraud alert and a victim's statement in your file. These two items indicate to those who look at your report that the request for credit they've received recently may not actually be from you. Generally, for a subsequent request for a new account or a change to an existing account, the creditor will contact you before approving the credit request.

A fraud alert is placed on your account for 90 days. Any new activity, including your own, is researched and reported to you. So if you open new credit lines during this time, you may notice a slower-than-normal approval process. Although this may slow you down just a bit, it's worth the extra red tape to be sure you and your identity are being protected.

If you aren't sure whether your identity has been stolen but you know the information necessary to steal it has been compromised, consider an *extended alert* on your credit report. An extended alert lasts seven years. Why use an extended alert? Say that your hospital's computer is hacked, and the hacker gets access to patients' Social Security numbers, birth dates, and credit information. The thief may not sell or use your information right away; he may save your information for future use. The extended alert covers a long enough time period to prevent the information from being used to open an account, say, next year. An extended alert can be a bit of a nuisance, because after you place an extended alert on your credit file, potential creditors are required to actually contact you, or meet with you in person, before they issue new credit in your name. Still, an extended alert warns you of any suspicious activity, even after you've forgotten about the original event that triggered you to establish the alert in the first place.

A small silver lining: After you put the extended fraud alert on your file, you're entitled to *two* more free copies of your credit report at any time during the next 12 months from all three agencies, not just the one you get with a simple fraud alert or the annual free report that everyone gets.

Blocking fraudulent credit lines

"Block that line" may sound like a football cheer, but blocking can be a powerful tool. Be sure to request that the bureaus block any lines of credit that you believe are fraudulent. You'll have to provide information for the account you want blocked and a copy of your identity theft report. The block prevents those accounts from being sold, transferred, or placed for collection. In addition, don't forget to ask the credit bureaus to remove any inquiries on your record as a result of those fraudulent lines. Those inquiries can hurt your credit score.

Finally, ask the credit bureaus to notify anyone who may have received reports over the last six months with the erroneous information and inquiries on them. Doing so helps alert creditors and other interested parties to the situation — and saves your reputation.

Getting and Using Credit after Identity Theft

As with any theft, break-in, or personal attack, as a victim of identity theft, you likely feel traumatized, battered, fearful, and angry. You may want to avoid any experience with credit and borrowing in the future.

But my advice is to recognize these feelings for what they are — feelings — and to not give up altogether. After all, credit — though it certainly can be abused and exploited — is a powerful and sometimes indispensable tool that can help you achieve personal and financial goals you may not achieve otherwise. I strongly suggest that you adopt a strong offense and move forward with your personal goals. Whether you're planning on buying a house or a car or you're simply taking advantage of a retail offer for 10 percent off with a new credit account, don't be afraid to use credit to your advantage. Here are some steps you can take to get your credit going again, without putting yourself at renewed risk for identity theft.

Closing and reopening your accounts

Whether your credit, banking, or other accounts were broken into, stolen, or just sniffed at, change all your passwords, user IDs, and account numbers. You'll probably have to close accounts and reopen them. Doing so may be hassle, but if you've been a victim of identity theft, you already know the real meaning of *hassle*.

Here's a list of which accounts to close and reopen:

- ✔ **Bank accounts:** When your information is compromised, you never know if or when trouble will pop up. Changing the account numbers results in a dead end for a thief. Place an alert on the new accounts so you're informed when certain transactions happen or dollar levels are exceeded, such as a debit of more than $1,000.

- ✔ **Credit card accounts:** When you contact the card companies, they'll ask you for proper identification. (This is good — you *want* them to be suspicious!) They're used to closing accounts and reopening new ones quickly and painlessly. I suggest that you only reopen those you use. As a rule, if I haven't used a card in two years, I begin to wonder why it's taking up space in my wallet or my sock drawer.

- ✔ **Other accounts:** Contact your Internet service provider, phone service provider, and utility companies to alert them of the identity theft and to get new account numbers.

Altering your PINs and passwords

When you change your bank accounts, change your personal identification numbers (PINs), too. And when you access money at ATMs or in public places, make sure that no one can see you enter the number. Getting close to the machine may block the sight of someone across the street using binoculars or a camera with a telephoto lens. (Yes, thieves really *do* go that far.) Using ATMs located in bank lobbies is better for your security.

For online access to bank, credit card, bill paying, and investment accounts, switch to a *pass phrase* instead of a password. A pass phrase uses a short series of words like "Mauiis#1" instead of a single password. Pass phrases tend to be longer and harder to crack. Include some capital letters, numbers, and characters in them for additional strength.

Changing your Social Security number and driver's license

If you can't seem to shake the damage done by the identity theft (either because new theft occurrences keep popping up or collectors keep landing on you like mosquitoes), you may need to take more-serious action. Consider contacting the Social Security Administration to inquire about getting a new Social Security number.

Getting a new Social Security number is a huge pain to everyone, including you. Imagine all the places you've used your old number. If you go this route, you need to change all your records yourself. For more information, visit the Social Security website at www.socialsecurity.gov or call 800-772-1213 (800-325-0778, TTY for the hearing impaired).

You won't be the first person who had to do this. Besides the storied federal witness protection program, Social Security numbers are also changed for domestic violence victims and others when warranted. But with all the emphasis on national security, changing your number isn't easy.

A few circumstances can prevent you from changing your Social Security number. You can't get a new Social Security number if

- You've filed for bankruptcy.
- You intend to avoid the law or your legal responsibility.
- Your Social Security card is lost or stolen, but there's no evidence that someone is using your number.

Be sure to document everything. This dog can have a very long tail. You may need to dig up some documentation a year or two after you thought all the dust had settled. Good records, with everything in writing and names and dates, are a godsend.

While you're at it, go down to the Department of Motor Vehicles and get your driver's license number changed, especially if someone is using yours as an ID.

Part V
The Part of Tens

The terms of our refinancing gave us a little extra cash to build an add-on to the back of the house.

In this part . . .

Everyone loves tens — the top-ten YouTube videos, ten-dollar bills, and ten ways to build great credit. In this part, you get my top-ten suggestions in short, concise, bite-sized portions to help you tame, improve, repair, and protect your credit. I condense my favorites into a few pages for your quick reference.

I include ten legislative acts that provide consumer protections for you and your credit that can be real life-savers. Also, look for ten action tips to improve your credit and make it shine. And I give you ten ways to successfully manage financial emergencies. Whether you can spare ten minutes for a quick read or just ten seconds for a look-up, these no-nonsense chapters are bound to help you and your credit.

Chapter 21

Ten Consumer Protections Everyone Needs to Know

....

In This Chapter

▶ Getting acquainted with laws that can help protect you

▶ Seeking aid from lawyers, counselors, and government agencies

....

*I*t has been said that a person can't be too good-looking or have too many friends. This has never been truer than in the world of credit — at least the part about friends. The world of credit can be complex, unforgiving, and expensive — very expensive! So as the credit-granting, credit-reporting, and credit-scoring industries have evolved to be used for everything from issuing credit cards to getting a job, legislators and consumer advocates have recognized that consumers need effective ways to keep errors, both yours and theirs, from seriously complicating your life. The result is a series of consumer laws, protections, and agencies whose sole purpose is to keep the credit game honest and give you as fair an opportunity as possible to access the American financial system. These protections may not always work as you'd like, but if they didn't exist, you'd be at the mercy of big business, and that's no place you want to be.

In this chapter I cover the big legal protection resources you have and some people who can offer you help and guidance in dealing with the world of consumer credit.

The Fair and Accurate Credit Transactions Act

Fairness is something you can hope for in your dealings with the credit bureaus and those other consumer-reporting bureaus that are increasingly in the news. But before the protections afforded in the Fair and Accurate Credit Transactions Act (FACT Act or FACTA) became effective, fairness was strictly in the eye of the beholder. And the beholder wasn't you! Congress acted to end a number of perceived or real abuses.

Congress understood that the nation's banking system was increasingly dependent on credit reporting; that inaccurate reports resulted in unfair and inefficient banking; and that you had a right to privacy. The result is that you now have more control over what's said about you in credit bureau files and who can access your information. You also have the right to dispute errors or out-of-date information and to get a free report from each bureau every year. Not bad for the crowd in Washington! Here are your main protections:

- ✔ You have to be told of any negative action taken as a result of information contained in your credit report, and you must be given free access to the same information. If the interest rate on your favorite credit card goes up, you get to see a copy of the report that had the data leading to that increase.

- ✔ You can find out what information is in your personal file. No more secrets! It's your information and your file, so you can look at it.

- ✔ You can get a free copy of your reports at least annually if you ask for one. Free is a wonderful thing, and you can get free reports every 12 months or whenever you're the object of identity theft or fraud, you're on public assistance, or you're unemployed but expect to apply for employment within 60 days.

- ✔ You have the right to know the score. Yes, your credit score. This score used to be as big a secret as what was in your bureau files. Score watching has become a favorite pastime for many and a profitable business for others.

- ✔ The data in your file must be accurate, verifiable, and not out-of-date. If data is incorrect or too old, you need only ask and it will be verified or removed pronto.

- ✔ Only those who have a legitimate business purpose can see your bureau file, and you can stop everyone from accessing your file if you like. Usually only a creditor, insurer, employer, landlord, or others with whom you do business get to see what's in your file. You can slam the door on everyone with a credit freeze if you like.

- ✔ Active-duty military service personnel and identity theft victims have even more rights.

Fair Debt Collection Practices Act

If you ever needed protection, when a debt collector comes a-calling is it! The Fair Debt Collection Practices Act (FDCPA) limits debt collectors' activities and spells out your rights. Highlights include:

- Prohibiting collectors from abusing you, being unfair, and trying to trick you into paying.

- Applying the law to most personal debts including credit cards, auto loans, medical debts, and debts secured by your home.

- Defining when and where a debt can be collected. For example, between 8 a.m. and 9 p.m., or not at work if you indicate otherwise.

- Requiring a validation notice that specifies how much money you owe and what you should do if the debt isn't yours or is paid already.

- Allowing you to just say no. If you don't want to hear from the collector again, you have the right to write to the collection agency and demand that it doesn't contact you again. This doesn't satisfy a legitimate debt but it ends collector contact. It may, however, begin a legal contact to sue you for the debt.

- Giving you the right to sue for breach of the rules. You have a year to bring action for violations.

Credit Card Accountability, Responsibility, and Disclosure Act

Fed up with tricky terms, excessive penalties, fees, and unfair banking practices, Congress enacted the Credit Card Accountability, Responsibility, and Disclosure Act (CARD Act) to give you a fair playing field in the area of credit cards. Here are your major protections:

- Credit card companies can't raise card interest rates except under specific circumstances, such as at the end of a promotional rate, or when a variable interest rate index to which your card is tied rises, or if you're 60 days late on a payment. Also, double cycle interest billing, which uses your average daily balance for the current and previous billing cycles to charge you more, is no longer allowed.

- If your rate or terms change, you have 45 days notice to plan what to do.

- You can opt out of changes you don't like. This may cause your account to be closed, but you can pay off under your old terms.

- The card companies can't issue cards to people under 21 who have no income. This sounds like a no-brainer, but for years creditors have been giving students credit despite their having no income to repay their charges.

- Creditors must give you at least 21 days after the bill is mailed to get your payment in. The due date can't be before the mail is delivered or on a weekend, holiday, or a day when the creditor is closed for business. If you're late, fees are limited to a maximum of $25.

- ✔ All payment amounts above the minimum payment due must be applied to the balance with the highest interest rate, not the lowest!

- ✔ If you exceed your credit limit, card companies must ask you whether you want to process that transaction and incur an over-limit fee. Saying "no thank you" results in the purchase being denied but also in no over-limit fee. Even if you say yes, the fee can't be more than the amount you exceed the credit limit. So if you exceed your limit by $10, the fee can't be more than $10.

Dodd-Frank Legislation

Reforming Wall Street isn't easy and the Feds know it, so they formed a new agency — the Consumer Financial Protection Bureau, or CFPB — to carry on the fight of protecting you long after the ink is dry on the Dodd-Frank Wall Street Reform and Consumer Protection Act (the legislation that created the CFPB). The CFPB sets rules for payday lenders, credit card issuers, and all the players in between. Here are the major protections this agency delivers.

- ✔ Anyone who issues credit or prepaid cards is required to give you better, more easily understandable terms-and-cost disclosures.

- ✔ If you have to sign it, you should be able to understand it. Paperwork has to be understandable to be allowed.

- ✔ Real estate or personal property appraisals must be fair and consistent.

- ✔ Transaction fees for interchange activity, like on your Visa or MasterCard, must be reasonable.

- ✔ Consumer credit counseling, debt settlement, and debt collectors are more closely regulated to keep you from being victimized.

The Federal Trade Commission

The Federal Trade Commission (FTC) is the alter ego of the Bureau of Consumer Protection (BCP). Although it doesn't deal with individual consumer complaints, it does protect consumers by accumulating and analyzing complaints and then taking industry-wide action to address issues that you bring to it. Some examples of BCP protections are your ability to get a free annual credit report, the National Do Not Call Registry to block unwanted telemarketing calls, and appliance disclosure stickers that show the energy costs of home appliances, to name just a few.

The BCP looks out for unfair, deceptive, or fraudulent practices in the marketplace. It investigates and sues companies and people who violate the law. It also develops rules to protect you and requires businesses to give you better disclosure of costs, your rights, and dispute-resolution options. It also collects complaints about consumer fraud and identity theft and makes them available to law enforcement agencies across the country.

Of the bureau's seven divisions, here are the five that I think you may find useful:

- ✔ **Advertising practices:** Enforces truth-in-advertising laws. If the offer seems too good to be true and it is, complain to the FTC.

- ✔ **Financial practices:** Protects you from deceptive and unfair practices in the financial services industry. This includes protection from predatory or discriminatory lending practices, deceptive or unfair loan servicing and debt collection, and credit counseling and debt settlement companies.

- ✔ **Marketing practices:** Responds to Internet, telecommunications, and direct-mail fraud; spam; fraudulent work-at-home schemes; and violations of the Do Not Call provisions of the Telemarketing Sales Rule.

- ✔ **Privacy and identity protection:** Protects your financial privacy, investigates data breaches, helps consumers whose identities have been stolen, and implements laws and regulations for the credit reporting industry, including the FACT Act.

- ✔ **Enforcement:** Sues to address issues on these practices.

Your complaint, comment, or inquiry may help spot a pattern of law violations requiring law enforcement action, but the FTC doesn't resolve individual consumer disputes.

Statute of Limitations

This protection is worthy of Perry Mason: "I object your honor, for this charge is too old." Well, maybe Perry didn't exactly say that, but he'd be happy to see that each state has a law called a *statute of limitations* (SOL) that sets a limit on how long you can be sued in court by a debt collector, depending on what type of loan you allegedly owe. This is only fair, because after several years, who keeps all those receipts and slips of paper? Either hurry up and sue me or forget about it!

This protection isn't automatic; you have to ask for it. What do you need to know and do? Read on.

- ✔ If your debt is past the SOL, you can't be successfully sued in court to collect it. But you must show up and prove the debt is too old.

- ✔ Credit reports show a delinquency for seven years. This has nothing to do with the time a debt is collectible.

> ✔ The period used to figure how old your debt is starts when you miss a payment and then never make another one. A payment may restart the SOL clock again depending on the state in which you live.

Your State Attorney General

Every state has a state attorney general. They all have at least one thing in common: One of their primary responsibilities is to enforce their state's consumer protection laws. Every state, including yours, has a consumer protection statute prohibiting deceptive acts and practices. These statutes include laws that address specific industries or practices. For example, many FACT Act protections, especially for credit reporting, may have stricter state regulations, giving you more rights and a local resource for help.

The state attorneys general love to go after abuses and illegalities in the marketplace. It's good press for them and good protection for you. These areas include deceptive trade practices, telemarketing and Internet fraud, fake charities, ID theft, and false or misleading advertising.

Generally, these public officials have a low tolerance for financial shenanigans of any type. So if you think you're being abused, taken advantage of, or have been scammed in a credit or personal finance transaction, this is the office to call.

I've had good luck working with the consumer protection sections of several state attorneys general. If you decide to pursue them for help, I suggest that you be organized, to the point, and have whatever pertinent information at hand. Attorneys general are no-nonsense law enforcement officials who appreciate you calling for their help but not wasting their time.

Consumer Credit Counseling

Sometimes, protection comes from helping you reach an agreement with your creditors rather than going through an exhausting collection and legal process. Consumer credit counseling services are nonprofit agencies that act as intermediaries on your behalf with creditors who won't listen to you. They've been helping consumers come to mutually satisfactory debt-repayment arrangements for more than 50 years, and they offer their services for free or for a nominal cost.

You can find a good agency at www.debtadvice.org or www.aiccca.org or by calling 800-388-2227 or 866-703-8787. Look for third-party accreditation and HUD certification. For more information about credit counseling, see Chapter 15.

Your Lawyer

Lawyers often get a bad rap in society, but if you want a very effective weapon in providing protection for a consumer, you need look no further. Whether your issue is a debt collector, a retailer who won't step up to resolve a problem, or a contract with unsuspected gotcha clauses, a knowledgeable and persistent attorney is hard to beat for results. Yes, I know, lawyers are expensive, but there are times when only the best will do. I reason that using a second-rate attorney to resolve a problem is like showing up at a gunfight with the second-fastest gunslinger. Better not to show up at all!

Here are some points to consider when looking for a top-flight consumer attorney.

- ✔ Nothing is better than a referral from a satisfied friend, colleague, or relative. Ask someone in whom you have confidence. You may get a great referral and maybe a solution you haven't thought of.

- ✔ Look for someone who does a lot of what you need. Like picking a heart surgeon, you want lots of experience here.

- ✔ If you already have a lawyer, ask him or her for a specialist recommendation.

- ✔ Check your local American Bar Association affiliate or attorney association. They often maintain lawyer reference services.

- ✔ Look for background information on prospective attorneys. Don't be afraid to contact an attorney because of cost. Many lawyers give you, for little or no charge, a consultation to see whether you need an attorney at all.

- ✔ When you visit an attorney, be organized. Have your problem defined as best you can. Look for someone your gut says you can work with. Ask yourself whether you like this person. Is the lawyer concerned with you and your problem? Always interview more than one attorney. It's your money and your problem, and this situation is important.

- ✔ Don't be completely deterred by hourly rates. A good attorney who charges more can be a bargain if you get resolution quickly and permanently.

- ✔ Get all agreements in writing to avoid miscommunication. Be sure to read the agreement before you sign it and ask about anything that's not clear to you.

Bankruptcy Abuse Prevention and Consumer Protection Act

The Bankruptcy Abuse Prevention and Consumer Protection Act (BAPCPA) aimed to cut back on what were seen by creditors as unwarranted and excessive losses caused by bankruptcy filings. A few of the major provisions in this law include

- ✔ Mandatory credit counseling before filing

- ✔ Stricter eligibility for Chapter 7 filing to encourage Chapter 13

- ✔ Fewer debts discharged and fewer state exemptions

- ✔ Tax returns and proof of income required for means test

- ✔ Mandatory five-year Chapter 13 plan if over your state's median income

- ✔ Mandatory financial management education after filing

- ✔ Time between Chapter 7 filings increased to eight years

Bankruptcy was designed to give you the ultimate protection of the courts from your creditors. The process can be as effective as it is damaging to your credit, and you should use it with great care and only if you've already considered less damaging courses of action.

In some states you can file your own bankruptcy petition (called *pro se*); in others you need an attorney. Regardless, I recommend that you use an attorney who does this for a living. A poorly thought out or executed bankruptcy can leave you with unresolved debts and deprive you of using this tool again for several years. A good bankruptcy attorney will spend a significant amount of time with you to compare bankruptcy with other possible ways of handling financial problems.

A quick checklist to see whether bankruptcy is for you includes these questions:

- ✔ Do you qualify for a Chapter 7 or a Chapter 13 bankruptcy? Chapter 7 can eliminate some debts, and Chapter 13 creates a repayment plan supervised by a court trustee.

- ✔ Are your debts dischargeable? Bankruptcy can discharge many but not always all debts. Debts that can't normally be discharged include taxes, alimony and child support, and student loans.

- ✔ Will bankruptcy really solve your problem going forward? Doing a budget analysis can help you see whether you can keep up with future living expenses after a bankruptcy. Calculate ongoing expenses and income to determine whether bankruptcy will end your problems once and for all.

- ✔ Will your bankruptcy affect others? If someone is a cosigner on your loans or you live in a community property state, you may not be the only one affected when you file for bankruptcy.

Chapter 22

Ten Tips to Achieving Stellar Credit

*T*he stars have been a source of mystery and beauty for as long as men and women have looked into the night sky. Even today, if you want to compliment someone's eyes, you tell her that her eyes sparkle like stars. And if you want to praise a great performance, you call it *stellar*.

The same applies to your credit. Stellar credit is not, however, perfect credit. It is as bright and shiny as you can make it given what you have to work with. So how to make the best out of what you have and keep it bright and sparkling? That's what this chapter is all about.

Paying on Time, Every Time

The most important thing you can do to achieve stellar credit is to pay your bills on time, every time, and to pay at least the minimum required payment. This simple practice is a major factor in credit scoring and a major item that lenders look for when they underwrite you for a loan or consider your application for a purchase, insurance, employment, or a rental or lease.

Performing Periodic Credit Checkups

You know you should get the oil in your car changed every so many miles. You don't wait until your engine seizes up before getting out the dipstick and measuring how much oil you have left in the crankcase. Well, a periodic peek at what others say about you on your credit report is financially just as important!

Review your report from one of the three major credit bureaus every four months for free by using www.annualcreditreport.com. Read the reports carefully to make certain that no inaccurate or outdated information is included and that none of the positive information is missing. Dispute all inaccurate entries and any negative items that are more than seven years old (but see Chapter 7 for some exceptions), and be sure to challenge the credit bureau on items you don't recognize because they can be signs of identity theft.

If you're checking credit reports because you think that someone may be looking at your report soon (for example, a lender or a prospective employer), check all three reports at once. The lender or employer could request any of the reports or a merged copy of all three, so you want to review all of them. You may have to pay for the reports if you've already taken your free annual credit reports and any extra ones that your state allows (see Chapter 8 for more details), but the cost is small, and you should consider it a maintenance expense. You may also be entitled to free, extra copies of your reports; see the next section for more info.

Taking Advantage of Surprise Credit Inspection Opportunities

Besides the free look you get at each of your credit reports annually, a number of situations allow you extra inspections for free. You're entitled to one if

✔ You were denied credit

✔ You're unemployed and seeking work or you're on welfare

✔ You believe you've been the victim of identity fraud or theft

✔ You didn't get the best rate from an insurer or lender

✔ You've had an interest rate increase or a credit line decrease

✔ You place an active duty military alert on your credit file

✔ You live in a state (Colorado, Georgia, Maine, Maryland, Massachusetts, New Jersey, or Vermont) that requires the bureaus to give you more than one free report each year; some require three free requests!

Strengthening Your Credit History Quickly

Trying to build or improve your credit? A loan or a line of credit may be just the ticket. Showing that you can use credit without messing up helps establish your credit and payment history.

Here are four easy opportunities to get some points on your credit scoreboard quickly:

- **Passbook loan:** These loans are a great way to build your credit. The loan is considered and reported as an installment loan because you borrow a specific amount with a defined monthly payment. Pay each month on time and you'll be well on your way to establishing your credit history.

- **Secured credit card:** These cards are issued by banks and credit unions and look just like any other credit card, but they have one big difference: They're backed by money that you have on deposit with the card issuer. The deposit guarantees that the lender gets paid if you forget to make a payment. But you won't forget, right? The account is reported to the credit bureaus as a revolving account.

- **Retail store card:** Retail cards are a great first step to building new credit muscle. Stores issue retail cards for purchases at their specific store. These cards are relatively easy to get and can boost your credit appeal. Use them for purchases you'd make anyway, and pay the balances on time and in full each month. The goal here is to establish accounts that reflect that you pay as agreed — a stellar mark in the credit good-looks department — not to charge up to your limit.

- **Authorized user account:** Adding your name to the account of a loved one or relative with a good credit history can enhance your credit. With an *authorized user account,* your name is added to the account and you're issued a card to use. The account's history is reported on both the account owner's credit report and yours. But choose wisely — the account owner's negative history becomes yours as well.

For more info on strengthening your credit history, flip to Chapter 9.

Reducing Balances on Your Revolving Credit Accounts

One of the fastest ways to improve your existing credit is to decrease your *credit-used-to-credit-available ratio* (or *credit utilization ratio*). Simply put, this means paying down the balances you carry over from the previous month on your revolving credit accounts.

For example, if you have a credit card with a credit limit of $5,000 and your balance is $2,500, your credit-used-to-credit-available ratio is 50 percent — you're using half of the credit you have at your disposal. Lenders think it's stellar if your ratio is lower than 25 percent.

FICO (www.myfico.com) will ding your credit score if your ratio is above 50 percent. So if you want to up your credit pizzazz, start by paying down your balances to below 50 percent of your credit limit and then shoot for a ratio of less than 25 percent to look even more desirable.

Pruning Your Credit to Keep It in Bloom

Like tending your garden, you want to trim unused lines of credit but keep the strong old credit lines you've been nurturing for years. Having credit lines that you don't intend to use can hurt your credit. All that unused credit can easily become unaffordable debt that can jeopardize your next loan payment. The result may be that a lender could be less comfortable giving you credit if you already have access to lots of the stuff. If you haven't used a credit card in a year or you don't intend to use it, consider closing the account.

Accounts older than ten years that have positive histories are the gold standard of good credit. Lenders like to see stability and loyalty, and they spell it *o-l-d*. So keep those accounts, especially if you open a new one. From a scoring standpoint, closing an account won't affect your longevity points because the closed account will continue to show on your credit report and be included in your score. Bureaus typically report closed credit card accounts with only positive information for ten years. Adding a new account, however, does hurt your score. Two of the characteristics of people that FICO calls *high achievers* (those with a score over 760) are that their oldest account is around 19 years old and that the average age of their accounts is between 6 and 12 years.

Avoiding Overapplying for Credit

In your enthusiasm to achieve stellar credit, don't overdo it. Don't apply for every offer that comes your way. First of all, you're only *preapproved;* you can still be turned down. When you ask for credit or a line increase, your score is lowered. If you apply and are turned down, that counts even more against you. Depending on which scoring model is used, getting turned down can count very, very heavily against you!

Getting Help Before You Need It

If you want to get some additional assurance that you're on the right track, you may want to look for free professional help. Here are two confidential sources you can tap into at different phases of your trip to stellar credit:

- ✔ A legitimate nonprofit credit counselor can help you come up with a comprehensive plan to manage your money and meet your goals. Part of that plan includes funding an emergency savings account. (See Chapter 15 for information on how to choose an agency.)

- ✔ When you're consistently paying all your bills on time, building new credit, and saving, an initial visit with a financial planner is the next stop for you. A good planner can give you the hope and incentive you need to balance today's spending and saving with tomorrow's needs. You have to pay a financial planner if you decide to work with one, but the first visit or two should be free.

Pledging Never to Cosign

In my 20 years of helping people with financial issues, I've rarely seen cosigning on a loan to be helpful to either the cosigner or the borrower. So raise your right hand and repeat after me: "I pledge never to cosign for anyone, anytime!"

Here's how cosigning works in theory: A person wants to borrow money for a good reason, but she has bad credit and can't get a loan, so she gets a person with good credit to cosign the loan. The loan is issued, the payments are made, and everyone lives happily ever after.

Here's how cosigning works in reality: A person wants to borrow money, but a professional who gets paid for making loans refuses to make the loan. The borrower has bad credit for a good reason. She gets a person with good credit to cosign the loan. The loan is issued, and the payments aren't made consistently or aren't made at all. Collectors come after the cosigner. The cosigner's credit is ruined. The cosigner pays the entire bill. The defaulting borrower blames the cosigner for not doing more or being more understanding. No one talks to each other ever again.

This theme has a lot of variations, but they almost always end badly.

Guarding against Identity Theft

Now that you're on your way to stellar credit, watch out, because someone may try to steal it all away from you. The last thing you want is for an identity thief to mess up what you've worked so hard to achieve.

To help protect yourself from identity theft, follow these tips:

- **Guard your account numbers.** Be careful with credit card statements, bank statements, and other financial documents. Shred any documents that you don't file away that contain account numbers or personal information.

- **Be wary of phone transactions.** Never supply credit card or Social Security numbers over the phone unless you initiated the call and you know whom you're dealing with.

- **Protect your Social Security number.** Don't keep your card in your wallet or purse.

- **Check credit reports for evidence of identity theft.** Review one of your credit reports every four months at www.annualcreditreport.com.

Check out Chapter 12 for more about protecting your identity.

Chapter 23

Ten Ways to Successfully Manage Financial Emergencies

In This Chapter

▶ Implementing a plan before an emergency strikes

▶ Drawing on resources you may not have considered

▶ Knowing who to turn to for help

*A*ll too many of you are vulnerable to unexpected financial emergencies. Beyond causing sleepless nights, many emergencies spill over into credit and debt trouble. Even people who responsibly pay their bills on time, pay off their entire credit card balance monthly, and always keep up with their mortgage payments can easily find themselves thrown into a financial crisis when life's surprises jump out and shout "Boo!" A serious illness or accident can rack up astronomical medical expenses in no time. A job layoff can eat up that last paycheck and your unemployment benefits before you can say "the rent is due again." And suddenly, you're running to keep ahead of a financial tsunami that threatens to overwhelm your good credit standing.

But a financial emergency isn't different from any other type of emergency. You can prepare for it and plan your response in ways that reduce the shock to your financial system and hasten your recovery. Consider this chapter's ten tips for tackling financial emergencies as your very own emergency-response plan that lessens the impact on your wallet and your credit.

Plan Ahead to Make a Difference

Companies develop disaster plans to ensure that situations such as fire, theft, and natural disasters are handled with the least impact to customers and the companies' bottom lines. But you don't need to be a corporation to plan for a disaster, big or small. As an individual or family, you too can benefit from a plan designed to handle unexpected financial emergencies. After all, you have homeowners insurance to protect you if your home has a catastrophe, and you have car insurance to cover damage and expenses that result from an accident. So in many ways you've already started on your plan without even knowing it.

Why is planning ahead so important? Because after a financial emergency strikes, you're under tremendous stress to fix problems and deal with unpleasant situations quickly. Making decisions before you become stressed makes for better decisions, more options, and, yes, less stress.

Begin your financial emergency planning by starting a savings plan with the goal of accumulating a cushion of six months to a year of living expenses. Review your insurance policies (auto, medical, homeowners, disability, and life) to make sure you have adequate coverage and know what is and isn't covered. And come up with ways to reduce your living expenses if needed to stay within your means. Check out Chapter 4 for more on establishing your spending plan.

Set Up an Emergency Account

You don't need to go to Switzerland or the Cayman Islands to set up an emergency savings account, but I do recommend that you have one and that you keep it separate from your regular checking and savings accounts. You need to have a safe place to keep your emergency cash stash where access is easy but not too easy! Choose a bank, credit union, or brokerage money market fund as the home for your soon-to-be-large emergency fund.

You're less apt to miss the money that's funding your emergency savings if you never see it. Therefore, request direct deposit of a portion of your check from your employer to your new account. Doing so may have an additional benefit because direct deposits may eliminate some bank fees. Don't get an ATM card, debit card, or checks to go with the account at first. You want to accumulate this money, not use it unnecessarily. If direct deposit isn't available to you, be sure to put the money in the account as soon as you're paid.

Pay Yourself First

The first rule of saving is to pay yourself first. In other words, don't wait until the end of the month to put aside savings because, more often than not, you may not have any money left. Instead, sock the money away as soon as you get paid. I strongly recommend that you make saving as automatic and easy as possible (see the preceding section). In addition, when you receive pay raises, bonuses, or tax refunds, have half the money direct-deposited if you can and keep half for yourself.

Imagine how you'll feel knowing that you're well on your way to meeting your goal of painlessly building a stockpile of six months to a year of living expenses in your emergency fund. You'll feel more prepared, more confident, and less stressed than most people. Your emergency fund won't build up overnight, but your regular efforts add up over time.

Spend Less and Earn More

Living within your means requires that you find a balance between your expenses and your income. Begin by calculating what you spend and what you earn. (Chapter 4 has more information on how to best do this.) Now figure out how to spend less, earn more, or do a little of both.

After you put together a spending plan (see Chapter 4), you immediately see areas you can trim. Cutting down on or cutting out tobacco and alcohol, eating out less, and not buying those lottery tickets are just a few of those areas.

Next, look for ways to increase your income. *Income* is what's left of your paycheck after nondiscretionary deductions for things like taxes, child support, and insurance. You can increase your income in two simple ways: Reduce your payroll deductions or make more money.

Start by scrutinizing your deductions carefully. Are you over-withholding for income taxes? Many people look at the IRS as a sort of savings account. They may purposefully claim fewer deductions than necessary in order to get that big tax return check each tax season. But if you get more than $600 a year back in refunds, consider squeezing this category a bit. You're better off having that money available (and earning interest on it) should you need it for an emergency than letting the IRS hold onto it (without paying you any interest).

Here are some ways you can earn more money to fund that emergency account:

- ✔ **Get a second job.** No, not another full-time job, and not another career, but a job with enough hours to kick-start that emergency fund. Look for one that's outside your normal occupation, maybe in line with an outside interest, which can serve the dual purpose of earning you extra cash and providing some interesting experiences. Sometimes a few extra hours on a Saturday is all it takes.

- ✔ **Work overtime.** Overtime hours can be a great way to increase your immediate earnings. I don't recommend building a budget that depends on overtime, but extra hours can help cover emergency expenses or fund savings.

- ✔ **Ask for a raise.** If it's been a year or more since your last raise, or if your job has changed significantly but your income hasn't, it never hurts to ask. You may be able to increase your chances of getting that raise by getting additional certifications or education.

Sell Some Assets

A financial emergency has a way of causing you to rethink the importance of some of your possessions. If you're struggling with a medical condition, you may not have time to enjoy your sailboat on the weekends. If you're out of a job, the extra monthly payments for your second SUV, your motorcycle, and your snowmobile become a burden.

Consider selling any big-ticket, unused (or underused) possessions. You can put the much-needed cash from such a sale toward your emergency expenses, and if you're still carrying a loan on the item, you eliminate that monthly payment as well as any insurance expense associated with it. Whether you sell your grand piano on eBay or hold a garage sale, you just may be able to offset some or all of your emergency costs by turning your nonessential possessions and clutter into ready cash.

Note that selling an item for which you're *upside down* on the loan (you owe more than what you can sell the item for) doesn't work for creating extra cash for emergencies.

Borrow against Your Home

If you've owned your house long enough, you may have built up adequate equity to tap. If you can afford an additional monthly payment, a home-equity line of credit may be just the ticket to help get you through a financial emergency. With a home-equity line of credit, you have access to the money if and when you need it but not before, so you incur interest payments only if you draw on the line of credit, and they may be tax-deductible.

Tread carefully and don't over-borrow against your home. I recommend that your mortgage not exceed 75 percent of your home's current value. Consider the line of credit as an investment in yourself — not investing for a vacation, but to get you through a rough financial spot before you sail into calmer waters.

Over-borrowing can lead to being *upside down* on a home loan — where you owe more than the house is worth — and this is not a place you want to be. If you need to sell the house to downsize or to move to take advantage of a job opportunity, you have to come up with the difference between the sale price and the balance on your loan.

If you're 62 or older and intend to stay in your home for the foreseeable future, you may want to research a *reverse mortgage* line of credit or income stream to help you deal with emergency funding needs. A reverse mortgage allows a homeowner to take out a nonrecourse loan against the value of the home with no repayment due until the house is sold or the borrower dies.

Rely on Friends and Relatives

A friend or a relative who has been more fortunate than you may be in a position to offer just the help you need to get through hard times. Some are more than willing to assist with a financial boost if asked. Before you do the asking, consider the importance of the relationship and whether you can really make good on your pledge to repay.

If you have a supportive clan who can afford to help you overcome a financial hardship, you're fortunate, indeed. But I don't have to tell you that if money issues can destroy a marriage, they can also ruin a friendship and create family feuds. So by all means turn to friends and relatives for help, but do so with a careful and considerate approach. Neither bended knee nor flattery is what's called for; responsibility and commitment are.

Here are some tips for borrowing from friends or family:

- ✔ **Make sure you put the terms of the loan in writing.** Get promissory notes in business supply stores or download them from suppliers like Nolo (www.nolo.com) for a fee. Or you can just type up a statement that lists the loan amount, the interest rate, the payment due dates, and any other details you work out. Make sure both parties get signed copies.

- ✔ **Pay interest just as you would with a traditional loan.** This can keep your friends or family from feeling as though they're being taken advantage of and help you keep things businesslike. A designated interest rate also keeps you out of trouble with the IRS for loans of more than $10,000. The IRS issues monthly minimum interest rates that must be charged on loans exceeding $10,000, called AFR *(applicable federal rate)*.

- ✔ **If you can't make a scheduled payment, communicate with the person immediately.** Offer whatever contingency plan you can, such as making a partial payment or scheduling a revised payment date.

Failure to pay back the loan may damage your relationship with the person loaning you the money. Do everything you can to set realistic terms and live up to them.

Defer Retirement Contributions

If you regularly contribute to a retirement savings plan — a 401(k), 403(b), or IRA, for example — you may want to consider suspending or reducing these contributions temporarily and funneling the money toward your emergency expenses.

Note: I advise this only as a short-term strategy. After all, the money in your retirement plan is tax-deferred (except in the case of Roth IRAs), and it grows while you sleep.

Additionally, you may receive an employer match when you contribute. If you don't make your regular contribution, you miss out on these benefits. You can, however, make a commitment to make up the contributions you missed at a later date, and I encourage you to do so.

Deferring your retirement contributions is definitely a better strategy than borrowing from your retirement account, which I don't recommend. But borrowing from your retirement account is an option if your situation demands it. If you do take money out of your account, you may incur penalties and taxes that can eat away 50 percent of the account's value. Plus, your qualified retirement plan assets may be protected from creditors and even bankruptcy. Use this resource only in the direst situations.

Call in the Experts

Some financial emergencies are extremely upsetting, and you may find that you need some professional help to think clearly and come up with a solution that fits your situation without over- or under-reacting. Visiting with a credit counselor to determine how best to meet your regular monthly obligations while at the same time funding your emergency expense may be a good option. Check out Chapter 15 for help on finding a qualified professional who can help you get back on track for free after a financial emergency derailment. If you have an existing relationship with a financial planner, you may want to consider getting advice from that person. Don't forget that you may have to pay the financial planner depending on what you choose to do, so be sure to take that into account.

Use Credit to Protect Your Cash

I know this may sound like heresy, but if you're facing a temporary financial emergency, especially from unemployment — a time when maintaining a positive credit report is very important — consider protecting your credit by using it, but only for essentials per your plan. Be sure to make your minimum payments on time and don't splurge until you're past the emergency. You may pay more in interest charges following this plan, but it makes your savings last longer and keeps your credit looking its best.

Try to spread balances over multiple cards or lines of credit to keep your borrowing as low a percentage of your maximum credit limits as possible to avoid damage to your credit score. After your emergency is over, make sure you pay down the balances on your credit cards and start saving again. Getting rid of the excess debt and building up a new savings cushion gets you in shape for the next financial emergency you have to face, which often arrives sooner than you expect.

Appendix

About the CD

*N*o book today is complete without references to the Internet and other media. This book is no exception. I include not only references to online materials but also a CD chock-full of useful links, forms, and examples. This appendix walks you through the CD that accompanies this book and also gives you the system and other technical specs you may need to get the most out of the information I've prepared for you.

System Requirements

Make sure that your computer meets the minimum system requirements shown in the following list. If your computer doesn't match up to most of these requirements, you may have problems using the software and files on the CD. For the latest and greatest information, please refer to the ReadMe file located at the root of the CD-ROM.

✔ A PC running Microsoft Windows or Linux with kernel 2.4 or later

✔ A Macintosh running Apple OS X or later

✔ A CD-ROM drive

If you need more information on the basics, check out these books published by John Wiley & Sons, Inc.: *PCs For Dummies*, 11th Edition, by Dan Gookin; *Macs For Dummies*, 11th Edition, by Edward C. Baig; *iMacs For Dummies*, 6th Edition, by Mark L. Chambers; and *Windows XP For Dummies, Windows Vista For Dummies*, and *Windows 7 For Dummies*, all by Andy Rathbone.

Using the CD

To install the items from the CD to your hard drive, follow these steps.

1. **Insert the CD into your computer's CD-ROM drive.**

   The license agreement appears.

   Note to Windows users: The interface won't launch if you have autorun disabled. In that case, choose Start⇨Run. (For Windows Vista, choose Start⇨All Programs⇨Accessories⇨Run.) In the dialog box that appears, type ***D:\Start.exe.*** (Replace *D* with the proper letter if your CD drive uses a different letter. If you don't know the letter, see how your CD drive is listed under My Computer.) Click OK.

   Note for Mac users: When the CD icon appears on your desktop, double-click the icon to open the CD and double-click the Start icon. Also, note that the content menus may not function as expected in newer versions of Safari and Firefox; however, the documents are available by navigating to the Contents folder.

2. **Read through the license agreement and then click the Accept button if you want to use the CD.**

   The CD interface appears. The interface allows you to browse the contents and install the programs with just a click of a button (or two).

What You'll Find on the CD

The following sections are arranged by category and provide a summary of the software and other goodies you'll find on the CD. If you need help installing the items on the CD, refer to the installation instructions in the preceding section.

For each program listed, I provide the program platform (Windows or Mac), plus the type of software. The programs fall into one of the following categories:

- ✔ *Shareware programs* are fully functional, free, trial versions of copyrighted programs. If you like particular programs, register with their authors for a nominal fee and receive licenses, enhanced versions, and technical support.

- ✔ *Freeware programs* are free, copyrighted games, applications, and utilities. You can copy them to as many computers as you like — for free — but they offer no technical support.

- ✔ *GNU software* is governed by its own license, which is included inside the folder of the GNU software. There are no restrictions on distribution of GNU software. See the GNU license at the root of the CD for more details.

✔ *Trial, demo,* or *evaluation* versions of software are usually limited either by time or functionality (such as not letting you save a project after you create it).

In addition, the CD includes a handy glossary of commonly used terms that are helpful in your daily use of credit. Even though I define these terms in the text where they first appear, this is a place where you can look up a term that has you stumped or to sharpen your credit knowledge skills.

Software

The files on the CD are in Adobe PDF, Microsoft Word, and Microsoft Excel formats. In case you don't have Adobe Reader, Microsoft Word, or Microsoft Excel on your computer, I include the following on the CD so that you can read all the files:

✔ **Adobe Reader:** Adobe Reader is a freeware application for viewing files in the Adobe Portable Document Format.

✔ **OpenOffice.org:** OpenOffice.org is a free multiplatform office productivity suite, similar to Microsoft Office. It includes word processing, spreadsheet, presentation, and drawing applications. It supports most file formats of other office software, allowing you to view and edit files created with other office programs.

Acts and legislation

If you're like me — a little strange — you may want to see the underlying legislation that spells out all the facts that apply to credit reports and debt collection. For all you kindred spirits, I include my favorite laws on the CD. If you're like my wife — normal, or so she says — you'll go on to the next section.

✔ **Credit Card Accountability, Responsibility, and Disclosure (CARD) Act.pdf:** This 2009 act was designed to prevent unfair increases in interest rates and changes in terms. Under the law, card issuers can't arbitrarily increase interest rates on existing balances or use universal default policies considered unfair or deceptive. What a lender can and can't do to you is specified in this important piece of consumer legislation. Of course, lower fees and interest rates may make cards more difficult for marginal borrowers to obtain, which is all the more reason for you to make your credit the best it can be!

- ✔ **Dodd-Frank Wall Street Reform and Consumer Protection Act.pdf:** This act is a sweeping piece of financial reform legislation with a big consumer credit impact. Among its main provisions are new consumer protections for mortgages, credit cards, and financial products. It also created the Consumer Financial Protection Bureau, which is charged with protecting you from abuse. It also allows unprecedented free access to credit scores in the case of an adverse action or risked-based pricing by a lender or insurer.

- ✔ **Fair and Accurate Credit Transactions (FACT) Act.pdf:** This is the famous FACT Act. It's an update to the Fair Credit Reporting Act, designed to give you tools to help prevent identity theft, improve the credit-report dispute process, improve the accuracy of your credit data, and give you better access to your credit information and your free annual credit reports.

- ✔ **Fair Debt Collection Practices Act.pdf:** The FDCPA is the rule book that collectors have to follow when contacting a person about a bill. What, when, and how collectors can do what they do is spelled out here. Your rights and what's fair and not fair in terms of collection practices are all topics that this act includes.

- ✔ **Mortgage Forgiveness Debt Relief Act of 2007.pdf:** If you owe a debt and it's forgiven, the lender issues you a Form 1099, and the forgiven debt is considered taxable income. This law excludes up to $2 million of Form 1099 income from taxes if the income comes from a discharge of mortgage indebtedness subject to certain criteria.

- ✔ **Servicemembers Civil Relief Act.pdf:** The SCRA is an update of the Soldiers' and Sailors' Civil Relief Act. It covers the special rights that servicepersons have that allow them to concentrate on defending the United States rather than defending *themselves* from creditors.

- ✔ **Summary of State Foreclosure Laws.pdf:** This handy reference chart gives you the state-by-state highlights of foreclosure laws including which states require court action to foreclose, which are recourse and non-recourse, and how long a foreclosure may take.

Bankruptcy info

The means test that determines what chapter of personal bankruptcy you may qualify for can be very confusing. The handy **Bankruptcy Code Filing Procedures Chart.pdf** is a graphic representation of the process used to determine which bankruptcy chapter an individual qualifies for under the Bankruptcy Abuse Prevention and Consumer Protection Act of 2005.

Credit-report letters

The CD contains samples of letters to get you started communicating effectively with credit bureaus and creditors. Everyone makes mistakes, including the credit bureaus and creditors. You're just helping them improve the quality of their records if you spot an error in your report.

- **Add 100-Word Statement to Report.doc:** This letter provides the format for adding a 100-word statement to your credit report explaining a negative item. This won't be picked up if your lender uses automated underwriting. The bureaus will assist you in writing a concise statement if you go over 100 words or (in the case of TransUnion only) if you ask them to.

- **Annual Credit Report Request Form.pdf:** When requesting your free annual credit report, using the official form to do so is important. Use the Request Credit File.doc letter (see the next bullet) as a cover letter.

- **Request Credit File.doc:** This is a generic letter that you can use to request a free credit report for various reasons. If you're requesting a free annual credit report, attach the Annual Credit Report Request Form. pdf (see the preceding bullet).

- **Request for Creditor to Remove Error.doc:** This letter is helpful if your original request to a credit bureau didn't remove a disputed item from your credit report. Asking the creditor directly may get you the attention you need.

- **Request to Remove Error.doc:** This provides the basics you need to dispute an erroneous or out-of-date item on your credit report.

Credit reports and credit scores

If you've never ordered a copy of your credit report or credit score, this section shows you what to expect. I include sample credit reports from Equifax, Experian, and TransUnion on the CD, as well as a sample credit score from Fair Isaac to help demystify the process.

- **ChexSystems Sample Report.pdf:** This PDF is a sample report that helps you manage and maintain your checking accounts.

- **Equifax Sample Credit Report.pdf:** This is a PDF of what you should expect to see if you order a credit report from Equifax.

- **Experian Rent Bureau Information.pdf:** This is a sample of the rental data that Experian now has available for its credit report users.

- **Experian Sample Credit Report.pdf:** This is a PDF of what you should expect to see if you order a credit report from Experian.

- **FICO Sample Credit Report.png:** This sample of a credit report order from www.myfico.com shows you the reporting format used and what you should expect to see if you order a report with a credit score from the site.

- **FICO Sample Score Report.png:** This is a copy of what you get if you order your FICO score from FICO, showing your relative score position and ways to improve it.

> ✔ **TransUnion Sample Credit Report.pdf:** This is a PDF of what you should expect to see if you order a credit report from TransUnion. This example shows all the code meanings.

Creditor letters

Communicating with your creditors can be a daunting task for many. This section has drafts of letters that can help you be precise, professional, and effective. In other words, they can help you get your way, with a minimum of fuss and worry.

Current accounts

As a valued customer, your satisfaction is a primary concern of your creditors. These letters help them help you.

> ✔ **Billing Error.doc:** This short and professional letter is aimed at getting billing discrepancies resolved quickly.
>
> ✔ **Change Due Date.doc:** Changing your due date with some creditors allows you to spread your payments out to better match your paydays. Here's a letter to do just that.
>
> ✔ **Credit Bureaus Sample Opt-Out Letter.doc:** This is a handy example of a letter you can modify and send to the three credit bureaus to get your name off their marketing lists.
>
> ✔ **Partial Payment Hardship Letter Current.doc:** This letter shows you how to communicate with your creditor if you can't make a full payment because of circumstances beyond your control.
>
> ✔ **Request to Lower Interest for Military Service Members.doc:** Service personnel on active duty can use the wording of this letter to reduce finance charges to the 6 percent legal limit allowed under the Servicemembers Civil Relief Act.
>
> ✔ **Unemployment Letter.doc:** When you can't make any payment to your creditors, telling them in advance is better than letting them guess why you didn't send in your payment. This letter helps set a professional and concerned tone for future communications with your creditors.

Delinquent accounts

This list of letters contains suggested wordings that you should feel free to modify to fit your situation and tone. Using a professional tone is always best, regardless of your level of frustration or emotion. A letter won't resolve the situation — only a payment will — but documenting your efforts at trying to work out a solution is very important if matters should escalate to a court action. If you copy (cc:) a lawyer, be sure the collector knows about it. If you ask your lawyer to send a letter, expect the collector's attorney to respond to your lawyer. And always be sure to send correspondence via certified mail with a return receipt requested to document your efforts.

✔ **Confirmation Letter to Creditors.doc:** Use this form to confirm a telephone conversation with a creditor regarding an agreement on an account.

✔ **Intend to File Bankruptcy.doc:** This is a short-and-sweet notice to your creditors that will stop any collection calls. Sending a letter stating your intention is usually easier and cleaner than trying to do so over the phone.

✔ **Offer to Return Secured Items.doc:** This letter puts you on record as trying to do the right thing in a difficult situation. Some items, like jewelry or hard goods, may be easier for the creditor to take back.

✔ **Partial Payment Delinquent.doc:** Contacting your creditors before you send in a short payment is a good idea. This letter asks that creditors contact you in writing rather than by phone. They may call you at home if they have a current number, but they shouldn't call you at work after they receive this letter.

✔ **Request a Settlement.doc:** Making an offer to settle an account for less than is owed is never the first choice of a creditor. Expect a push back from the creditor unless you haven't made a payment in a long time. Also be prepared to answer the question of how you can come up with a lump-sum payment but not an installment. (Perhaps a family member is willing to help out or you have a small windfall.)

✔ **Request No Future Contact.doc:** This letter stops the phone calls but not the collection activity. Expect that the creditor will continue to want its money and will probably refer the matter to its lawyers.

✔ **Request No Future Contact from Collection Agency.doc:** If you decide to renegotiate your debts with the original creditor, use this letter to instruct the collection agency to cease all contact.

✔ **Request to Stop Harassment.doc:** If you're being harassed, going on record with as much detail as possible is important. The FTC won't investigate, but your letter may help identify a trend with some collection companies, which may move them to action. If you include your lawyer's name, be sure to run the letter by your lawyer first.

✔ **Request to Stop Work Calls.doc:** This letter stops calls at work, but telling creditors where and when they *can* contact you is important. They have the right to contact you, but only when doing so is convenient. If you don't let them know when it's convenient for them to contact *you,* they'll do it when it's convenient for *them.*

Forms and worksheets

This section contains some handy tools to help you keep track of your communications with creditors and your money at home.

✔ **Conversation Log.doc:** Good records are essential in getting a dispute or other request resolved. This form helps you keep track of who you speak with or receive communication from and what you agree to.

- ✔ **Cutting Expenses.doc:** This worksheet helps you track your efforts to cut expenses. Having a goal on paper is much more powerful than having a goal in your mind because you can measure the progress you're making.

- ✔ **Debt Repayment Tracking Worksheet.xls:** This handy worksheet helps you track your progress as you pay down debt.

- ✔ **Future Plans and Goals.xls:** This worksheet gives you the elements you want to include as you set goals and track your progress. Be sure to go back and make changes as necessary to keep your goals realistic and achievable.

- ✔ **Household Budget Plan.doc:** This worksheet is a great way to start thinking about how much money comes in and goes out of your household and where it ends up. You can make adjustments and see the results.

- ✔ **IRS Form 982 Avoid Debt-Relief Taxes.pdf:** The IRS may view the amount of debt that's "forgiven" by your lender as income for that tax year. If you owe $300,000 on your home and you and your lender accept an offer for $250,000 (a short sale), the IRS views the $50,000 difference as regular earnings in that tax year. So you'd owe taxes on the $50,000. This is a simplistic example, and most cases are more complex. However, the main point is that you need to be aware of the potential tax liability involved in a short sale.

- ✔ **IRS Form 9465 Installment Agreement Request.pdf:** This is the form you fill out to request an installment agreement with the IRS. You can request a payment plan of five years or more. Plus, if you owe more than $10,000, you can't be turned down for installment payments as long as you meet the simple criteria listed on the form. Instead of filling out Form 9465, if you owe $25,000 or less in combined tax, penalties, and interest, you can apply online for a payment agreement at www.irs.gov.

- ✔ **Money Gobblers.doc:** In the normal course of your day, you probably spend money almost as naturally as you breathe. Recognizing which money gobblers you really want to keep versus those you don't need is an important part of controlling your spending. The objective is to use this form to track where your cash goes so you can spend money on those things that you really want, not just on whatever comes along.

- ✔ **Monthly Expense Worksheet.doc:** The essential ingredient in controlling your expenses is knowing where your money is going and deciding whether you want that pattern to continue. This form, which you can customize to your needs, gives you a good starting point for identifying monthly expenses and beginning a livable budget.

- ✔ **Monthly Income Worksheet.doc:** The second essential ingredient in a good budget (see the preceding bullet for the first) is knowing exactly how much you have to spend. Be sure to look at deductions from your paycheck to see whether you can reduce them to increase your take-home pay. Use this customizable form to track your income.

- ✔ **Out-of-Pocket Expense Tracking Worksheet.doc:** Use this handy form to record your cash expenses so you can get a better handle on why your money is disappearing.

✔ **Outstanding Debts.doc:** Fewer people than you'd expect actually know how much they owe. This form helps you get a handle on the size of your debts and gives you a reality check on which to base your solutions.

Identity theft documents

Identity theft is on everybody's radar these days. This section provides tools to use to keep the damage to a minimum if you think you've been a victim of identity theft.

✔ **Fraud Alert Letter to Credit-Reporting Agency.doc:** Quick and concise notification of possible identity theft is essential to limiting damage to your credit and those creditors who may be victimized as well. This letter has all the essential ingredients you need to stop identity theft from going any further and to begin to recover from it.

✔ **Chart Your Course of Action.pdf:** This sample format gets you started on the path to organization while tracking all your contacts with credit bureaus, creditors, and law-enforcement agencies.

✔ **Identity Theft Letter to Institutions Directly Involved.doc:** Your identity has been stolen and so have your creditor's products or services. Quickly letting creditors know about a theft not only helps your credit report but also limits both your and the creditor's losses.

✔ **Identity Theft Letter to Institutions Not Directly Involved.doc:** Use this letter when you suspect your identity has been compromised but before you *know* someone is using it illegally. Placing passwords and safeguards on your account can help keep your credit and your identity safe from a thief who has your personal information.

✔ **Letter of Complaint of Identity Theft to the FTC.doc:** Use this letter of complaint to inform the FTC about a credit bureau's failure to remove fraudulent accounts opened in your name because of identity theft. Be sure to send the credit bureau a copy of your FTC complaint letter so the bureau knows that you're complaining. This may spur a second look at your file.

Troubleshooting

I tried my best to compile programs that work on most computers with the minimum system requirements. Alas, your computer may differ, and some programs may not work properly for some reason.

The two likeliest problems are that you don't have enough memory (RAM) for the programs you want to use or that you have other programs running that are affecting the installation or running of a program. If you get an error message such as `Not enough memory` or `Setup cannot continue`, try one or more of the following suggestions and then try using the software again:

- ✓ **Turn off any antivirus software running on your computer.** Installation programs sometimes mimic virus activity and may make your computer incorrectly believe that it's being infected by a virus.

- ✓ **Close all running programs.** The more programs you have running, the less memory is available to other programs. Installation programs typically update files and programs, so if you keep other programs running, installation may not work properly.

- ✓ **Have your local computer store add more RAM to your computer.** This is, admittedly, a drastic and somewhat expensive step. However, adding more memory can really help the speed of your computer and allow more programs to run at the same time.

Customer Care

If you have trouble with the CD-ROM, please call Wiley Product Technical Support at 800-762-2974. Outside the United States, call 317-572-3993. You can also contact Wiley Product Technical Support at `http://support.wiley.com`. John Wiley & Sons, Inc., provides technical support only for installation and other general quality control items. For technical support on the applications themselves, consult the program's vendor or author.

To place additional orders or to request information about other Wiley products, please call 877-762-2974.

Index

SOFTWARE LICENSE AGREEMENT

Important: Read carefully before opening software package.

This is a legal agreement between you, the end user, and John Wiley & Sons, Inc. ("Wiley"). The enclosed

Wiley software program and accompanying data (the "Software") is licensed by Wiley for use only on the terms set forth herein. Please read this license agreement. Registering the product indicates that you accept these terms. If you do not agree to these terms, return the full product (including documentation) with proof of purchase within 30 days for a full refund. In addition, if you are not satisfied with this product for any other reason, you may return the entire product (including documentation) with proof of purchase within 15 days for a full refund.

1. **License:** Wiley hereby grants you, and you accept, a non-exclusive and non-transferable license, to use the Software on the following terms and conditions only:

   (a) The Software is for your personal use only.

   (b) You may use the Software on a single terminal connected to a single computer (that is, single CPU) and a laptop or other secondary machine for personal use.

   (c) A backup copy or copies of the Software may be made solely for your personal use. Except for such back up copy or copies, you may not copy, modify, distribute, transmit, or otherwise reproduce the Software or related documentation, in whole or in part, or systematically store such material in any form or media in a retrieval system; or store such material in electronic format in electronic reading rooms; or transmit such material, directly or indirectly, for use in any service such as document delivery or list serve, or for use by any information brokerage or for systematic distribution of material, whether for a fee or free of charge. You agree to protect the Software and documentation from unauthorized use, reproduction, or distribution.

   (d) You agree not to remove or modify any copyright or proprietary notices, author attribution, or disclaimer contained in the Software or documentation or on any screen display, and not to integrate material from there with other material or otherwise create derivative works in any medium based on or including materials from the Software or documentation.

   (e) You agree not to translate, decompile, disassemble or otherwise reverse engineer the Software.

2. **Limited Warranty:**

   (a) Wiley warrants that this product is free of defects in materials and workmanship under normal use for a period of 60 days from the date of purchase as evidenced by a copy of your receipt. If during the 60-day period a defect occurs, you may return the product. Your sole and exclusive remedy in the event of a defect is expressly limited to the replacement of the defective product at no additional charge.

   (b) The limited warranty set forth above is in lieu of any and all other warranties, both express and implied, including but not limited to the implied warranties of merchantability or fitness for a particular purpose. The liability of Wiley pursuant to this limited warranty will be limited to replacement of the defective copies of the Software. Some states do not allow the exclusion of implied warranties, so the preceding exclusion may not apply to you.

(c) Because software is inherently complex and may not be completely free of errors, you are advised to verify your work and to make backup copies. In no event will Wiley, nor anyone else involved in creating, producing, or delivering the Software, documentation, or the materials contained therein, be liable to you for any direct, indirect, incidental, special, consequential, or punitive damages arising out of the use or inability to use the Software, documentation, or materials contained therein even if advised of the possibility of such damages, or for any claim by any other party. In no case will Wiley's liability exceed the amount paid by you for the Software. Some states do not allow the exclusion or limitation of liability for incidental or consequential damages, so the above limitation or exclusion may not apply to you.

(d) Wiley reserves the right to make changes, additions, and improvements to the Software at any time without notice to any person or organization. No guarantee is made that future versions of the Software will be compatible with any other version.

3. **Term:** Your license to use the Software and documentation will automatically terminate if you fail to comply with the terms of this Agreement. If this license is terminated you agree to destroy all copies of the Software and documentation.

4. **Ownership:** You acknowledge that all rights (including without limitation, copyrights, patents, and trade secrets) in the Software and documentation (including without limitation, the structure, sequence, organization, flow, logic, source code, object code, and all means and forms of operation of the Software) are the sole and exclusive property of Wiley and/or its licensors, and are protected by the United Sates copyright laws, other applicable copyright laws, and international treaty provisions.

5. **Restricted Rights:** This Software and/or user documentation are provided with restricted and limited rights. Use, duplication, or disclosure by the Government is subject to restrictions as set forth in paragraph (b)(3)(B) of the Rights in Technical Data and Computer Software clause in DAR 7-104.9(a), FAR 52.2227-14 (June 1987) Alternate III(g)(3)(June 1987), FAR 52.227-19 (June 1987), or DFARS 52.227-701 (c)(1)(ii)(June 1988), or their successors, as applicable. Contractor/manufacturer is John Wiley & Sons, Inc., 111 River Street, Hoboken, NJ 07030.

6. **Canadian Purchase:** If you purchased this product in Canada, you agree to the following: the parties hereto confirm that it is their wish that this Agreement, as well as all other documents relating hereto, including Notices, have been and will be drawn up in the English language only.

7. **Technical Support:** Wiley will respond to all technical support inquiries within 48 hours.

8. **General:** This Agreement represents the entire agreement between us and supersedes any proposals or prior Agreements, oral or written, and any other communication between us relating to the subject matter of this Agreement. This Agreement will be construed and interpreted pursuant to the laws of the State of New York, without regard to such State's conflict of law rules. Any legal action, suit, or proceeding arising out of or relating to this Agreement or the breach thereof will be instituted in a court of competent jurisdiction in New York County in the State of New York and each party hereby consents and submits to the personal jurisdiction of such court, waives any objection to venue in such court, and consents to the service of process by registered or certified mail, return receipt requested, at the last known address of such party. Should you have any questions concerning this Agreement or if you desire to contact Wiley for any reason, please write to: John Wiley & Sons, Inc., Customer Sales and Service, 111 River Street, Hoboken, NJ 07030.

Apple & Macs

iPad For Dummies
978-0-470-58027-1

iPhone For Dummies,
4th Edition
978-0-470-87870-5

MacBook For Dummies, 3rd
Edition
978-0-470-76918-8

Mac OS X Snow Leopard For
Dummies
978-0-470-43543-4

Business

Bookkeeping For Dummies
978-0-7645-9848-7

Job Interviews
For Dummies,
3rd Edition
978-0-470-17748-8

Resumes For Dummies,
5th Edition
978-0-470-08037-5

Starting an
Online Business
For Dummies,
6th Edition
978-0-470-60210-2

Stock Investing
For Dummies,
3rd Edition
978-0-470-40114-9

Successful
Time Management
For Dummies
978-0-470-29034-7

Computer Hardware

BlackBerry
For Dummies,
4th Edition
978-0-470-60700-8

Computers For Seniors
For Dummies,
2nd Edition
978-0-470-53483-0

PCs For Dummies,
Windows
7 Edition
978-0-470-46542-4

Laptops For Dummies,
4th Edition
978-0-470-57829-2

Cooking & Entertaining

Cooking Basics
For Dummies,
3rd Edition
978-0-7645-7206-7

Wine For Dummies,
4th Edition
978-0-470-04579-4

Diet & Nutrition

Dieting For Dummies,
2nd Edition
978-0-7645-4149-0

Nutrition For Dummies,
4th Edition
978-0-471-79868-2

Weight Training
For Dummies,
3rd Edition
978-0-471-76845-6

Digital Photography

Digital SLR Cameras &
Photography For Dummies,
3rd Edition
978-0-470-46606-3

Photoshop Elements 8
For Dummies
978-0-470-52967-6

Gardening

Gardening Basics
For Dummies
978-0-470-03749-2

Organic Gardening
For Dummies,
2nd Edition
978-0-470-43067-5

Green/Sustainable

Raising Chickens
For Dummies
978-0-470-46544-8

Green Cleaning
For Dummies
978-0-470-39106-8

Health

Diabetes For Dummies,
3rd Edition
978-0-470-27086-8

Food Allergies
For Dummies
978-0-470-09584-3

Living Gluten-Free
For Dummies,
2nd Edition
978-0-470-58589-4

Hobbies/General

Chess For Dummies,
2nd Edition
978-0-7645-8404-6

Drawing
Cartoons & Comics
For Dummies
978-0-470-42683-8

Knitting For Dummies,
2nd Edition
978-0-470-28747-7

Organizing
For Dummies
978-0-7645-5300-4

Su Doku For Dummies
978-0-470-01892-7

Home Improvement

Home Maintenance
For Dummies,
2nd Edition
978-0-470-43063-7

Home Theater
For Dummies,
3rd Edition
978-0-470-41189-6

Living the
Country Lifestyle
All-in-One
For Dummies
978-0-470-43061-3

Solar Power Your Home
For Dummies,
2nd Edition
978-0-470-59678-4

Internet

Blogging For Dummies,
3rd Edition
978-0-470-61996-4

eBay For Dummies,
6th Edition
978-0-470-49741-8

Facebook For Dummies,
3rd Edition
978-0-470-87804-0

Web Marketing
For Dummies,
2nd Edition
978-0-470-37181-7

WordPress
For Dummies,
3rd Edition
978-0-470-59274-8

Language & Foreign Language

French For Dummies
978-0-7645-5193-2

Italian Phrases
For Dummies
978-0-7645-7203-6

Spanish For Dummies,
2nd Edition
978-0-470-87855-2

Spanish
For Dummies,
Audio Set
978-0-470-09585-0

Math & Science

Algebra I
For Dummies,
2nd Edition
978-0-470-55964-2

Biology For Dummies,
2nd Edition
978-0-470-59875-7

Calculus For Dummies
978-0-7645-2498-1

Chemistry For Dummies
978-0-7645-5430-8

Microsoft Office

Excel 2010 For Dummies
978-0-470-48953-6

Office 2010 All-in-One
For Dummies
978-0-470-49748-7

Office 2010 For Dummies,
Book + DVD Bundle
978-0-470-62698-6

Word 2010 For Dummies
978-0-470-48772-3

Music

Guitar For Dummies,
2nd Edition
978-0-7645-9904-0

iPod & iTunes For
Dummies, 8th Edition
978-0-470-87871-2

Piano Exercises
For Dummies
978-0-470-38765-8

Parenting & Education

Parenting For Dummies,
2nd Edition
978-0-7645-5418-6

Type 1 Diabetes
For Dummies
978-0-470-17811-9

Pets

Cats For Dummies,
2nd Edition
978-0-7645-5275-5

Dog Training For Dummies,
3rd Edition
978-0-470-60029-0

Puppies For Dummies,
2nd Edition
978-0-470-03717-1

Religion & Inspiration

The Bible For Dummies
978-0-7645-5296-0

Catholicism For Dummies
978-0-7645-5391-2

Women in the Bible
For Dummies
978-0-7645-8475-6

Self-Help & Relationship

Anger Management
For Dummies
978-0-470-03715-7

Overcoming Anxiety
For Dummies,
2nd Edition
978-0-470-57441-6

Sports

Baseball
For Dummies,
3rd Edition
978-0-7645-7537-2

Basketball
For Dummies,
2nd Edition
978-0-7645-5248-9

Golf For Dummies,
3rd Edition
978-0-471-76871-5

Web Development

Web Design
All-in-One
For Dummies
978-0-470-41796-6

Web Sites
Do-It-Yourself
For Dummies,
2nd Edition
978-0-470-56520-9

Windows 7

Windows 7
For Dummies
978-0-470-49743-2

Windows 7
For Dummies,
Book + DVD Bundle
978-0-470-52398-8

Windows 7 All-in-One
For Dummies
978-0-470-48763-1

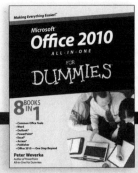